THE AUTHORS J. M. Barwise works as a secondary school History teacher in Wirral and her research interests are in the international history of South East Asia. N. J. White is Professor of Imperial & Commonwealth History at Liverpool John Moores University. He is the author of *Business, Government, and the End of Empire: Malaya, 1942-57*, *Decolonisation: the British Experience since 1945* and *British Business in Post-Colonial Malaysia, 1957-70*. Both authors have travelled extensively in the region.

SERIES EDITOR Professor Denis Judd is a graduate of Oxford, a Fellow of the Royal Historical Society and Professor of History at the University of North London. He has published over 20 books including the biographies of Joseph Chamberlain, Prince Philip, George VI and Alison Uttley. His most recent book is the highly praised *Empire: The British Imperial Experience from 1765 to the Present*. He is an advisor to the BBC *History* magazine and reviews and writes extensively in the national press.

Other Titles in the Series

THE TRAVELLER'S HISTORY SERIES

'Ideal before-you-go reading' *The Daily Telegraph*

'An excellent series of brief histories' *New York Times*

'I want to compliment you ... on the brilliantly concise contents of your books' *Shirley Conran*

Reviews of Individual Titles

A Traveller's History of France

'Undoubtedly the best way to prepare for a trip to France is to bone up on some history. *The Traveller's History of France* by Robert Cole is concise and gives the essential facts in a very readable form.' *The Independent*

A Traveller's History of China

'The author manages to get 2 million years into 300 pages. An excellent addition to a series which is already invaluable, whether you're travelling or not.' *The Guardian*

A Traveller's History of India

'For anyone ... planning a trip to India, the latest in the excellent Traveller's History series ... provides a useful grounding for those whose curiosity exceeds the time available for research.' *The London Evening Standard*

A Traveller's History of Japan

'It succeeds admirably in its goal of making the present country comprehensible through a narrative of its past, with asides on everything from bonsai to *zazen*, in a brisk, highly readable style ... you could easily read it on the flight over, if you skip the movie.' *The Washington Post*

A Traveller's History of Ireland

'For independent, inquisitive travellers traversing the green roads of Ireland, there is no better guide than *A Traveller's History of Ireland*.' *Small Press*

A Traveller's History
of Southeast Asia

A Traveller's History of Southeast Asia

J.M. BARWISE & N.J. WHITE

Series Editor   DENIS JUDD
Line Drawings   PETER GUESSLER

Interlink Books

An imprint of Interlink Publishing Group, Inc.
Northampton, Massachusetts

This edition published in 2015 by
INTERLINK BOOKS
An imprint of Interlink Publishing Group, Inc
46 Crosby Street, Northampton, Massachusetts 01060
www.interlinkbooks.com

The front cover shows Harvest Scene, Indonesia, *(Balinese painting). Private collection/Bridgeman Art library.*

Library of Congress Cataloging-in-Publication Data
Barwise, J.M.
    A traveller's history of Southeast Asia/by J.M Barwise and N.J. White. – 1st American ed.
            p. cm. – (Traveller's history series)
Includes bibliographical references and index.
    ISBN 978-1-56656-439-7
    1. Asia, Southeastern–History. 2. Asia, Southeastern–Description and travel.
I. White, N.J. II. Title. III. Series: Traveller's history.
DS525 .B3 2015
959–dc21

                        2001006351

Printed and bound in the United States of America

Contents

Preface

This is stunning work of concise and fascinating historical writing. It is often hard enough to describe vividly and accurately one country's history, but here the authors have taken on a whole, far-flung region, and made sense of it. They begin, reasonably enough, with defining South East Asia. Excluding Burma and the Philippines, they are still left with a huge and complex region, consisting of Thailand, Laos, Vietnam, Cambodia, Indonesia, Malaysia, Singapore, and Brunei. For myself, Indonesia alone is a baffling hotchpotch of territories, ethnicities and religions – with its thirteen thousand islands, its population of 220 million and its two hundred ethnic groups. True experts in their fields, however, the authors swoop with apparently effortless scholarship and enormous energy between the patchwork of the South East Asia region, enlightening and informing us as they go.

The average Western traveller surveying the region will, I suspect, only have a random smattering of information, much of it deriving from the clichés of popular culture and a few scraps of historical information. The Vietnam War, in all its horror and confusion, has left an indelible stamp on our collective memory, but perhaps largely through a number of fine feature films, mostly American in origin. British readers will be aware that Malaya, Singapore and Brunei were once part of the Empire, though exactly how and when may be more tricky to recall. Thailand has a less than enviable reputation as one of the pioneers of sexual tourism, with all its tacky and lurid overtones, though a more wholesome image is conjured up by the hit musical *The King and I*. Laos and Cambodia may seem as obscure as the other side of the moon to many westerners, though its friendly people and lovely landscapes will amply repay closer examination. Indonesia has far too often recently forced its way into our consciousness through the televised pictures of rioting crowds, either demanding the overthrow of local tyrants or expressing passionate support for Muslim causes on the other side of the world.

There is also something sultry, silky and sexy about the region. Behind the social formalities it is easy to imagine seething passions and the timeless interplay of ambition and intrigue. The writings of Joseph Conrad, and on a less exalted scale, those of Somerset Maugham, introduce the reader to exotic locations, obscure local traditions, the murky ebb and flow of emotion, and the bitter-sweet of European exile amid a people both alluring and compliant but also strange and menacing. It is perhaps no coincidence that one of the most devastating and unexpected volcanic eruptions of modern times occurred at Krakatoa, east of Java.

South East Asia has been a magnet for European traders and commerce ever since the Age of Discovery, and the huge profits that could be gained from the spice trade. More recently the region has been a major producer of the oil, rubber and tin that has been crucial to industrial and manufacturing developments. The western impact was felt early and with great intensity. In these circumstances, it is not surprising to learn that 'South East Asians – since the beginning of recorded time – have been extremely adept at absorbing, manipulating and adapting external cultures and technologies to maintain their own cultural autonomy and distinctiveness.' So a characteristic of the region is 'present-mindedness ... a willingness to embrace and act upon new things.' This means that the visitor will find a challenging and at the same time reassuring blend of the familiar and the unfamiliar – in a word, Coca-Cola and satai, the baseball cap and the sarong.

Those travellers who take their holidays in South East Asia will experience a cultural diversity, a love of life and a traditional warmth that will surprise and enrapture them. If they are also equipped with this clear and intelligent history, then their enjoyment and understanding will be greatly enhanced.

Denis Judd
London, 2001

CHAPTER ONE

Defining South East Asia

Variety and Diversity

Most popular images of South East Asia, in the west at least, derive from feature films about the Vietnam War. American movies such as *Apocalypse Now* (1979), *Hamburger Hill* (1987) and *Full Metal Jacket* (1987) have presented a South East Asia in which innocent and naive peasants are at the mercy of either United States soldiers or communist guerrillas. This is one of the stereotypical myths about South East Asia's past that will be debunked in this book. It is actually very difficult to generalize about a region made up of the countries of Burma (Myanmar), Thailand, Laos, Vietnam, Cambodia, Indonesia, Malaysia, Singapore, Brunei, the Philippines, and South East Asia's newest nation, East Timor. We take a narrower focus by excluding Burma and the Philippines (which are less frequently visited by tourists). Even so, for our slimmed-down South East Asia, there remains a huge variety and diversity of peoples and cultures between the different countries. To use Vietnam as a benchmark for the region is misguided because, at the north eastern extremity of South East Asia, the country remains distinct from the rest of the region as a consequence of China's long influence on its politics and culture. But variety is also found within countries: the island nation of Indonesia is comprised of 13,000 islands, which are home to a population of 220 million drawn from over 200 different ethnic groups. Not surprisingly, Indonesia's national catchphrase is 'Unity in Diversity'. Even Laos – one of the smaller countries of the region with a population of about 5 million – contains some 47 ethnicities.

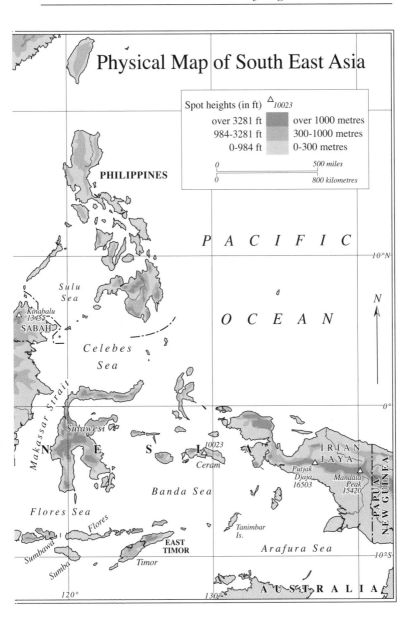

Physical Map of South East Asia

Spot heights (in ft) △*10023*

over 3281 ft	over 1000 metres
984-3281 ft	300-1000 metres
0-984 ft	0-300 metres

0   500 miles
0   800 kilometres

PHILIPPINES

P A C I F I C

10°N

*Sulu
Sea*

*Kinabalu
13455*
SABAH

N

O C E A N

*Celebes
Sea*

Makasar Strait

Sulawesi

N   E   S   I   A

Ceram

10023

IRIAN
JAYA

*Putjak
Djaja
16503*

*Mandala
Peak
15420*

PAPUA
NEW GUINEA

Banda Sea

0°

Flores Sea

Flores

*Tanimbar
Is.*

Sumbawa

Sumba

EAST
TIMOR

Timor

Arafura Sea

10°S

A U S T R A L I A

120°   130°

RELIGION

A convenient way of imposing some order on the chaos of South East Asia is to divide the region in religious terms. Vietnam, Laos, Cambodia and Thailand can be classified as 'Buddhist' since Buddhism has been the dominant religion in the 'northern' states since classical times. To the south, Malaysia, Indonesia, Brunei and Singapore might be classified as 'Muslim', reflecting the dominance of Islamic thinking since the sixteenth and seventeenth centuries. But this is to engage in a misleading generalization. Bali and Lombok in Indonesia retain their Hindu culture. Moreover, mass immigration from China and India in the nineteenth and twentieth centuries laid the basis of 'plural societies' in the 'southern' states; the result in Singapore being a island republic with a non-Muslim, Chinese majority. Significant pockets of Christianity can be found throughout Malaysia and Indonesia alongside the survival of much older tribal religious practices in the more remote areas, such as Sarawak in East Malaysia and Irian Jaya in eastern Indonesia. In the Buddhist world, there is perhaps more of a case for religious homogeneity but even here there remain important Muslim, animist and Christian communities.

LANGUAGE

The diversity of religious practice and belief is matched by the variety of languages spoken throughout South East Asia [see map]. Today's states of Malaysia and Indonesia are united by common use of forms of Malay as the basis of their national languages. Malay is the most dominant of the Austronesian languages that developed out of a common parent language about 5,000 years ago. Even so, Acehnese, Batak, Minangkabau, Javanese, Bugis and Makassarese remain important distinct, local Austronesian dialects within Indonesia. The easternmost islanders of the archipelago, meanwhile, speak non-Austronesian, Papuan languages. In Malaysia, there are many local languages still spoken amongst non-Malay tribal peoples. The 40,000-strong Orang Asli communities of the Malay peninsula converse in Austro-Asiatic mother tongues (also about 5,000 years old). Khmer – the dominant indigenous language of Cambodia – has similar Austro-Asiatic roots to Aslian, pointing to the likelihood that most people on the mainland of South East Asia once spoke similar languages. Although its tones have developed relatively recently, Vietnamese too is an Austro-Asiatic language related to Khmer. But the Cham minorities of central Vietnam and eastern Cambodia are both ethnically and linguistically closer to the Austronesians of the island world. Moreover, in what are today Thailand and Laos, Austro-Asiatic speakers were slowly pushed out from about 600 BC by *Tai*-speaking peoples; Thai and Lao being the two modern versions of these languages. Thai is a distinct language within the Tai language group (which also includes Lao). Yet, even within populations who speak the same tongue, there can often be a huge variety of dialects. It is only in the last two centuries, for example, that Thai has become standardized. Even then, great geographical differences in pronunciation remain, particularly between urban and rural dwellers. In Malaysia, the Malay spoken in rural, traditionalist Kelantan on the east coast of the peninsula still differs markedly from the dialect of the cosmopolitan capital, Kuala Lumpur. Linguistic diversity is further complicated in the towns and cities of South East Asia by the presence of large overseas Chinese and Indian communities, which retain their own cultures and dialects. It is this diversity and variety that make South East Asia such a fascinating region to study and to visit.

The Autonomy of South East Asia

Films about the Vietnam War also distort reality because they present the region and its peoples as being externally acted upon and lacking in initiative. Indeed few films of the conflict between 1965 and 1975 show things from the Vietnamese side. Even Oliver Stone's admirable *Heaven and Earth* (1993), which is supposed to be a portrayal of the life of a Vietnamese peasant woman, actually ends up making the American experience of the war the central focus. Clearly, the American military presence during the 1960s *did* have a huge impact on the Vietnamese people, as *did* the much longer Chinese occupation of northern Vietnam from the first to the eleventh centuries. Located pivotally between East Asia and the rest of the world, South East Asia in general has been unable to avoid external cultural, political and economic forces crashing

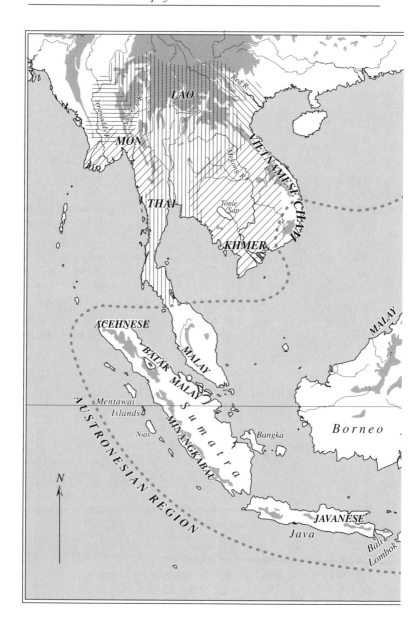

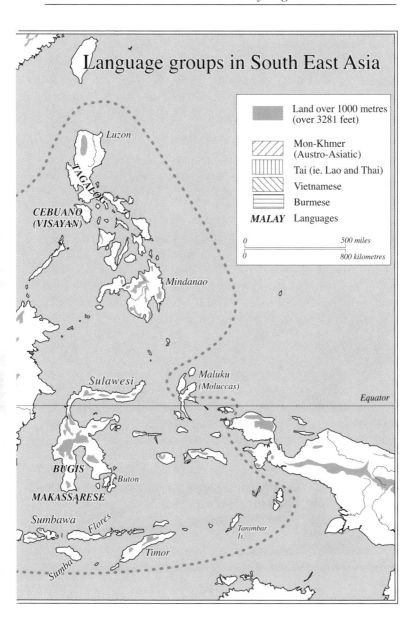

Language groups in South East Asia

Land over 1000 metres (over 3281 feet)

Mon-Khmer (Austro-Asiatic)

Tai (ie. Lao and Thai)

Vietnamese

Burmese

MALAY Languages

0 — 500 miles
0 — 800 kilometres

Luzon

TAGALOG

CEBUANO (VISAYAN)

Mindanao

Sulawesi

Maluku (Moluccas)

Equator

BUGIS

Buton

MAKASSARESE

Sumbawa

Flores

Sumba

Timor

Tanimbar Is.

their way through it. From the earliest times, most of the major world religions established themselves in the region. First Hinduism and Buddhism, then Islam and finally Christianity came to overlay indigenous animist beliefs. In economic terms, the spice trade attracted merchants from China, India, the Middle East and Europe. Portuguese and Dutch interest in spices during the sixteenth and seventeenth centuries gave way to full blown colonialism in the nineteenth century, when almost all the region was carved up between the European powers. This loss of political autonomy coincided with a new economic dependence as South East Asia became a major producer of raw materials for western industry. Decolonization in the second half of the twentieth century restored political independence. But international influence only reached a new height as, by the 1950s, the region became a front line in the 'struggle for existence' between the communist and capitalist worlds with their respective centres in Moscow-Beijing and Washington. The most visible example of this internationalization of South East Asia was United States troop deployments and aerial bombardments in Vietnam, Cambodia and Laos. More recently, South East Asia's growing absorption into the world economy – a process described as 'globalization' – has further submerged local cultures. Malaysians and Indonesians choose to consume Coca-Cola

Muslim women at prayer in Indonesia

and French fries rather than coconut milk and satai. Malay women wear baseball caps, T-shirts and designer jeans rather than the traditional headscarf and sarong. With such an international bombardment since earliest times, how, you might well ask, could anything uniquely South East Asian survive?

Yet, a central theme of this book is the degree to which South East Asians – since the beginning of recorded time – have been extremely adept at absorbing, manipulating and adapting external cultures and technologies to maintain their own cultural autonomy and distinctiveness. Even at the height of external influence – the apogee of European colonialism between the 1870s and the 1930s – alien rulers were forced into 'collaboration' with local elites and compromises with local cultures. As the historian Tim Harper has pointed out, a key South East Asian characteristic is 'present-mindedness', a 'willingness to embrace and act upon new things'. South East Asians were (and are) unlikely to be bamboozled. Indeed, in the era of European imperialism possibilities abounded. Anticolonial movements came to fashion new nation-states from the 1940s, which drew on older precolonial traditions. But the new regimes also embraced the opportunities provided by the modern world, notably interaction with the international capitalist economy. This adept interaction with the outside world has a long pedigree in South East Asia. It has also engendered another South East Asian trait: tenacity and resourcefulness in the face of adversity.

Autonomy has not always been an accepted interpretation of South East Asia's past, and the '*Apocalypse Now* view' reflects a long tradition in western portraits of the region. Colonial historians once tried to argue that the dominant influence upon South East Asia's early history was Indian; the only exception being northern Vietnam, which had fallen under Chinese political and cultural dominance. The prevalence of Indian-style inscriptions, architectural styles and religions (Hinduism and Buddhism), as well as local translations of the Sanskrit epics, all pointed to wholesale colonization by South Asian peoples in the early centuries AD. Sir Thomas Stamford Raffles, the celebrated British colonial administrator of the early nineteenth century, believed that the medieval temple complex at Borobudur on Java could not have been built by the Javanese without Indian assistance. Sandwiched between

The traditional Chinese ribbon dance

India and China, South East Asian cultures and traditions were seen as mere fusions and imitations of Chinese and Indian civilizations. Indeed, the British came to refer to their colonial territories as 'Malayan India'; the Dutch styled theirs' 'Netherlands India'; while, the French preferred 'Indochina'. It was during the Second World War that the term 'South East Asia' was first used to describe those territories under the Allied command of Admiral Lord Louis Mountbatten. Previous to this, South East Asia had never been seen as a distinct region; it was a mere appendage to either India or China.

Yet, other Asians had long seen South East Asia as 'different'. The Chinese called the region the Nanyang (the Southern Seas). The Japanese similarly knew it as the Nanyo. Arab, Indian and Persian traders described South East Asia as the 'lands below the winds,' given that the seasonal monsoon carried their ships to the ports of the region across the Indian Ocean. It was by trade and the peaceable travels of holy men, not formal colonial conquest, that Indian influences came to

South East Asia. The only recorded Indian military victory over a South East Asian kingdom was when forces from south India sacked the capital of the Srivijaya empire on Sumatra in the eleventh century; and this was not followed by colonization. Indian civilization was not forced upon an unsuspecting South East Asia. Rather, clever local elites took on elements of Indian culture that they found useful and adapted religious and political ideas to local traditions. Similarly, Vietnam was not completely subsumed by China but, from the eleventh century, actually acted as a barrier to Chinese expansion into the region. Vietnamese resistance to Beijing's imperialism forced the Chinese to come to South East Asia by sea and not as military conquerors but – like the Indians – as peaceable commercial travellers.

Even the external influence of Chinese and Indian sea-borne commerce should not be overestimated. As the historian Anthony Reid has argued, by the middle of the fifteenth century a huge intraregional trade network had been established linking all the major ports of South East Asia, evidenced by the widespread use of Malay as the language of commerce. South East Asia's position as a largely self-contained economic unit was to be blown apart by European imperialism, beginning with the arrival of Dutch East India Company in the seventeenth century. Yet South East Asian traditions still survived and, as the Dutch historian, J.C. van Leur, came to realize in the 1930s external influences on the region had always been little more than a 'thin and flaking glaze'. For example, despite the cultural onslaught from all the world religions, many South East Asians have maintained their belief in spirits – some malevolent, some benevolent – which inhabit and animate trees and wild animals. South East Asians continue to 'borrow' from other cultures those values and practices that they find useful but not to the extent that local identities and values are lost.

The Physical and Natural Environments

Variety and diversity of peoples notwithstanding, the South East Asia region is provided with a certain coherence by the physical and natural environments, and the ways in which they have impacted upon human

Lake Toba, a volcanic crater lake in northern Sumatra

history. As recently as 15,000 years ago, sea levels were some 219 yards (200 metres) lower. This meant that the present-day islands of Sumatra, Java, Bali and Borneo were once joined to the mainland, explaining why the plant and animal life of the larger Indonesian islands remained quite similar to the mainland into contemporary times. For example, before the expansion of human settlement and the European colonial mania for hunting, the tiger was widespread from Vietnam to Bali. But the postglacial rise in sea levels divided the region into two halves – 'mainland' and 'island'.

THE MAINLAND

Mainland South East Asia comprises Burma, Thailand, Indochina (Vietnam, Laos and Cambodia) and peninsula or West Malaysia. The major geographical features of the mainland are a series of vast river systems – the Irrawaddy and Salween in Burma, the Chao Phraya in Thailand, the Mekong which forms the border today between Thailand and Laos (before running through Cambodia and southern Vietnam), and the Red or Hong in northern Vietnam. All run roughly north to south and have their sources in the eastern Himalayas – the mountains that effectively seal South East Asia off from China. The other major geographical delineators are the mountain ranges that separate Vietnam from Laos and Thailand from Burma. A mountain range also splits the eastern and western halves of the Malay peninsula. In general terms, then, the mainland region is made up of a series of lowland river and coastal plains separated by highlands.

THE ISLANDS

The island realm – the other physical half of South East Asia – is made up of today's Indonesia, Brunei, East Malaysia, East Timor and the Philippines. (Given West Malaysia's and Singapore's geographical proximity and cultural complementarity these two areas are also often linked with the island world to form 'maritime South East Asia'.) Distinctions between upland and lowland are important in island South East Asia too, but the major physical differences are concerned with those land masses deemed 'stable' and those termed 'volcanically active'. The Malay peninsula, Borneo, and eastern Sumatra are all stable terrain while the huge Sunda-Banda arc from west Sumatra to the Maluku Islands (Moluccas) has had volcanically active 'hot spots' into recent times. The most famous eruption, and resulting tidal wave, was in 1883 around the islands of Krakatau (Krakatoa), which contrary to the claims of the spatially challenged makers of the 1968 adventure film, are to be found not *east* but *west of Java* in the Sunda Straits. However, a worse natural catastrophe – indeed, the biggest natural explosion previously known – occurred in 1815 at Mount Tambora on the island of Sumbawa (this time definitely east of Java!). Twelve thousand died in the blasts and the lava flows. But more than 80,000 others lost their lives in the aftermath as volcanic ash covered the rice fields of Sumbawa and surrounding islands such as Bali. Another volcanic arc runs from Sulawesi to the Philippines archipelago.

In terms of botany and zoology, however, the island world is split in two by Wallace's Line. This is named after the English naturalist Alfred Russell Wallace who, in the 1850s, devised an explanation for the distinctive flora and fauna of eastern Indonesia; ideas which would have a profound influence upon the theory of evolution associated with Charles Darwin. In terms of mammals, Wallace observed on Java and Borneo that 'the forests abound in monkeys of many kinds, wild cats,

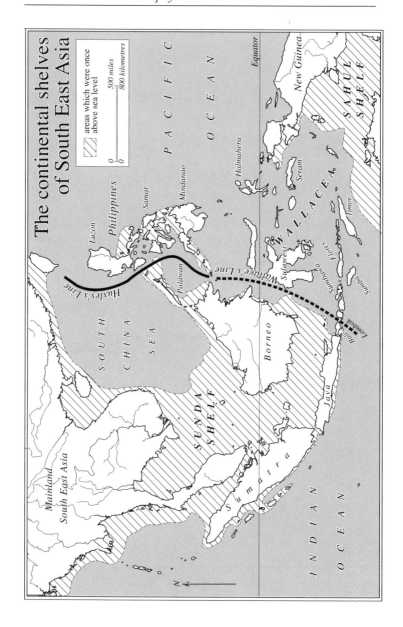

The continental shelves of South East Asia

areas which were once above sea level

500 miles
800 kilometres

PACIFIC OCEAN

Equator

New Guinea

SAHUL SHELF

Halmahera

Seram

Luzon

Philippines

Samar

Mindanao

WALLACEA

Timor

Flores

Sumba

Sumbawa

Palawan

Huxley's Line

Wallace's Line

Lombok

Bali

SOUTH CHINA SEA

Borneo

SUNDA SHELF

Java

Sulawesi

Mainland South East Asia

Sumatra

INDIAN OCEAN

N

deer, civets, and otters, and numerous varieties of squirrels are constantly met with'. But on Sulawesi and the Maluku Islands 'none of these occur; but the prehensile-tailed Cuscus is almost the only terrestrial mammal seen, except wild pigs, which are found in all the islands, and deer [which have probably been recently introduced]...' Because of the deep sea trough between Bali and Lombok and between Kalimantan and Sulawesi, all the islands of present-day Indonesia from Sulawesi and Lombok eastward were never joined to the mainland. According to Wallace, this fact explained why eastern Indonesia developed flora and fauna more akin to Australasia than Asia. Wallace likewise used his line to explain the ethnographic differences of the Malays to the west and the Papuans to the east. The line was later extended to the west of the Philippines by Huxley. Although Wallace's botanical ideas have been challenged, the theory still remains as a generally accepted explanation of the zoological differences between west and east Indonesia.

CLIMATE AND VEGETATION

Perhaps the greatest claim to regional coherence surrounds South East Asia's shared weather patterns. The whole region is located within the tropics, with the Equator dissecting the larger Indonesian islands of Sumatra, Borneo and Sulawesi. Temperatures are therefore uniformly high. The only cool areas are to be found in the highlands, which is why the colonial rulers of the nineteenth and twentieth centuries – in the days before air-conditioning – typically built their exclusive retreats on hilltops to escape the sweltering heat of the lowlands. Malaysia – lying between one and seven degrees north of the Equator – is fairly typical with temperatures ranging from 25.5 degrees Celsius to 33 degrees Celsius. Moreover, temperatures are high all year round: the passing of the seasons in South East Asia is not distinguishable by changes in temperature as in northern Europe. Rather, it is rainfall that varies, particularly in the intertropical zone north of Indonesia and Malaysia. Here, there is a winter dry season as a result of the cycle of the monsoons. Yet in equatorial Indonesia and Malaysia, there are few areas that experience a dry period: rainfall occurs year-round.

Generally, then, South East Asia is wet and hot, providing ideal

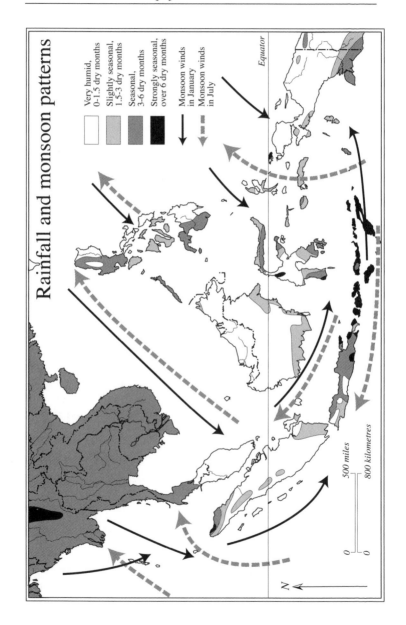

Rainfall and monsoon patterns

Very humid,
0-1.5 dry months

Slightly seasonal,
1.5-3 dry months

Seasonal,
3-6 dry months

Strongly seasonal,
over 6 dry months

Monsoon winds
in January

Monsoon winds
in July

Equator

500 miles

800 kilometres

conditions for the development of evergreen rainforests. Only in the areas of the severest dry season – in northern Indochina and Thailand and on the southeastern islands of Indonesia from Java to Timor – is there an absence of rainforest. Although constantly being eroded by the pressures of population growth and economic development, much of South East Asia is still covered by primary jungle and, in contrast to most of the developed world, the forest remains a major influence on the environment.

THE ENVIRONMENT AND HUMAN HISTORY

As Anthony Reid has argued, the abundance of forest in the region can explain much about the life styles of South East Asians. Historically wood, bamboo and palm were the preferred materials for the construction of houses. Universally, South East Asian dwellings were raised off the ground by stilts to avoid floods and attacks from wild animals. Towns were frequently at risk from fire but, on the other hand, the ease with which wooden houses could be put up allowed settlements to be swiftly rebuilt or relocated; this South East Asian ability to be flexible in the face of the unexpected has survived into modern times. At the same time, the absence of grasslands – and therefore grazing livestock – led to common diets throughout premodern South East Asia. Rice was, and continues to be, eaten everywhere in the region as the staple food, supplemented by the fruits of the coconut and sugar palm. Fish, not meat, was the main source of protein. This diet underlines the other great 'natural' influence on human behaviour: water. Before the end of the nineteenth century, transport over any long distance was along the inland rivers or the coastal seas, and every household possessed a boat. The kindness of South East Asia's seas – with their uniformly warm temperatures and predictable and moderate winds – also made the region a boon to international and intraregional traders, travellers and missionaries. This further explains the long influence of maritime exchange on the 'lands below the winds'.

In addition to the role of wood and water, the terrain of South East Asia had a profound influence upon human settlement patterns. From the beginning of recorded time in Thailand and Indochina, the presence of great river basins and mountain ranges forced mankind to settle in concentrations on the river plains and estuaries, which provided the irrigated water and fertile soils necessary for rice cultivation. It was around the Mekong estuary (today in southern Vietnam) and along the Red River plain (in northern Vietnam) that the earliest civilizations in South East Asia sprang up, while the Menam plain of central Thailand has long been the centre of Thai power. In the struggles for the best agricultural land, less-efficient societies were pushed out on to the marginal uplands – a process that still continues today as the Orang Asli of West Malaysia or the Chams of central Vietnam and eastern Cambodia will testify.

In the island world, however, it is the volcanic heritage that explains the concentration of populations in particular areas. Previously volcanic regions produced rich soils, which, combined with high rainfall from the monsoon climate, supported a booming rice culture and some of the world's highest population densities from the early centuries AD. Java, which even today holds half of Indonesia's population, is the classic example of this phenomenon. By way of contrast, the interiors of Borneo and east Sumatra have traditionally had very low populations, with only small pockets of settled agriculture, because of the infertile soils found in these nonvolcanic zones.

Climate can explain much about human settlement too. Before modern times, the largest population centres tended to be in the intertropical zone – that is, north of Malaysia and on the southern Indonesian island chain from Java to Timor. In these regions, good soils were boosted by a three-month period of lower rainfall in which rice could 'ripen'. Even today, a country such as Malaysia finds it difficult to grow enough food to feed its population and is reliant on imports. The earliest human fossil remains in South East Asia have been found in Java and Thailand. This is no coincidence, for again the more amenable intertropical climate permitted the presence of larger numbers of edible animals, such as wild cattle, in the days before the development of agriculture.

As hunting and gathering gave way to settled agriculture on the mainland (excluding the Malay peninsula), four main civilizations developed with their own language and culture – from west to east, Burmese, Thai, Khmer, and Vietnamese. Their distinctiveness reflected the role of the north–south mountain ranges, which effectively isolated the four cultures and allowed them to develop separately. Maritime South East Asia was much more open, however, and as a result came to develop a far more homogenous language and culture. The navigable straits and seas of the island world acted as cultural, intellectual and linguistic conduits, in contrast to the untraversable mountain ranges of the mainland. This probably explains why Malay, and other similar Austronesian languages, established themselves over a wide area of present-day Malaysia, Brunei and Indonesia. It was by maritime routes too that Islam, from the 1400s onwards, came to dominate the religious life of much of this area.

At the same time, however, geography played an important part in leaving South East Asia politically fragmented, lacking in strong, centralized states until recent times. The river basins and estuaries of the mainland and on Java developed great clusters of people, but even in these areas villages were often cut off from one another by forests, hills, and coastal mangrove swamps. The physical separation of communities was further exacerbated in Indonesia by the thousands of islands that make up the archipelago. As such, before colonial times, few individuals would venture beyond their own locale. On the Malay peninsula, for example, because the interior mountain range posed a formidable barrier, the focus of settlement tended to be on the coastal lowlands. The major Malay settlements were established on the rivers, and it was from their principal river that most of the peninsular states took their name – for example, the state of Pahang is named after West Malaysia's longest river. The result was the lack of any central authority for the whole peninsula. Into the twentieth century, a region roughly the size of England was composed of some nine tiny and separate states. Indeed, it was only in the second half of the twentieth century that the nation-states now known as Malaysia and Indonesia came into being. The central cores of today's Vietnam, Thailand, Cambodia, and to a lesser extent, Laos have a premodern lineage. But those of Malaysia and Indonesia do not, while before the nineteenth century the island of Singapore was a sparsely inhabited swamp. One paradox of maritime South East Asia's history is that colonial rule – both wittingly and unwittingly – forged unity from diversity.

CHAPTER TWO

Early South East Asia, Prehistory to c. 500 AD

In reconstructing the earliest human history of any part of the world, archeologists and anthropologists face a very complex task. These inherent difficulties are exacerbated in South East Asia where there is an absence of 'indigenous' written sources before the early Christian era in Europe. Skeletal remains tell us something about the earliest humans in the region, while the discovery of stone tools and arrowheads sheds a little light on the technological sophistication of the earliest communities. The bronze drums found throughout the region, but particularly in northern Vietnam, suggest a metal-working culture and the development of sophisticated, stratified and settled societies as early as the fourth century BC. Yet, because of the patchy and scarce nature of the evidence, there remains much speculation about the earliest human history of South East Asia.

Nevertheless it is clear that the period before 500 AD in South East Asia witnessed developments that would have an important influence on future epochs: notably, the beginnings of long-distance sea travel from as early as 40,000 years ago; the domestication of rice from as long ago as 3000 BC; the remarkable migrations from southern China, which established today's ethnic and linguistic map of South East Asia; the acquisition of sophisticated metal-working techniques throughout the South East Asian region by 200 BC; the development of centralized and class-based societies, which preceded South East Asia's growing contacts with India and China; and, finally, the establishment of indigenous belief systems, which have survived in places beneath the veneer of the world religions into recent times. Before 500 AD, South East Asia may have lacked the great cities, empires and civilizations of contemporaneous China and Mediterranean Europe, but South East Asians as skilled farmers, metal workers and sailors-cum-traders still made significant contributions to early world history.

From Homo Erectus to Homo Sapiens

JAVA MAN

In 1891 an archeologist named Eugene Dubois first discovered the remains of what became known as 'Java Man' by unearthing the skull of a *Homo erectus* in central Java, Indonesia. Remains of *Homo erectus* have also been found in northern Vietnam, but the island of Java continues to provide the most important human fossils in the region. The general consensus is that the development of pre-*sapiens* began in Africa, from where *Homo erectus* expanded into Asia more than 1 million years ago. Precisely how *Homo erectus* (as well as *Homo sapiens* later) came to arrive on Java is a mystery. Some have postulated that *Homo erectus* actually evolved first in Asia. It appears more likely, however, that lower sea levels than today meant that for much of the Pleistocene era (about 1.8 million to 10,000 years ago) Java as well as Sumatra and Borneo were joined to the Asian mainland. Via an extraordinarily slow migration, *Homo erectus* literally 'walked in' to Java via the Malayan peninsula between 1.7 million and 1 million years ago. The path of *Homo erectus* family groups was also unimpeded by thick jungle, because climatic differences in the Pleistocene meant that there were considerable stretches of open vegetation.

More debatable is how 'Java Man' actually lived. Did he or she use stone tools, for example? The dental remains of Javanese *erectus* populations have shown that they were probably vegetarians and it is likely that they only used bone tools at first. The employment of stone tools is usually associated with *Homo sapiens* groups (also originally from Africa). Javanese *erectus* may not have been completely replaced by the *Homo sapiens,* armed with their stone tools, who arrived in South East Asia after *Homo erectus*. Instead, rather than replacement by the more technologically advanced *Homo sapiens*, it may be that *Homo erectus* evolved and adapted over time to become the very distant ancestors of modern South East Asians. It has been claimed, for example, that *Homo erectus* was using stone tools in Thailand some time between 600,000 and 800,000 years ago. What we do know is that 100,000 years ago the first South East Asians were using stone tools in Java and they should be regarded as among the antecedents of today's South East Asian populations. These early humans probably lived outside the tropical forests in sparse and isolated communities, and over time, began hunting or scavenging for edible animals.

THE AUSTRALO-MELANESIANS

Archeologists and anthropologists can be clearer about the evolution of human society in South East Asia from about 40,000 years ago, because of a greater abundance of dateable skeletal remains as well as stone tools and arrowheads. The indigenous groups inhabiting the region between 40,000 and 7,000 years ago are usually referred to as Australo-Melanesians (or tropical Australoids). They were hunters and gatherers, rather than settled farmers, and were the first peoples to colonize eastern Indonesia through sea travel from Java and Borneo. (Islands such as Sulawesi were not joined to the mainland in the late Pleistocene era and therefore must have required a sea crossing for human settlement). The earliest evidence of Australo-Melanesian life in South East Asia is between 20,000 and 40,000 years old, and comes from Niah Cave in Sarawak on the island of Borneo. Between 14,000 and 8,000 years ago, these cave dwellers were engaging in complex burial rituals and hunting and scavenging meat from more than 50 species of mammals, ranging in size from rodents to rhinoceroses. Pigs, porcupine and monkeys were actually the main food source, but the Australo-Melanesians of Niah were opportunists who effectively ate whatever they caught (with the assistance of arrows and spears) or found already dead.

On mainland South East Asia, however, it seems that 13,000 years ago Australo-Melanesian communities made pottery, grew crops and kept animals as well as continuing to engage in traditional hunting and gathering activities. First discovered in the Hoa Binh province of northern Vietnam in the 1920s, this semi-agricultural culture is termed the Hoabinhian. Hoabinhian communities may also have extended as far southwards as peninsular Malaysia and northern Sumatra. Island South East Asia was predominantly populated by hunter-gatherer societies, but they continued to exist alongside these semi-agricultural communities. The complete shift to agriculture is usually associated with the spread of Austronesian and Austro-Asiatic migrants into lowland and coastal South East Asia between 10,000 and 500 BC. Descendants of Australo-Melanesian groups can still be found, however, amongst the peoples of Maluku and Irian Jaya (Indonesia) plus certain Orang Asli groups in West Malaysia. Similar hunter-gatherer communities have survived in the remoter parts of South East Asia into contemporary times.

The Beginnings of Agricultural Societies

AUSTRONESIANS AND AUSTRO-ASIATICS

The development of settled agriculture, and especially rice cultivation, in South East Asia is usually associated with the slow spread of speakers of Austronesian and Austro-Asiatic languages into areas previously inhabited by hunter-gatherers. Both of these southern Mongoloid groups originated in southern China and brought with them knowledge of rice, millet, yam, taro and sugar-cane cultivation as well as experience in the domestication of pigs, chickens, dogs and cattle. Indigenous South East Asian crops – such as bananas and coconuts – were brought into the Mongoloid agricultural system as it moved south but the real key to Austronesian and Austro-Asiatic success lay with rice cropping. Under the 'slash and burn', shifting agriculture of the Australo-Melanesians, millet had been the staple crop. The great advantage of rice was that it was both nutritious and high yielding. The most productive wet-rice system could support population densities 100 times greater than those of the Australo-Melanesian hunter-gatherers. Rice cultivation seems to have originated in China about 8,000 years ago and underpinned the development of the earliest Neolithic societies there. Yet, the development of wet-rice cultivation, first in swampy riverside areas and later in irrigated fields, demarcated by

Rice farming in Sumatra

embankments, may well have been an 'indigenous' modification, originating entirely within South East Asia.

In island South East Asia, it was once believed that Australo-Melanesian communities were replaced swiftly by Austronesians originating in China. The success of the Austronesian colonization was allegedly underpinned by their more efficient agricultural systems and superior seafaring skills (particularly the use of sailing canoes). The hunter-gatherers were forced onto marginal interior and high lands. A more realistic scenario sketches out a longer, slower process of intermarriage, integration and adaptation between communities rather than a sudden, wholesale overrunning of the outmoded Australo-Melanesians. This process is evinced by the continued presence today of populations exhibiting both 'Australoid' and 'Mongoloid' characteristics in eastern Indonesia. What is certain, though, is that between 3000 and 500 BC agricultural societies speaking Austronesian languages became dominant throughout present-day Malaysia, southern Vietnam, and Indonesia (bar Papuan-speaking Irian Jaya and parts of Timor). The original source area for this diaspora was probably Taiwan (although the original Taiwanese Austronesians may first have sailed from the Chinese mainland before 4000 BC). Seaborne Austronesian migration continued into the Christian era in Europe and, remarkably, reached as far east as Easter Island in the Pacific and as far west as Madagascar off the coast of Africa. These prehistoric Malayo-Polynesians were clearly skilled sailors, capable of harnessing the monsoon winds to travel thousands of miles and to navigate by the fluctuations in these winds as well as swell and wave patterns, cloud formations, birds and even sea life. This maritime knowledge was orally transmitted from generation to generation and allowed for the large-scale 'island-hopping' integral to the Austronesian diaspora in South East Asia. Given the great skill of their mariners, it was probable that Malay trading vessels, and not those of Indian or Chinese traders, were responsible for nurturing South East Asia's earliest international trade links to China by the third century BC, to India sometime in the last two centuries BC, and to Africa approximately 2,000 years ago.

The importance of settled farming, as well as seafaring, to all the speakers of Malayo-Polynesian languages is confirmed by the common words found for food crops (especially rice), domesticated animals, pottery and canoes. The unearthing of pottery shards, as well as evidence of forest clearance and burning in Java and Sumatra, also suggest the dispersal of both agricultural techniques and Austronesian vocabularies into much of island South East Asia from the third millennium BC.

On the mainland, outside the Cham-populated areas of southern Vietnam, agriculturalists who spoke non-Austronesian languages came to predominate. Native speakers of Mon, Khmer, Vietnamese and Aslian today can claim descent from these Austro-Asiatic migrants who brought agricultural techniques to South East Asia. The origins of this diaspora were also probably Chinese. A common feature of Austro-Asiatic vocabulary is a knowledge of rice, and these languages were once spoken widely in southern China. Agricultural settlements, dated from between the third and second millennia BC, have been found along tributaries of the great rivers of mainland South East Asia: the Chao Phraya, the Mekong and the Red. The remains of these sites share common characteristics: evidence of wet-rice cultivation in surrounding swamp areas, the raising of domestic animals, burial tombs, pottery, shell jewellery and the heads of stone tools. It may be that

Austro-Asiatic speakers were once found throughout mainland South East Asia, and as far south as Malaysia and northern Sumatra, but were eventually pushed back by the spread of Tai and Austronesian dialects.

Bronze and Iron

As with the languages and technology of basic agriculture, the development of metal-working communities in South East Asia probably relied upon the dissemination of knowledge from China. In northern Thailand this development allowed for the appearance of bronze manufacture by about 1500 BC. The wider adoption of this technology probably followed quite rapidly down the coast and rivers of mainland South East Asia. Bronze was produced by casting the copper and tin alloy and the molten metal was subsequently moulded into axes, spearheads, bracelets, beads, fishhooks, bells and bowls. Producing bronze was no easy feat and involved a high level of technological sophistication for the inhabitants of northern Thailand. Open fire furnaces, encouraged by clay-nozzled bellows, were employed to liquefy the metals in clay melting pots. The molten bronze was then poured into stone moulds. Alternatively, it has been suggested that bronze-working skills were developed autonomously in South East Asia, and that they hinged on the use of hollowed-out bamboo trunks to act as 'fire pistons', producing sufficient heat to melt the ores.

The most famous example of South East Asian bronze work comes from northern Vietnam and was produced by the Dong-son culture, named after the site where exquisite bronze ceremonial drums have been discovered in Thanh Hoa province. This was an area increasingly under Chinese political influence from the third century BC. But the Dong-son drums may date from as early as 600 BC, which suggests an indigenous South East Asian cultural origin, as well as a centralized chiefdom in the Red River valley area of Vietnam from around 400 BC. The decorations on the sides of the drums tell us much about social organization in northern Vietnam. What concerns us here is that the drums exhibit significant technical skills on the part of the Vietnamese bronzesmiths who made them. The largest of the drums weighs in at an impressive 100 kilograms, or 220 pounds, and measures nearly one metre, or about 3.2 feet, in height with a flat face, domed upper sides and tapered lower sides to amplify the sound, and handles joining the upper and lower sides so it could be easily carried. The whole drum would probably have been cast in a single moulding, with the decorations ingeniously engraved in negative, using wax. Smaller, intricately fashioned bronze items have also been found in northern Vietnam; notably, a finely cast bronze lamp, representing a man kneeling down while holding a bowl with outstretched arms, which is also indicative of well-honed metal skills. This figure exhibits affinities with bronze figure sculptures from Chow China, but, like the drums, the lamp holder may also be representative of a purely Vietnamese style. Iron working on the mainland of South East Asia is usually dated to between 600 and 500 BC, coinciding with growing Chinese contacts in the north of the region. Typical items fashioned from iron at this time included bracelets and spearheads.

In island South East Asia the development of metal-working tech-

Bronze lamp-holder representing a kneeling man from the Dong-son culture of Vietnam

nology lagged behind the mainland. Bronze and iron arrived pretty much simultaneously in present-day Indonesia between 500 and 200 BC. The dissemination of this technology probably relied upon trade contacts with the mainland, particularly Vietnam, given the large number of Dong-son-style drums found in the island world. Commercial exchanges with Tonkin allowed for the rise of important bronze-making industries in Indonesia by the first century AD, indicated by bronze drums found on both Java and Bali. The most striking of these is the magnificently cast, 'Moon of Bali', the largest of South East Asia's decorated ritual kettle drums, found near Pedjeng on Bali and generally believed to be about 2,000 years old. Although clearly influenced by Vietnamese designs, the stone-mould fragments for smaller bronze items found on Bali suggest that the 'Moon' could have been manufactured locally. A number of ceremonial axes, also of Dong-son style, have been found throughout the archipelago. A particularly fine example comes from Pulau Roti, an island off the south west coast of Timor in eastern Indonesia.

The diffusion of iron-working technologies in both mainland and island South East Asia during the last centuries BC, as well as the earlier development of bronze, points to the need for technological change to support increases in agricultural productivity and higher populations as a result. Metal ploughshares and reaping tools, for example, were far more effective than their stone equivalents. More intensive agricultural techniques also suggest a shift towards more centralized societies, stratified by wealth and status. The path was being paved for the birth of South East Asia's first organized polities or 'states'.

The Rise of Centralized Societies

EARLY TRADE

In the past, historians of ancient South East Asia attributed the rise of states and kingdoms in the region to increasing trade and political-cum-military contacts with India and China by the first century AD. But it is quite possible that Indian and Chinese notions of kingship and hierarchy simply reinforced political trends with long indigenous roots in

South East Asian societies. Archeological digs in north eastern Thailand have unearthed the remains of burial grounds, dated between 1400 and 1000 BC, which suggest a hierarchical society composed of at least two distinct social groups defined by both wealth and rank. Into the Bronze Age, the villages in mainland South East Asia remained essentially independent of each other, but were increasingly interlinked by complex trade networks, which exchanged luxury goods such as tin, copper, bronze, high-quality pottery and stones, and shell jewellery. Early internal South East Asian trade also developed between highland hunter-gatherer communities and their lowland, rice-cultivating counterparts: traditional forest products, such as rare woods, lacquer and bamboos, might be bartered for salt from coastal areas. Indeed, within these trade networks, particular lowland villages became specialists in a certain craft, such as pottery making or the fashioning of shell bracelets. By 1000 BC trade networks in Thailand, dealing in metal goods, may have extended beyond South East Asia to link up with China and India too. Through these trade links, South East Asians became interlinked and interdependent.

CO LOA: THE FIRST STATE IN VIETNAM?

Trends towards greater, political centralization around the great rivers of the mainland only became manifest from 500 BC. In this connection, the Dong-son drums of northern Vietnam provide not only an important glimpse of the technological level reached by early South East Asians but also a tantalizing view of the nature of their society. The ornate decorations on the sides of the drums depict scenes from life on the Red River floodplain. Images of axe-wielding warriors with feathered headdresses, boats equipped for warfare, human sacrifice, horse riding, allegiance ceremonies to a paramount chief, and dancers and musicians are all testament to a centralized and hierarchical society, which placed great stress on organized ritual. The function of the drums was probably ceremonial. These so-called thunder drums produce an impressive volume of sound on being struck and perhaps they were used by 'rain-makers' in ceremonies to bring on the thunderous monsoon. Relief designs of the sun and water-loving animals such as frogs on the faces of some of the Vietnamese drums emphasize their significance vis-à-vis the annual agricultural cycle. But the kettle drums may also have had a central use in elaborate funerals for monarchs or important chieftains, who would be buried in wooden boat-shaped coffins surrounded by weaponry, bronze bells and painted wooden boxes to ensure a comfortable existence in the 'Kingdom of the Dead'. In addition, the drums probably served as gifts to lesser lords as a means of cementing the authority of the centre over the outlying regions. The ability to manufacture one of the larger drums in the first place also indicates a centrally organized society, because the drums required a massive seven tons of copper ore. Although Chinese written sources depict Vietnamese peoples as inferior, dangerous barbarians, they also confirm that northern Vietnam was under the control of an aristocratic elite (a contradiction overlooked by Chinese chroniclers, no doubt). Vietnamese legend has it that the mysterious Hong-bang dynasty of kings dates back to as early as 2879 BC.

The political centre or monarchical seat of this 'first Vietnamese state' by the third century BC is likely to have been Co Loa, on the floodplain of the Red River, ten miles north west of present-day Hanoi. Excavations have revealed a city of some 1,500 acres, or 600 hectares, in size surrounded by ramparts and a moat. A Chinese census of 2 AD recorded a population of some 1 million people in northern Vietnam. The Red River area certainly could have supported a substantial population because the good soils and plentiful rainfall were conducive to growing two rice crops per year. Discoveries of bronze ploughshares (which would have been drawn by water buffalo), as well as Chinese references to ricefields, irrigated by canals, in the first century BC, illustrate that this was an area of intensive and innovative agriculture. Through its ability to produce a rice surplus, the agricultural system of northern Vietnam could easily support an upper class who did not need to work the land. This was a phenomenon replicated throughout South East Asia. Increased agricultural efficiency led to greater social divisions and economic activities became specialist occupations. Agricultural work became associated with lower-status 'commoners', war captives and debt slaves. Occupational differences based upon gender also emerged.

The mere fact that more than 200 Dong-son-style drums have been found throughout South East Asia suggests that, firstly, Co Loa may not have been particularly unique, confirmed by archaeological discoveries in Thailand and Laos, and, secondly, that Co Loa itself had tapped into coastal and river trade routes, requiring a high level of regional economic coordination and integration. The finding of so many Dong-son bronzes spread over wide areas suggests that an extensive and well-organized intraregional trade network in South East Asia existed long before large-scale Indian and Chinese commercial intercourse. Certainly, the idea that South East Asia was a political and economic desert – prior to the infusion of Chinese and Indian modes of authority and trading techniques – requires qualification. South East Asians lived and traded under stratified and hierarchical political dynasties long before the expansion and adaptation of Chinese and Indian influences over the region.

Nevertheless Vietnam's earliest state was unable to remain as an independent entity, given increasing Han Chinese incursions from about 300 BC onwards. The Chinese were attracted to Vietnam in the hope of gaining access to the southern trade in goods such as pearls, incense, elephant tusks, rhinoceros horn, tortoiseshell, coral, and, for their beautiful feathers, parrots, kingfishers and peacocks. The area around the Red River was conquered by Chinese armies in 111 BC. By the first centuries AD, the Vietnamese aristocrats increasingly collaborated with, and administered on behalf of, their Han overlords in the new Chinese province of Giao-chi. Under Chinese influence, the previous system of communal landownership gave way to private landholding and further class divisions based upon the ownership of property emerged. A merged Sino-Vietnamese elite culture also took shape.

FU-NAN: THE FIRST STATE IN CAMBODIA?

As northern Vietnam increasingly fell under Chinese hegemony, an independent polity was emerging further south, on the border between present-day Cambodia and Vietnam. This is referred to in Chinese sources as the kingdom of Fu-nan and it seems to have risen to prominence in the first century AD. The Chinese believed that the kingdom was founded by Kaundinya, who had been guided there by a dream that had revealed his destiny. With the aid of a magic bow,

Kaundinya was able to transfix the boat of Liu Yeh (willow leaf), and defeat her. The union of Liu Yeh and Kaundinya resulted in the creation of a dynasty that ruled over Fu-nan for 150 years after Kaundinya's death. Indian legend, however, suggests that Kaundinya was given a sacred javelin, which he threw to mark the spot of Fu-nan's capital. When Kaundinya married Soma, the *naga* (cobra) king's daughter, he encouraged her to wear her hair in a knot and, because she wore no clothing, Kaundinya designed a simple garment with a hole for the head, which was worn by all women. The landing site of Kaundinya's mythical javelin was Vyadapura, which was near Ba Phnom in today's Prei Veng province, Cambodia. Excavations have revealed a walled seaport, which served the kingdom commercially, at Oc-eo on the Mekong River, now in Vietnam. Oc-eo was linked by a network of canals to other settlements in the kingdom.

Fu-nan's success was clearly connected to its emergence as a centre for international trade: discoveries from the first and second centuries AD of Roman medallions, Greco-Roman jewellery, Persian coinage, Indian seals and rings, and a Chinese mirror reveal that Oc-eo was an important port on the global trade network that linked China to India to the Middle East and, ultimately, to Roman Europe. Indian and Persian sailors would have stopped off at Oc-eo waiting for favourable winds to transport them to China and exchange Mediterranean, Middle Eastern, Indian and African goods for Chinese silk.

Oc-eo also served as an important collecting point for South East Asian products (for example, copper and tin) and as a manufacturing centre for jewellery; items which could be exchanged for international goods with Indian and Chinese traders who visited the port. Located on the great Mekong Delta, Oc-eo was able to exploit its hinterland for rice, which grew in abundance in fields naturally irrigated by the river's flood waters. This rice surplus fed not only the population of Fu-nan but also supplied the sailors and merchants on passing ships. Oc-eo also possessed locational advantages thanks to its tranquil position relative to the rough seas around the coast of southern Vietnam. Before 350 AD, the India-China trade route from the Bay of Bengal passed overland at the Kra Isthmus (in present-day southern Thailand) rather than negotiating the longer sea-route via the Melaka or Sunda Straits. The

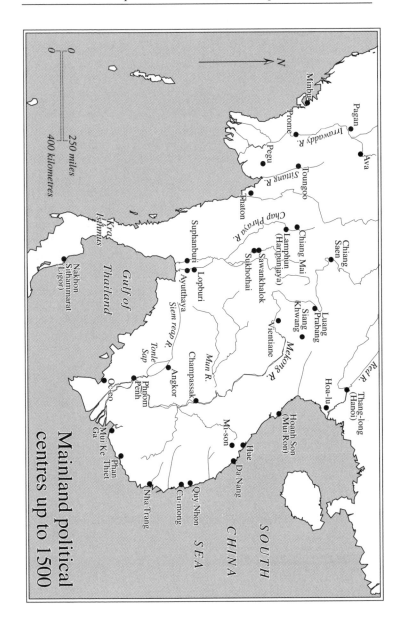

Mainland political centres up to 1500

trade then passed around the rim of the Gulf of Thailand to Oc-eo, where a set of canals led on to a river transit route through the lower Mekong. The final leg of the journey to southern China proceeded along the Vietnamese coast.

Fu-nan was a cosmopolitan trading kingdom and Indian influences, in particular, were significant. Chinese visitors to the Mekong Delta in the third century AD reported that Fu-nan's writing system resembled that of other Indian-influenced societies. Fu-nan's king was keen to expand his kingdom. According to the Chinese, in the early third century King Fan Shiman 'used troops to attack and subdue neighbouring kingdoms, which all acknowledged themselves his vassals'. Fu-nan's military power and wealth, infused with Indian notions of monarchy and vassalage, allowed the kingdom to control the coastal rim of the Gulf of Thailand from the Mekong Delta to the land route across the Kra. Chinese visitors also reported that Fu-nan's people 'lived in walled cities, palaces and houses', devoting themselves primarily to agriculture, but the elite was literate and kept books and archives. Customs duties at Fu-nan were 'paid in gold, silver, pearls, and perfumes'. The Chinese were successful in persuading the 'ugly, black, frizzy-haired naked' people to adopt clothing, which took the form of a piece of cloth, wrapped around the waist.

By the mid-fourth century, however, Fu-nan was on the defensive as Chinese and Indian merchants increasingly chose the sea route via new rival ports on the islands of present-day Indonesia. International traders were also attracted to Java and Sumatra by their ability to supply something that Fu-nan could not produce: spices – nutmeg, cloves, pepper, and mace – from the islands of Maluku (the Moluccas). The decline of the overland route to southern China was confirmed by the sixth century, when Fu-nan seems to have been absorbed into the Khmer kingdom (known to the Chinese as Chen-la).

CENTRALIZED SOCIETIES IN THE AUSTRONESIAN WORLD

In contrast to the mainland, the evidence for the existence of state-like polities in the Indonesian and Malay world is less clear before 500 AD. On Java, for example, it would seem that it was not until the seventh century that a number of Indian-influenced principalities emerged. Nevertheless, there clearly were trends towards stratified and more complex societies in island South East Asia even before cultural and commercial exchanges with India. The Malay word for a king or queen, *ratu*, for example, is assumed to have its origins in prehistoric times. So-called megalithic cultures, epitomized by the burial chambers lined with large stones found on the Pasemah Plateau of southern Sumatra, also suggest the development of complex societies by the early Christian era. The most interesting relics found here are carved boulders, illustrated with images of people variously clad in loincloths and tunics and also sporting such items as bracelets, anklets, ear plugs, helmets and necklaces, again indicating social divisions based on wealth as in mainland societies. Similar stratified societies probably also existed on Java and Bali, which, like Sumatra, had fostered trade contacts with India by the first century AD. Gold items, acquired from Indian traders, stand out as the status symbols for aristocrats and monarchs.

SAWAH

The trend towards more centralized societies was aided by the development of more intensive systems of agriculture, particularly on the islands of Java and Bali, where the wet-rice cultivation system known as *sawah* was well-established by the beginning of the first millennium AD. Rice had already replaced millet as the staple grain in shifting agriculture systems in the upland areas. Patches of forest were cleared annually and then planted with rice grains using sharpened sticks. Lowland, wet-rice exploitation by transplanting, however, was far more productive and could support much larger populations on the islands. The *sawah* system (still practiced today) involved five main stages. Firstly when the rainy season was about to start, the rice seed was sown in seedling beds. While the seeds germinated, the farming community would prepare the main fields for cultivation with wooden, stone and, increasingly, metal-tipped tools. In the second stage, as the monsoon rains began to water the fields, the seedlings were transplanted at suitable intervals to allow space for rapid growth. Thirdly the fields were irrigated by the heavy monsoon rains, which allowed for the maturation of the crop. Fourthly the end of the heavy rains allowed for the sun to ripen the grain and, then, the final harvesting of the crop. Afterwards, the fields would be cleared in the dry season, which was also traditionally the time for the celebration of festivals and marriages.

The *sawah* system supported dense populations because of the relatively high rice yields. Rice, alongside fish and coconut, represented the main staple in a diet that was supplemented by fowls, pigs, and vegetables raised in the villages. From the beginning of the first millennium, the productivity of the *sawah* system was further enhanced by the use of the great unsung hero of Indonesian agriculture, the water buffalo. While ploughing or clearing the fields, dung from these majestic beasts revitalized the soils.

Surplus food production also facilitated the development of early polities on islands such as Java and Bali, for it allowed for the feeding of officials, religious leaders and traders who did not have time to produce food. Another important connection between sedentary agriculture and the development of states was that settled cultivators were easy to tax – in other words, food surpluses could be extracted from the population to support the nonfarming ruling elite. In return, this developing Javanese aristocracy provided law and order and places of worship. Before 500 AD, however, no large towns or metropolitan areas emerged – typically small village communities peppered the Javanese landscape. It is also important to appreciate that, in what is now Indonesia, *sawah* agriculture could not be developed everywhere, for the system was dependent upon a delicate interlocking of three variables: firstly, extremely fertile volcanic soils; secondly, an abundance of water to irrigate those soils; and thirdly, manure from buffaloes to fertilize the ricefields. Thus traditionally the islands of Borneo and eastern Indonesia, with their far poorer soils, have not been able to support large populations; even today the attempts of the Indonesian government to develop Kalimantan as a 'rice bowl' have largely failed. On Borneo and the islands of the eastern archipelago more primitive 'slash and burn' agriculture, combined with hunting and gathering, survived much longer than on Java, Bali and Sumatra. As a result, the Bornean and eastern Indonesian societies took longer to develop into centralized polities and remained far more egalitarian.

Popular Beliefs Before the Advent of Hinduism and Buddhism

ANIMISM

It is very difficult to reconstruct indigenous belief systems before the spread of the world religions to the region in the early centuries AD. Nevertheless, from the reports of the earliest Christian missionaries who entered the remoter islands of eastern Indonesia – barely touched by Hinduism, Buddhism or Islam – in the sixteenth and seventeenth centuries, it is possible to present a picture of animist ideas, which were probably once common throughout South East Asia. Most early South East Asians believed that the terrestrial world was largely the plaything of a huge variety of 'spirits' who lived in mountains, trees, seas, rivers, lakes, and caves. The appeasement of these spirits was all-important because they exercised great power and were capable of both good and evil deeds. At Parapat on the shores of Lake Toba, Sumatra, a great festival is still held annually among the Batak people who inhabit the area; reputedly this entertainment originated in an attempt by Toba's king to placate the spirits of those drowned in the lake. One of the most potent signs that the spirits were not happy was the failure of harvests and/or rains. To guard against bad fortune, and to soothe angry spirits, gifts were offered in ceremonies: blood offerings, for example, were thought to be an especially effective guarantee of fertile soils and plentiful harvests. Human sacrifice was not common in early South East Asia, however, and those unfortunate people who were offered to the spirits on odd occasions were usually prisoners of war or the victims of slave raids.

On a more personal basis, protection and favours might be sought by individuals from powerful ancestors or former chiefs and warrior heroes. The masks that encircle the 'Moon of Bali' kettle drum probably represent such ancestor spirits. In fact, important figures were assumed to have become spirits on death and might inhabit the earthly form of tigers, elephants or crocodiles. Defence against malevolent deities could be assured by the wearing of amulets – a particularly powerful protection was believed to emanate from bezoar stones

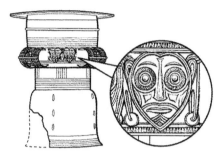

'The Moon of Bali', Pedjeng, Bali, Indonesia. This is the largest of the bronze drums at a height of over 6 feet and with a diameter of 5 feet, 3 inches and is about 2000 years old

(known in Malay as *mestika galiga*). These are still found in the stomachs of wild pigs and deer and, well into the modern period, remained an important trade item in areas such as Sarawak.

Funerals – particularly of community leaders – were very important events and involved much ceremonial, because of the need to ensure the safe passage of the dead individual's spirit into the afterlife. Bodies were carefully prepared and dressed and provided with possessions – such as jewellery, food, drink, clothing and even boats – which would all be required in the spirit world. It was assumed that an individual's temporal status would be replicated in the 'Kingdom of the Dead', so that a king on earth would become a kind of spirit monarch on death. Myths about the founding of peoples and kingdoms have much to tell us about the earliest indigenous, animist ideas. According to Vietnamese legend, the line of Lac lords, who ruled in the Red River region during the first millennium BC, were descended from the union of the dragon spirit with a Vietnamese queen, Ao Co. This myth imbued Vietnamese rulers with supernatural powers. Similarly, snake cults legitimized royal authority in Cambodia whose founding monarch, it will be recalled, was supposed to have married a Cobra princess. Khmer kings maintained the wellbeing of the people through consummation with a nine-headed cobra. In the *naga* (cobra) cult – which is found throughout the South East Asian region – Indian ideas simply blended with much older, local religious concepts.

Indigenous beliefs proved remarkably resilient into classical, modern and contemporary times. In thirteenth-century 'Buddhist' Thailand, for example, rituals at spring sites were designed to appease spirits in order to keep the realm well watered and prosperous. Considerably after the spread of Islam to the Indonesian island of Sulawesi, it was common for families still to keep images of the sun and the moon in their homes to appease these mighty deities. Sacrifices to powerful mountain spirits in Cambodia survived into the nineteenth century. Indeed the world religions essentially had to adapt themselves to much older traditional practices and ideas, and the new gods continued to exist alongside local deities. The French ex-rubber planter, Henri Fauconnier, published *The Soul of Malaya* in 1931. The book provides a fascinating insight into Malay culture, in which Islamic precepts continued to co-exist with an eclectic cornucopia of spirits. The most frightening of these pre-Islamic deities was known as the Penanggal and manifested itself as the head and entrails of an unfaithful wife! As Fauconnier perceptively observed: 'The conversion of a people to a new religion does not modify the character of that people. It is a process of painting wood to look like wood'. Today many tourists visit Torajaland in Sulawesi. This highland community is nominally Christian, but the principal fascination for westerners with the Toraja people lies with their elaborate funerals, in which a number of pre-Christian ideas predominate and provide a contemporary window on the earliest South East Asian belief systems. Most notable is the concept of a huge, prolonged and noisy ceremony, including the spilling of pig and buffalo blood, to ensure the safe passage of the dead person's spirit to the world beyond. Many South East Asians clung on to their own spirits because quite often Buddhism, Hinduism, Islam or Christianity only provided solutions to big, long-term questions. Ancestor spirits, on the other hand, which might inhabit an impressive tree in a village or a tiger prowling in the nearby jungle, could be called upon to assist in more immediately relevant issues, such as illness, childbearing, the rice crop, the rains, warfare and trade.

THE ROLE OF WOMEN

Women had a central place in many of the early rituals. It was assumed that women had special powers and were particularly adept at communicating with the spirits. Women were approached to cure disease, avert crop failures and expand trade opportunities. The central religio-cultural role for women reflected their general political and economic status, which was probably better than in equivalent Asian societies such as India or China. Evidence from archaeological digs in Thailand suggests that before the Bronze Age high status was afforded to women, who were traditionally the producers of pottery. Through barter of their pottery, women accumulated wealth – for example, in the form of jewellery – and, on death, were given prestigious burials. Women were pivotal in early trade systems and remained prominent as merchants until the sixteenth and seventeenth centuries AD in much of the island world – again in contrast to India or China.

In the elite political realm too, women exercised significant power and rights. In the early kingdoms of South East Asia, succession to the throne was rarely clearly established and could be through either the male or the female line. Rights of inheritance were not exclusively along the male line and bride wealth frequently passed from male to female. The common and excruciatingly painful male practice of implanting penis balls to heighten female sexual pleasure, is another example of the considerable power and influence held by women in early South East Asia. The freedom and enhanced position enjoyed by women only began to erode with the spread of the world religions to the region after 500 AD.

CHAPTER THREE

Classical South East Asia,
500–1500

The so-called classical era of South East Asian history roughly corresponds to the medieval period in Europe. Far more is known about the 500–1500 period, than the earliest era of South East Asian history, mainly due to the survival of a greater stock of written source material, generated both within and without the region. Chinese and Indian sources are particularly abundant, as are the chronicles left by the literati in countries like Vietnam. Between the sixth and sixteenth centuries AD, a number of monarchies and empires rose (and sometimes fell): the most famous of these were, Dai Viet, Champa, Angkor, Ayutthaya, Srivijaya, Majapahit, and Melaka. This classical political heritage has often been drawn upon by modern South East Asians to furnish the independent nations of the region with a pre-colonial legitimacy. At the same time, with ever-expanding global trade contacts, South East Asia gained international repute due, particularly, to the trade in spices from the Maluku Islands (Moluccas) in present-day Indonesia. In recognition of the region's fantastic wealth potential, Indian and western traders depicted South East Asia as the 'Golden Khersonese' or 'Land of Gold'. By the eleventh century, according to the historian Kenneth R. Hall, 'all world trade was more or less governed by the ebb and flow of spices in and out of South East Asia'. The millennium after 500 also constituted a period of great cultural significance for South East Asia, for this was the era in which Hindu and Buddhist ideas spread throughout much of the region, and in the last centuries of the classical period we can also witness the beginnings of Islam's religious hegemony over much of the island world.

Dai Viet

THE STRUGGLE AGAINST CHINESE DOMINATION

The kingdom of Dai Viet, based upon the city of Hanoi (Thang-long) in today's northern Vietnam (Bac Bo or Tonkin), was proclaimed by the later Ly dynasty in the eleventh century. Prior to this, Vietnam's history had been dominated by a struggle against Chinese overlordship. It is interesting to note that the Vietnamese sense of national identity has traditionally been defined through the assertion of independence from a Chinese alien, 'Other' in what the Vietnamese call the '1000 War'. This sense of being different from China, while, at the same time, borrowing and adapting Chinese ideas, proved an important factor in the final emergence of an independent Dai Viet. The chiefdom established around the Red River had become a Chinese province by the earliest centuries AD. But Chinese control was never absolute, and the Han soldier-lords essentially ruled in collaboration with the Vietnamese aristocracy. Intermarriage between Chinese soldier-administrators and leading Vietnamese families was common, and soon a fusion of Chinese and Vietnamese cultures occurred. If not all pervasive, Chinese influence was nevertheless crucial to the evolution of Viet society. In an attempt to expand the tax base to support an ever-growing administration, the Chinese mandarins promoted increases in agricultural productivity (for example, through the digging of irrigation canals around the Red River delta) and also a shift from communal usage to private ownership of land. The result was the emergence of a Sino-Viet aristocratic landowner class and a landless peasantry: the inability to pay taxes often forced peasants to sell their land and become tenant farmers on the big private fiefs. Status and wealth were increasingly determined by how much land a particular family owned.

The localized nature of rule meant that at times of imperial weakness the Vietnamese could throw off the Chinese yoke, for example, in the sixth century. Yet, by the seventh and eighth centuries, the Tang dynasty reasserted Chinese administrative dominance over the Red River region and established a protectorate known as An Nam, in which the Vietnamese elite once again co-operated with the Chinese colonizers via the former's favoured position in the bureaucracy. Under Tang rule, Hanoi emerged as the political capital of the Vietnamese province, largely due to its commanding strategic location at the centre of the Red River network, which was the main communications artery for northern Vietnam. From Hanoi the Tang administration was to promote further improvements in Vietnam's wet-rice economy, through the extension of dykes along the Red River delta.

The disintegration of imperial authority, which followed the fall of the last Tang emperor in 907, permitted another bid for Vietnamese independence, so that in 939 a Vietnamese army won a significant victory over forces of the Southern Han dynasty at Canton (Guangzhou) in southern China. By the 960s the major political force in northern Vietnam was a warrior named Dinh Bo Linh who led brigades of peasants. Aided by a productive wet-rice economy and expanding internal and international trade, Vietnam's 'first emperor' succeeded in establishing a modicum of political hegemony at his capital, Hoa-lu, on the southern edge of the Red River plain. But Dinh's system of warrior-kingship was always transient, lacking both bureaucratic efficiency and cultural vitality. As a result, in the eleventh century, an alternative elite focus of Vietnamese unity had emerged, involving an alliance between the aristocracy and the increasingly important Buddhist monkhood. The leading monks had previously been advisers to the warrior-kings at Hoa-lu, and they were an important source of support for these regimes from the 960s to the early 1000s because they could furnish the monarchy with labour and other resources, as well as peasant acquiescence. But the monkhood became increasingly disenchanted with the system of military rule it had helped establish at Hoa-lu and looked instead to the traditional aristocracy to lead a cultural and political renaissance. Military power alone, the monks reasoned, was not enough to resist China. Hanoi was resurrected as the capital, but with a new identity as the centre of the royal court of the self-proclaimed Ly dynasty. A reunified China – as represented by the Song dynasty after 960 – attempted to reassert its dominance. But the Vietnamese elite, albeit utilizing modes of administration, culture and learning introduced by their Chinese overlords, now proved capable of full autonomy.

THE LY DYNASTY

The rule of the Ly kings between 1009 and 1224 is regarded as a period central to the development of Vietnam for four main reasons. Firstly, the Lys developed the concept of an ethical, responsible monarchy based upon Buddhist precepts, linking the king to the heavens above and the people below. Secondly, they sanctioned the worship of a set of indigenous, 'national' spirits as defenders of royal authority. Thirdly, the Ly kings adapted Chinese political concepts to define Hanoi as the seat of a 'southern emperor', who ruled the 'southern kingdom' by virtue of the 'mandate of heaven'. Fourthly, under Ly rule, the tendency towards the greater internationalization of the Vietnamese economy was intensified.

Ly Tai To

The founder of the Ly dynasty of Dai Viet was Ly Tai To (originally Ly Cong Uan). Born in 974, Ly Tai To was highly educated, thanks to the teachings of Buddhist monks. Ly had a short career as a praetorian guard at Hoa-lu before grabbing the throne for himself and relocating the royal court to Hanoi, between 1009 and 1010. With the ever-present influence of his spiritual advisors, particularly one Van Hanh, Ly's rule was both efficient and ruthless. Ly consolidated his rule and his new empire by conquering rebels and bringing the hill people into line, while the enforcement of efficient taxation brought Ly rewards for his efforts. Given his reliance on the monkhood, it is no surprise that Ly Tai To proved himself a great supporter of Buddhism. But in continuing patronage of a number of indigenous spirit cults, Ly successfully initiated a cultural revival, which further cemented monarchical authority. Another important feature of Ly Tai To's seminal reign was the development of an ethical basis to his kingship. According to the Vietnamese chronicles, Ly Tai To attacked the Dinh and Early Le dynasties of Hoa-lu for being too arrogant and too despotic; for ignoring the 'will of heaven' and 'plundering and injuring the people'.

Instead, Ly Tai To aimed at a monarchy that ruled in harmony with both the heavens and the masses.

Ly Tai Tong

Ly Tai To was succeeded as king in 1028 by his son Ly Tai Tong, who ruled until 1054. Ly Tai Tong continued his father's work both as a reformer and a successful military commander. He was, however, much more independent of the monkhood than Ly Tai To. Ly Tai Tong's greatest achievement was the institutionalization of monarchical authority through a book of laws, the *Minh-dao* or 'Clear Way', published in 1042. Edicts concerned with military discipline, oaths of loyalty, theft of royal property, slavery, corruption, famine relief, the protection of high-born women, and offences against the king indicate that Ly Tai Tong was principally concerned with increasing the bureaucratic efficiency of his administration. Confucianism – the moral code based upon the teachings of the ancient Chinese philosopher, Confucius (K'ung Fu-tse) – became a kind of state ideology and was a central part of the syllabus for the state examinations that state administrators or mandarins had to pass. Ly Tai Tong's energetic rule, which also included a highly successful, sea-launched plunder raid against the kingdom of Champa to the south in 1044, earned him a fearsome reputation. According to legend, in 1043, he had caused a leaning pillar to straighten by the power of thought alone. Ly Tai Tong's reign was also an era of economic expansion, which was so successful that taxes were actually reduced. Economic development projects, such as the building of roads and the settling of 5,000 Cham war captives on frontier lands, were initiated. Meanwhile, new internal and international markets developed, as Dai Viet emerged as a major supplier of gold and silver to Angkor, the Malay States, Srivijaya and Java, in exchange for spices and other international trade goods. The Buddhist devotion of this most celebrated of the Ly kings is confirmed by the building of Hanoi's famous 'One Pillar Pagoda' (Chua Mot Cot) in the final years of Ly Tai Tong's reign.

Ly Thanh Tong

Such was the reverence afforded Ly Tai Tong that his son, Ly Thanh

Tong, was able to succeed to the throne unchallenged on his father's death in 1054. In the Ly tradition, Ly Thanh Tong was scholarly, musical, warlike, religious but, at the same time, a ruthless defender of royal power. The authority of the monarchy over the regional lords was upheld by oathing ceremonies, feasts and elaborate royal-birthday celebrations. Ly Thanh Tong also further encouraged the development of a national culture and adaptation of local traditions that emphasized the role of the king as an intermediary between the heavens and the people; the rice crop and the prosperity of Dai Viet became intimately associated with the monarchy. Ly Thanh Tong's deliberate aping of the imperial court in China, aroused Song displeasure as a haughty rival 'southern emperor'. Sensibly, however, Ly Thanh Tong avoided confrontation with imperial China over the contentious border issue and focused his overseas adventurism to the south in another successful military expedition against Champa in 1069. This struggle for naval supremacy in the South China Sea was again indicative of the Ly desire to open up international markets, because the Chams were an obstacle in the path of Dai Viet's expanding trade with Java.

VICTORY OVER CHINA

China still remained a formidable problem for Dai Viet and in 1075 under the boy-king, Ly Can Duc, the Viet general, Ly Thuong Kiet, led a fantastic campaign against a divided Song China in which the Chinese navy and several cities were decimated. Ly Thuong Kiet was a great strategist and favoured a pre-emptive strike against China; having divided his 100,000 strong army he launched a successful two-pronged attack and occupied several citadels in southern China. Some Viet forces were welcomed as liberators sent by father Ly from the southern country. But the successes were short lived, and it was not long before the Chinese launched a counterattack. Again, the military genius of Ly Thuong Kiet proved decisive. Dai Viet was blessed with the natural defence of the Cau River which Ly skilfully capitalised upon. The Viet forces successfully held a 25-mile line, and were aided by the navy and some guerrilla forces who prevented the Chinese from getting supplies and reinforcements through to their front line. Legend tells a more interesting story of terrified Chinese forces listening to the prophetic poem of the river genie, which foretold doom and certain annihilation for the invading Chinese. The river genie in this instance was said to be one of Ly Thuong Kiet's officers, sent to a temple to recite a poem that Ly himself had scripted. After the unsuccessful Song attempt at retaliation, negotiations ensued, which eventually fixed the Sino-Vietnamese border (where it roughly remains to this day). Hanoi was still regarded by the Chinese as having vassal status and tribute was paid on a regular basis, but Dai Viet had won an important concession. In essence, the political principle had been established that the northern, Chinese emperor's 'mandate of heaven' only extended as far as the border with Vietnam. The defence of this sacred frontier increasingly underpinned Viet identity.

Despite this considerable achievement against China, the authority of the Ly dynasty slowly ebbed away in the course of the twelfth and thirteenth centuries. The death of the childless Ly Can Duc in 1127 ushered in a period of weak government in which a group of ministers exercised de facto authority. Internecine disputes and lack of charismatic royal leadership increasingly paralyzed Ly rule. In 1225 a new dynasty, the Tran, began its rule of Dai Viet, which lasted until the 1400s.

THE TRAN DYNASTY

The Tran were a powerful aristocratic clan from the coastal region of Dai Viet. Their naval skills allowed for the eventual domination of the Red and Black rivers in the civil wars that afflicted the country in the 1200s. Although never proclaimed king, their initial leader was Tran Thu Do. According to Tran thinking, the basic problem that had weakened Ly royal authority, was the dangerous influence of the maternal family at court. Eradicating this danger was easy. Tran kings were simply not allowed to marry outside their own clan and, to cement clan loyalty, were encouraged to rule in concert with their male relatives. Dai Viet became a Tran family affair, in which lesser members of the Tran family were favoured in the regional administration, and the Tran royal estates were expanded to encompass more lucrative rice-growing land. The thirteenth century saw the growing power of the great estates (*trang-dien*). This development was aided by an official sanction of Tran Thanh Tong in 1266, which ordered vagabonds and the unemployed into bondage to clear and develop new lands in the south to be owned and administered by the mighty Tran magnates. In addition, the Tran dynasty rescinded the orders of the earlier Ly dynasty, which had forbidden the sale of children into slavery.

The Lys had developed an efficient bureaucracy, but the Trans went further in introducing a Chinese-style examination system as a means of selecting mandarins, educated in neo-Confucian thinking. The Tran era witnessed the rise of a literati-administrator class. The stability of the Tran realm was to be threatened, however, by Dai Viet's old adversary, China. But China was not merely the same the old force with which to reckon. It had taken on a frighteningly novel dimension because after 1279 the empire was fully under the control of the fearsome Mongol warriors. In 1284 the armies of Kublai Khan invaded Dai Viet and, as would be repeated in 1287–88, fearless Tran resistance on both land and sea repulsed the would-be colonizers.

The defeat of the Mongols in the 1280s has entered into Vietnamese national mythology, but this represented the apogee of Tran power, because from the 1340s Dai Viet was subject to a number of fissures and revolts. These reached their peak in 1369 when the death of the childless Tran Du Tong ushered in an almost inevitable succession dispute. Such was the weakness of the royal authority that Cham invaders were able to sack Hanoi three times in the course of 1390, and the Tran actually lost power to the Ho dynasty for a short period between 1400 and 1407. Worse still, in 1406, Ming Chinese armies occupied Dai Viet in yet another attempt to incorporate China's defiant southern neighbour into the empire. It was the Chinese threat that brought to power a new Vietnamese dynasty, the Later Le.

THE LATER LE DYNASTY

Resistance to the Ming occupation of northern Vietnam was led by Le Loi, a powerful landowner from Thanh Hoa on the Ma River plain, south of the Red River. Le Loi also enjoyed the support of the gifted politician and poet, Nguyen Trai. The siege of Ming forces at Hanoi in 1427 was the prelude to full Chinese withdrawal one year later, followed by the triumphant proclamation of the Later Le dynasty. Le Loi died just five years after becoming king, but he did initiate a new era of stability in which a number of agricultural, legal and ideological-cum-cultural reforms were introduced. The reforming zeal of the Later Le dynasty culminated in the much-vaunted reign of Le Loi's grandson, Le Thanh Ton from 1460. Le Thanh Ton laid the basis of the bureaucratic system, based upon the Confucian philosophy of loyalty to established hierarchies and efficiency, which would underpin Vietnam's governance through to the nineteenth century. The stability of Le Thanh Ton's rule also permitted an intellectual revival. Thanh Ton was himself a poet and a patron of poets, and there remain to this day classic works of poetry, folklore, history, law and government that originate from the period of his reign. There was a revival also of military power, and campaigns in Champa and Laos resulted in the expansion of territory. The decisive victory over Champa in 1471 held major economic advantages for it removed at a stroke the possibility of any further Cham plunder raids. It also provided new territory for agricultural expansion to be settled by the 30,000 Cham war captives. Moreover the annihilation of Champa now allowed Vietnamese access to the highland sources of forest products – such as ivory, rhinoceros horn, tortoiseshell, pearls, peacock and kingfisher feathers, spices, aromatic woods, and even gold – much coveted by international merchants. Indeed, following on from the Hoa-lu warrior-monarchs and the Ly dynasty, the Le kings seized upon the potential of commerce as an alternative source of taxation. Thanh Ton was, in particular, extremely proud of having reduced taxes on the overburdened peasantry. Le Thanh Ton also used convicts to open up the southern provinces, and in the early sixteenth century the highlands were incorporated into the Dai Viet state by utilizing the local chieftains as district officials.

During the fifteenth century, the 'golden age' of Dai Viet, the stability of Le rule allowed Hanoi to emerge as the region's largest city, with a population in excess of 100,000, at the heart of South East Asia's most centralised and populous state. Manufacturing was centred in Hanoi. Within the expanding city, quarters dedicated to particular crafts emerged, while Le kings engaged skilled craftsmen to build magnificent temples and palaces. Dai Viet may have been riding high, but Le Thanh Ton's death in 1497 soon witnessed Dai Viet descend, yet again, into a maelstrom of anarchy and self-destruction. Le Thanh Ton was probably the last truly popular Viet king, and during his reign the monarchy achieved a security both for itself and its realm that would never be witnessed again.

Champa

UNITY AND DISUNITY

In contrast to the north, political authority in the kingdom of Champa in central, coastal Vietnam was far more dispersed. The diverse peoples of the various Champa polities were descendants of Austronesian settlers and formed several Malay-style river-mouth states along the coastal enclaves of their mountainous region. The Chams were ethnically quite different from their northern neighbours and engaged in various economic activities from rice growing to fishing, to trade and to piracy. The first organized Cham polity seems to have been centred around modern Hue; a state known as Lin Yi to the Chinese from the second century AD. It became an important international centre for trade but, in 446, Lin Yi was sacked in a Sino-Vietnamese invasion.

By the late ninth century, the centre of Cham power had shifted south to the modern-day city of Da Nang. Amaravati is the name used to describe the Indian-style temples, sculptures and inscriptions found in this area and that represent both Hindu and Buddhist themes. The major site for Amaravati artefacts is Mi-son, the Cham spiritual capital and centre of royal ceremony, upriver from the ancient city of Indrapura (modern-day Tra-kieu). Indian influences on Champa may have arrived indirectly via trade contacts with Java from the eighth century. Similar bas-reliefs to those on temples at Mi-son can be found at the great temple complex of Borobudur on Java, and in the early 1300s the Cham king, Jayasinhavarman II, married a Javanese princess named Tapasi. Champa's Indo-Javanese relics are indicative of the important religious basis to Cham kingship. The right to rule was intimately linked to the monarch's close relations with traditional ancestor spirits as well as the 'new' Hindu and Buddhist deities.

Mi-son remained the cultural heart of the Cham realm and the main

Eighth-century bronze Buddha from central Java, Indonesia

focus of Cham unity. But, between the eleventh and fifteenth centuries, the most important power centre became Vijaya, near present-day Quy Nhon. The Chams managed to sack Angkor in 1177 but, during the eleventh, twelfth and thirteenth centuries, Cham lands were subject to repeated incursions from both Dai Viet and Cambodia. The decline of Tran power in the north, however, led to the sacking of Hanoi in 1390 by Cham forces under King Che Bong Nga. Indeed, lacking extensive wet-rice cultivation or international trade links, Cham kings were highly reliant on war booty from raids against their neighbours to generate the wealth required to cement alliances with their leading subjects.

DEFEAT AND SURVIVAL

Champa's superiority over its northern neighbour was short-lived. In 1471, Vijaya was seized by the resurgent Viet armies and northern Cham lands were occupied. The essential problem for Champa was the decentralized nature of Cham political authority, which did not allow for the retention of Cham territory in the face of both Viet and

Cambodian aggrandizement. Lacking a centralized bureaucracy, the Cham kings relied on their leadership of various religious cults to mobilize the population. The death of a particular king was often followed by a period of anarchy and pillage before the emergence of another powerful leader to take the throne. Even so, a Cham kingdom, around the modern city of Nha Trang, survived the defeat of 1471 and Cham kings and princes ruled under Viet overlordship until 1832. Today, most of Vietnam's Cham population can be found in the central highlands province of Thuan Hai. They remain discriminated against and a marginalized population but, increasingly, a degree of wealth is filtering through to the Cham people through growing tourism. Despite the destruction of the formal kingdom, the idea of Champa has survived into contemporary times, as witnessed by revolts of ethnic minorities against Vietnamese governments in the 1960s and 1970s.

Angkor

THE ESTABLISHMENT OF THE KINGDOM

The kingdom of Angkor, in modern-day Cambodia, emerged in the ninth century following the decline of Chen-la. By the early 1200s Angkor's rule was the golden age of Cambodia, extending its influence not only over present-day Cambodia but also the Mekong Delta and large areas of modern Laos and Thailand. Before the early 800s, however, the Khmer peoples of the lower Mekong basin lacked a political or cultural centre, and authority in Cambodia was fragmented into various small coastal and riverine trading kingdoms. Angkor, located inland in north west Cambodia, filled this void, and differed from Fu-nan and Chen-la before it by basing its wealth not on international commerce but on domestic agriculture. Angkor's prime location on the north west shore of the great inland lake, Tonle Sap, provided the kingdom with superb water-transport possibilities, which meant that Angkor was perfectly located to command the labour and land resources of the surrounding rice fields. It remained the seat of Khmer royal power until the fifteenth century. Several Cambodian

Economic centres up to 1500

Tonplun
• Pagan
• Manbu

Pegu

Thaton

Irrawaddy R.

Red R.
Black R.

Thang-long
(Hanoi)
• Bo-hai
Hoa-lu

Nghe-an

Mekong R.

Quang Tri

Chao Phraya R.

Lopburi

Prah Vihar

Siem reap R. Angkor

Tonle Sap

Mergui

Yang
Prong

Hue • Tra-kieu (Indrapura)
Mi-son • Dong-duong
• Quy Nhon (Vijaya)
Cheo Reo

• Nha Trang (Kauthara)

Phan Rang (Panduranga)

Gulf of Thailand

Chaiya
Takuapa

Suratthani

Oc-eo Vyadhapura

SOUTH

CHINA

SEA

Samudra
Pasai

Straits of Melaka

Melaka

Brunei

Equator

N

INDIAN

OCEAN

Jambi
Palembang
• Kotakapur

Musi R.

Palas
Pasemah

Sunda Strait Ho-ling

Mataram

Java Sea

Majapahit
Singhasari

Kadiri

| 0 | 500 miles |
| 0 | 800 kilometres |

leaders had attempted to establish a capital amidst the rice fields, but the founding of Angkor is usually associated with King Jayavarman II, who was proclaimed universal monarch of the Khmer people in 802.

The first Khmer king to actually live at Angkor, however, was Yasovarman I who ruled from 889 to 900. A central prop to Yasovarman's power was the building of monasteries and temples, carefully designed and located to create a *Mandala* – a representation of the universe on earth. The three great religious cult figures of Angkor – Siva, Vishnu and Buddha – all sanctified royal authority. Through these cults developed the concept of individual kings being divinely endowed with superior powers and skills by the Hindu (and later Buddhist) deities. The Brahmanical priests were part of a clearly defined Angkorean hierarchy, which further enhanced regal authority by placing the king at the pinnacle. The king bestowed land upon the leading aristocratic families in a system that has been likened to European feudalism. Although royal power was still largely personalized by the end of Yasovarman's reign, the centralized authority of the Khmer kings was sufficient to mobilize labour on a large-enough scale to build awe-inspiring temples and support military campaigns against Angkor's rivals.

Under the reign of Yasovarman I's grandson, Rajendravarman II, between 944 and 968, the aristocracy was tied further to the monarchy by marriage into the royal house. Like his grandfather, Rajendravarman was both a great builder in support of royal power and a great general, orchestrating a decisive victory over Champa. The expansionist tendencies of the Angkor kings were confirmed in the first half of the eleventh century under Suryavarman I. He extended Angkor's authority to the north but, most notably, to the west, over the entire lower Chao Phraya plain of today's Thailand. This western focus to Angkor's expansionist attentions was mainly the result of Suryavarman's desire to open up a trade route to India via Lopburi and the Kra Isthmus. At home, meanwhile, Suryavarman promoted greater efficiencies in royal governance through the Khmer temple network. Essentially, this entailed the land-holding elite becoming state officials through their administration of local temples: in return for this official recognition, the big families, through their own temples, transferred a share of local rice production to temples under royal control, contributing to greater monarchical wealth. So temples had more than just a spiritual function and, as well as acting as warehouses in which to store rice, they were also centres for technology, management and craftsmanship. It was under the direction of temple inhabitants that land cultivation was successfully extended in the tenth and eleventh centuries.

The real key to the success of early Angkor kings was their ability to mobilize agricultural resources. Rice productivity in the realm was greatly enhanced by an irrigation network of earth dams, which ran east–west and north–south and which transferred water to the paddy fields from the hill of Phnom Kulen, some thirty miles north west of Angkor. Phnom Kulen, understandably, became the centre of the *devaraja* cult, which symbolized the unity of the Khmer realm through the association of the king with Angkor's water supply and its prosperity. The system of royal and elite-owned temples that covered the realm was central to Angkor's economic development because land, and the bonded labourers (*knum*) who worked it, were tied to the religious establishments.

ORDER AND DISORDER

Between the 1050s and the 1430s, the story of Angkor is punctuated by intermittent bouts of anarchy, following the death of an authoritative charismatic king. Although monarchs such as Suryavarman I achieved greater centralized authority than the rulers of Champa, they did not permanently institutionalize their personal power along the lines of the Ly dynasty in Dai Viet. In contrast to the Chinese threat to northern Vietnam, Angkor faced few external challenges, save for the occasional Cham incursion. Perhaps, Cambodian kings felt no urgency to shore up central government.

On the death of Suryavarman I in 1050, power passed to his son Udayadityavarman II, who left an important architectural legacy: notably the vast Saivite temple–mountain at Angkor, the Baphuon. Asceticism aside, Udayadityavarman seems to have been a weak king: he faced three major internal challenges from the leading Khmer aristocrats, exacerbated by Cham military pressure, in his politically turbulent reign, which ended in 1066. The period of instability was broken, however, by the emergence of Suryavarman II as king in 1113. Suryavarman II's military achievements were considerable: Champa was subjugated in 1145 and Angkor's authority even extended into the Malay peninsula. Recognition from the Southern Song court in China was indicative of Angkor's growing international status. It is Suryavarman's constructions that are most celebrated: he ordered the building of the magnificent temple complex of Angkor Wat, the crowning glory and culmination of centuries of fine Khmer architecture. Angkor Wat was built as the king's funeral temple and reveals Suryavarman's devotion to the Hindu deity, Vishnu. As in Champa, there were significant Indo-Javanese influences on both art and ideas in classical Angkor.

Yet once Angkor Wat had served its intended purpose in 1150, the Khmer realm again descended into political chaos. In 1177, the Chams

The Khmer king's celestial concubines – or *apsarases* – as shown in a twelfth-century relief sculpture at Angkor Wat, Cambodia

took advantage and overwhelmed Angkor in a water-borne invasion. Once again, however, a powerful Khmer leader emerged out of disaster. The celebrated Jayavarman VII claimed the throne in 1181, and counterattacks against the Chams were so successful that in the early thirteenth century Champa was formally incorporated into the Angkorean empire. Under Jayavarman VII, Angkor's sway also extended as far north as Vientiane in present-day Laos. Jayavarman was another of Angkor's great architect–kings, possibly the most prolific. In celebration of his penchant for Mahayana Buddhist deities, as the fount of royal power and Angkor's wealth, Jayavarman built the Bayon temple–mountain – symbolizing the cosmic Mount Meru, the abode of the great Hindu gods and centre of the universe – in a new walled city, Angkor Thom, begun about 1200. He was also a great road builder, and inscriptions at Angkor celebrate Jayavarman's establishment of hospitals, Buddhist shrines and resthouses throughout the kingdom as further testament to his piety. Certainly under Jayavarman VII the royal temples flourished: at Angkor Wat, Ta Prohm, the vast Buddhist temple complex dedicated to the king's mother, was built around 1186 and, at its height, reputedly had over 12,000 inhabitants – including priests, officials, learned hermits, students and female dancers – sustained by the surpluses of the surrounding villages and lesser temples.

But, despite his 40 years on the throne, Jayavarman VII relied on the cult of personality and was no more successful than his predecessors in securing the permanency of Khmer royal authority. Indeed, from the 1220s, Angkor entered into a troubled phase of terminal decline. In the economic sphere, the trade route to India opened up by Suryavarman I in the eleventh century was blocked from the late twelfth century by Burmese expansion into the Kra Isthmus. As a result, the Khmer economy – along the lines of similarly ill-fated Champa – became more and more dependent upon looting raids in the east. At the same time, no leader of Suryavarman I, Suryavarman II or Jayavarman VII's personal capability arose to infuse the monarchy with the necessary innovative energy to reverse the downward spiral. The lack of monarchical dynamism is reflected in the absence of great building projects and the replacement of Mahayana with the more egalitarian Theravada

Buddhism from the end of the thirteenth century. Angkor was finally abandoned in the 1430s, following the city's sacking by the Tais of Ayutthaya. By this time, the political capital of Cambodia had shifted to the south east, to the vicinity of the modern city of Phnom Penh, which had better access to trade with Ming China, as well as greater security vis-à-vis the expanding Tais. Nevertheless, the traditions of Angkor were to be continued at Phnom Penh and re-invented in the context of the most powerful of the Tai kingdoms, Ayutthaya.

The Tai Kingdoms

LAN NA

While Cambodia was generally united under a single monarch at Angkor, as late as the thirteenth century, the Tai-speaking peoples of present-day Thailand and Laos remained decentralized under a number of chieftains amidst the upper reaches of the Mekong River. The Mongol incursions into South East Asia from the 1280s, however, provided opportunities for enterprising Tai leaders to cobble together coalitions of chiefdoms and expand their authority, at the expense of Angkor to the south and Pagan (Burma) to the west. One such figure was Mangrai who in 1259, at the age of 20, became the chief of Chiang Saen (located today on Thailand's border with Laos). He later shifted his seat of power south west to Fang (now on the Thai border with Burma). Mangrai built alliances with other Tai leaders to conquer the ancient Mon kingdom at Lamphun, just south of Chiang Mai, between 1290 and 1292. This allowed Mangrai to begin building a new power centre at Chiang Mai, where he is remembered as the founder of the kingdom of Lan Na. Earlier, the Mongol conquest of Pagan in 1287 had allowed Mangrai to expand his authority into modern-day Burma. Mangrai died in 1317, but, in successfully resisting Mongols for two decades and introducing a set of Buddhist-style laws, he laid basis of a distinct northern Tai cultural identity at Chiang Mai. In the early 1400s, Ming Chinese invasions were repelled as were the ambitions of the southern Tai kingdom of Ayutthaya during the reign of Lan Na's King Tilok between 1441 and 1487. The Chiang Mai region remained separate from the rest of Thailand until the nineteenth century.

SUKHOTHAI

In 1287 Mangrai of Lan Na had concluded a pact of friendship with another influential Tai chief to the south, Ramkamhaeng of Sukhothai. Sukhothai is traditionally regarded as Thailand's first capital and appears to have been occupied by Tai-speaking peoples in 1238, when the commander of this north western outpost of the Angkorean empire was overthrown. During the 1240s Angkor's influence was further eradicated from the Chao Phraya plain of central Thailand by Tai armies under the direction of Ramkamhaeng's grandfather. The occupation of Sukhothai was just one part of the slow, but relentless, southern migration of Tai settlers, often at the expense of Mon-Khmer populations, which had its origins in southern China in the sixth century BC. In 1279 Ramkamhaeng, or 'Rama the Brave', the greatest of Sukhothai's kings, succeeded to the throne. He was a great warrior and, through victories on the battlefield, Sukhothai's writ came to run throughout much of modern-day Thailand and Laos. As an inscription of 1292 claims, 'Ramkamhaeng is sovereign lord of all the Tais... He has conquered the multitude of his enemies, possessing spacious cities and numbers of elephants'. Ramkamhaeng came to govern his realms through a feudal-style system, in which vanquished local lords were made Sukhothai's vassals. But Ramkamhaeng was a great statesman as well as a soldier. Most of his subjects were probably Mons and Khmers, and it was from their older civilizations that he borrowed a script to put the Tai language into writing for the first time. Through trade contacts the Tais had come into contact with Chinese and Indian Buddhism and at Sukhothai Ramkamhaeng also fostered a Tai culture based upon Buddhist-inspired literature and sculpture. Ramkamhaeng's descendants continued to rule Sukhothai independently until 1419. But the great king's death in 1298 ushered in the steady transfer of Sukhothai's authority to another Tai kingdom further to the south, Ayutthaya.

AYUTTHAYA

Occupying an island in the great river, the Chao Phraya, between the chiefdoms of Lopburi to the east and Suphanburi to the west, Ayutthaya was established by one U Thong. U Thong came from a wealthy Chinese merchant family and, ingeniously, he had strategically married into both the Lopburi and the Suphanburi ruling houses. Ayutthaya emerged as a unified Lopburi-Suphanburi kingdom when U Thong proclaimed himself King Ramathibodi in 1351. There occurred at Ayutthaya a creative blending of three strengths: martial experience and manpower resources from the Tais of Suphanburi; administrative traditions, derived from Angkor, from the Mons and Khmers of Lopburi; and the abilities of the local Chinese as merchants. Ayutthaya was a well-placed typical pre-modern South East Asian capital: it was surrounded by numerous wet-rice growing villages and, at the same time, was accessible by sea for international trade.

Under Ramathibodi's reign, which lasted until 1369, Ayutthaya asserted its independence from Angkor. According to a Cambodian source, the Khmer capital was even occupied by Ayutthaya between 1353 and 1357, forcing Angkor's king into exile in Laos. In the fifteenth century, Ayutthaya was finally victorious in the struggle for regional overlordship: in 1431, under King Borommaracha II, Angkor was overwhelmed and finally abandoned by the Khmer kings. To the north, the rulers of Ayutthaya were also partially successful in combining the Tais under a single power centre. By 1419 Borommaracha's father, Intharacha, had reduced Sukhothai to vassal status and, from that date on, the rulers of Sukhothai were merely hereditary governors within the Ayutthayan provincial administration.

King Trailok, Borommaracha's son, failed to subdue Lan Na in the far north. Nevertheless, during his reign from 1448 to 1488, Trailok succeeded in laying the basis of a more durable, organized system of government, which may have owed much to Angkorean precepts. Each person was allotted a clearly numbered position in the Ayutthayan hierarchy, from slaves at the bottom to the king at the top. Through this, an individual's rights and obligations were established under law. Meanwhile, officials were grouped into sections, each responsible for a specified sphere of government business. It was these firm administrative foundations, combined with a sound economy based upon extensive irrigated rice cultivation in the Chao Phraya plain and flourishing international commerce with Ming China, which guaranteed Ayutthaya's independence and prosperity into the modern era. The lands ruled over by Ayutthaya were known as 'Siam' – the name by which Thailand would be known until the 1940s.

LAN SANG

Alongside Lan Na, another Tai kingdom survived, independent of Ayutthaya's enveloping suzerainty, amongst the Lao of the mid-Mekong area. Lan Sang was founded in 1353 by Fa Ngum as the great Lao centres of Luang Prabang and Vientiane slipped from the grasp of declining Sukhothai. Fa Ngum had previously been exiled at the Angkor court and had married a Khmer princess. Lan Sang, at its height, managed much of modern-day Laos and north eastern Thailand. But, beyond its ability to muster armed forces, Lan Sang never equalled the power and authority of Lan Na or Ayutthaya. During the fifteenth century, as in recent times, Laos was subject to repeated pressures from northern Vietnam and in the 1470s, an invasion from Dai Viet forced King Sainyachakkaphat to flee his realm. Lao independence was restored in 1479 by Sainyachakkaphat's younger brother, Suvanna Bulang. Ultimately, however, the Lao kingdom was unable to survive as a unified entity and in 1707 Lan Sang was bifurcated into Vientiane and Luang Prabang. These smaller, weaker units increasingly came under the sway of Bangkok until the arrival of the French colonialists in the 1880s.

Srivijaya

THE BEGINNINGS OF AN EMPIRE

Srivijaya was the first major Malay maritime trading empire. It was centred on south eastern Sumatra from the seventh century and remained the dominant political and economic centre in the Malay world until the 1200s. Palembang, about 30 miles upstream from the sea on the Musi River, essentially mushroomed out of growing Malay engagement, from the fourth century, with the India–China trade via the Melaka and Sunda straits. Palembang, and also Jambi to the north, began life as a small estuarine port where merchant sailors could exchange international goods for products from the Sumatran hinterland. Through trade contacts, these river-mouth polities developed cultural links with India as early as 350 AD, allowing for the transmission of Buddhist religious, monarchical and imperial ideas. In the seventh century, however, Srivijaya emerged as dominant over the surrounding ports, permitting the channelling of the agricultural, forest and ocean products of the Malay world into one principal entrepot. Jambi, Palembang's main rival, was subjugated some time between 671 and 685, allowing access to the hinterland trade of the Hari River system as well as the Musi.

The key to Palembang's dominance was probably the agricultural productivity of the Musi River valley, which could support a large non-farming population as well as feed visiting merchants and sailors. Although hardly comparable with the lower Mekong, the best rice land in south east Sumatra is still to be found near the modern city of Palembang around the hill of Bukit Seguntang, where the great relics of Srivijayan civilization have been discovered. In recognition of its fertility, Bukit Seguntang was probably both the ceremonial and commercial centre of the empire, as well as the residence of the religious elite. In addition, the Palembang area was blessed with an excellent natural harbour and an inland river system, navigable to about 50 miles. Even so, Srivijaya's imperial authority outside the Musi River valley was more imagined than real: the ruler of Palembang was essentially a Malay overlord who forged alliances with the leaders of the other riverine ports of Sumatra, the Malay peninsula and west and north Java. These lesser lords shared with Palembang a common interest in the free flow of merchant ships through the island world. Only in the immediate vicinity of Palembang did the Srivijayan king rule directly through a retinue of royal officials and peasant farmers; the latter being both royal bondsmen and imperial soldiers. Beyond the Musi River system, Srivijaya relied on its efficient navy to subdue potential rivals and maintain supremacy. But, force alone could not guarantee Srivijaya's hegemony in the Malay world: the Srivijayan king also depended on elaborate oath-taking ceremonies, often infused with Buddhist symbolism. The building of monasteries and the depositing of inscriptions were further means of maintaining allegiances in Srivijaya's diverse realm. An inscription dated 775 from the east coast of Malaya also records that the king at Palembang was 'the patron of the snakes', an ancient Malay symbol of authority. Indeed, this latter example emphasizes the cultivation of traditional Malay ideas by the rulers of Srivijaya to cement relations with their subjects and vassals. The king was believed to be so powerful that he bathed in water treated with flower petals to avert floods and also avoided eating grain on special days to prevent famine. Ruination would necessarily follow the king's departure from his realm. As lord of both 'Mountain' and 'Isles', the king was also in direct communication with the dangerous and powerful 'Spirit of the Waters of the Sea'. To appease the sea spirit, the king threw gold bricks into the Musi estuary.

Specific details of Srivijaya are lacking, but, from the evidence of both Srivijayan inscriptions and Chinese records, it appears that Palembang was already a flourishing international port by the last decade of the seventh century. In the eighth century its importance is confirmed by the sending of missions to Tang China. Ships on both the India and China routes used Palembang as a resting point while they waited for favourable winds. As a consequence of a strategic marriage alliance with the Buddhist Sailendra rulers of Java, the Sumatran king in the mid-ninth century was of that line. This connection with the west Javanese, 'rice bowl' was a further buttress to Srivijayan power, for Java provided additional food supplies to provision the ships berthed in Palembang's harbour.

THE DECLINE OF THE EMPIRE

From the eleventh century, Srivijaya faced increasing difficulties. The Malay maritime empire was a victim of its own success because its wealth aroused the jealousy of powerful rivals. Several military challenges from Java from the late tenth century were effectively rebuffed by a retaliatory plundering of the island in 1016. But, concurrently, the Cola rulers of Tamil Nadu in southern India wished to end Srivijaya's stranglehold over the Melaka Straits and in 1025 Palembang was raided and virtually destroyed. The real problem for Srivijaya, however, was the growing presence of Chinese shipping in the straits, encouraged particularly by the Southern Song dynasty (1127–1279). Malay merchant power declined and dispersed to a number of smaller centres, such as Jambi, which broke free of the Srivijayan grip. On the Malay peninsula, meanwhile, new regional powers emerged to usurp Srivijaya's authority in ports such as Kedah. In the fourteenth century both Ayutthaya to the north and Majapahit (Java) to the east encroached on Srivijaya's former vassals. Of more long-term significance was the foundation and rise of Melaka in the 1400s as the new Malay super-port under the protection of Ming China. Java's dominant position in the island world would also eventually be threatened by the rise of the Melaka sultanate.

Java

MATARAM

A sophisticated rice-cultivation system, known as *sawah*, had developed on the rich soils of Java by the classical era. Yet in contrast to northern Vietnam or southern Cambodia, kingdoms seem to have been slower to develop (although Chinese sources refer to some significant political centres in west Java as early as the second century AD). By the end of the sixth century, however, at Mataram in central Java a political centre had been established, based upon the rice resources of the Kedu River plain. During the sixth century, *sawah* rice communities were increasingly co-ordinated within kingdoms given the need to manage the supply of irrigated water from village to village. As a by-product of trade contacts with India, Buddhist and Hindu symbolism was employed to differentiate kings (who had direct links with the deities) from commoners (who did not). From the seventh century, north and west Javanese ports fell under the sway of Srivijaya, but the area around the rice-producing Kedu plain remained independent, supplying food to the regional and international markets controlled by the Sumatran empire.

In the 730s, a powerful king called Sanjaya established himself at Mataram. His descendants, however, became vassals of a line of Buddhist kings, the Sailendras. It was these kings who, around 800, directed the building of Java's most famous historical site, the Borobudur, near the modern-city of Yogyakarta. A colossal stupa-style temple-mountain of square and circular terraces built upon a hill in the Kedu plain, the Borobudur's terrace walls are all decorated with a vast series of bas-reliefs showing scenes from Buddhist stories, of Javanese court life, and of sea-borne trade. The rulers of Mataram were clearly lovers of all things Indian, but the Borobudur also reflects an indigenous Javanese style. The Borobudur served to legitimize royal authority as the centre of a monarchical cult. The temple was also a Buddhist teaching centre with the stories depicted on the terrace walls being used to illustrate each lesson.

The Sailendra rulers clearly exercised considerable authority to mobilize the labour resources necessary to build such a magnificent, awe-inspiring monument. The construction work was highly organized: an army of bondsmen undertook the actual building and transporting of stones following the plans drawn up by priest and monk architects while skilled artisans carved the statues and bas-reliefs. Finance for the temples of central Java came via a system of donations that reflected the piety of individual donors. Once built, the temples were sustained through an entitlement to a share of local produce and, much like contemporaneous Cambodia, the Javanese temples directed labour in the construction of dams, bridges and roads to improve the productivity of local agriculture. The Sailendras adopted the Indian title Maharaja (Great King) in the eighth century to emphasize their superiority over other local chiefs and the Sanskrit writing skills of the royal priests at Borobudur were central to efficient administration. The power of the Sailendra kings was also enhanced by their right to tribute in the form of rice from community chiefs. Rice was subsequently exchanged by the royal chancellery for goods at the northern ports: gold, silver and Indian textiles, which could, in turn, be redistributed to local leaders to build alliances and coalitions.

However, the Borobudur fell into a state of neglect from the mid-ninth century as the Sailendras were exiled to Sumatra. These events followed the rise of a Hindu king, descended from Sanjaya and called Pikatan. It was Pikatan's descendants who built the other famous Javanese temple complex of Prambanan, also near the modern city of Yogyakarta. Prambanan served as a kind of Hindu equivalent of Borobudur.

EAST JAVA

Mataram continued to flourish until the eleventh century but as early as the 950s the Javanese power centre was slipping eastwards to the Brantas River plain, where ambitious rulers could oversee greater rice production. The Brantas River also offered Javanese kings better access to the interisland trade routes of maritime South East Asia, notably with Bali, Maluku, Sumatra and the Malay peninsula. An inscription dated 927 refers to a mysterious river-mouth port called Goreng Gareng. The king of this port apparently oversaw a fleet of 135 craft and used local as well as Sri Lankan, south Indian and Burmese merchants to collect taxes in the villages that surrounded the port. Eastern Java's growing involvement in international trade inevitably trod on the toes of Srivijaya and, lacking Palembang's naval resources, the independent Javanese core entered into a period of decline.

Nevertheless, Java re-emerged as a force to be reckoned within the eleventh century under the direction of the celebrated monarch, Air-langga, son of a Balinese king and Javanese princess. Airlangga appears to have ruled most of Java for a 30 year period after 1019. He also ruled on Bali, an important rice-producing island, after 1025. Taking advantage of Srivijaya's weakness after the sacking of Palembang by Cola, Airlangga successfully established dominance over his rivals in central Java between 1025 and 1037. Javanese tradition tells us his success also resulted from the king's victory over a number of demons through the superior power of Hindu meditation. Certainly Hindu symbolism was an important prop to Airlangga's right to rule and he portrayed himself as an earthly incarnation of the god Vishnu. At his mausoleum he was portrayed on a statue as Vishnu riding the mighty bird, Garuda.

From his capital on the Brantas River delta near modern Surabaya, Airlangga improved Java's international standing by marrying his family into the Srivijayan royal house. As a consequence of this diplomatic success, more Javanese ports were opened to international trade. Java entered into a period of economic growth based principally on its ability to attract international shippers to buy spices. The spices were not grown on Java but were transhipped from the islands of Maluku; the spice islanders being attracted to Java in the first place by its copious rice supplies. Before 1600, the rare tropical evergreen trees, clove and nutmeg, grew exclusively on the eastern Indonesian islands. Due to seasonal winds, which kept spice islanders and international merchants apart, Java maintained an effective stranglehold over this ever-expanding trade. International trade was certainly growing largely due to the efforts of the Song dynasty in China, which vigorously promoted the southern trades in porcelain and silk. Moreover to the west, the spice trade with the Mediterranean was secured by the restoration of political stability in the Middle East under the Fatimid caliphate, which after 973 controlled Egypt. The royal monopoly over the distribution of luxury items, such as Chinese ceramics, enabled Airlangga to reward powerful allies.

Airlangga's greatness was also underpinned by economic development projects, most notably the damning of the Brantas River which prevented flooding, encouraged settlement and improved irrigation and navigation. Expanding royal revenues from trade were also employed in the provision of military forces, which, on both land and at sea, were deployed to subdue rival regional powers and suppress unruly pirates and brigands. Royal wealth supported a large scholarly community as well as the building of temples and the celebration of festivals. Airlangga was clearly a lover of the arts: it was in his reign that a famous Javanese version of the Sanskrit epic, the *Mahabharata*, was written. Known as the *Arjunavivaha*, it used the story of the Indian prince, Arjuna, as an allegory for Airlangga's own reign. The story remains one of the most popular productions of the Javanese shadow theatre, the *wayang*. Additionally, Airlangga proved an able bureaucrat, centralizing power through codifying a number of Javanese customs and developing a unified administrative system to preside over numerous villages and ports.

Airlangga's epoch of relative political stability witnessed a reflowering of Javanese culture, particularly literature. Yet, like many a powerful Cham and Khmer monarch, Airlangga's abilities did not infuse his successors and political power in Java once again fractured. The great king's death in 1049 witnessed the division of his realm into two halves: Janggala in the east and Kediri in the west. Even so, trade and literature continued to flourish without Airlangga or political unity. The late twelfth century was a period in which great Javanese epic poems and further Indonesian versions of the *Mahabharata* stories were written. Meanwhile, Javanese ports continued to expand their trade with the spice islands and attracted merchants from as far away as Gujarat on the west coast of India. In the early thirteenth century, the spice trade with Java was so large that it caused a huge drain of copper coinage from China. In 1292, the Italian adventurer, Marco Polo, passed through South East Asia and commented that 'the treasure of this island [Java] is so great as to be past telling'.

SINGHASARI AND MAJAPAHIT

East Java was politically reunited in the early thirteenth century as Singhasari under the rule of Ken Angrok, 'he who upsets everything'. Of lowly background, Ken Angrok became King Rajasa in 1222, with his capital at Janggala. His achievements were continued by Visnu-vardhana who ruled between 1248 and 1268. He fully subjugated the kingdom of Kediri and laid the foundations for the establishment of the last Hindu kingdom to rule on Java, Majapahit.

However, the first king mentioned in the epic poem of Majapahit, the *Nagarakertagama*, written in 1365 by a Buddhist monk, was Kertanagara who ruled between 1268 and 1292. Kertanagara is a fascinating character whose abilities and energies, allegedly, relied upon his observance of Tantric rituals involving much intoxication and copulation. Whether or not this is true, under Kertanagara the Javanese attempted to assert their authority beyond their shores and in the 1270s and 1280s succeeded in extending influence to Sumatra, Madura and Bali. Here was born the idea of a great Javanese-controlled island empire, *nusantara*. Such aspirations, however, only angered China, now under the control of the Mongol Yuan dynasty. But Kertanagara was not to be intimidated: Mongol envoys sent by Kublai Khan to secure

Java's allegiance returned tattooed and disfigured. Understandably infuriated by such insolence, the Great Khan assembled a massive naval force to punish the Javanese king. Before the Mongol ships arrived, however, Kertanagara was murdered in 1292, as Kediri rebelled against Singhasari. Facing the Mongols and dealing with a disintegrating empire was left to Kertanagara's son-in-law, Kertajasara, who established a new capital at Majapahit in 1293. Its remains can be seen today scattered around the town of Trowulan, some 35 miles south west of Surabaya. In a remarkable episode, Kertajasara persuaded the Mongol navy to suppress Kediri. In the meantime he mustered an army, turned on his new-found Chinese allies and expelled them from his realm.

With the Chinese threat eliminated, Majapahit became an economic powerhouse, as the expanding European appetite for Indonesian spices was exploited. At Majapahit's commercial centre, Bubat, Chinese and Indian merchants negotiated and exchanged with Javanese traders acting for the king. This trade was increasingly monetized: copper coins being the accepted currency. Bubat was also the locus of culture and ceremony where music, dancing, martial arts, and the shadow theatre all flourished and great festivals were celebrated. Majapahit's king would receive tribute – in the form of luxury goods and agricultural products – at Bubat from both international traders and empire producers; this tribute was subsequently redistributed to appease regional lords. During the fourteenth century, Majapahit claimed to rule over most of modern-day Indonesia and Malaysia. Majapahit's naval forces were the key to controlling this far-flung empire, while members of the royal family or prominent courtiers ruled in each 'colony' (after 1343, for example, Bali was governed by a Javanese prince). Like Srivijaya, however, Majapahit's imperial control should not be exaggerated. Certainly, at the peak of its power in the 1360s and 1370s, Majapahit dominated Java, Bali and Madura. But its political influence in the rest of maritime South East Asia was actually very limited.

Majapahit's greatness was also short-lived and was largely based upon the skills of the remarkable chief minister, Gaja Muda, who was pre-eminent on Java's political scene for three decades after 1330. If the chronicles are to be believed, Gaja Muda was indeed an extraordinary talent – he conquered Bali, introduced legal and administrative reforms,

and trapped and killed a visiting king from west Java. Yet the death of
Gaja Muda in 1364, marks the beginning of Majapahit's decline. In the
early fifteenth century, the core of the Javanese realm was overtaken by
civil war. In 1428 control was lost over the western half of the island.
Worse still, a coalition of north Javanese Muslim ports attacked the east
Javanese kingdom in 1513. In 1528 the royal family was forced to flee
to Bali, where the last remnants of Hindu culture in Indonesia remain
to this day. An idealized image of Majapahit's greatness lived on,
however, in the imagination of twentieth-century Javanese nationalists
who wished to emulate Kertajasara's concept of *nusantara* through the
establishment of a united island-nation, 'Indonesia'.

Melaka

FOUNDATIONS

With the rise of Melaka after 1400, Majapahit was increasingly outmoded both economically and ideologically; the north Javanese ports
broke free of eastern Java's grip and, like Melaka, often embraced Islam
as a symbol of that autonomy. Melaka was the first major power on the
Malay peninsula, whose small riverine port-states had previously been
under the domination of Angkor, the Tai kingdoms, Sumatra or Java.
The Malay empire was founded by a Sumatran prince called Paramesvara. During the 1390s he attempted to throw off Javanese domination of his realm at Palembang by founding a new power-base on
the Malay peninsula, beyond the jurisdiction of Majapahit. This
Paramesvara tried first at Tumasik on modern-day Singapore island.
Tumasik, however, proved too vulnerable to challenges from Ayutthaya, leading Paramesvara to try his luck at Melaka on the mainland
instead. At the same time, however, Paramesvara courted China, which
was emerging reunified and reassertive overseas under the rule of the
Ming emperors. As part of a remarkable series of Ming overseas
voyages, a fleet under the command of Admiral Cheng Ho was despatched in 1405 to assert Chinese authority over pirate-infested
Sumatra. Paramesvara seized his chance and, in return for acknowl-
edgement of Ming overlordship, the Melakan prince concluded a

protective agreement with Cheng Ho. It was this close relationship with the Ming navy which was the key to Melaka's independence vis-à-vis Thailand and, in 1411, Paramesvara actually visited China personally to pay homage to the emperor. Melaka remained under direct Chinese protection until the 1430s and quickly became a new version of the Srivijaya-style Malay port for Sumatran and Javanese trade goods. Melaka established supremacy over the other Malay centres, achieving for the first time a loose political unity in west Malaysia. Not surprisingly, therefore, Melaka has passed into Malaysian mythology as the beginnings of the nation. Certainly Melaka remains very important to Malay identity today because it was probably the first polity on the peninsula to adopt Islam. (Although from inscriptions found in Terengganu, it is possible that an Islamic state was established on the east coast of Malaya from the 1300s.) It is unclear when precisely this occurred, but the Islamization of Melaka is usually believed to have taken place in the reign of Paramesvara's son, Sri Maharaja, between 1425 and 1445. From Melaka, Islam spread to other parts of the Malay world.

SUCCESS

Besides being a centre for the dissemination of the Muslim faith in South East Asia, Melaka's power was based upon commerce. Alongside the visiting junks from China, the port-city also had a close relationship with Gujarati and other Indian merchants who, in turn, had access to Middle-Eastern and European markets. Melaka was a truly cosmopolitan city by the 1480s: given the seasonal winds, ships from China, Japan, India and Persia might spend at least one year in the port, meaning that its streets were thronged with visiting traders from throughout Asia. Melaka, with its excellent command of the straits between the Malay peninsula and Sumatra, was able to monopolize the supply of Maluku spices via the north Javanese ports. In return, the Melaka emporium became a major centre for the importation of Indian cloth. And, lacking a food-producing hinterland of its own, Melaka imported numerous shiploads of rice from Java, Ayutthaya and Burma. It was this trade-based affluence that would ominously attract the

Portuguese in the early sixteenth century but, until then, Melaka maintained its autonomous supremacy as the international trade emporium for the entire South East Asia region. According to the sixteenth-century Portuguese chronicler, Tomé Pires, Melaka was 'of such importance and profit that it ... has no equal in the world'. The rulers of Melaka certainly recognized the importance of trade. As Sultan Mansur Shah observed in 1468, 'we have learned that to master the blue oceans people must engage in commerce and trade, even if their countries are barren ... Life has never been so affluent in preceding generations as it is today'.

Melaka's success also hinged on dynamic political leadership. Paramesvara himself was clearly an enterprising individual and this energy was bequeathed to his successors. The Malay hero, Tun Perak, a brother-in-law of one of Paramesvara's descendants, led armies which withstood Ayutthaya in the first half of the fifteenth century, later becoming the *bendahara*, or chief Malay official. By 1500, Melaka's expansionism ensured that it was the major power on the Malay peninsula and its influence was likewise felt over much of the east coast of Sumatra. To avoid the accumulation of wealth by Malays, who might become so affluent that they could mount challenges to the sultan's authority, the Melaka rulers utilized and encouraged foreign merchants, not Malay ones. Gujarati merchants and south Indian moneylenders (*chettiars*) were particularly prominent in the foreign commercial community. A long tradition of Malay management of trade rather than direct involvement in entrepreneurship began. Melaka was certainly a well-ordered state: the Melaka legal codes were established in the reign of the last and wealthiest ruler, Sultan Mahmud, between 1488 and 1511, providing for security of property and regulating commerce. Crimes against the royal house carried especially draconian punishments. The rulers of Melaka were also careful not to alienate the indigenous ethnic groups of the peninsula, the Orang Asli; their leaders were incorporated into the administrative and military hierarchy. Melaka's traditions of royal absolutism, court ceremony and bureaucracy were bequeathed to the other Malay peninsula states and even to Brunei in northern Borneo. The role of Islam in Melaka underlines the importance of religious developments in classical South East Asia.

Religious Developments in the Classical Era

HINDUISM

Buddhism eventually came to dominate the religious life of mainland South East Asia while Islam was victorious in the struggle for souls in most of the island world. Yet, the two main world religions frequently absorbed or were forced to tolerate much older, indigenous concepts. They also shared religious space with 'Hinduism' – the convenient, conventional moniker used to describe a mixture of Brahmanism and the cults of Saivism (the worship of Siva) and Vaisnavism (the worship of Vishnu). In classical Java and classical Angkor, there were both Hindu and Buddhist state-sponsored priests. Royal ceremonies, such as funerals, involved a remarkable fusion of Hinduism, Buddhism and animism. Common to all forms of Hindu religion in South East Asia was the concept of Jambudipa, the universe as a central continent, which contained a central cosmic mountain, Mount Meru. As an abode

Sandstone statue of a Hindu deity from the Fu Nan civilization of sixth-century southern Vietnam and Cambodia

of the gods, the sun, moon and stars revolved around Mount Meru's peak. Above Mount Meru there were endless heavens; below it multiple hells. Over vast epochs of time, life was conceived as a perpetual cycle of creation and destruction: it was the role of Hindu kings, therefore, to maintain order (*dharma*) in the face of the dangerous machinations of Kali, the universal destroyer. Meanwhile, mortals were subject to successive rebirths, each one determined by the balance of good and bad deeds committed in the previous life. The cycle of rebirth was finally broken when the human soul was cleansed of all evil and was able to fuse with the divine. There existed a vast pantheon of Hindu deities, but the most important in South East Asia were the high gods, Siva and Vishnu. Siva worship, throughout South Asia and South East Asia, may actually predate Hinduism proper and stones associated with the deities were probably worshipped from Neolithic times. Siva was the god of creation and destruction and was an incarnation of creative energy. His symbol was the *linga*, a stylized representation of the phallus, while the personalities of his two wives – Paraiti, the benevolent, and Durga, the 'Black One' – were indicative of the two dimensions to Siva's power (*sakti*). His mount was the magnificent bull, Nandi. Vishnu, meanwhile, was the beneficent ruler of human destiny. His beautiful wife Laksmi was the goddess of good fortune and his mount was the giant bird, Garuda. Vishnu was incarnated as both Rama and Krishna. In the epic Indian poem, the *Ramayana*, it is Rama who leads an army of monkeys to Sri Lanka to rescue his wife, Sita. Krishna, meanwhile, was a Hercules-style superman who slayed terrible beings and whose deeds are retold in the vast collection of writings known as the *Mahabharata*. Both the *Ramayana* and the *Mahabharata* continue to inform the traditional Indonesian performing arts, especially the shadow play.

Brahmanism is the type of Hindu religion based on the pre-eminence and sacred role of the Brahman priestly caste, a spiritual elite by birth. Brahmans – whether of Indian or indigenous origin – from the earliest centuries AD established themselves as important counsellors to kings; indeed they were central to government given their Sanskrit-writing and administrative skills. The Brahmans also served as royal priests, central to the legitimization of monarchical power, particularly in early Angkor. On Java, from as early as the fifth century, Brahmanic Hindu ceremonies – carried out by both Buddhist and Hindu priests – were performed at both royal consecrations and funerals. However, in nominally Buddhist societies on the mainland, such as Sukhothai in central Thailand, Brahmans also shared ceremonial functions with Buddhist monks. Even when Angkor fully embraced Buddhism in the thirteenth century, Jayavarman VII still built a temple for his Hindu court sacrificial priest as well as his Buddhist scholar-priest. Brahmanism was popular with upper-class South East Asians, particularly in the Indonesian world, because it offered opportunities to escape the daily grind and live a life of ascetic contemplation at ashrams, such as on the Dieng Plateau in central Java. The Brahmans also found an easy appeal because their ideas melded with existing Austronesian belief systems, such as the worship of ancestors or tiger, crocodile and mountain spirits.

As distinct from the teachings of the Brahmans, the cult of Siva (Saivism) was very strong in classical Cambodia and Champa, where it was used to legitimize royal power. *Linga* cults, which are found throughout the region, may have their cultural origin long before the influence of Indian travellers was felt. But the *linga* came to be the emblem of Siva as the god of creation and fertility; the latter being of particular significance for rice-growing societies. Mainland kings liked to emphasize their vital roles as guarantors of prosperity and often sponsored *linga* worship at special shrines, for example, as late as the twelfth century in Cambodia. Siva was also supposed to supply spiritual energy to kings in Cambodia and even Dai Viet during the Ly dynasty.

The real centre of Saivism in classical South East Asia was Java, however, where it was the dominant form of Hindu worship up to the sixteenth century. The remnants of that culture can still be seen today on Bali and Lombok. Statues and temples dedicated to Siva and his associated deities, Durga (Siva's eight-armed spouse), Ganesa (the tremendously strong, four-armed elephant god) and the Guru (the teacher), can still be observed throughout Java. Siva was usually portrayed with four arms, three eyes and a number of accoutrements including a trident and a snake. Another favourite image found at Saivite temples on Java is of the goddess Durga, slaying the demon inhabiting a buffalo. The typical portrayal of Siva surrounded by three fellow, but lesser, deities may have been meant as a spiritual parallel of the temporal world: the divine equivalent of a Javanese court with a king accompanied by a queen, a chief minister and a religious mentor. In other words, the hierarchical ordering of Javanese society was legitimate precisely because this was how the deities ruled in heaven. The idea that the supernatural world mirrored the temporal world was reflected in the huge Saivite temple-mountain of Loro Jonggrang at Prambanan, which was constructed as a hierarchically-ordered *Mandala* (an earthly representation of the universe). Siva worship went through a revival in the fourteenth-century flowering of Majapahit, epitomized by the charming Panataran temple complex near Blitar in east Java, which was dedicated to Siva as 'Lord of the Mountain'. Again we have the Saivite concept of an idealized heavenly kingdom because Panataran is built in the style of a royal palace.

Nowhere in South East Asia did the Vishnu cult achieve the same status as Siva worship. Nevertheless, in twelfth-century Java, Vaisnavism had a significant influence at the royal court, not least because kings were regarded as semi-divine, earthly-versions of Vishnu. Incarnated as both Krishna and Rama, Vishnu was worshipped as a heavenly king. Vishnu's huge steed, Garuda, is remembered as the name of Indonesia's national airline. Vishnu's wife, Laksmi or Sri, was also venerated as the goddess of good fortune and fertility – in west Java she is still celebrated today. Vishnu was also honoured on the mainland; for the early rulers of Angkor this was because of his association with the sun. The great Angkor Wat illustrates the importance of Vishnu for the Cambodian royals of the twelfth century. This 'Mountain of the Gods' (*Mahameru*) was strategically placed in the centre of the kingdom and bas-reliefs depicted stories of Vishnu and his incarnation of the heroic (and erotic) Krishna.

BUDDHISM

Judging from the dateable Buddha images found in South East Asia, Buddhism was spread by wandering scholars and pilgrims, throughout the region, between the fourth and sixth centuries. Buddhism, of course, had been established much earlier – during the sixth and fifth centuries BC – in India where an order of monks, the Sangha, revered the Buddha (formerly Gautama Siddhartha) as their supreme, enlightened teacher. The Buddha is supposed to have lived between 563 and 483 BC. According to South East Asian tradition, he was a north Indian prince who abandoned his comfortable life – including his wife and young son – to gain enlightenment. This Gautama achieved by resisting temptation for 49 nights under the bodhi tree at Gaya. He then taught the law (*dharma*) to his disciples near Banaras. Essentially, Buddhist thinking aimed at individual deliverance from the sorrows of everyday life through a strictly planned existence, which involved reflection and meditation as well as abstinence from earthly pleasures, such as sex, intoxication and the possession of valuables. The Buddha was believed to be merely one in a long line of human beings who had achieved supreme virtue and wisdom by living the right kind of life while on earth. Sometime in the third century BC, Buddhist doctrine was standardized as the Three Baskets of Law, or *Tripitaka*. This set of scriptures includes stories of the Buddha's predecessors, rules laid down by the Buddha, and a detailed analysis of moral virtues, the *dharmapada*.

The main source region for Buddhist ideas and statues in South East Asia was probably Sri Lanka rather than India. There may have been Chinese influences too; pilgrims from China would often spend time in South East Asia en route to India. Certainly the planting of Mahayana Buddhism in northern Vietnam from the seventh century, as with Confucianism from the eleventh century, relied heavily on the Chinese connection. But the general progress of Theravada Buddhism – the form of Buddhism dominant today in mainland South East Asia outside Vietnam – was from west to east, entering modern Thailand and Cambodia from the Mon kingdoms of Burma. Until the thirteenth century Mahayana Buddhism, associated with compassion and the worship of the deity, the 'Lord Who Looks Down', Avalokitesvara (Lokesvara), remained dominant in mainland kingdoms such as Angkor. But with the decline of Mahayana in its spiritual home, India, and the rise of Sri Lanka as the new centre of Buddhist orthodoxy, the Theravada variety gained ascendancy by the end of the classical era. In Angkor by the mid-fourteenth century the royal court was wholly influenced by Theravada concepts. Theravada, or the 'Lesser Vehicle', is usually associated with the saffron-robed monks that can be observed today throughout most of mainland South East Asia. It is actually the older, simpler form of Buddhism, which places stress on individual salvation through extreme piety to break the circle of reincarnation and so achieve nirvana. Mahayana, or the 'Great Vehicle', on the other hand, focuses on the public veneration of a vast galaxy of Buddhas and also Bodhisattvas. Bodhisattvas are usually, but not exclusively, humans on the brink of full Buddhahood; the most popular in South East Asia being Avalokitesvara. Theravada Buddhism was also distinguished from Mahayana because its texts were written in the sacred language of Pali as opposed to Sanskrit. Theravada Buddhism is also usually taken to be less hierarchical. Nevertheless, the Tai, Cambodian, and Cham kings were keen supporters of Theravada Buddhism because of the quasi-divine characteristics it could confer on them. Buddhist kings were not worshipped as gods while they were still alive, but their superiority was assumed to be derived from their special links to and relationships with the supernatural world. For this reason, Tai monarchs despatched hundreds of monks to Sri Lanka in the fourteenth and fifteenth centuries to learn from Sinhalese Theravada teachers. As important props to royal power, then, monasteries often became very rich and, paradoxically, sometimes aroused the jealousy of insecure monarchs, most notably in Angkor.

The Theravadans had very little impact on maritime South East Asia, however, where Mahayana Buddhism prevailed in most of Sumatra, the Malay peninsula and western Borneo before the arrival of Islam in the sixteenth and seventeenth centuries. On Sumatra the Srivijaya kings, although unfortunately leaving few temples to prove this, were serious Mahayanans. Under the patronage of Srivijaya's Buddhist ruler, Palembang was also an important religious centre where novice monks from as far away as China came to study under Indian gurus. Srivijaya may have financed the building of a monastery in north-eastern India at Nalanda, the area around which the Buddha is traditionally believed to have gained enlightenment.

In Java, however, Mahayana Buddhism had a less firm hold over allegiances given the strength of Hinduism. Only really during the Sailendra era (c. 750–850) did Buddhism achieve pre-eminence, when the great Borobudur temple-mountain was built as a teaching centre and example of the piety and authority of the Sailendra kings as 'Lords of the Mountain'. Mahayana Buddhism received another burst of life on Java, albeit alongside Saivism, in the height of the Singhasari-Majapahit era (c. 1250–1400). King Kertanagara was posthumously revered as 'Siva-Buddha' and, while alive, was certainly a keen participant in a sexually hedonistic form of Buddhism. Buddhist temples survive from Kertanagara's reign – for example, the fabulous ruins of Candi Jago at Tumpang near Malang, east Java, dating from c. 1270–80. It was Islam, however, which would supersede both Buddhism and Hinduism as the major world religion in Indonesia and the Malay world.

ISLAM

Islam gained its first toehold in South East Asia in the late thirteenth century when the ruler of Pasai, on the north coast of Sumatra, became a Muslim. This was some 600 years after the beginnings of the Islamic religion, based upon the teachings of the Prophet Mohammed who died in the Middle East in 632. As the Seal of Prophecy, Mohammed was the vehicle of Allah's (God's) revelation, the basis of which is contained in the Muslim holy book, the Koran. The spread of Islam in island South East Asia proved a slow process, however, given the resilience of the Hindu and Buddhist island kingdoms and empires. Islamization was not fully complete by the sixteenth century. Islam's diffusion probably relied upon the increasing presence in the straits of Muslim traders from northern and southern India. According to Malay legend, the Melaka hero, Hang Tuah, was taught to recite the Koran by a merchant from southern India's Coromandel coast. Chinese Muslims may also have played their part as missionaries, especially in Java and Brunei. The conversion of the Melaka king, probably through the influences of Indian Muslim traders, in the early fifteenth century, provided an excellent window of opportunity for Islamic proselytization: powerful Melaka acted as a jumping-off point for Islam into the sultanate's network of commercial allies. By the sixteenth century, most of the rulers of the coastal port-states of east and west Malaya and east Sumatra, as well as Patani in southern Thailand and Brunei in northern Borneo, had become sultans under the Melakan model. Indeed, Islam became so ingrained in Malay cultural identity that 'to become a Malay' (*masuk melayu*) was synonymous with becoming a Muslim. Moreover, as Melaka developed as a regional centre for Islamic scholarship and missionary work, the Malay language became the medium through which the Koran was taught and recited.

There were significant gains to be made from royal conversion in states like Melaka. For one, more Indian Muslim traders would be attracted by an Islamic-controlled port. But, even more importantly, Persian notions of kingship accompanied the Muslim faith: because he was a sultan, the ruler of Melaka instantly had a higher status than the mere rajas of surrounding ports. As a Muslim king, the sultan of Melaka was Allah's representative on earth and bore the illustrious title, 'Helper of the World and of the Religion'. Unquestioning obedience was due to the sultan as a central tenet of Muslim doctrine. But Islam in island South East Asia also had a genuine mass appeal, especially via the brand of Sufi mysticism disseminated by Indian traders. Sufi merchant-teachers – who often claimed to be distant descendants of the founder, Mohammed – sponsored a form of worship, which aimed at unity with the Divine. This might involve dancing, singing, musical renditions, meditation and recitation of the Koran: activities that all fit in with existing patterns of worship and ideas of interaction with the super-natural. Allah, as a supreme god, as well as angels, prophets and saintly teachers, were new powerful additions to the existing spirits, which could be invoked for assistance and protection. In this way, Islam was not seen as an alien religion but merely an extension of traditional South East Asian culture. Mysticism was particularly attractive to the Javanese because of its stress on contemplation and meditation along the lines of existing Hindu and Buddhist concepts. In Malaysia Islam did not completely eradicate Hindu traditions. For example, in 1933 the son of the Sultan of Kelantan (on the east coast of the Malay peninsula), was carried to his circumcision ceremony on a bird called Petalawati. Petalawati was clearly a modern manifestation of the ancient Hindu god Garuda, the trusted steed of Vishnu.

Yet, by 1500, outside of the Malay world, Islam was not firmly established. On Java, its progress was certainly patchy. A number of mystical *wali*, or preachers, spread the faith in the northern ports where the influence of Melaka was also strong. Only in 1524, however, did the ruler of the leading port, Demak, take the title of sultan. Muslims featured at the court of Majapahit during the fifteenth century. But not until the defeat of Majapahit in the 1520s by the Banten–Demak–Gresik axis of sultanates was Islam able fully to infiltrate both inland and beyond Java into eastern Indonesia. Even then, progress was often slow and uneven: in contemporary Indonesia the process of Islamization continues as indigenous beliefs maintain a strong hold over remoter areas. Bali and Lombok, of course, have remained predominantly Hindu. Muslims also had very little influence on the mainland of South East Asia: pockets of Islamic teaching existed in Champa and Cambodia, but Theravada Buddhism generally stood firm.

Moreover, even where Islam was dominant, like Hinduism and Buddhism earlier, it did not sweep all before it; it merely slotted into the existing multi-layered jigsaw of South East Asian belief. Being a 'Good Muslim' and leading a pure life – through performing prayers (*salat*) five times a day, reciting the Koran, paying alms, fasting during the ninth month of the Islamic year, Ramadan, making the hajj (pilgrimage) to Mecca, avoiding eating pork or drinking alcohol, and responding to the call for holy war (*jihad*) – did not obfuscate the continued observance of customs of previous millennia. The Javanese shadow puppet theatre, based upon the Hindu *Mahabharata* and *Ramayana*, is a case in point. Indeed, the *wayang* essentially exhibits a very old Austronesian concept of viewing the temporal world as a kind of theatrical stage. Islamic law or *sharia* was extremely flexible so that in Melaka, for example, two penalties might exist for the same crime – one for custom (*adat*) and one for the law of Allah. Beneath the Islamic veneer, *adat* remains to this day as a powerful way of ordering society, for example, amongst the Minangkabau people of west Sumatra. The view of Islam as an intolerant creed is myth: indeed, a remarkably tolerant Muslim faith has always predominated throughout maritime South East Asia. Islam in the region stressed the subordinate position of women, but females in South East Asia probably enjoyed, and continue to enjoy, less restrictions on their dress and conduct than in the Middle East and the Indian subcontinent. Tolerance notwithstanding, Muslim proselytizers were certainly not prepared simply to sit back in the face of challenges from the European 'infidel'. After 1500, the growing pre-sence of Europeans in the region gave a new urgent impetus to the spread of Islam, as a 'scramble for souls' ensued between Christian and Islamic missionaries. The Muslim faith provided a strong symbol of resistance to, and independence from, the encroaching Europeans.

CHAPTER FOUR

Early-Modern South East Asia, 1500-1800

The early-modern period between 1500 and 1800 was an era of mixed blessings for South East Asians. On the mainland, there was a general process of political coalescence between 1500 and 1800, which laid the basis of today's nation-states in Vietnam and Thailand and confirmed the dominance of these two states over the lesser kingdoms of Cambodia and Laos. In the areas of South East Asia that now make up the modern states of Malaysia and Indonesia, on the other hand, political authority remained much more fractured, and, in comparison to the mainland, no large-scale kingdoms emerged. The island world was united by widespread use of the Malay language – Malay was the language of inter-island trade and European visitors heard Malay words such as *amok* (a frenzied thirst for blood and the origin of the English expression 'running amuck'), *gudang* (warehouse), *perahu* (boat), and *kris* (dagger) throughout ports of the archipelago. Likewise the dominance of the Islamic faith permitted the emergence of a shared Malay culture amongst the religious and political elites of early-modern Malaysia and Indonesia. But the Malay-Muslim port-based states often remained bitter rivals for trade and Islamic leadership. Aceh and Johor vied with each other for dominance over Sumatra and the Malay peninsula; Brunei's preeminence on Borneo was challenged by Sulu; Bugis and Makassar remained at odds on Sulawesi; Java was divided between the interior dominated by Mataram and a number of Islamic coastal ports; Hindu Bali, meanwhile, kept its distance from the rest of the Muslim-dominated archipelago.

Yet, as well as being at odds with each other, the various kingdoms of the island world had to deal with an alien threat in the guise of

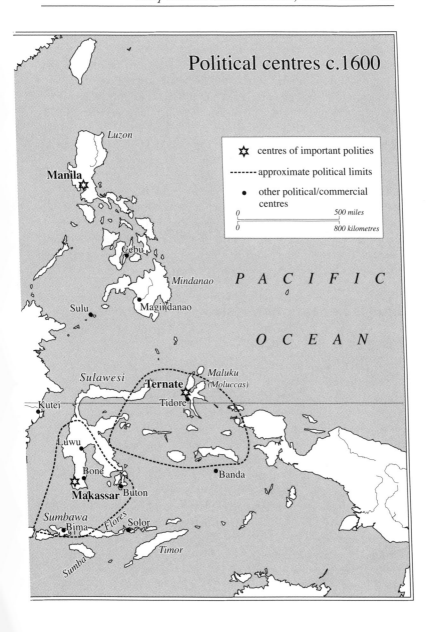

Political centres c.1600

☆ centres of important polities

------ approximate political limits

● other political/commercial centres

| 0 | | 500 miles |
| 0 | | 800 kilometres |

Luzon

Manila ☆

Cebu

Mindanao

P A C I F I C

Sulu

Magindanao

O C E A N

Sulawesi

Ternate ☆

Maluku *(Moluccas)*

Kutei

Tidore

Luwu

Bone

●Banda

Makassar Buton

Sumbawa
Bima Flores Solor

Timor

Sumba

European traders, missionaries and soldiers. Chinese merchants and settlers were also venturing into South East Asia on a scale never witnessed before, but it was the Europeans who now represented the most powerful aliens in the region. The mainland kingdoms too were coming into increasing contact with Europeans, but only really in the Malay world were distinct European-controlled permanent cities and trading arrangements established from 1511 onwards. The expanded alien presence in South East Asia was not necessarily disastrous, for it did offer opportunities for South East Asians to learn and to adapt from European and Chinese ideas to benefit their own lives. Moreover, European rule was far from all pervasive: up to 1800, the leaders, at least, of most South East Asian societies were still in control of their own destinies. But, even in the mainland kingdoms, there were ominous signs by the end of the eighteenth century – particularly, in the fields of commerce and warfare – that South East Asians were not adapting swiftly enough to resist further alien encroachment.

Europe in South East Asia

THE PORTUGUESE

Indian and Chinese traders had long been visiting the region, but what made the new European intrusion so much more formidable after 1500 was the far greater support European merchants and adventurers received from their governments. Moreover, as time wore on, Europeans were increasingly in possession of larger, swifter ships and more powerful weaponry than the Chinese, Indians and indigenous South East Asians. Portuguese enterprise in South East Asia certainly had strong backing from its monarchs, who initiated and secured the finance for the first voyages in search of pepper, cinnamon, cloves, nutmeg and mace. In an attempt to bypass the stranglehold of Muslim traders in the Middle East over Asian trade, the celebrated Vasco da Gama rounded the coast of Africa, ending up in India in 1498. South East Asia was not reached, however, until Don Afonso de Albuquerque established a Portuguese power-base in Asia at Goa on the west coast of India. From Goa the conquest of Melaka was planned and eventually executed in 1511, forcing the sultan of Melaka into exile at Johor on the southern tip of the Malay peninsula. Melaka was taken, however, only after a furious battle both at sea and on land. The Portuguese were faced with a large number of Malay heavy cannons, which were equivalent to European weapons and which caused considerable loss of Portuguese life and limb.

Melaka was a treasured jewel for the Portuguese because of its fabled wealth as a thriving international commercial centre, with its command of the straits between Sumatra and the Malay peninsula. Once conquered, it naturally served as Portugal's main centre in the region. A stone fortress was quickly put up on the ruins of the sultan's palace, followed later by the erection of various administrative and religious buildings. The ruins of the church of St. Paul, which stood on a hill in the centre of the city, can still be observed today. Melaka came to be run by a sophisticated administration headed by a captain and a council. But Portuguese manpower was limited – as a result, prominent Indian merchants were often appointed to official positions. An absence of European women also led to frequent interracial contacts in the bedroom. The Portuguese administration openly encouraged marriages of Portuguese men and local women who had converted to Christianity, because Asian wives proved important sources of trade contacts and information on local politics. This allowed for the rise of a Eurasian, *mestizo* community. A 'Portuguese' community still exists in today's Melaka.

Portuguese adventurism was clearly motivated by a search for profit from monopolizing the spice trade. China had previously been the main market for South East Asian spices, forest and ocean products. From the end of the fourteenth century, however, there was growing European demand for pepper and cloves to make food more appetising in an age before refrigeration. Ever-growing demand produced high prices, making the spice trade a highly profitable business: as early as 1518 over one-third of royal revenues in Portugal were derived from the spice trade. In search of further booty, Portuguese merchants branched out from Melaka to reach the spice islands of Maluku in 1512, Timor in 1522 and northern Java in 1532. The Portuguese merchants were disappointed to discover, however, that, save for silver, gold and firearms, there was limited South East Asian demand for the European goods they offered. Like their Asian counterparts, therefore, the Portuguese shifted into the trade in Indian cottons in exchange for the much-coveted spices.

Alongside economic incentives, the Portuguese adventurers satisfied a search for national glory as well as a strong Christian crusading impulse. Indeed, the pope in Rome decreed in 1493 that it was the duty of all Catholic kings to convert 'heathens' everywhere, and the following year the Treaty of Tordesillas divided the world between Portugal and Spain. The religious dimension to Portuguese imperialism is testified by the building in Melaka of a cathedral, a bishop's palace and residences for various Catholic orders. The co-founder of the Jesuit order, Francis Xavier, arrived in Melaka in 1546. Xavier energetically set about spreading the gospel in the spice islands and, despite language barriers, by 1555 there were about 30 'Christian' villages on the island of Ambon alone. By the seventeenth century, many spice islanders had reverted to their former religious beliefs and practices. However, the Dominican missionaries from the 1560s achieved more permanence to their conversions on the islands in the Nusa Tenggara chain – notably Timor and Flores – where significant Catholic communities remain to this day.

In the sixteenth century, Portugal had a rival for trade, national aggrandizement and the saving of souls in Catholic Spain. Ferdinand Magellan, during his epic circumnavigation of the globe, reached the spice islands in 1522 only to find that, like Captain Scott, his rivals had been there before him. Spain was forced to give up its claims in eastern Indonesia and confined its Asian realm to the Philippines, centred on the city of Manila. It was not merely the Spanish who could not compete with the Portuguese. As the latter increasingly built bigger, more powerful and more heavily-armed ships, the indigenous peoples of the island world abandoned ocean-going, large-scale trade.

Yet despite the momentous efforts of Albuquerque, Xavier and their followers, the impact of Portugal on South East Asia was relatively insignificant. Attempts to halt the progress of Islam through conversion to Christianity only served to encourage Muslim missionaries as a sign of resistance to the 'infidels'. The Portuguese goal of monopolizing the spice trade also failed, as Muslim merchants dispersed to Melaka's rival ports and even in Portuguese-controlled areas 'black markets' were rife. Moreover, by the seventeenth century, the Portuguese were superseded by rivals from northern Europe.

THE ENGLISH

The main arm of the English presence in South East Asia was a joint stock company, which had a monopoly of trading rights endowed by the crown, the East India Company (EIC). Founded in 1600, the EIC established outposts in South East Asia between 1611 and 1615 at Ayutthaya and Patani. More significant, however, was the opening of a factory on the eastern Indonesian island of Sulawesi at Makassar (Ujung Pandang), permitting access to the lucrative trade in nutmeg, mace and cloves from the Maluku Islands. The English merchants soon found themselves in the same dilemma as the Portuguese, however: South East Asians had little need for their manufactured goods. The solution, therefore, was to establish an English headquarters at Surat on the west Indian coast, as a means of procuring textiles that could be bartered for Indonesian spices, and Indian traders found themselves squeezed out by the English in the shipping of cloth to South East Asia.

Yet, Albion soon found itself up against a formidable European rival: the Dutch expelled the English from Ambon in 1623. The English position in Thailand was also relinquished, leaving the factory at Banten on Java as the EIC's principal South East Asian base. In 1682, however, Banten was likewise abandoned as a consequence of Dutch military pressure. The EIC presence in South East Asia was now confined to the pepper trade of west Sumatra from its base at Bengkulu. India – completely by accident – would emerge as the main focus of British power in Asia until the middle of the twentieth century. Even so, from India, the EIC became more and more involved in South East Asian trade as part of its greater promotion of the India–China trade during the eighteenth century: Indian textiles and opium were bartered for the archipelago's spices, pepper, tin, birds' nests and sea cucumbers, which could all be sold on to the Chinese at Canton. Ports such as Aceh, Kedah, Kuala Selangor, Riau and Kuala Terengganu were enriched by their position on the EIC's India–China trade route. Even so, it was only with the confirmation of English supremacy in the British Isles, industrialization and the development of a sophisticated financial capital based on the City of London, the expansion of empire in the Indian subcontinent, and victories over France and Holland in the Napoleonic wars, that Britain emerged as the paramount power in South East Asia by the early years of the nineteenth century. Until then, the EIC was no match for its more efficiently organized Dutch equivalent.

THE DUTCH

Liberated from the Catholic Habsburg Empire in Europe in the course of the sixteenth and seventeenth centuries, the Protestant-dominated Dutch Republic became an international trader *par excellence*. It was only a matter of time before the Dutch burghers dabbled in the trades of southern Asia. The first fleet despatched from Amsterdam reached Indonesia in 1596, and a consolidation of companies interested in the spice trade resulted in the formation of the Vereenigde Oost-Indische Compagnie (VOC) or United Dutch East India Company in 1602. Dutch control of the spice trade was secured by a combination of business acumen, millions of guilders of capital, and the willingness of the Dutch navy to use force to support the VOC's interests. In 1619, under the direction of Governor-General Jan Pieterszoon Coen, the VOC seized Jakarta from the Javanese sultanate of Banten and established the city of Batavia as the Dutch centre of operations in maritime South East Asia. Batavia occupied an excellent strategic position because it controlled the Sunda Straits between Sumatra and Java. Besides the Portuguese-dominated straits of Melaka, the Sunda Straits was the other principal route to the west in maritime South East Asia. The Dutch were not content with Batavia alone, however, and did not flinch at using further force to expand their commercial realm in the Indies. The peoples of the Banda Islands in Maluku discovered this to their cost in 1621. As punishment for refusal to grant the Dutch monopoly rights over the nutmeg trade, hundreds of Bandanese were massacred and Banda became dominated by Dutch-owned plantations worked by slaves. It was not only indigenous societies that encountered Dutch ruthlessness: the Portuguese, English, and Spanish were all forced to abandon their positions in the spice islands in the course of the seventeenth century. Meanwhile, Portuguese Melaka was conquered by Dutch forces in 1641. Two of the other major ports of early-modern Indonesia, Makassar and Banten, fell under Dutch control in 1669 and 1682 respectively. By the 1700s most Indonesian trading cities were either under direct VOC control or were forced into trading agreements with the company.

Dutch success relied not only on conquest but more importantly the ability to hold on to power. VOC dominance was maintained by a network of forts, garrisons, trading stations and a system of information gathering. Moreover, the Dutch also established in South East Asia a permanent fleet of warships. At Batavia once a fort had been built, Dutch-style canals, merchant houses and a town hall were established. Likewise, Dutch buildings are still notable in the centre of Melaka. In Batavia, the top administration was dominated by Dutchmen in the guise of the governor-general and the Council of the Indies. Dutch

Javanese men and woman and child going to the market at Banten as represented by a Dutch engraver at the end of the sixteenth century

officials and military commanders likewise controlled the outstations and reported back to Batavia. The Hollanders were less concerned to proselytise than their Portuguese forbears. The VOC was concerned, however, to eradicate the influence of Catholic missionaries in the eastern archipelago. By 1624, for example, there were only twelve Jesuits left in Maluku. The Dutch did tend to favour Christian kings over non-Christians and on Ambon, for example, this gave an impetus to the revival of Christianity there (albeit now in Protestant form). Yet the VOC generally tolerated other faiths, and Indonesia remained far less Christianized than the Philippines under Spanish rule.

Like the Portuguese before them, the Dutch relied on immigrant Asian groups for lower-level administrative and trading activities. Mistrusting Indonesians and Muslim Indians alike, the Dutch encouraged the Chinese as retail traders and managers of agricultural estates growing export crops such as sugar. The beginnings of the Dutch empire in Indonesia coincided with an ever-growing influx of Chinese merchants and sailors, most notably from the southern area of Fujian. This was particularly the case after 1683 when the Qing dynasty lifted previous bans on overseas voyages to the South Seas or *nanyang*. By the early eighteenth century, the Chinese easily outnumbered the Dutch in Batavia, making up about 60 percent of the city's population. They were administered by their own *Kapitan China* (kapitan, meaning captain, being a word derived from Portuguese). When the VOC diversified out of trading into agricultural production in the eighteenth century, it was the Chinese who benefited most as the managers of the sugar mills – worked by landless labourers supplied by the local aristocrats – that sprang up all over the north Javanese coast. Under this Dutch-Chinese economic partnership sugar replaced pepper as South East Asia's most important export by 1800. Chinese merchants also invariably acted as customs officials and revenue-farmers throughout Indonesia. The system of revenue-farming was a means of the Dutch administering cheaply and with limited personnel: annual auctions amongst the leading Chinese, or *towkay*, would determine who would win the right to retain customs duties and taxes on salt, opium or gambling in return for the payment of a fixed fee to the Dutch overlords. The system was replicated in British-administered South East

Asia as well as in some of the independent monarchies of the region (most notably in Thailand).

As with the Portuguese, the absence of European women encouraged intermarriage between Dutch men and South East Asian women to produce a unique Eurasian culture in the Dutch-controlled ports. Dutch military forces in the Indies were made up of Indonesian and other Asian mercenaries, and manual labour in Batavia and Melaka was carried out by slaves from all over the archipelago. Beyond Batavia's immediate environs, the Dutch did not rule directly but signed treaties of friendship with Javanese and Malay rulers. The Dutch became experts at playing off sultanates and chiefdoms against one another and thereby accentuating local jealousies and rivalries. Despite intermittent calls for *jihad* (holy war) by religious and political malcontents, no regional anti-Dutch, Muslim coalition in the island world emerged. Indigenous rulers, instead, were lured into collaboration with the colonial regime. Javanese aristocrats were used to oversee the growing of export crops to be delivered to the VOC at agreed, artificially low prices. Coffee, an increasingly popular beverage in eighteenth-century Europe, was the prime success of this arrangement in western Java, where it was grown from 1707. By the 1730s, Java was the world's leading producer of coffee. Delivery contracts for coffee were arranged via negotiation with local aristocrats, whose bondsmen subsequently planted, tended and supplied the crop as part of their unpaid labour duties to their overlord (what was known in feudal Europe as *corvée*). The British operated a similar system in west Sumatra for the delivery of pepper production.

It would be very wrong, therefore, to view European power in South East Asia as all embracing. Indeed, beyond a few enclaves on the coast of Indonesia and western Malaysia, Portuguese, English and Dutch authority was remarkably weak and ineffectual, forcing the Europeans into co-operation with indigenous rulers. European influence merely scratched the surface of South East Asian cultures and even the Dutch in Indonesia were (to borrow J. D. Legge's phrase) simply 'fitting into', rather than dominating or transforming, existing trading patterns and political conditions. Pockets of agricultural production, for international export only, impinged upon a tiny percentage of the archipelago's population. As the historian Anthony Reid has observed of the eighteenth century: 'South East Asians were not groaning under the effect of Western oppression'. As Reid has also pointed out, the coming of the European after 1500 was not an apocalyptic turning point because economic change had been in 'full flight' since the 1400s, given the huge expansion of South East Asia's trade with Ming China. In addition, the commercial decline experienced in South East Asia during the seventeenth century may have had more to do with worldwide meteorological problems, such as lower-than-usual rainfall, than the activities of the VOC. Moreover, European political and economic authority was confined to a few outposts in the island world: on the mainland, it was South East Asians who clearly continued to determine their own destinies.

Vietnam Divided

THE LE AND MAC DYNASTIES

The strong political and cultural influence of China on Vietnam had, paradoxically, engendered a strong sense of Vietnamese identity by the 1500s. In other words, the Vietnamese had developed a clear sense of being non-Chinese. This sense of difference was accentuated by encounters with the Chams of central Vietnam who were regarded as inferior barbarians and who were increasingly pushed out to the southern fringes of the Vietnamese realm. This sense of unity, however, was insufficient to prevent an era of civil war in the first half of the sixteenth century that culminated in Vietnam being divided into two separate kingdoms. In 1527, the Le king was deposed by the head of the powerful Mac family. This situation infuriated the leaders of the Mac's equally powerful rivals, the Nguyen clan, who championed the Le dynasty as the rightful rulers of the realm. The civil war finally came to an end in the 1550s when Vietnam's overlord, the Chinese emperor in Beijing, brokered an agreement that decreed that the Mac should rule in the north of the country, leaving the south to be governed by the Le kings in alliance with the Nguyen family.

THE TRINH AND THE NGUYEN

The compromise soon broke down, however, as the Nguyen were challenged by an even more powerful clan, the Trinh. Both families tried to oust the Mac and establish themselves as the true defenders of the Le. In the fifteenth century, Le Thanh Ton had introduced numerous administrative reforms that enhanced royal authority. Nevertheless, considerable power remained in the hands of Vietnam's nobility, epitomized by the struggle between the Nguyen and the Trinh. Remaining loyal to the Le, Trinh forces had managed to force the Mac dynasty out of most of northern Vietnam by 1592. This did not lead to unification of the realm, however. In the name of the Le kings, the Trinh administered the north and by the seventeenth century the Trinh family head had assumed the title of a hereditary prince or *vuong*. The Nguyen, meanwhile, continued to guard the Le kings in the south. From 1627 there was open warfare between the two clans, and the Trinh and Nguyen zones were demarcated by the building of two huge walls north of the Nguyen capital at Hue in 1631. Both armies in the Vietnamese civil war were vast in number and, schooled by European gunsmiths, employed muskets and cannon of a high calibre and on a grand scale. The northern forces were probably better equipped. But despite the launching of four massive campaigns against Hue between 1643 and 1672, the Trinh were unable to subdue the south. A state of uneasy entente was finally achieved during the 1670s, allowing for the establishment of two separate, and mutually hostile, realms.

Yet, despite this 'cold war', both families pursued remarkably similar administrative policies in their different zones. The crux of reform was to re-establish royal control, whether Le-Trinh or Le-Nguyen. To prevent the accumulation of local power, royal family members were prevented from governing the regions, while the landed bureaucrats or mandarins were no longer allowed to administer in provinces where they had been born. There was a clampdown on the power of village leaders, whose authority had grown under conditions of civil war. After 1660, in both Trinh and Nguyen zones, village chiefs and elders were made responsible for delivering taxes and labour to the central administration. The Trinh went further in 1669 in decreeing that the title of village leader should now be *xa quan* (village mandarin) rather than *xa truang* (village chief). Central authority was also revitalized by a revival of Confucianism as a state ideology, often at the expense of Buddhist ideas and the indigenous spirit cults, in the administration and in everyday life. In the north, the ruler Trinh Tac, between 1657 and 1682, was particularly keen on Confucian precepts as a means of legitimizing his family's claims in the face of the Nguyen and also as a means of reversing a perceived moral decline, which it was believed had led to the civil war. Trinh district leaders had to be Confucian scholars who would both disseminate knowledge of the great Confucian texts and act in a suitably pious manner. In the Trinh-controlled villages, a new moral code, 'The Path for Religious Improvement', was introduced as early as 1663. It stressed how to be a good subject – not surprisingly to be achieved by showing unquestioning obedience to Trinh authority!

The Nguyen, meanwhile, began to feel the constraints of their lands around Hue, narrowly squeezed between the sea and the mountains. Blocked by the Trinh to the north, the Nguyen increasingly supported Vietnamese expansion to the south through the founding of military settlements (*don dien*) at the expense of both the Chams and the Cambodians. The process began in 1620 with the occupation of Saigon – formerly the Cambodian city of Prey Nokor – and migration to the Mekong River delta grew apace in the eighteenth century. By 1760 six Vietnamese delta provinces had been established in which thousands of ethnic Khmers were subject to 'Vietnamization'.

THE TAYSON REBELLION AND THE REUNIFICATION OF VIETNAM

Despite royal reform and military expansion, both north and south Vietnamese rulers faced increasing problems in administering their lands. A state of anarchy prevailed in the north Vietnamese countryside by the 1730s, epitomized by large-scale tax evasion and corrupt village administration. The 'robber barons' once again reigned supreme, grabbing communal lands and property and levying taxes on the defenceless peasants with impunity. Village life was increasingly miserable and when famines occurred (for example, in 1735) peasants, merchants, bandits and ethnic minority groups needed little encouragement to join the spate of rebellions aimed at expelling the Trinh and restoring the Le in northern Vietnam. Rebel leaders – monks, teachers, doctors and wandering holy men – appealed to the concept of the 'mandate of heaven'. As in China, this was the traditional Confucian idea that natural disasters, such as floods and famines, and popular unrest were signs that the deities and spirits were not happy with the emperors on earth. The approval of the heavens had been withdrawn and it was legitimate to revolt against the monarchy.

It was in the southern Nguyen territory that protests against misgovernment found their greatest expression. In 1773 three brothers from the village of Tayson in south-central Vietnam began a successful rebellion that culminated in their rule from Hue between 1778 and 1801. The Tayson rulers bore the family name, Nguyen, but were in no way related to the Nguyen aristocracy for they were of lowly, peasant background. The Tayson rebellion had wide support and swiftly undermined Nguyen power in the south, crippled anyway by chronic mismanagement under the regime of Chua Vo Vuong. By 1778 the Tayson rebels were in effective control of the Nguyen zone, including Saigon. Even greater triumphs followed under the leadership of the middle brother, Nguyen Hue. A veritable charmer, Nguyen Hue, according to Vietnamese tradition, had 'a voice musical as a bell and a look bright as lighting'. He also proved himself a brilliant military strategist, taking full advantage of Trinh weakness during a succession dispute – as well as another devastating famine – to achieve victory in the north in 1786. Two years later, Nguyen Hue successfully fought back a Chinese invasion to try and restore the Trinh and subsequently proclaimed himself emperor with the title of Quang-trung. His son, Quang-toan, succeeded him in 1792. A remarkable lower-class Vietnamese family had thus achieved the reunification of north and south Vietnam. Not surprisingly, Vietnamese nationalists in the twentieth century, such as Ho Chi Minh, would draw inspiration from the Tayson rebels in their campaigns for national rejuvenation based upon popular support.

Although the Tayson rulers declared themselves kings, they attempted to capture the mandate of heaven and rule as just and enlightened monarchs, as venerated in the ancient Confucian texts. In this sense, Tayson philosophy differed radically from the old order dominated by the emperors, nobles, and mandarins: if not democratic, rule was still to be based on the consent of the people and, remarkably for their time, the Tayson brothers declared that rich and poor were equal. There were certainly well-meaning attempts at reform, particularly in agriculture where land was redistributed and new lands were brought into cultivation. Trade and industry flourished at Hanoi and Saigon, assisted by a unified currency system.

Yet, economic modernization aside, the Tayson rulers, like so many Vietnamese leaders before and after them, failed really to relieve the problems of poverty and landlessness amongst the rice-producing peasants. Moreover, after Nguyen Hue's death, his son proved a weak leader unable to crush a challenge from Nguyen Anh, grandson of Chua Vo Vuong. Nguyen Anh had escaped from Hue in 1778 and planned his return under the patronage of the Thai kings. Nguyen Anh was helped by the Thais, as well as Chinese pirates and Cambodian mercenaries, to re-establish himself in Saigon as early as 1788. From Saigon he planned the conquest of Hue, which finally fell in 1801 and he was proclaimed emperor in 1802. To symbolize the unification of north and south Vietnam under the Nguyen aristocracy, Anh tactfully took the title of Gia-long, derived from a combination of Gia Dinh (the old name for Saigon) and Thang-long (the old name for Hanoi). The revamped Nguyen administration quickly turned back the clock, reinstating the nobility and the landed bureaucratic classes as well as the old elite Confucianist thinking to bolster monarchical authority. In contrast to the Thai kings, the emperors at Hue would prove themselves much more inward looking and incapable of adapting fast enough to the pressures of European encroachment in the nineteenth century.

Ayutthaya Becomes Siam

CONSOLIDATING THE REALM IN THE SIXTEENTH CENTURY

By 1500 the Thai monarch based at Ayutthaya dominated what is now central Thailand – some 20 kings were said to pay Ayutthaya allegiance. Following on from King Trailok's administrative zeal in the fifteenth century, territories under Ayutthaya's suzerainty were divided into a number of provinces, each with its own governor. The Portuguese came to regard Ayutthaya as one of the major powers in Asia. The process of centralization was further helped by growing involvement in international trade, particularly with China, as well as the similarity of dialects spoken from province to province. A greater sense of Thai identity was reinforced by the various Buddhist monasteries dotted around Ayutthaya's realm. By the 1600s, Ayutthaya's empire was being called 'Siam', the name by which Thailand would be known until the middle of the twentieth century. Previously, the term Siam had only referred to the kingdom of Sukhothai, which itself was now firmly in Ayutthaya's grip. Ayutthaya's growing power over weaker vassals, for example, the sultanates of the northern Malay peninsula, was further assisted by the employment of European firearms and soldiers of fortune.

But, in knitting together Tai-speaking peoples, Ayutthaya faced a formidable external threat in the guise of the Burmese monarchy, which was also seeking to expand its influence. The 200 or so years of intermittent warfare between Burma and Siam from the mid-sixteenth century were violent struggles to grab manpower and land but also sprang from an internecine Buddhist conflict, in which the Burmese and Thai kings vied with each other to take the title of *cakkavatti*, or Universal Monarch. (The wars are depicted in numerous Thai pictures and carvings, in which a Thai prince, king or general defeats his Burmese counterpart after a duel on the back of elephants). In 1569 Ayutthaya's power was severely weakened when the Burmese pillaged the Thai capital and took thousands of prisoners.

Faced by devastation, as well as a humiliating series of Cambodian raids, King Naresuan set about rejuvenating Ayutthaya after 1590. After strengthening the city's defences, Naresuan repulsed a Burmese invasion in 1593 and ensured Ayutthaya's self-proclaimed independence. Ayutthaya was reconfirmed as the most powerful state in the Tai-speaking world not least because its northern rivals, Lan Na and Lan Sang, continued to suffer at the hands of Burmese armies. Dominance over Cambodia was reasserted by the sacking of the seat of the Khmer kings at Lovek in 1594.

Central to this Siamese rehabilitation was a set of administrative reforms, which placed authoritarian controls upon the every day lives of average Thais. All male 'free' commoners (*phrai som*) had to register in a specific district with a particular local leader (*nai*) – the latter being either a noble or a royal prince. A tattoo on the wrist of each *phrai som* identified the *nai* to whom he owed six months service each year. The *nai*, in return, assumed general responsibility for the welfare of his *phrai som*. Meanwhile, the king retained servicemen of his own, *phrai luang*, who were also required to undertake the six months *corvée* (in the army, for example). Women and monks were exempt from the unpaid labour system but both groups were still required to register with a lord: when monks returned to the lay world, they would revert to service with a particular *nai*, while the registration of women established precisely to whom Thai children owed service. Effective though this system was, it still presented the king with a knotty problem: his own *phrai* tended to evade service by either seeking sanctuary in monasteries or reregistering with the princes and nobles because the king's *corvée* demands were regarded as more exacting. As a means of circumventing provincial power, therefore, the princes and nobles were prevented from holding regional office by their forced residence at court. In this way, the *nai* were split off from their *phrai* and the provinces were now administered by the king's own appointees.

To reinforce royal authority, spies kept an eye on provincial and town governors for the king, and the development of a professional standing army in the service of the king was a further deterrent against both internal and external challenges. On his death in 1605, then, Naresuan had succeeded in laying the basis for a permanent and efficient system of royal administration. Thus visitors from Louis XIV's

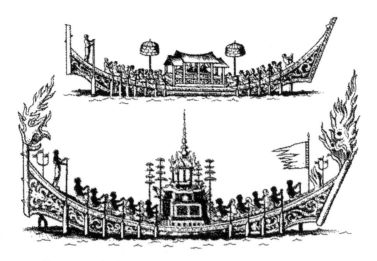

Siamese royal galleys as represented by French artists in the 1680s

France in the 1680s admiringly reported that, 'in the distribution of responsibilities they [the Siamese] pay most attention to the merits, the experience and the services that one has given, and not to birth; which ensures that everyone applies himself to earning the favour of the prince'.

TRADE, WAR AND EXPANSION IN THE SEVENTEENTH CENTURY

By the 1600s Siam was not only a major military power in Asia, but its capital at Ayutthaya was also a great centre of international trade, underpinned by the widespread use of silver coins known as *baht*, the name by which Thailand's currency is still known today. Despite the ravages of the Burmese invasion of 1569, Ayutthaya's population had recovered by the 1600s, so much so that English observers thought it 'as big a city as London'. Living in mainly wooden houses, the city of Ayutthaya probably contained about 100,000 people – roughly ten percent of Siam's total population. With Hanoi, Aceh, Banten, Makassar and Mataram, this concentration made Ayutthaya one of

South East Asia's largest pre-modern cities. Its size was made possible by the huge rice surpluses of the Chao Phraya plain, the desire of Thai kings to surround themselves with retainers for military and status purposes, and Ayutthaya's easy access by river to the sea, which encouraged the growth of international trade. It was Ayutthaya's large Chinese community, however, which dominated in commercial activities. Led by two *kapitan*, the Chinese were pig breeders, artisans, physicians, actors, and even Siamese officials and the captains and navigators of royal ships, as well as traders and merchants. The Chinese found themselves in a very fortunate position in Siam because they were not obliged to register in the *nai-phrai* system and were exempt from *corvée* labour duties. In this way, the Chinese used the royal capital at Ayutthaya as a base from which they freely developed trade and investment networks both within the Siamese kingdom and overseas. The revenue-farming system saw the Chinese frequently employed as tax collectors in the provinces and they also ran enterprises, on behalf of the king and court, in activities such as tin mining and international trade.

Yet seventeenth-century Thailand was still beset by external threats. In 1622 the Cambodians achieved a remarkable victory in which Ayutthaya lost between 4,000 and 5,000 men. In 1634 the southern tributary state of Patani also defeated Siamese forces. Even more alarming was the revival of the wars with Burma during the 1660s and, despite the importation of large amounts of European muskets and cannon, the Siamese were unable to prevent the northern Tai state of Lan Na falling under Burmese control. The Siamese had occupied Lan Na's capital, Chiang Mai, after its ruler appealed to Ayutthaya for protection. But by 1664 Lan Na was confirmed as a Burmese vassal or *pyi*. The Burmese now installed their own governors in Lan Na, filled their armies with Chiang Mai's subjects and further cemented their hegemony by controlling the local monasteries.

Blocked by the Burmese to the north, Ayutthaya increasingly turned south in the seventeenth century – as far as the Malay peninsula – to satisfy its expansionist cravings. Here Ayutthaya's links with the European powers – Portugal, Holland, France and England – were crucial in the supply of superior arms and military advice. The northern

Malay state of Kedah was forced to submit to Siam during the reign of King Prasat Thong (1630–56). In 1651 the Muslim ruler of Songkhla made the mistake of refusing submission to Ayutthaya. A fleet of some 120 Siamese ships was subsequently despatched to the southern port. Each ship was reputedly hung with human heads and smeared with blood to terrify the people of Songkhla. Wisely, in 1679, the ruler of Songkhla agreed to pay the Siamese king homage.

THE DESCENT INTO FRAGMENTATION, 1688–1767

Despite royal centralization, economic growth and the expansion of authority in the south, there remained a central problem for the Siamese kings. This was the tradition whereby the heir to the throne was a brother rather than a son of the monarch. The uncertain nature of succession created all sorts of opportunities for court intrigues, as occurred in the 1680s, at the end of the reign of King Narai. In 1688 a group of Siamese nobles championed Narai's foster brother, P'ra P'etraja as heir to the throne. The aristocratic rebellion, involving thousands of armed Siamese, was directed against foreign influence at court. From the 1650s, Narai had skilfully played off the Dutch, English and French against each other to secure the independence of his realm. But in the course of this diplomacy, the Greek adventurer, Constantine Phaulkon, had emerged as a major adviser to Narai – a situation which had irritated many a Siamese noble. P'ra P'etraja was made regent on behalf of Narai, who had fallen seriously ill, while Phaulkon was arrested and executed. When Narai died in August 1688, P'ra P'etraja became king.

P'ra P'etraja was able to found a dynasty which lasted some 80 years, noted for its relative political stability. Under the reigns of Thai Sra and Borommakot between 1709 and 1758, Siam recovered from the chaos wrought by the succession dispute of the late seventeenth century as well as the global downturn in economic activity. Borommakot's reign after 1733 is particularly noted for its Buddhist revival, in which Christianity was virtually outlawed. Only former Buddhist monks could now become nobles and Ayutthaya emerged as an important centre of Theravada Buddhism.

But Borommakot's piety was not enough to prevent another wave of internal unrest and external threats from the 1750s. Rebellions led by 'holy men' and rival princes involving several thousand men became commonplace as royal *phrai* increasingly entered the service of nobles and ministers. Royal weakness was also manifest in the restlessness of the Malay tributaries to the south. These centrifugal tendencies within the Siamese empire were exacerbated by the revival of Burmese pretensions after 1760. Despite the marshalling of huge land and naval forces by Siam, Ayutthaya was brutally sacked by the Burmese in 1767 – a deep historical wound, which has left a scar on Thailand's national consciousness. With its buildings destroyed, military hardware plundered, and population killed or captured, Ayutthaya could no longer control the provinces and the realm split into some five separate regions. For the first time in nearly 400 years, central Thailand lacked a political centre.

TAKSIN, RAMA I AND SIAM'S LATE-EIGHTEENTH CENTURY RENAISSANCE

As often seems to be the case in Thailand's history, a charismatic leader emerged from disaster. The military commander, Phraya Taksin, the son of a wealthy and influential Chinese merchant and a Thai mother, founded a new capital at Thonburi about 50 miles south of Ayutthaya on the Chao Phraya river. Taksin reunified the country after 1767, aspiring to *cakkavatti* status and to be 'greater than the king of Ava [Burma]'. He relied on Chinese trade, food production, construction skills and capital to rejuvenate Siamese power. The Chinese were particularly effective in draining the marshy land around Thonburi to provide an excellent area for food cultivation. Under Taksin's patronage a privileged group of 'royal Chinese' or *chin luang* emerged. Replicating the Dutch system in the Indies, port revenues, gambling, tin mining, as well as provincial governorships and military commands were farmed out to leading Chinese, in return for an annual payment to the crown. These *chin luang* might eventually pass into the Siamese nobility.

In reconstructing Siam's power, Taksin also initiated a policy of territorial expansion, building up a circle of border provinces allied to the capital at Thonburi. In this way, the southern territories of Nakhon Sithammarat (Ligor) and Songkhla were to return to vassal status. In the north, meanwhile, Chiang Mai fell under Siamese control as Burmese military might receded.

But Taksin ultimately became hoist with his own petard – through his study of mysticism he became convinced of his own Buddha-like divinity. The idea that kings were deities, however, was contrary to traditional notions of Thai kingship: it was only accepted that Buddhist kings might become divine on death. The monkhood or *sangha*, therefore, refused to sanctify Taksin's claims to supernatural status and, for their disobedience, the increasingly tyrannical king had some 500 monks flogged and sentenced to hard labour. The religious hierarchy's disapproval of Taksin played a large part in his downfall in 1782.

Another former general, P'ra P'utt'a Yot Fa Chulalok or Chakri, who ruled between 1782 and 1809, would prove a more tactful ruler than Taksin. Chakri took the title of Rama I on being raised to the throne. His legacy is still felt in modern-day Thailand, for it was Rama I who engineered another shift of the Siamese capital to the opposite bank of the Chao Phraya from Thonburi to found the modern city of Bangkok. He also founded the Chakri dynasty, which has ruled Thailand for more than 200 years. Like Taksin, Rama I was linked to the Chinese merchant elite through his mother, Dan Ruang. Bangkok swiftly became a new centre of Chinese enterprise, based particularly on the two rice crops per year from the surrounding river plain, and rice once again became a major Siamese export to China. Rama I also continued Taksin's strategy of military expansion, both up the Chao Phraya river and down the Gulf of Thailand to the Kra Isthmus. The Malay Muslim port of Patani was subdued in 1791, while Chiang Mai was permitted the privilege of administering the far north and Nakhon Sithammarat and Songkhla supervised the south of the nation. Bangkok's control over the various provinces was guaranteed by forcing the sons of provincial governors to reside at court as royal pages. With a more relaxed interpretation of his role as 'Universal Monarch' than Taksin, Rama I was more easily able to coax the Lao states of the north east, Cambodia to the south east and the sultanates of the northern

Malay peninsula into Chakri vassalage to form important buffer zones. Mirroring the neatly ordered hierarchy of Thai society, Rama I's empire graded each of the provinces from one to four, defining their obligations and responsibilities to Bangkok. The least independent, fourth-class *muang* were the old territories of the Ayutthayan empire, which were directly controlled by Bangkok and could expect the highest demands for manpower, military obligations and taxes from the centre. At the other extreme, the first-class *muang*, such as Cambodia and the Malay states, were permitted virtual independence in return for their recognition of Siamese overlordship.

Rama I's reign was also one of celebrated religious reform predicated on the belief that Ayutthaya's destruction by the Burmese had resulted from moral decay. Appreciating Taksin's errors, Rama I went out of his way to resurrect the monarchy's links with the *sangha* by decreeing that Thai kings should not intervene in religious disputes until the matter had been extensively discussed by the leading monks. Brahmanical and animist practices in royal ceremonies were now downgraded in favour of Buddhist precepts, and the worship of *lingas*, dating from pre-Buddhist Thailand, was abolished. Most notably, Rama I opened the fabulous royal temple of the Emerald Buddha within the palace grounds at Bangkok as a centre for Buddhist instruction. Rama I and his court also presided over a drastic overhaul of the Buddhist 'bible', the *Tripitaka*, between 1788 and 1789. This was a task involving more than 200 monks and more than 30 laymen living and working within the palace grounds. From these reviews resulted texts that remain central to Thai Buddhism, and which were translated from the ancient Pali into Thai for lay readers. In what the distinguished scholar of Thailand, D.K. Wyatt, calls both a 'subtle revolution' and a 'Buddhist "reformation"', Rama I provided Siam with a solid intellectual and cultural framework to face the challenges emanating from imperialist Europe in the nineteenth century. One source of division, remained, however: the continued reliance by the kings of Siam on the Chinese community, particularly in economic affairs, may have avoided the rise of alternative power centres from within the indigenous Thai community, but it also led to an increasing exclusion of the indigenous population from large-scale commercial activity.

Laos and Cambodia: Buffer States

THE SURVIVAL AND SPLITTING OF LAN SANG

Lan Sang (roughly corresponding to the modern state of Laos) survived as an independent entity until the early eighteenth century. This endurance was aided by geographical factors: the kingdom was surrounded by inaccessible mountains that served as natural barriers and accentuated Lan Sang's sense of remoteness from the centres of both Burmese and Siamese authority. Indeed traffic on Laos's major international trade route via the Mekong River had to circumvent the Khone Falls on the border with Cambodia by going over land before rejoining the great river to reach the capital at Vientiane. Despite its isolation, however, Vientiane, under the stable 57 year reign of King Soulignavongsa after 1637, reached a population of around 50,000.

Nevertheless in 1707 Lan Sang was split into two separate kingdoms, with capitals at Vientiane and Luang Prabang while the southern city of Champasak maintained a *de facto* independence. Squabbles between the three Lao centres notwithstanding, a sense of Lao distinctiveness in relation to their Thai neighbours developed. A feeling of local pride was reinforced by Lao possession of the fabulous 'Emerald Buddha'. (Actually carved from green jasper, the 'Emerald Buddha', was originally brought to Vientiane by King Setthathirat in 1564 from Chiang Mai via Luang Prabang).

As the eighteenth century wore on, however, the Lao principalities experienced growing pressures from their expansionist neighbours who frequently exploited divisions between the states. Luang Prabang finally broke free of its 43 years of Burmese domination in 1778, but only to find itself faced with a resurgent Siam. During 1791–92 the Siamese manipulated Vientiane to force the complete submission of its northern Lao rival. At the end of the century, Vientiane provided Siam with further support to prevent Burmese attempts to recapture northern Thailand and Laos. The Lao principalities found themselves increasingly reduced in status vis-à-vis Bangkok, becoming mere third-class *muang* in Rama I's imperial hierarchy. The trend of Lao submission to Siam had been indicated earlier when in 1779 Taksin's armies had carried off the Emerald Buddha to Bangkok, where it remains as one of the main sights. The Lao states also had to deal with the Vietnamese to the north west. Vientiane adopted a strategy of 'dual allegiance', allying with Emperor Gia-long in his struggles with the Tayson rebels in the 1790s. As a result, Vientiane was paying tribute to both Bangkok and Hue by the nineteenth century.

THE KHMERS UNDER THAI AND VIETNAMESE DOMINATION

Like Laos sandwiched between Siam and Vietnam, Cambodia remained a weak, enfeebled entity compared to its expanding neighbours. But while Laos was shielded by its mountains, Cambodia lacked any natural barriers to keep out marauding armies. The Khmer kings, despite a brief resurgence in the early seventeenth century, were never able to revive the splendours and power of Angkor and increasingly fell under the influence of Thailand. Indeed, in 1594 the Thais of Ayutthaya dealt a punishing blow to the Khmer capital at Lovek, despite a Cambodian appeal for assistance to the Spanish at Manila. According to legend, during the plundering of Lovek, the Thais captured holy books, which allowed them to become 'superior in knowledge to the Cambodians'. Khmer Buddhism was flourishing at the end of the sixteenth century and in the 1620s the Cambodians did manage to shed Ayutthaya's suzerainty with a shift of their capital to Udong, just south of Lovek, under King Chey Chetta II. But this was only to be followed by a period of internecine struggle after 1643 when King Chan, who had a Malay wife, converted to Islam and changed his name to Ibrahim. A coup restored a Buddhist to the throne, Batom Reachea, in 1659. Yet, the troubled kingdom continued to be plagued by court intrigues, coup attempts and frequent Siamese or Vietnamese interventions.

In the eighteenth century, the shared Angkorian past, as well as continued Theravada Buddhist links, engendered a sense of Thai paternalism towards the Khmer kings, particularly when Cambodia was threatened by Vietnamese encroachments. Cambodia, like Laos, became an important Thai buffer state between Thailand proper and Vietnam. Thai influence at Udong, which had been reduced after Burma's crushing of Ayutthaya in 1767, was revived as Vietnam became embroiled in another civil war between the Tayson and the Nguyen after 1771. Siam took sides in the Cambodian civil war of the 1780s when Rama I nurtured the exiled boy-King, Ang Eng, as a 'priceless jewel' in Bangkok. Ang Eng, when he reached maturity in 1794, was restored as Khmer king at Udong, backed by a Siamese army. By this time, the western Cambodian provinces of Battambang and Siem Reap had been absorbed into the Siamese empire. Any attempt at revitalising Cambodian power would have been thwarted by the country's poor resource base. Its lack of manpower, commercial wealth, and military hardware was further undermined by the loss of the lands and peoples of the Mekong estuary, south of Phnom Penh, to the expansionist Nguyen of Vietnam during the seventeenth and eighteenth centuries. Cambodia's only port of significance, Kampot, was hardly on a par with Bangkok, Saigon or Hanoi.

Fragmented Malaysia

THE FALL OF MELAKA

The experience of Cambodia and Laos between 1500 and 1800 was replicated in the island world, although here the predators were Europeans rather than South East Asians. An Italian observer of the great battle of 1511 between the Portuguese and Melaka described the Malays as 'most valiant men, well trained in war, and copiously supplied with every type of very good weapon'. This was not enough, however, to prevent the catastrophic fall of the sultanate. This Portuguese intrusion into the peninsula, followed by the Dutch in the seventeenth and eighteenth centuries and then the British from the 1800s, fractured Malay political power and made any moves towards political unity in western Malaysia problematic. Malay economic power also splintered: the population of Melaka, probably about 100,000 at the port's heyday in the 1480s, was reduced to about 25,000 in the sixteenth century as Muslim traders scattered around the ports of the Malay peninsula, Java, Sumatra, Borneo and Sulawesi.

Melaka's royal family was forced into exile at Johor, on the southern tip of the peninsula. At Johor, there were attempts to recreate Melaka's power and traditions. But, with the Portuguese controlling the straits, it proved impossible for the Melaka sultans to maintain dominance over their former client states in Malaya and Sumatra, and individual sultanates, such as Perak, now moved out of Melaka/Johor's orbit. Johor's attempts to lead a religious war against the Portuguese – to recapture Melaka and reunite the peninsula under its leadership – foundered on its rivalry with the north Sumatran sultanate of Aceh. Perak, Pahang and Kedah had all fallen under the influence of Aceh by the early seventeenth century, and Johor even allied with the Portuguese in a war with Aceh in 1568. Seemingly accepting that

The Dutch church at Melaka, Malaysia dating from 1753

Melaka could never be recaptured, Johor even made a pact with the Dutch in 1641 during the latter's successful ousting of the Portuguese from the peninsula.

JOHOR-RIAU: THE FROGS AND THE COBRAS

As the seventeenth century drew to a close, Johor was increasingly riven by internal strife, often exploited by foreign interlopers, which culminated in the extraordinary events of the late seventeenth and early eighteenth centuries, beginning with the assassination of the sadistic and perverted Sultan Mahmud in 1699 by his nobles. Mahmud was the last of the Melaka royal line, and he was replaced as king by his former chief minister or *bendahara*, Abdul Jalil. Many Malay and Orang Asli leaders – whose loyalties had their origins in the Melaka 'golden age' – were so unhappy with this situation that a Minangkabau prince from Sumatra, Raja Kechil, was able to seize the throne in 1717, claiming to be a son of the murdered Mahmud. But Raja Kechil had made an enemy of a powerful Bugis leader, Daing Parani, exiled from his native Sulawesi. Daing Parani allied with the deposed Abdul Jalil, eventually forcing the Minangkabau raja to flee in 1722. Abdul Jalil's son became sultan, but de facto power was now in the hands of the Bugis immigrants. The new dynasty was also located off the mainland on the island of Riau (today in Indonesia). The Melaka royal line had reached its somewhat inglorious denouement. The events of the early-eighteenth century in Johor-Riau are remembered in the nineteenth-century Malay satirical poem about a naive frog-king (i.e., the Johor ruler) who is bamboozled by a devious cobra-king (i.e., the Bugis prince) to the extent that the cobra-king eventually devours all the frogs in the kingdom, including the frog-king and his chief minister!

Under Bugis control, the islands of the Riau archipelago did flourish as a major centre for the production of gambier – a plant extract used in tanning – and attracted large numbers of Chinese and Bugis cultivators from the 1740s. But economic dynamism aside, the rulers of Johor-Riau, rather like their Vietnamese and Javanese counterparts, retreated into inward-looking conservatism and in 1784 the kingdom was split in two as Riau was captured by the Dutch.

THE MALAY STATES UNDER THAI AND DUTCH DOMINANCE

Partly because of the conservatism of their ruling elites, the Malay states were also easy prey for both European and South East Asian predators because of their small size. The rice-producing sultanate of Kedah on the north east of the peninsula, for example, contained a population of only 20,000 in the 1700s. Kedah shook off Aceh's governance in the 1640s only to replace this with Dutch economic dominance. By the end of the eighteenth century, Kedah and the other northern states, Terengganu and Kelantan, were increasingly subservient to Bangkok. The Malay states proved difficult vassals, however, due to the Muslim faith and other cultural differences and often had to be coerced into paying tribute by Buddhist Siam. Perak, with its abundant supplies of tin ore, was also coveted by Siam but in 1746 signed a treaty with the Dutch, which granted the VOC a monopoly over the purchase of Perak's tin in return for protection against Siam and other potential aggressors.

BABAS AND NONYAS

Despite political fragmentation in the peninsula, there remained plenty of opportunities for economic development, attracting increasing numbers of enterprising Chinese. As in Johor-Riau, Chinese entrepreneurs were present throughout the ports of the peninsula, often marrying into Malay society and converting to Islam. With the males known as *baba* and the females as *nonya*, these assimilated Chinese produced a unique fusion of Malay and Chinese culture, notably in their delicious cuisine. Tan Cheng Lock, the twentieth-century leader of the Malayan Chinese, was a Melaka *baba* descended from late-eighteenth century immigrants. As well as successful merchants and planters, the Chinese also gained a reputation as great miners and smelters in the eighteenth-century Malay world, forming partnerships (*kongsi*) and settlements in the interior to develop western Malaysia's tin fields.

BRUNEI, SULU AND BORNEO

One 'Malay' state that did flourish after the fall of Melaka was the kingdom known as Brunei, which emerged in the sixteenth century on the north west coast of Borneo. Brunei is usually regarded as a Malay kingdom, but its rulers may actually have been descended from the indigenous Bisaya and Murut peoples of the area. Even so, Malay connections were important as the Brunei ruler converted to Islam some time between 1514 and 1521, probably as a consequence of the arrival of Muslim traders and Malay officials from Melaka after 1511. (Although, according to tradition, a Muslim sultan has been ruling Brunei since 1360.) With a population approaching 50,000 in the late sixteenth century, Brunei had achieved remarkable wealth, becoming one of the largest cities of the 'Malay' world and attracting traders from China as well as from all over the region. It even aroused the jealousy of the Spanish at Manila: in the 1520s Magellan reported on an illustrious court, clothed in fine silks and gold, and in 1578 the Spanish even sent an expedition to incorporate the country into its empire (the attempt had to be abandoned, however, due to the European susceptibility to disease).

Brunei's trade contacts with China stretched back to the fifth century, given the kingdom's ideal location as a stopping-off point for ships in the Nanyang (as China called South East Asia) trade. By the early-modern era, Brunei flourished as a central collecting point for the unique sea and jungle products much coveted by Chinese merchants. Brunei was also central in the northern trade route to the spice islands of Maluku. As well as an economic powerhouse, the Borneo sultanate emerged as a major centre for Islamic missionary work.

But Brunei's paramountcy on Borneo was challenged in the seventeenth century by its former vassal to the north east, the sultanate of Sulu (the Sulu archipelago is today part of the Philippines). In supporting the successful claimant in a Brunei succession dispute, Sulu obtained rights over large areas of the modern-day, East Malaysian state of Sabah. These north eastern concessions comprised over half of Brunei's territories. Worse still, the ceded lands were the source of much of Brunei's wealth from the forest and sea produce sought by international traders. By the eighteenth century, the growing economic and political strength of the Sulu archipelago allowed it not only to resist Spanish attempts to Christianize the southern Philippines, but also to force Brunei to relinquish authority over the Bajau sea people. Even so, until the 1830s, Brunei remained suzerain over the huge territory of what is today the East Malaysian state of Sarawak. *Pangeran*, or nobles, were appointed by the sultan theoretically to administer the Dayaks, Malays, Melanaus and other ethnic groups of diverse Sarawak.

Fragmented Indonesia

THE RISE AND DECLINE OF ACEH

Once the Palembang-centred empire of Srivijaya had declined by the thirteenth century, Sumatra lacked a dominant political and economic core. Marco Polo during his sojourn through Indonesia in the 1290s counted 'eight kingdoms and eight crowned kings' in northern Sumatra, with each polity having 'a language of its own'. This situation was to change, however, from the 1520s when the north Sumatran state of Aceh, whose ruler had converted to Islam in the mid-fifteenth century, began to spread its tentacles down both east and west coasts of Sumatra. As heir to the first Muslim state in South East Asia, Pasai, Aceh also led campaigns of conversion against the animist Bataks of the interior. Indeed, Aceh increasingly saw itself as carrying on Melaka's work – a base for Muslim trade and missionary work after the Portuguese intrusion. As a self-styled 'Verandah of Mecca', Aceh became a major centre of Islamic thought in the sixteenth century where the Koran and other Arabic texts were translated into Malay. Aceh also benefitted from contacts with the wider Muslim world: Turkish mercenaries from the powerful Ottoman empire of the Middle East and eastern Europe were incorporated into Aceh's armies. In the 1560s, Aceh sent missions to try and interest the Ottoman sultan, Suleiman the Magnificent, in a *jihad* against the Portuguese infidels of Melaka. The Turks, occupied with their own holy wars in Europe, did not become officially involved but did supply men, firearms (especially cannon) and messages of support for Aceh's subsequent (unsuccessful) attacks on the European-controlled port between 1566 and 1568.

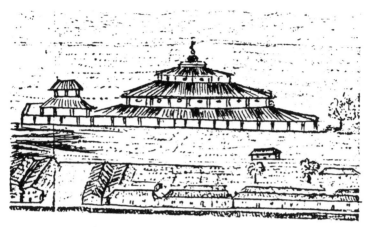

A sketch, *c.* 1650, of the great mosque of Aceh

Aceh's most acclaimed sultan was Iskandar Muda who ruled between 1607 and 1636. Iskandar Muda's reign is famous for its ruthless expansionism in a further series of campaigns on Sumatra plus new military expeditions on the Malay peninsula, which confirmed Aceh's status as the wealthiest and most powerful state in the island world. Aceh's awesome military machine sacked Johor twice in 1613 and 1615. And, although Iskandar failed in his campaign to 'liberate' Melaka from the Portuguese, by 1620 Kedah, Perak and Pahang had all submitted to Aceh's authority. With more than 2,000 cannon and guns – of both Sumatran and European origin – in Iskandar's mighty arsenal, Aceh's force was unrivalled. During Iskandar's attack on Kedah in 1619, for example, the capital was laid waste with its surviving inhabitants carried off to Aceh. In the following year, 5,000 people were captured from Perak – their fate was to be left to die in the streets of Aceh.

Aceh's power during the reign of Iskandar Muda also derived from its fabulous wealth. Aceh exported huge quantities of pepper, cloves and nutmegs as part of its key position in the 'Islamic' trade route to the Middle East and the Mediterranean. Here Aceh's close relations with the Ottoman Turks were crucial in circumventing the spice trade route around Africa controlled by the Portuguese 'infidels'. Aceh was also famous for its export of betel (or areca) nuts. Betel was an intoxicant that bypassed the Muslim prohibition on the consumption of alcohol and also acted as a means of suppressing hunger pangs. The narcotic properties of betel were released on chewing a combination of a small piece of the nut of the areca palm, a fresh leaf of the betel vine and a pinch of lime. As a consequence of trade-derived wealth, Aceh grew to be one of the largest cities in the archipelago by the 1600s, and its role as a major trade centre was underpinned by the low interest rates prevailing in Iskandar Muda's reign as well as the widespread use of small gold coins known as *mas*.

Iskandar Muda was a shrewd economist but, at the same time, a bloodthirsty tyrant who frequently added to his personal fortune by executing his wealthier subjects and confiscating their assets. Royal power was certainly increased at the expense of the Iskandar's most significant subjects through a system of centralization. In the 1580s, Aceh remained effectively an oligarchy in which a clique of aristocratic merchants known as the *orang kaya* (literally, 'rich men') possessed fabulous wealth and a great number of arms and slaves. Iskandar Muda understandably regarded the *orang kaya* as a threat and sought to curtail their independent power. The elite were heavily supervised through their enforced attendance at court as well as through prohibitions on the independent building of houses, which might be used for military purposes and the keeping of cannon. The royal princes, meanwhile, were replaced by royal officials called *panglima* who reported annually and were subject to periodic appraisal by other officials. To enhance administrative efficiency, Aceh was divided into a number of *mukim*, or parishes, and a set of legal reforms created a sophisticated network of courts based on Islamic law. The development of an elite palace guard – composed of some 3,000 women – further secured against any challenges from disaffected Acehnese. Gruesome punishments were meted out to those who were deemed to have transgressed. As a French visitor to Aceh in the 1620s reported, 'every day the King would have people's noses cut off, eyes dug out, castrations, feet cut off, or hands, ears and other parts mutilated, very often for some very small matter'. His tyranny notwithstanding, Iskandar Muda is revered today in Aceh as a great hero and symbol of Aceh's vanished greatness.

The triumph of royal absolutism proved short-lived, however. Iskandar Thani, Iskandar Muda's son-in-law, who ruled between 1636 and 1641, continued the process of centralizing royal power. But after his death, effective power returned to the *orang kaya*, who managed to install four queens to rule Aceh from 1641 until the end of the century. The oligarchs opted for female rulers – a situation which did not please the Islamic leaders, the *ulama* – because they feared a resurgence of the royal despotism of the Iskandars. In the 1680s a Persian visitor to Aceh reported that, 'every corner shelters a separate king or governor and all the local rulers maintain themselves independently and do not pay tribute to any higher authority'. Northern Sumatra's trade continued to flourish, but with a lack of central cohesion, Aceh found it increasingly difficult to compete with the growing economic and military power of the VOC in the straits. The reality of Dutch power on the Malay peninsula was signalled in 1641 when Johor allied with Holland in the successful siege of Portuguese Melaka. This was followed by a Dutch blockade of Aceh in the 1650s and full-scale warfare in the 1660s. By this time, the VOC had usurped the sultanate's control of the pepper trade of west Sumatra as well as the tin exports of the Malay peninsula. With these major sources of Aceh's prosperity in European hands, decline had clearly set in by the eighteenth century.

MINANGKABAU, 'THE VICTORIOUS BUFFALO'

Even at the height of its power in the 1620s and 1630s, Aceh had not been able to control the whole of Sumatra. The Acehnese had rivals amongst the Minangkabau peoples of west Sumatra. The origins of the Minangkabau kingdom are obscure but the reputed founder of the realm in the third quarter of the fourteenth century was one Aditya-varman, an observer of Buddhist Tantric ceremonies involving various bloodcurdling and erotic acts. According to Minangkabau tradition, the name of the people derives from a medieval conflict with the Javanese, the outcome of which was decided by a battle between a tiger (representing the Javanese) and a buffalo (representing the Sumatrans). Since the buffalo killed the tiger, the west Sumatrans took the name

Minangkabau, meaning 'the victorious buffalo'. In the course of the sixteenth and seventeenth centuries, the Minangkabau converted to Islam. But, despite being Muslims, the strength of traditional, *adat* inheritance laws – which passed property from female to female – encouraged ambitious enterprising young Minangkabau males to leave their homelands and form communities all over Sumatra, such as at Siak near the east coast, and even on the Malay peninsula, as in the modern West Malaysian state of Negeri Sembilan. In this way, Minangkabau influence spread over a very wide area of Sumatra and the Malay peninsula, and a Minangkabau prince even challenged for the throne of Johor in the early eighteenth century. Where the Minangkabau differed from the Acehnese, however, was in their general reluctance to back up influence with armed force (although Minangkabau gunsmiths manufactured large quantities of firearms). Also in contrast to Aceh, Minangkabau accommodated itself to the presence of the VOC, following the latter's victory over Aceh in 1667. A Dutch treaty confirmed Minangkabau overlordship in west Sumatra. The price for Minangkabau, however, was the appointment of a Dutch adviser at the capital, Padang, as military commander on behalf of the sultan.

MAKASSAR AND BUGIS

As on Sumatra at the western end of present-day Indonesia, so in the eastern islands of the archipelago, ever-growing trade pushed towards greater political consolidation in the early-modern period. Most notably, this occurred at Makassar (Ujung Pandang), south west Sulawesi, which in the seventeenth century became a major locus for regional commerce. The spread of Islam to eastern Indonesia also played an important part in the rise of Makassar, which was actually a fusion of the kingdoms of Goa (N.B. This has no connection with Goa in India) and Tallo. The long-standing work of Muslim traders and missionaries on Sulawesi was finally rewarded in 1605 when the ruler of Tallo, Karaeng Matoya, adopted the Muslim faith. Concurrently, the ruler of Goa took the title, Sultan Alauddin, and the two newly-converted kingdoms merged. Makassar acted as a new base for missionary teaching in eastern Indonesia, and a number of victorious religious crusades (assisted by Makassarese skill in the manufacture of cannon and muskets) were fought against Makassar's Bugis rival, Bone, which also succumbed to Islam in the 1600s. By the 1640s Makassar was the supreme lord of all the small states of south western Sulawesi that, like Bone, also took on the Muslim faith. Only the Toraja people of the inaccessible interior highlands resisted Makassar's grip and retained their animist beliefs.

Makassar's power also spread beyond Sulawesi to envelop the island of Sumbawa to the south, which, by the 1640s, had accepted both Makassarese dominance and Islam. Makassar's wealth was based on its ability to attract international traders, eager to restock their food supplies on their voyages further east to the spice islands. Karaeng Matoya, who ruled until 1637, shrewdly introduced measures to increase rice production and so guarantee an adequate surplus of rice for sale to the ships in Makassar's busy harbour.

But as was the case for so many rich states in the island world, it was not long before the Dutch sought to control Makassar. Between 1666 and 1669, then, the Dutch allied with the Bugis from Bone, under their celebrated leader Arung Palakka, to defeat Makassar. In appropriating the Makassar king's title of Torisomape, the 'Venerated One', Arung Palakka was recognized by the Dutch as suzerain of all Sulawesi and in return the Bugis agreed to expel all other European traders from Makassar. Oaths of loyalty required of the Bugis were now taken to both the Bugis king and the VOC. The Bugis became the major ethnic group in the city of Makassar (as remains the case in contemporary Ujung Pandang), as the Makassarese migrated en masse. The Bugis community of Wajo, however, remained loyal to the Makassar sultanate and joined the Makassarese in what would prove to be an incredibly successful Bugis diaspora to rival that of the Minangkabau of west Sumatra. Bugis communities established themselves in Java, Sumatra, the eastern coast of Borneo and even in Siam and Cambodia. The Bugis, with their small, light and fast *perahu*, proved themselves highly skilled seaborne, regional traders (even after the displacement of the *perahu* by bigger, more heavily armed Chinese and European vessels in the long-distance trades). The Bugis were also fearsome warriors and pirates, skilled in the use of both chain mail and modern firearms.

Having accumulated wealth and power around much of the

archipelago, the Wajo Bugis returned to Sulawesi in 1737 to free their homeland from Bone. In the first half of the eighteenth century Bugis chiefs, with weaponry much admired by Europeans, then succeeded in taking control of the sultanates of Perak and Selangor on the Malay peninsula as well as the islands of Riau to the south. They even staged an unsuccessful attack on Dutch Melaka in 1756. Meanwhile the Bugis women of southern Sulawesi had developed major markets throughout the archipelago for their low-cost, fine-woven cotton sarongs, which sold at half the price of Indian cottons offered by the Dutch. But as in other parts of the archipelago in the eighteenth century, the actual carriage of Sulawesi's trade became increasingly dominated by Chinese-owned vessels.

BALI: THE REJUVENATION OF HINDUISM

Unique in early-modern Indonesia, the small island of Bali, and its eastern satellite, Lombok, remained an outpost of Hinduism, despite being positioned between Islamic Java to the west and Islamic Sulawesi to the north east. The vitality of Balinese Hinduism was assisted by the unification of the island under the kingdom of Gelgel in the sixteenth century. Bali had been part of the Javanese Hindu empire of Majapahit. But, whereas Java converted to Islam and shattered into a number of small states, Bali remained united and Hinduism went through a renaissance. While not completely hostile to Islam, Bali's leaders resisted its wholesale adoption because of the Muslim faith's link with Javanese aggrandisement. Bali's wariness of its western neighbour has survived in present-day Indonesia. Majapahit's Hinduism was 'reinvented' on Bali as a strict caste system developed. In this, the priests, kings and nobles were together known as the *trivangsa* (the three castes) and were strictly separated from the lumpen masses, the *sudras*. Religious rituals stressing Siva as manifested by the sun, the making of holy water, the recitation of mantras from the sacred scripts and ceremonial feasting can all still be observed on Bali today. So resilient was Bali in the sixteenth and seventeenth centuries, that Gelgel's influence extended into eastern Java as well as to Lombok and Sumbawa to the east. Gelgel finally collapsed in the mid-seventeenth century and Bali split into a number of competing kingdoms. Even so, Bali's unique culture survived and many of the unique Balinese rituals and arts of today, such as the Balinese shadow play, developed during the 'golden age' of the seventeenth and eighteenth centuries. And, as today, the Balinese remained committed to keeping their distance from the rest of the Muslim-dominated archipelago.

JAVA: THE FAILURE OF MATARAM

The great Java-based empire of Majapahit came to an abrupt end in 1527, when an alliance of Muslim ports in north Java, under the dominance of Demak, defeated the Hindu kingdom. But, in contrast to Bali, no Javanese kingdom emerged to replace Majapahit and reunify the island. Demak's dominance only lasted to the middle of the sixteenth century. From 1582 it was left, therefore, to a resurrected kingdom of Mataram in central Java to attempt a reunfication of Java under King Senapati and his successors. Senapati's vision of a united Java was partially realized under the Muslim king, Agung, who ruled between 1613 and 1646. Mataram's armies forced the subservience of the northern or *pasisir* ports, most notably Mataram's principal rival, Surabaya, in 1625, when Dutch observers reported that 'not more than 500 of its 5,000–6,000 people were left, the rest having died or gone away because of misery and famine'. By Sultan Agung's death, Mataram had also extended its influence to Madura, southern Sumatra and southern Borneo. Mataram's military superiority hinged on the presence of a number of Portuguese military advisers in the kingdom and, by the mid-seventeenth century, Mataram was not only making its own gunpowder but also manufacturing muskets at the impressive rate of 800 every three months. But, as in the days of Borobudur, the real key to central Java's success lay in the revenues derived from its role as a rice bowl: Java was South East Asia's largest rice exporter, with quantities of 11,000 tons shipped from the port of Japara every year to food-deficient kingdoms such as Aceh. Unique among South East Asia's early modern states, Mataram possessed a high-quality road network, which permitted the relatively swift transport of rice by bullock carts from the central plains to the north coast near modern-day Semarang.

Once Agung died in 1646, however, Mataram was caught up in a spiral of decline. Agung's son, Amangkurat I, who ruled between 1646 and 1677, made the haughty claim that he was the supreme monarch 'to whom all the kings of the Javanese and Malay lands pay homage'. But, despite the cunning ploy of replacing local officials with royal appointees to key positions in the administration of Java's ports, Amangkurat could not resurrect the authority commanded by his father. Amangkurat's heavy-handed approach towards potential opponents did not help things. The widespread assassination of aristocrats and religious leaders eventually culminated in a full-scale rebellion, beginning in east Java in 1670, against Amangkurat's authority. The rebels were a powerful bunch of malcontents, led by a prince from Madura called Trunajaya and including the crown prince of Mataram, various religious dignitaries, and a band of Makassarese refugees. They looked forward to the rule throughout Java of a less-despotic, kindly king who would bring about prosperity as well as the expulsion of the Dutch infidels from the island.

Indeed the anti-Dutch dimension to the rebellion of the 1670s is a reminder that Mataram had a rival for economic and political dominance on Java, in the form of the VOC based at Batavia. Even under the great Agung, the Dutch presence meant that Mataram never completely controlled Java: Agung's siege of Batavia between 1628 and 1629 was an abject failure. The Dutch resisted completely crushing Mataram but circumscribed the central kingdom's power in more subtle ways, principally by interfering in its internal politics. The VOC actually decided to support Mataram in the civil war of the 1670s, given the anti-European sentiments of the rebels, and, in the last year of his reign, Amangkurat committed Mataram to a military alliance with the VOC. In the short term, this pact proved beneficial for Mataram because it allowed King Amangkurat II to kill Prince Trunajaya in 1680. In the longer term, however, it confirmed Mataram's increasing subservience to the Dutch as the price of VOC support and the passing of more and more of the Javanese coast into European hands. Mataram's satellite status vis-à-vis Batavia was confirmed in 1749 when King Pakubuwana III was installed by the Dutch governor-general. Mataram now had to accept a Dutch resident at court, the outer provinces of the realm were ceded to direct Dutch control, and the VOC – in league with a compliant aristocracy – demanded more and more coffee, timber, indigo and rice from the down trodden peasantry. Attempts by members of the Javanese elite to get a better deal for Mataram only encouraged further Dutch machinations at Mataram's expense, as the kingdom was split into the sultanates of Surakarta and Yogyakarta in 1755. Despite the dreams of some Javanese aristocrats and religious leaders, rivalries between the courts prevented any reunification of Mataram or Java more generally.

Ultimately, then, Mataram was no match for the Dutch. In commercial affairs, Mataram's kings made the fatal error of neglecting, and becoming increasingly hostile to, international trade. They made no attempt to develop the trade of the *pasisir*. Indeed, rulers such as Amangkurat I were determined to destroy all commercial rivals, lest they provide potential opposition to his increasingly despotic rule. Talented Javanese entrepreneurs increasingly left Java for other trade centres, such as Banjarmasin, Banten, Palembang, Patani and Makassar, where they melted into the existing 'Malay' trading communities. The result was the virtual end of the Javanese shipping industry: by the 1730s, for example, Chinese traders owned over 60 percent of vessels reaching Batavia from the north coast towns. The Chinese also became successful 'middle men' traders, supplying goods to the sugar and coffee labourers of north and west Java, while controlling many of the toll-gates as well as tax, opium and gambling. Thus commenced the huge economic disparities between the Javanese and the Chinese, which still plague today's Indonesia.

Yet it was in the science of warfare that Mataram's obsolescence was most clearly marked. In the course of the eighteenth century, the technological gap between Europeans and South East Asians became a gaping chasm, especially as institutions such as the VOC placed embargoes on the passing on of industrial secrets to non-Europeans. Even where South East Asian armies were well equipped with modern, European-style firearms, as in Mataram, this rarely altered the anti-quated way in which military forces fought. On Java, then, the principal means of combat remained frozen in the classical era with the pike and the *kris*. The case of Java starkly illustrates how, by the end of the eighteenth century, South East Asians had lost the ability to adapt quickly enough to prevent economic and military dominance passing to alien groups.

CHAPTER FIVE

Colonial South East Asia, 1800–1941

The colonial era represented a difficult and contradictory period for South East Asians. On the negative side, all of the region – with the notable exception of Thailand – fell under European control. The European presence before the mid-nineteenth century was confined to coastal belts and enclaves. By the 1910s, virtually the whole region had been 'colonized'. Today's independent countries of Malaysia, Singapore and Brunei were ruled by Great Britain; Cambodia, Laos and Vietnam became French territories; while, the Dutch extended their realm to encompass the sprawling island chain that is present-day Indonesia. Top decision making was in the hands of aliens as European-style bureaucratic government replaced the charismatic and personalized rule of kings, sultans and chiefs.

Imperialism was not merely a radical re-drawing of the political map; as an accompaniment to colonial rule, there was an economic revolution. South East Asia had always been a participant in the international economy but western capitalism, fuelled by tremendous factory-based industrial expansion that spread from Britain to the rest of Europe and the United States, was now so powerful that it transformed the region. European-controlled companies came to dominate the colonial export economies, and even independent Thailand was not immune from this economic transformation.

As a side benefit, however, colonial rulers – both wittingly and unwittingly – provided a framework for the emergence of nation-states in the second half of the twentieth century. Even for 'Asia-centric' analyses of South East Asia's past, such as that by D.R. Sardesai, the impact of the colonial period was more than a mere 'interlude' in the

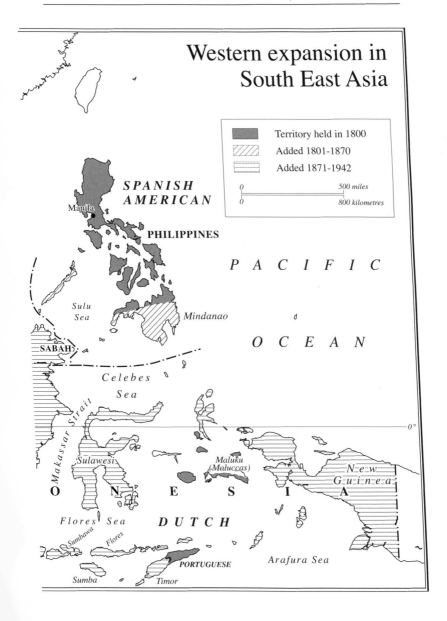

Western expansion in South East Asia

	Territory held in 1800
	Added 1801-1870
	Added 1871-1942

0   500 *miles*
0   800 *kilometres*

SPANISH
AMERICAN

Manila

PHILIPPINES

P A C I F I C

Sulu
Sea

Mindanao

O C E A N

SABAH

Celebes
Sea

Makassar Strait

0°

Sulawesi

Maluku
(Moluccas)

N-e-w
G-u-i-n-e-a

O   N   E   S   I   A

Flores Sea

D U T C H

Sumbawa

Flores

PORTUGUESE

Arafura Sea

Sumba

Timor

region's history: 'most of the present-day economic, communications and educational patterns of the region's independent states owe much to the colonial period... Today's nation states largely correspond to the administrative boundaries imposed by the European powers'.

British Malaya and British Borneo

RAFFLES AND SINGAPORE

Although hard to imagine today, by the 1800s Britain was the world's superpower. Through the industrial revolution Britain became the 'workshop of the world', the financial growth of the City of London added the title 'clearing house of the world', while the supremacy of the Royal Navy ensured Britain was also 'ruler of the waves'. Following Britain's final victory over Napoleon Bonaparte's France in 1815, Albion was easily the paramount power in Asia, based upon the East India Company (EIC) territories in India. British power was being felt further east too. As early as 1786 the EIC's growing commercial involvement in the archipelago, as a consequence of the opium-for-tea trade between India and China, led to the securing of a toehold off the coast of northern Malaya. The island of Penang was acquired from the sultan of Kedah by Captain Francis Light as a naval base to protect British merchant ships passing through the Straits of Melaka. The British were drug dealers *par excellence* in this period, and Penang became the main distribution centre in the archipelago for Bengali opium.

The formative growth of British power in South East Asia is usually associated with the celebrated Sir Thomas Stamford Raffles. Like Light, Raffles was a servant of the EIC, and he was despatched to Java in 1811 to occupy the Dutch colonial possessions (Holland had fallen under Napoleon's influence). Remarkably short in stature but adventurous and intellectual, Raffles was a fascinating character, imbued with the tremendous British self-confidence of his age. The son of a merchant seaman, he joined the EIC in London as a clerk aged just fourteen in 1795. Here he began his study of Malay language and culture, a personal passion that would become his life's work. Working his way

A statue of Sir Stamford Raffles, the founder of Singapore

up through the ranks of the EIC, Raffles was permitted to go to Penang in 1805. Here Raffles's self-education in all things Malay soon paid off as the governor-general of the EIC recognized his remarkable talents and appointed him governor of Java. On Java he introduced a number of reforms to the restrictive Dutch economic system, and as part of his studies on Javanese history, Raffles initiated several expeditions, one of which 're-discovered' the majestic medieval temple of Borobudur.

At the end of the wars with France, Java was returned to Holland – much to Raffles's chagrin. Sir Stamford was compensated with the lieutenant-governorship of Bengkulu in west Sumatra. It was on Sumatra that Raffles developed his idea of founding a British base at the south end of the Malay peninsula as a means of controlling the straits. With the permission of the EIC, Raffles acquired rights from the rajas of Johor in 1819 to develop a trading post on the island of Singapore.

As a free-trade port, Raffles hoped that Singapore would serve as a model for the rest of the Malay world. Britain's paramountcy in the straits was confirmed five years later when, as part of an Anglo-Dutch treaty, Bengkulu was swapped with Holland for Melaka.

Raffles's ultimate vision – compromised by Holland's reoccupation of the Indies – was the unification of the Malay world under British 'superintendance' and 'interference'. For although Raffles had a genuine concern for the peoples of the archipelago, he believed that there was an essential defect in the Malay character, epitomized by wide-scale piracy and slave trading (symptoms also, Raffles believed, of restrictive trading practices on the part of both indigenous and Dutch rulers). The task of the British was to revitalize South East Asian societies and guide them towards progress, civilization, and free trade on the British model. As Raffles hoped in a famous poem, Britain would be remembered not 'as the tempest whose course was desolation, but as the gale of spring reviving the slumbering seeds of mind and calling them to life'. This was a humanitarian but also exceedingly patronizing and potentially authoritarian impulse, which would influence many a colonial administrator after Raffles. Sir Stamford and his ilk deeply cared for the peoples of South East Asia but ultimately, 'British was Best'.

Raffles died virtually penniless in England in 1826 at the age of 45, and he did not live to see Singapore eclipse Penang as Britain's premier port in South East Asia. From the 1830s, blessed by its geographical position, the island was transformed from little more than a tiger- and pirate-infested swamp, with a population of less than 200, into a bustling colonial port, boasting a population of nearly 100,000 by the 1870s. The colony attracted many a British merchant, establishing firms known as agency houses. All sorts of trades became concentrated on early colonial Singapore: Lancashire textiles, Chinese tea, Bengali opium, Malayan tin, Sumatran pepper plus local plantation and forest produce. Singapore overtook Bangkok as the major South East Asian port on the China route, while also serving as the centre of intra-archipelago trade promoted by the energetic Bugis.

Three-quarters of the town's inhabitants were Chinese immigrants – merchants, gambier and pepper planters, labourers (known as 'coolies'), as well as the prostitutes to service the male population. The rich

Chinese merchants or *towkay*, like their European counterparts, lived in palatial mansions on the outskirts of the city. In stark contrast, the mass of the Chinese populace were jam-packed into insanitary, squalid houses, often containing upwards of 150 people. Rickshaw pullers and coolies frequently shared beds on a shift basis. As a Singapore guidebook at the end of the nineteenth century described the town:

> The streets . . . are crowded and busy at all hours of the day, and in the native quarters at nearly all hours of the night as well. Carriages, hack-gharries, bullock-carts, and jinrikishas pass and re-pass in a continual stream; native vendors of various kinds of foods, fruits and drinks, take up their position by the roadsides, or, wandering up and down the streets proclaim the excellence of their wares; carriers and messengers come and go: all is bustle and activity.

To police the Chinese population, the colonial administration in Singapore – and Penang and Melaka also – ruled through the leading 'Straits Chinese' merchants, *kapitan*, secret society headmen and revenue farmers. The opium revenue-farmers – whose status was only outlawed in the 1900s – exercised remarkable power over the coolies. The English-educated Straits Chinese, especially the graduates of the exclusive Raffles Institute, would eventually inherit power in postcolonial Singapore.

Yet, despite Chinese demographic dominance, Singapore was a truly international city, recreating the Melaka emporium of the sixteenth century. As the Singapore guide book continued:

> In half-an-hour's walk, a stranger may hear the accents of almost every language and see the features and costumes of nearly every race in the world. Amongst the crowds that pass him, he may see, besides Europeans of every nation, Chinese, Malays, Hindus, Madrassees, Sikhs, Japanese, Burmese, Siamese, Javanese, Boyanese, Singhalese, Tamils, Arabs, Jews, Parsees, Negroes, &c., &c.

BRITISH INTERVENTION IN THE MALAY STATES

In 1826 Singapore was federated with Penang and Melaka to become the colony of the Straits Settlements, and after 1832 Singapore became the colony's capital. In recognition of the growing importance of these three British possessions, the settlements were passed from the responsibility of the government of India to the Colonial Office in London in 1867. Yet, the British showed little inclination to expand further on to the Malayan mainland, which was still composed of a number of small sultanates. The northern states paid homage to Bangkok, and indeed in 1821 the British at Penang merely stood by as Kedah was depopulated by a Siamese army. Perak was wealthy as a result of its tin, but it lacked a large population. Selangor had fallen under the control of Bugis leaders in the eighteenth century while today's Negeri Sembilan was fragmented into nine minute Minangkabau chiefdoms. Johor in the south had been split off from Riau by Dutch and British aggrandizement and had also lost its hold over the larger but thinly-populated Pahang.

However, during the 1870s and the 1880s Britain's policy of non-intervention was scrapped and the so-called Resident System to advise the sultans was initiated on the peninsula. Furthermore, in the 1890s the British pressured the chiefs of Negeri Sembilan ('Nine States') to combine. With the other three states that had accepted residents – Perak, Selangor, and Pahang – a federation was formed known as the Federated Malay States (FMS). Under the FMS, the residents in the states were now under the central direction of the high commissioner in a new capital, Kuala Lumpur. In 1909 the northern Malay states – Terengganu, Kelantan, Kedah and Perlis – were formally passed from the protection of Siam to the protection of Britain. Patani, however, remained a part of Siam. The rulers of Johor, in detaching themselves from the Bugis pirates who had captured power there in the eighteenth century, also associated themselves more and more with the British in Singapore. A British adviser was finally appointed to Johor in 1914 but, as with the ex-Siamese territories, the fiercely-independent state did not join the FMS, remaining one of the Unfederated Malay States (UMS).

One of the reasons behind British intervention was commercial. Malaya was emerging as the world's most important source of tin, especially after the opening of the Suez Canal in 1869, which halved travelling times between Europe and the Far East, reducing the price and increasing the demand for Straits tin. But the tiny states were far from a safe bet for European merchants and investors. Malaya was a veritable 'wild east', in which a fundamental lack of individual rights allowed the rich and powerful to terrorize the meek. Malayans themselves were disturbed by the condition of the Malay states. Raffles's former scribe, Munshi Abdullah, returned to the Straits Settlements after a visit to Kelantan, Pahang and Terengganu in 1838 and lamented:

> Is it God's will that one man should take another's goods against his will? Or that he should take a man's wife or daughter by force? Or that he should kill a man without cause? Is it God's will that a man should treat the servants of God as he pleases, just because he is a Raja? I say that all these evil things were done in the Malay States. . . I thank God ten thousand times that I was born under the English flag and can live in peace, instead of being a man who has never known anything but grief and oppression and folly and wickedness.

The state of lawlessness was exacerbated by bands of pirates, operating from as far as away as Borneo, who disrupted trade along the rivers. Worse still, many of the states were plagued by civil war; a situation intensified by the presence of the Chinese tin miners. From the 1840s, many more Chinese were drawn to the valleys of the western states as rich deposits of tin were discovered. In Selangor, Kuala Lumpur was founded in 1857 by an expedition of 87 Chinese miners at the confluence of the muddy Gombak and Klang rivers. These miners, in their competition for tin-bearing lands, often backed Malay rivals in dynastic feuds. Malay chiefs too were more likely to fight each other for the rights to lucrative tin revenues. In such a chaotic environment, there was little guarantee for the long-term security of British investments.

But the major headache for the Colonial Office in London was that another big European power – recently unified and rapidly industrializing Germany – might take advantage of the unrest in the Malay states and gain economic or military concessions. Pangkor, an island off Perak, or Tioman, an island off Pahang, were seen as possible sites for a German naval base. A German presence in or around the peninsula would threaten Britain's paramount position in the straits, regarded since the days of Raffles as a vital national interest as the means of guaranteeing free passage of British ships between India and China.

In 1873 Colonial Secretary Lord Kimberley, authorized the new governor of the Straits Settlements, Sir Andrew Clarke, to take action that eventually resulted in British control being established over three of the west coast states, Perak, Selangor and Sungei Ujong (later part of Negeri Sembilan). Yet, the British were reluctant imperialists, concerned to limit their involvement as far as possible. The instructions given to Clarke were merely concerned with appointing advisers to the rajas, along the lines of the existing British practice in India. There was no intention of annexing the states as colonies. Rather, the British hoped to exercise influence through 'collaboration' with the established political leaders in the states. Except for a brief period after the Second World War, the sultans were never displaced as the sovereign authorities in their states. The British 'residents' – as the model treaty of 1874 with the Perak chiefs laid down – were simply 'advisers' on all matters except religion and traditional Malay custom. Because Islam and traditional custom governed a vast swathe of activities in the Malay States, the sultans and their religious and aristocratic advisers retained considerable local powers. For Malay rajas and *bendaharas* (chief ministers), British recognition could elevate them to the status of sultan, guaranteeing their positions over rival claimants!

There was some resistance against the imposition of British 'advice'. The first resident in Perak, J.W.W. Birch, was murdered in 1875 by leading Malays, outraged by increases in taxation and fearing complete annexation. The British military expedition that followed, however, restored the system of co-operation by exiling the recalcitrant Sultan Abdullah and appointing Raja Yusuf as regent. Birch's successor, Hugh Low, formed a council made up of the regent, the Malay chiefs, Chinese leaders, and himself to initiate reforms. This executive council would serve as the political model for British administration in the other states. In Pahang, the appointment of a resident in 1888 also produced violent resentment amongst Malay chiefs especially when Hugh Clifford ordered one of them dismissed. Yet, Sultan Ahmad was persuaded of the wisdom of collaborating with the British and resistance soon petered out. In the twentieth century, there were popular rebellions in the east coast states of Kelantan and Terengganu in 1915 and 1928 respectively. Again, however, these were fairly short-lived untroubling affairs. In contrast to the Dutch in Indonesia, the British proved far more adept at ruling through the traditional leadership and minimizing conflict. The extent of British official concern in the states was merely to institute the rule of law, to reform Malay society and so phase out 'abhorrent native practices' such as slavery and *kerah* (forced labour), as well as the general abuses of power by the Malay rulers and aristocracy that imperilled the rights of the individual. As architect of the FMS and doyen of the Malayan Civil Service (MCS) Sir Frank Swettenham convinced himself by the end of his career, British intervention in Malaya was 'a duty forced upon England', and while it might have some benefits for British trade, it sprang 'from motives of humanity alone'. The British residents came to greatly admire the Malays, for they seemed to live in a rural utopia and embody a gentlemanly chivalry akin to a lost England. Hugh Clifford was so elated to return to Malaya in 1927 as high commissioner that he stood outside naked during a thunderstorm as his train carried him from Penang to Kuala Lumpur!

The Malay elite, for their part, did not necessarily cherish British rule or individuals like Clifford but pragmatically adjusted to the international realities of the late nineteenth century. As a fellow pragmatist, King Chulalongkorn of Siam, appreciated, 'It is a big misconception when the British say the Malays respect and support them... If Malay leaders have sought British assistance, it is because Great Britain is a great power'. As time wore on, British administration did expand as more and more European administrators were appointed to the state bureaucracies. The residents evolved from mere advisers to full-blown administrators as they, and their underlings, took over the functions of law enforcement, legislation, and tax collection. In the process, the MCS lost its amateur feel as an examination system selected recruits from the private schools and universities. Yet this bureaucratic expansion was the result of unplanned factors; notably the expansion of the rubber industry from the 1900s. The skin-deep nature of British authority was reflected in the basic lack of uniformity to the constituent parts of 'British Malaya'. The governor of the Straits Settlements in

Singapore was regarded as the co-ordinating supremo for the region, but three quite distinct administrative systems operated by World War One in a territory about the size of England: the three Straits Settlements and the four FMS had a certain coherence of their own. But the five UMS sultans jealously guarded their independence and refused to join the FMS, only accepting advisers not residents. Indeed a strong sense of independence remains – in Kelantan and Johor particularly – in present-day Malaysia. The UMS advisers had far fewer powers than FMS residents with each sultan maintaining their own independent administrative services. The sultan of Johor even had his own army. At the same time, Singapore's wealth and status as British headquarters in South East Asia was always resented in Kuala Lumpur and Penang. The fragmented nature of British rule has a fair degree of responsibility for the military defeat of 1941–42 at the hands of Japan. The lack of coherence to Britain's presence in South East Asia was further exacerbated by the idiosyncratic administrative arrangements, which sprang up on Borneo.

THE WHITE RAJAHS OF SARAWAK

A bizarre dynasty of white rajahs ruled the vast territory of Sarawak for 100 years after 1841. A buccaneering merchant adventurer in the Raffles mode, James Brooke set sail from England in 1838 intent on reforming the Borneo polities under British guidance. Brooke sought to suppress such practices as piracy, slavery and headhunting, as well as exploitative commercial monopolies controlled by the Brunei elite. An antidote to these problems, Brooke believed, was free trade and British morality. He attempted, therefore, to interest the British government in taking over the territory of Sarawak. Brooke made a second trip to Borneo in 1840, during which he suppressed a revolt of Sarawak Malays against their Brunei overlords. In return, Sultan Omar of Brunei made James 'rajah' in Kuching and granted him his first slice of Sarawak. But, although appointed Brunei agent and knighted in 1844, the British government in London remained highly sceptical concerning Brooke's claims about the unlimited commercial potential of Borneo. Disheartened, Brooke further extended his realms, at the expense of Brunei, in the 1850s and 1860s. This exercise of power was completely independent of the British state and Brooke ruled Sarawak as his personal fiefdom. He co-opted the Malays into his administration as virtual joint rulers, utilized the martial skills of the Dayak 'head-hunters' in the military and police forces, who further expanded and pacified the realm, while leaving Chinese immigrants to develop the economy. The Chinese, however, were always mistrusted and discriminated against given an uprising of heavily taxed gold-miners in 1857 in which Europeans were killed.

James died in 1868. Yet, the Brooke absolute rule was continued by James's nephew, Charles. Charles expanded the boundaries of the Sarawak raj to its present-day limits and continued the policy of pacification so that headhunting amongst the rival Dayak clans was virtually eliminated. With the French now established in Vietnam and Cambodia, on the opposite side of the South China Sea, and Germany threatening to gain concessions on Borneo, the British government finally extended protection to Sarawak in 1888. But this treaty only covered foreign relations, and the Brookes maintained their jurisdiction internally. Brooke autocracy continued with Charles's son, the third and last rajah, Vyner, after 1917. Only in 1941 – on the centenary of Brooke rule and, somewhat ironically, on the eve of the Japanese invasion – was Sarawak finally granted a Constitution.

COMPANY RULE IN NORTH BORNEO AND THE SURVIVAL OF BRUNEI

In the course of 1846 and 1847 Britain annexed the island of Labuan off the north west coast of Borneo island, as a coaling station on the India-China route, and made a treaty with Brunei. Yet there was no further British involvement in what is today the East Malaysian state of Sabah until the 1880s. It was the heightened atmosphere of European economic and military competition that dragged a reluctant Albion into northern Borneo. Foreign intervention, whether from Germany or the United States, in a huge territory still nominally ruled by a fragile Brunei worried Britons in London and Singapore. The presence of Germany, especially, in close proximity to Malaya, disturbed Lord Kimberley who feared the Germans would 'seriously weaken and embarrass our position by unsettling the minds of the natives'. But there still remained a British desire to avoid costly entanglements in areas of dubious commercial value. The quintessential 'colonialism-on-the-cheap' option, therefore, was to encourage the British North Borneo Company to acquire concessions from the sultans of Brunei and Sulu. Officially 'chartered' by the British crown in 1881, the company was permitted a commercial monopoly in Sabah in return for maintaining law and order at its own expense. Indeed in its early years, the company faced ruination. Rice was in short supply and had to be imported at great cost, and the company was only saved financially in the 1900s by the growth of tobacco exports.

Moreover the company was confronted with unruly subjects cut off from their traditional overlords in Brunei and Sulu. Unlike the Brookes in Sarawak, who emulated Malay rajas, the company represented an alien government, which lacked local legitimacy. Not surprisingly, when company agents tried to implement taxes in the interior there was insurrection from 1895. This was co-ordinated by the enigmatic Mat Salleh, born of mixed Bajau and Sulu parentage. His movement was partly Islamic in character for he appealed to Sabah's Muslims as the *mahdi*, the future saviour. But Mat Salleh also exploited local animist notions to support his authority – his mouth allegedly spewed forth fire while his *parang* (curved cleaver) produced lightning. Gaining little help from the British government, the company's officers on the spot sought to appease Mat Salleh in 1898 by recognizing him as an 'up country' chief. The London board, however, could not countenance such an arrangement and a series of expeditions were launched to quash the rebels. Mat Salleh was killed in 1900, but he is revered today as one of Sabah's greatest heroes. Given widespread opposition to its early rule as well as the huge variety of peoples that made up Sabah, the company's grip on the interior remained nebulous. In 1915 another rebellion broke out, leading to a considerable reappraisal of company administration. The feeling that government had been somewhat overbearing in the interior led to a policy of rapprochement with native society and institutions. In the 1920s and 1930s, a more 'indirect rule' had emerged with the company ruling in concert with a Native Chiefs Advisory Council. Although today part of Malaysia, the peoples of Sabah have maintained their strong tradition of independence.

Brunei was once the pre-eminent power on Borneo. With the loss of its lands to the Brookes of Sarawak and the British North Borneo Company, the sultanate was reduced to its present tiny size. Brunei's complete disappearance was prevented, however, by the 1888 treaty of protection signed by the British with Sarawak and the North Borneo Company also. In 1906 the Malayan-style residency system was extended to Brunei. The discovery of oil in 1929 at Seria, however, more than compensated for Brunei's shrunken land mass and eventually made the sultans the world's richest men.

French Indochina

THE END OF VIETNAMESE INDEPENDENCE

Britain's intervention in South East Asia was partially dictated by the expanding French presence in the region. French Catholic missionaries had been nibbling at the fringes of the Vietnamese realm since the seventeenth century, and by 1848 – despite periodic clampdowns by Vietnamese emperors on Christians and Christianity – there were close to 70,000 Catholic converts. In 1787 Paris had claimed the central Vietnamese port of Da Nang. But defeat in the revolutionary wars put paid to any further gains. A resilient and reunified Vietnam, under the emperors Gia-long (r. 1802–19) and Minh-mang (r. 1820–40), wished to keep foreign influences at a minimum and placed severe limits on the activities of the missionaries. In 1855 Emperor Tu-duc (r. 1848–83) went even further when he ordered the execution of a Spanish bishop. Enraged, Napoleon III of France set about delivering Vietnam 'from a hateful yoke' while, at the same time, asserting Bonapartist *gloire* overseas. Early in 1859 Saigon was swiftly captured and French forces founded a colony, known as Cochin-China. Tu-duc and his court at Hue did little to assist those Vietnamese partisans who resisted.

A new phase of French expansionism began in the final quarter of the nineteenth century. This French 'new imperialism' was psychologically underpinned by a desire to prove to the world, as well as to France itself, that France was still a great power. This was particularly the case following Germany's crushing victory over Paris in 1870–71.

The new Third Republic sought imperial expansion as compensation for loss of status and territory in Europe. As the republic's former prime minister, Jules Ferry, lectured the Chamber of Deputies in Paris in July 1885, a new French overseas empire would provide markets and fields of investment for French businesses, but more importantly, to stand back from imperial expansion 'would mean that we should cease to be a first-rate power and become a third- or fourth-rate power instead'. Indeed, the French empire emerged as expression of an increasingly intolerant French nationalism in which ideas of *liberté, egalité, fraternité* were bastardized into what then came to be called the *mission civilisatrice* (civilizing mission). As Jules Ferry also believed the so-called 'superior races' had 'a duty to civilize the inferior races'. So confident were French imperialists of the superiority of French culture that they arrogantly sought to 'assimilate' Asians and Africans, to transform them into good French men and women.

Specific to northern Vietnam, meanwhile, there was also a vague French notion that the Red River would provide access to the fabled economic riches of southern China, especially after French adventurers had discovered that the upper reaches of the Mekong – through present-day Laos – were not navigable. French statesmen and businessmen were particularly obsessed with unwrapping the potential markets and raw materials source of Yunnan province, which bordered Tonkin (as the French came to call north Vietnam). North Vietnam, for the French, was merely a stepping stone, a transit lounge to far more remunerative destinations. If possible, Paris wished to secure the Yunnan trade without political control of the north. But Tonkin was in a state of anarchy as Red River shipping was disrupted by Vietnamese pirates and Chinese renegades. Fearing that Britain or Germany might intervene instead, Admiral Dupré, the governor of Cochin-China, despatched a military expedition to the north in 1873 under Francis Garnier. Garnier took the city of Hanoi briefly but was killed by a Sino-Vietnamese counterattack. In 1883 a second French mission was despatched under the leadership of Henri de Rivière, which, in repetition of the 1873 expedition, occupied Hanoi only to repulsed by a retaliatory force. Rivière was captured and decapitated. The government of Jules Ferry in Paris, however, was determined not to be humiliated a second time and an all-out assault on Tonkin was ordered. French protectorates were declared over Tonkin and Annam (central Vietnam) in 1884. Annam included the court at Hue; Tu-duc and his entourage were thrown into a state of panic. Having failed to resist the French takeover of the southern provinces in the 1850s, the emperor now chose to exploit his status as a vassal of China and requested Chinese intervention to save central and northern Vietnam from France. At the same time, Vietnamese troops from Annam crossed into Cochin-China. French forces now found themselves in a ten-month war with China, only formally ended in June 1885 by the Treaty of Tien-Tsin, which confirmed the defeat of China. Beijing also gave up its historic claims to be Vietnam's protector in favour of France.

Vietnamese soldiers as depicted by a French artist in the 1870s

The war to pacify Tonkin continued, however, until 1895, eating up a large slice of the French budget in Indochina. Moreover, the expenses of policing the unruly north were not met by the much-hoped-for trade with southern China. The Yunnan trade proved a total red herring, and the search for an Eldorado in southern China was abandoned after a trade mission to Yunnan from Lyon in the late 1890s reported on the province's dismal economic prospects. The French had expended vast resources for a mythical pot of gold, which turned out to be just that – a myth. Even so, the French remained ensconced in Vietnam, having a massive influence upon its culture and politics. In Cochin-China, the aristocratic mandarins were replaced by ordinary Vietnamese as civil servants. In Annam and Tonkin, however, the existing hierarchy of Confucian-trained mandarins was left intact. Yet, a parallel government service, comprised of French administrators was organized alongside the traditional Vietnamese arrangements, depriving the latter of any real authority. Further administrative reforms between 1897 and 1902 introduced a second wave of European civil servants as the 'protectorate' of Tonkin became a de facto colony along the lines of Cochin-China. Pacification and administrative efforts finally paid off in the twentieth century, when Vietnam became France's most treasured overseas possession, as it emerged as a major exporter of rice and rubber.

THE FAILURE OF THE NGUYEN DYNASTY

Vietnam's loss of independent status had a lot to do with the conservatism of its monarchy. The Nguyen clan had reunified the realm in the 1800s and in so doing had established itself as the imperial house. Vietnam was larger and more powerful than ever before. But in creating a united policy, the Nguyen dynasty attempted to turn back the clock and eradicate the reforms of the populist Tayson rulers. The old aristocracy and landed mandarins came back as administrators and props to royal power. Controls and heavy taxes – designed to funnel wealth to the imperial court at Hue – stifled economic activity. A new drive at centralization divided the realm into a number of centrally directed provinces and districts. But Hue's actual control over its realm remained tenuous, as was demonstrated by the huge number of peasant uprisings, particularly in the north. Popular religious movements in the south also challenged the regime by the 1850s.

The greatest failing of the Nguyen emperors was intellectual. The relative religious freedom of the Tayson days was scrapped as a ruthless devotion to an extremist, Chinese-style Confucianism was officially enforced. There was a greater borrowing of Chinese imperial ideas and styles than ever before, epitomized by the Beijing-style royal palaces and citadels put up to shut off the ruling elite from the mass of the population. Chinese cultural values produced an inward-looking philosophy. Cocooned within Hue's walls, the court refused to accept the international realities of the nineteenth century. It ignored the huge technological gap that had opened up between East and West. Under Gia-long and Minh-mang a national standing army and navy came into being through conscription and equipped with Western weaponry. But the tactics and *raison d'être* of the Vietnamese military remained hopelessly outmoded, conceived not to resist an outside imperialist aggressor but to put down internal insurgencies. Thus the Vietnamese completely underestimated the strength of the French military machine or the determination of French patriotism. Like the proverbial ostrich the Vietnamese buried their heads in the sand, believing, arrogantly, that the West had little to offer, save for a few steamships and modern weapons. The Siamese kings and the Malay sultans were able to come to terms with the West and see opportunities in collaboration with the colonials. The emperors might have placated the French with a trade treaty that guaranteed access to southern China. But the Vietnamese elite were unable to perceive this. They were little interested in expanding trade anyway, given that Vietnam was the South East Asian state least dependent on international commerce. Increased trade contacts with the West, the Nguyens reasoned, would only upset the existing social order. The situation was summed up by a Vietnamese Catholic priest in the 1860s:

> If, instead of directing our efforts and time to polishing our style or to embellishing our calligraphy, we were to study current affairs – battle plans, for example, or the methods of building citadels and firing cannons – we should probably be in a position to resist our enemy.

Instead, Emperor Tu-duc and his court looked to Vietnam's suzerain, China, to save them. But the Qing dynasty was now a spent force, like its Vietnamese junior counterpart also retreating into isolated self-delusion, and the Chinese armed forces were in no position to block French advances.

Vietnamese popular resistance to the French intruders came to very little. In the 1880s there was an upsurge of anti-colonial protest when anti-French mandarins fled from Hue with the boy-emperor, Duc Duc. But the French merely placed a more pliant member of the imperial family, Hiep-hoa, on the throne and subsequently captured and exiled Duc Duc. There were further anti-French and anti-Catholic scattered uprisings through to the 1900s. But both mass and elite resistance movements were easily crushed. The French retained the monarchs as powerless puppets in Annam until 1954, and Cochin-China and Tonkin were ruled independently of the dynasty. In similar fashion, the monarchies of Cambodia and Laos were preserved by French 'indirect rule'.

Vietnamese cartoon of the 1930s showing peasant resistance to French colonial rule

'INDIRECT RULE' IN CAMBODIA AND LAOS

In taking over Vietnam, the French claimed that they inherited the suzerain rights of the Nguyen dynasty over Cambodia and Laos. Cambodia had been squashed between Siamese expansion to the west and Vietnamese expansion to the south and east. By the nineteenth century, the loss of Khmer lands and manpower had reduced Cambodia to a shadow of its former mediaeval, Angkorian imperial glory. The court at Phnom Penh now paid tribute to both Hue and Bangkok. There was a huge anti-Vietnamese revolt in the 1840s, protesting at the Vietnamese exiling of Cambodia's queen and her followers. In 1848 the monarchy was restored but only as a consequence of Thai and Vietnamese acquiescence. In many senses, then, the French saved Cambodia from domination by its more powerful neighbours. Certainly, there was little Cambodian resistance to the imposition of colonial rule. From their foothold in southern Vietnam, the French challenged Siam's dominance of Cambodia by offering King Norodom their protection. He accepted, and in 1867 Siam finally gave up its claims over Cambodia in return for the western provinces of Battambang and Siem Reap (Angkor). In 1907, however, the French insisted on the return of the western provinces to their Cambodian protectorate.

The French chose to expand into Laos during the 1890s for essentially strategic reasons: since the British had occupied Upper Burma in 1885–86, and the French themselves were in the process of occupying Tonkin, Laos came to be regarded by the French as a necessary safeguard against British, and also German, expansion into Siam and northern Vietnam. Laos, like Cambodia, was a defensive buffer to protect France's main interest in Vietnam. In the process, Siam again lost out as the supposed protector of the small, rival Laotian principalities. Vientiane, Luang Prabang and Champasak had been easy prey for their overlord in Bangkok. In 1827 when Vientiane's ruler Chao Anu attempted to throw off the Thai yoke by marching on Bangkok, Siam's retaliation was furious. Vientiane was destroyed and the whole left bank of the Mekong was depopulated either through massacre or the forced movement of captives. As in Cambodia, then, France emerged as a benevolent protector of the Lao against the predations of Siam and Vietnam. While the Laotians did not adore the French, like the Cambodians they did at least see the European presence as the lesser of two evils. Furthermore, under the reforms of the governor-general of Indochina, Paul Doumer, between 1897 and 1902 the French created the basis of modern Laos by organizing, for the first time, a unified administration for the principalities with a capital at Vientiane.

Cambodia and Laos were joined with the three Vietnamese territories in the 1890s to form French Indochina. Yet, in both Laos and Cambodia the French continued to rule 'indirectly'. The royal courts were maintained alongside a network of French officials. The French ruled in Cambodia and Laos as the British did in Malaya, merely providing an additional layer of government between king and populace.

The Netherlands East Indies (NEI)

THE REASSERTION OF DUTCH RULE ON JAVA

The Dutch recovered the centre of their Indonesian empire, Java, at the end of the Napoleonic Wars. Their position was confirmed by the Anglo-Dutch Treaty of 1824, which delineated Dutch and British spheres of influence through the Straits of Melaka and south of Singapore. This artificially split the Malay world in two; as a Pahang chief lamented, 'parting brother from brother, father from son and friend from friend'.

Yet, if the external threat from the British had diminished by the 1820s, an internal threat to the Dutch from the Javanese themselves soon presented itself. The heavy-handed return of the Dutch culminated in the Java War after 1825. This rebellion was led by Prince Dipanagara of the Yogyakarta royal house, supported by the Islamic elite. Dipanagara sought to restore a purified Islam to Java through the expulsion of the European infidels and their aristocratic collaborators. His movement attracted huge numbers of peasant followers, disaffected by the economic extortions of the new Dutch regime. The rebels took five years to suppress at vast cost to the Dutch treasury. Rebellions led by holy men, looking to end the hierarchical order of Dutch officials and Javanese aristocrats continued to punctuate nineteenth-century Java. But the consolidation of Dutch political power after 1830 was unmistakable: the rajas' courts were stripped of their vast territorial holdings and reduced to mere ceremonial centres. Meanwhile, the Javanese aristocratic or *priyayi* class became more deeply embedded in the colonial administration as they lost their role as the hereditary feudal chiefs of individual territories and became instead full-blown bureaucrats serving the Dutch.

Meanwhile, the colony was seized upon by the Dutch as a means of staving off their economic decline in Europe. Reform of the economy had been initiated by Raffles, who abolished the role of the aristocrats as production and labour brokers and introduced a land tax payable in cash as a stimulus to free and increased production by the peasants. Yet agricultural production actually declined. So, the post-revolutionary Dutch administration evolved an intensified version of the old Dutch East India Company (VOC) system of forced deliveries. This was known as the Cultivation System, beginning in 1830 under Governor-General Johannes van den Bosch. These agricultural dictates forced peasants, under the direction of village heads and local Javanese officials, to grow and process crops, coffee and sugar particularly. The produce was then sold in Europe by the government-owned Netherlands Trading Company, formed in 1824 as successor to the VOC. Each village was paid for the crops it grew and harvested. But the price paid was substantially below the prevailing market price. In addition, peasants were forced to produce by the requirement for villages to pay a land rent to the Dutch administration. At the same time, of course, each village had to maintain itself through rice production. Failure to abide by the Cultivation System could result in village headmen being whipped and cultivators stripped and exposed to the blazing hot sun. The system benefited few Javanese, save for the village headmen whose authority was greatly enhanced. The Cultivation System was wound up in the later years of the nineteenth century in the belief that free rather than coerced labour would produce export crops more efficiently. But at its height in 1850, the system had generated massive profits for the Dutch, providing over one-third of Holland's state revenue. Java was the 'cork on which the Netherlands floats' as one governor-general put it. And in the early twentieth century, the cultivation directives were merely replaced by a much more systematic land rent system, which, as Dutch officials themselves admitted, taxed Java's peasants to the limit.

Java was always the 'jewel' in Holland's South East Asian 'crown'. Yet, the increased economic and military rivalry between the European powers of the late nineteenth century pushed the Dutch into extending their political presence on what became known as the outer islands: Sumatra, Borneo, Sulawesi, Bali and the Nusa Tenggara chain.

TROUBLESOME SUMATRA

Outside Java and a few of the spice islands, Dutch authority before the 1850s was not direct but relied instead on trade treaties with indigenous rulers. On Sumatra this informal rule gradually gave way as the 1824 treaty with Britain confirmed Holland's predominance on the largest of the Indonesian islands. The rest of the century saw Dutch rule gradually extended – often as a consequence of resistance by Sumatra's proud and independent-minded peoples.

In the south west, a strong anti-colonial movement sprang up amongst Minangkabau Muslims, leading to war with Holland during the 1820s and 1830s. As on Java, the rebels were influenced by the Wahhabi movement of eastern Arabia, which sought a return to the pure teachings of the Koran and declared a *jihad* against anything that deviated from their purified vision of Islam. The movement in Sumatra was given the name Padri after the port of Pedir, from where Minangkabau pilgrims set sail for Mecca where they came into contact with the Wahhabi clerics. On their return from the Middle East, the Padris sought to cleanse their homeland of cockfighting, gambling, alcohol, betel and tobacco consumption, as well as impose the Islamic legal code. This radical threat to established authority alarmed the Minangkabau chiefs, who appealed to Batavia. The Dutch were equally alarmed by the Padris, given the latters' control of the lucrative coffee trade. The concurrent Javanese revolt meant that the war could not be prosecuted fully until 1837. The following year, however, Minangkabau was incorporated into the NEI. By this time also most of the east-coast sultanates had prudently recognized Dutch sovereignty, and in 1871 another Anglo-Dutch Treaty removed all British objections to Holland's territorial control of Sumatra in return for free trade. The Dutch now began to develop their plantation belt along the east coast, centred on the sultanate of Deli and the city of Medan.

From the 1870s the Dutch pacification of Sumatra moved north. The resistance of certain Batak political and religious leaders of the highlands was undercut by the 1900s, thanks largely to the Bataks converting to Christianity. However, Aceh remained independent. As a Dutch ethnologist put it in 1906, the Acehnese were 'the least well mannered of the inhabitants of the Archipelago'. Envious of the sultanate's pepper trade with British Penang, the Dutch were increasingly annoyed by the stubborn Islamic defiance of the Acehnese. Worse, Aceh might succumb to another power. 'As long as it [Aceh] does not recognize our sovereignty foreign intervention will continue to threaten us like the sword of Damocles', wrote one Dutch official in 1873. Indeed, the sultan had appealed to both Italians and the Americans, offering naval bases and commercial preferences in exchange for political protection. In 1873 a four-decade long war began. The first attack on Banda Aceh was driven into the sea. The next year, however, the Dutch succeeded in occupying Aceh and abolishing the sultanate. The mantle of Acehnese resistance was merely taken up, however, by the regional chiefs. They were in turn suppressed. But in the early 1900s, it was the Islamic village leaders or *ulama* who transformed the war against the Dutch into both a populist religious crusade and a guerrilla war. Buoyed up by moral support from the rest of the Islamic world, the *jihad* tied down most of the NEI army and nearly bankrupted Jakarta. Only in 1913 was the resistance effort broken. Even so, as late as the 1930s the *ulama* were still taking oaths of allegiance promising the fruits of paradise to those recruits who attacked Dutch personnel and property. Aceh was never fully absorbed into the NEI, which in large part explains the sense of separateness from the rest of Indonesia that still exists in North Sumatra.

THE OTHER OUTER ISLANDS

A similar desire to seal off native states from international contacts, and so provide a protective shield to Java, encouraged the Dutch to incorporate the eastern islands of the archipelago into the Dutch East Indies from the 1870s. The Dutch also came to the islands with their own version of the 'civilizing mission', seeking to end arbitrary rule, opium smuggling, headhunting and slavery. Fears of German activities in the Pacific led to demands being placed on the Balinese king of Lombok to accept a Dutch agent. Following internal revolts against the king, the Dutch invaded the island in 1894 on the pretext of restoring 'law and order'. A tragic and bloody final battle ensued in which the king's followers were slaughtered in suicide attacks or *puputan*. This was a foretaste of what would happen on Bali itself where Dutch forces were sent to force the submission of the island's kings in 1906, following the plundering of a shipwreck. Clothed completely in white and armed with only lances and daggers, the Balinese aristocrats, including women and children, were mown down by the Dutch guns. Only pausing to kill their wounded, at least 1,000 died in Bali's *puputan*. Here is a haunting image of how the technological gap between

The Balinese ruler with his scribe about to write a message on a palm leaf.
Taken from a photograph of 1865

Europeans and South East Asians made colonial rule possible. The final conquest of Sulawesi occurred also in 1906 when the resistance of the Makassarese and Bugis states finally ended. The Dutch now extended their power inland also over the animist and headhunting Toraja people. Bitter resistance gave way to partial Christian conversion.

Perhaps aware of Lombok and Bali's fate, many rulers scrambled to sign up to Dutch rule in the 1900s. This was assisted by Holland's 'Short Declaration' whereby any chief who accepted Dutch authority was confirmed as the legitimate ruler of his/her territory. Between 1898 and 1911, then, some 300 native states came under Dutch control. The expansion of the Dutch realm was also assisted by further agreements with other powers. On Borneo, the agreement of 1891 settled the frontier between the Dutch territories – now Kalimantan – and the three British protectorates of Sarawak, North Borneo and Brunei. The Dutch presence in Kalimantan was not fully accepted, however, by its inhabitants and princes from the royal house of Banjarmasin led Islamic resistance from the 1850s to the 1900s. In 1902 the Dutch took the western half of New Guinea (now Irian Jaya), dividing this island of primitive peoples between Holland, Britain and Germany. In 1913 Timor was formally partitioned into Dutch and Portuguese halves.

The Dutch had created their 'girdle of emeralds' by the First World War, stretching from Sabang off the coast of northern Sumatra to Merauke in the south of New Guinea. The NEI was easily Holland's most important colonial possession, so much so that the slogan 'Indies gone, prosperity done' was a common one in early twentieth century Holland. Yet in the Indies administrations the 'outer islands' were merely regarded as defensive shields to the number one priority, Java. Indeed, the Dutch focus on Batavia (Jakarta) promoted an economic and political imbalance, skewed in favour of Java, which persists to this day. The 'outer islands' were there to serve Java; a view which dies hard today amongst certain sections of the Javanese-dominated Indonesian military.

AN ETHICAL POLICY?

In this sudden expansion of authority, the Dutch equally suddenly became aware of their responsibility for the welfare of a vast diversity of

'Indonesian' peoples. The Ethical Policy was devised in 1901 in an attempt to promote economic development, village democracy and social welfare. Schools were established to train Indonesians as officials and doctors as part of the policy of encouraging greater Indonesian participation in professional life and administration. At the political centre, meanwhile, a partially elected parliamentary body, the Volksraad, was launched in 1918. This went far beyond any political institutions available in the British or French territories. The new departure in Dutch policy involved a massive expansion in the bureaucracy and government expenditures, consistently running the NEI budget into deficit.

But this outlay achieved very little, particularly in the field of health care. In Lombok in 1931, for example, there were only three qualified doctors for a population of more than 750,000, and European medicine could not prevent the influenza pandemic of 1918, which killed more than 1.5 million Indonesians. Meanwhile the limited nature of the political reforms only served to frustrate Indonesia's young nationalists. The Volksraad was merely a consultative body, with no legislative powers and where little criticism of government was tolerated. As a result, the Indonesian nationalists withdrew from the Volksraad and became more militant in their demands and activities. By the 1930s the Ethical Policy was effectively ditched.

The Independence of Siam

RAMA II AND RAMA III

Unique among South East Asian states, Siam managed to avoid being colonized in the nineteenth and twentieth centuries. Siam's elite, in contrast to Vietnam's, evolved a flexible approach to the West, which allowed for compromise while at the same time preserving the basis of Siamese culture. This combination of change and tradition – very reminiscent of Japan after 1868 – had been initiated by the economic and intellectual reforms of Taksin and Rama I in the late eighteenth century. The reforms were continued by Rama II (r. 1809–24) and Rama III (r. 1824–51). International trade flourished as the aristocratic elite were encouraged by the kings to engage in commerce and intermarry with leading Chinese entrepreneurial families. Restrictions placed on European economic activity in Siam, however, could have led to Siam falling under the sway of an imperial power. The British, anxious to expand trade from India via Penang, were particularly frustrated. The haughty king of Burma had lost a slice of his territory in 1826 following a war with Britain. With one eye on the fate of his uncompromising neighbour and arch-rival, Rama III wisely chose to compromise with an EIC mission led by Henry Burney. The Anglo-Siamese Treaty of 1826 began the process of opening up Siam – without formal conquest – by allowing Western merchants to operate in the kingdom. The Siamese door was now partially ajar.

MONGKUT

Prince Mongkut was actually the rightful heir to the throne after the death of Rama II in 1824, but his half-brother usurped this position to become Rama III. Mongkut's years out of power, however, led to a remarkable broadening of horizons for the young prince – he was educated by European teachers and as a monk he travelled widely. This education stood Mongkut in good stead. When Rama III refused to sign an additional trade treaty, Mongkut was seized upon by the British as the key to a completely open door in Siam. Mongkut was backed by the British for succession to the throne in 1851 when Britain's envoy, Sir James Brooke (the rajah of Sarawak), described the prince as 'a highly accomplished gentleman, for a semi-barbarian'. Britain reaped the rewards: four years after becoming Rama IV, Mongkut signed the Bowring Treaty of 1855. The wisdom of accepting the *pax Britannica* had again been hammered home by Burma's second loss of territory to Britain in another war. The new treaty ended state monopolies, opened up the rice trade, allowed for the appointment of a British consul and for extraterritorial jurisdiction (i.e. Britons in Thailand were not subject to the laws of Thailand and could only be tried for offences in their own courts). This 'unequal' treaty was the price that Siam had to pay for its independence – Mongkut sacrificed control over Thailand's economy in order to preserve the core of his kingdom intact. Indeed, the independence of Siam was confirmed by a royal letter from Queen Victoria in 1856.

The Bowring Treaty also initiated the process whereby European advisers entered the kingdom to lead reforms of economy and society. Most famously, the celebrated English governess, Anna Leonowens, was employed in 1862 as tutor to the royal children. Anna was immortalized in the 1956 film, *The King and I*, but probably had less influence on Mongkut than is supposed. (The film is banned in Thailand because of its alleged lack of respect for the Chakri dynasty, and the 1999 re-make, *Anna and the King*, had to be filmed in Malaysia for the same reasons.) Anna's appointment was significant for the expansion of Western commercial interests in Siam, however. It was the British agency house, the Borneo Company (not to be confused with the British North Borneo Company), which introduced Anna to the king in the hope of currying favour at court. The initiative bore fruit in the concessions now granted to the Borneo Company and other European firms to cut teak from the northern forests.

Mongkut also led a new phase of Thai intellectual renaissance. During his years as a monk he founded the Thammayut movement, which attempted to modernize Buddhist thinking; to make it more intellectual and less ritualistic; to reconcile Siamese philosophy to the advances being made in science and technology in the West. Emphasis was placed on a new official Buddhist education for elites and masses alike; a process that also aided centralizing power in Bangkok through eliminating and de-legitimizing popular, unorthodox Buddhist texts and teachers who might pose a threat to the monarchy.

CHULALONGKORN

At the age of only sixteen, Prince Chulalongkorn took on the momentous responsibility of defending Siam's independence when he succeeded his father and became Rama V in 1868. Chulalongkorn had been taught by Anna Leonowens in the early stages of his Western education, and Anna constantly impressed upon him the need for various social reforms. Certainly one of Chulalongkorn's first acts when he became king, in his full right in 1873, was to proclaim the gradual phasing out of slavery. His subjects were also instructed that it was no longer necessary to approach the king on their hands and knees. From 1899 peasants were no longer required to perform their compulsory annual labour duties to the king; they paid a money tax instead.

Chulalongkorn intensified the strategy of what historian Nicholas Tarling calls 'defensive modernization'. The young king introduced European-style governance and fostered intensive economic development. The political reforms were designed to further centralize authority at Bangkok and curb the powers of the hereditary aristocracy who controlled provincial government. A new professional class of Bangkok-trained civil servants replaced the old elites in a new hierarchy of central, provincial and district administrations. Administration at the top of the governmental hierarchy was a family affair, however. The new ministries were headed by Chulalongkorn's brothers and half-brothers – the only individuals who had received a modern education. Prince Damrong, for example, became minister of the interior in 1892, the year in which all the brother ministers first met as a cabinet under Chulalongkorn's direction. Bangkok was confirmed as the centre of the Siamese state, backed up by the architectural symbols of national unification like the Temple of the Emerald Buddha and the royal palaces. British-financed railways further knit the realm together, radiating south, north and east from Bangkok. Such transport improvements, in turn, stimulated economic expansion, particularly in the south, where Western and Chinese firms set up tin and rubber enterprises.

The traditional aristocracy also lost military status as European advisers trained a new professional army, its numbers swelled by the introduction of universal conscription in 1902 and its firepower improved by the purchase of up-to-date weaponry. The Thai army was defeated in Laos by the French in 1893, but it proved an extremely effective instrument for suppressing the regional protests against the imposition of taxation and formal incorporation into the Siamese state – for example, around Chiang Mai from the 1880s and in Patani after 1902. In this sense, Chulalongkorn's modernizing monarchy acted as a colonial regime imposing 'law and order' and efficient, centralized administration upon its unruly subjects.

The success of Chulalongkorn's reforms relied on more than mere coercion. Strong links were fostered between king and populace via state-sponsored Buddhism. Following on from Mongkut's lead, further reforms of Siamese Buddhism were led by another of Chulalongkorn's brothers, Prince Wachiranan. In this process, the educative role of the village monasteries was harnessed to spread new ideas such as Western-style mathematics and science as well as a new Thai cultural nationalism through the medium of a standardized Thai script.

But there was a price to be paid for independence and moderniza-tion. During the last two decades of Chulalongkorn's reign, Siam lost over 300,000 square miles of territory to the European imperialists. Laos and Cambodia fell under French sway while the northern Malay states (bar Patani) passed under British protection. Siam became a kind of buffer zone between the British and French spheres in South East Asia. A 'special relationship' was developed particularly with the United Kingdom, epitomized by a secret agreement signed in 1897 during Chulalongkorn's visit to Queen Victoria: in return for British protection, Siam promised to offer no concessions on the Malay peninsula to another power without British consent. Yet Chula-longkorn was no European puppet. Like his predecessors he engaged in a game of *realpolitik*, playing off one imperial power against another, avoiding absolute subservience to any single country. Chulalongkorn took advice from Europeans of various nationality. If relations with Britain were especially close this merely served the purpose of staving off the French who the Thais calculated were the weaker power and therefore were the more likely to attempt to annex Siam. As Chula-longkorn's father Mongkut had shrewdly appreciated, the choice facing Siam was 'to swim upriver and make friends with the crocodile [the French] or to swim out to sea and hang on to the whale [the British]'. In swimming with the whale's school, Chulalongkorn and his successors skilfully avoided the greater evil of becoming crocodile fodder. In similar vein, Thailand would accommodate itself to Japan during the Pacific War and the United States in the Cold War. Certainly Chulalongkorn had no desire to ape the West, for he retained the absolutist monarchy of his forebears and resisted the introduction of British-style parliamentary institutions. To his death in 1910, the stubborn king dismissed the demands of European-educated officials

and princes for democratic institutions. The country, said Chulalongkorn, was not yet ready.

CONSTITUTIONAL MONARCHY

Chulalongkorn's successors, Vajiravudh (Rama VI, r. 1910–25) and
Prajadiphok (Rama VII, r. 1925–35), proved far less adept at managing
domestic disaffection with the absolutist system. Increasing challenges
from the emerging Siamese middle classes eventually led to the
establishment of a constitutional monarchy from 1932. Twenty years
earlier, however, Vajiravudh followed his father's example and resisted
demands for parliamentary government. As a substitute for democracy,
he set about trying to develop a new Thai inclusive nationalism with its
slogan, 'Nation, Religion, King'. Here was another attempt to preserve
the essence of 'Siam'. Western technology and institutions could be
absorbed but not at the expense of shattering the vertical linkages
between king and people, cemented by orthodox Buddhism. The Thai
kings certainly did not want the process of modernization to create a
European-style society in which class-based politics became the norm.
Alongside the defence of tradition, there was a less admirable xenophobic strain to the official nationalism. Reflecting popular Sino-
phobia, Vajiravudh described the Chinese as the 'Jews of the East', and
slogans like 'Siam for the Siamese' struck fear into the non-Thai
population. At the same time, Siam was attempting to be more assertive
on the international stage. Vajiravudh took Thailand into the First
World War in 1917 on the side of its traditional protector, Britain. But
this was part of a strategy to gain a seat at the League of Nations and so
revise the unequal treaties with the Western powers.

Patriotism was not enough, however, to save the absolutist monarchy under Vajiravudh's brother, Prajadiphok. Pressures for change
escalated after the Wall Street crash of 1929, which had a devastating
impact on Siam's economy through reducing the export price of rice.
The depression induced unrest among the Siamese peasantry,
encouraged by a nascent communist movement as well as more traditional millenarian, 'holy men'. More importantly, the economic crisis
spurred on a group of non-royal members of the new military and
civilian bureaucracy. Many of these malcontents had studied in France

where they had been influenced by republican ideas. Their civilian, liberal leader was Pridi Phanomyong who developed a leftist critique of Thailand's problems – basically, impoverishment was the product of royal collusion with the Western imperialists. In June 1932, little more than 100 determined individuals led a coup. A National Assembly was created to rule in concert with the king. Prajadiphok eventually abdicated in 1935 in favour of his ten-year-old nephew, Ananda, who was represented by a three-man Regency Council. As well as a centre-left civilian faction, the plotters of 1932 were made up of more conservative military figures. When Pridi presented a radical left-wing manifesto, which alluded to nationalization of the Thai economy, Minister of Defence Marshall Phibun Songkhram took over the reigns of power. In late 1938 Phibun became Thailand's prime minister and set about establishing a military dictatorship.

Phibun initiated a new aggressive, almost fascist, phase in Thai nationalism, in which the king became an inconsequential figure. Phibun as both prime minister and commander-in-chief styled himself, 'The Leader'. There was increased discrimination against the Chinese accompanied by growing restrictions on the activities of Europeans in Siam. The country now changed its name to Thailand (i.e. 'land of the free') to reflect this new assertiveness, and certain occupations were reserved for Thais. Xenophobia, militarism and an intolerant strain of Buddhism had a negative impact on the Malay areas of the south too, where bans on Malay dress, names and language were instituted. The increasingly anti-European stance culminated in an alliance with Japan from 1940, in which an expansionist programme sought the recovery of the so-called 'lost territories' in French Indochina and British Malaya. This 'Greater Thailand' would be achieved – with Japanese backing – for a brief period during the Pacific War.

Economic and Social Change under Colonial Rule

The Russian Marxist revolutionary, V.I. Lenin, regarded imperialism as the 'highest stage of capitalism', resulting, as he saw it, from an insatiable scramble for markets and raw materials on the part of the European 'magnates of capital'. Yet, if European imperialism was a search for profit, this was only part of a broader, genuinely humanitarian (albeit misguided) notion that South East Asia needed to be reformed, needed to be saved from itself. In the Malay world, there was a commonly held belief amongst Europeans that the riches of the mythical 'Land of Gold' were being squandered by decadent and corrupt rajahs. In Joseph Conrad's classic *fin-de-siècle* adventure story, *Lord Jim*, the European hero, Jim – based upon the first white rajah of Sarawak, James Brooke – is juxtaposed with Rajah Allang of Patusan. Jim is a blonde, 'stalwart figure in white apparel', whereas the Rajah is a 'dirty, little, used-up' drug addict, whose moral decay is symbolized by the piles of rotting rubbish that lie under his house. Jim's right to rule, therefore, is based upon his moral and physical superiority.

Yet even if capitalism was not the engine behind imperial expansion in South East Asia, colonialism did provide the stability, security and certainty required for the establishment of large-scale export industries. European banks, trading houses, plantations and mining ventures took advantage of the opportunities provided by new frameworks of Western-style 'law and order'. Such stability permitted the influx of capital to exploit South East Asia's natural resources, the opening up of new markets for European industry, and the importation of migrant labour on a scale far beyond anything witnessed before. The introduction of Western cultural and educational systems also threw up new Asian elites, shaped in the European image, and which acted as intermediaries in the capitalist export economies. At the same time, colonial states undertook transport improvements – for example, the building of railways in Malaya, Sumatra and Java – which enabled exports to reach the waiting ships in the colonial ports.

The greatest success of this capitalist revolution was the development of the rubber industry. The rubber tree, *Hevea brasiliensis*, was not indigenous to South East Asia but was introduced from Brazil via Kew Gardens and Sri Lanka to the Botanic Gardens in Singapore during 1877. The combination of large tracts of uncultivated land, stable colonial administration and favourable soil and climatic conditions made the Malay states ideal for the development of large-scale rubber plantations. But to make these factors count a mass demand was required for the latex, which oozed from the diagonal cuts made in the bark of the *Hevea* trees. It was not until the 1910s that the swift expansion of the automobile industry – particularly after the introduction of Henry Ford's mass production techniques in the United States – created a massive demand for rubber tyres. Channelling venture capital from the profit-hungry City of London, the Singapore agency houses now promoted vast new estates organized by rugged European managers. In Malaya, the land area under plantation rubber expanded almost 250-fold between 1900 and 1921, to 1.4 million acres, representing an investment of probably £100 million. Rubber came to overshadow completely the Chinese-owned pepper and gambier plantations or the earlier attempts of European planter-pioneers to grow sugar and coffee. From the 1920s, rubber also took off in southern Vietnam and Cambodia as French companies, such as

H.N. Ridley, who introduced rubber planting into Malaya, pictured with an assistant next to a rubber tree, *c.* 1905

Michelin, poured some 700 million francs-worth of capital into the French territories. By 1927 French Indochina had nearly 315,000 acres devoted to rubber production. But it was not only on large, European-owned estates that rubber trees flourished. Much to the irritation of European planters and district officers, indigenous smallholders in Malaya and Sumatra planted *Hevea* seeds alongside their traditional food crops. So successful were the rubber smallholders of Indonesia that their production completely undermined British attempts of the 1920s to restrict rubber output and so raise prices. The plantation belt along the east coast of Sumatra grew rubber on European-owned and -managed estates too, but also palm oil, tea, sisal and, most famously, tobacco leaves, which resulted in exquisite cigars.

Meanwhile the extraction and processing of South East Asia's minerals became concentrated in the hands of European firms. By the 1920s, the introduction of bucket-dredging recovery techniques in the Malayan tin fields allowed the British companies to overtake the Chinese *kongsi* (business co-operatives) as the principal extractors and smelters of the ore. Demand for tin had increased massively thanks to the growth of the canned food industry, and the Chinese simply could not entertain the huge investments, as well as the technological know-how, required for dredging and smelting. Western firms were also favoured by the state bureaucracies in the release of large chunks of land for tin prospecting. The tin belt also extended south to the Indonesian islands of Bangka and Belitung and north into southern Thailand. This region accounted for two-thirds of the world's tin production by the 1930s. Oil production too came under the control of huge multinational combines such as Royal Dutch Shell and Standard Oil in south-east Sumatra and throughout British and Dutch Borneo.

Another South East Asian natural resource coveted by the West was timber extracted – again largely by large Western firms – from northern Siam, Sarawak and British North Borneo (modern Sabah). A process was initiated, which has caused the region massive ecological damage. The rice-growing potential of South East Asia was also exploited as never before: the Mekong delta became a major centre for rice exports, assisted by huge French schemes for the construction of canals to provide irrigation and an excellent means of transporting rice to Saigon for export by Chinese merchants. Rice production increased 90 per cent between 1900 and 1937, making Vietnam the third largest rice-exporting country in the world. The crop was grown by peasants, renting their fields from a newly enriched, rentier class of absentee Vietnamese landlords. Independent Siam too witnessed a rice revolution between 1860 and 1930 when, also boosted by massive water-works construction and land reclamation, the volume of rice exports increased 25-fold. Cultivation was expanded from the central plain to the north and north east. Siamese peasants farmed the rice but the transportation and export business was shared between European and Chinese firms. Sugar on Java, meanwhile, was grown on land hired from peasants. The milling, however, took place at technologically advanced mills owned by Dutch firms.

Only in Sarawak did a disdain for the intrusions of Western capital develop, given the belief of the eccentric Brooke rajahs that this would exploit the native population and disturb the imagined social harmony of their realm. Sarawak was therefore preserved as a kind of huge living, anthropological museum. Outside of Sarawak, there were also vast swathes of remote South East Asia that remained untouched by Western capitalism and where lifestyles changed very little. Even in Malaya and Sumatra, smallholders remained essentially subsistence farmers who now tapped the odd rubber tree as a side interest.

PLURAL SOCIETIES

The economic developments that accompanied colonial rule did bring profound changes to the ethnic mix of many South East Asian societies. Chinese and Indians had been visiting, and often settling in, the region since the earliest times. But now they came in greater numbers than ever before to make up for labour shortages. There was a belief amongst colonial administrators that the indigenous peoples – the Malays, particularly – were 'lazy' and unsuited to wage labour or that their idyllic rural life-styles would be corrupted by the workplace. The Malay Reservations Act of 1913, for example, aimed at protecting the *bumiputera* (the 'princes of the soil'), and confirmed their role as rice farmers and fishermen. In the Brooke raj too, the Malays and Dayaks were discouraged from pursuing trade, which was left instead to avaricious aliens.

China emerged as a major source of manpower for colonial economic development. By the early twentieth century, floods of Hokkien, Hakka, Teochew, Cantonese and Hailam Chinese were herded through Singapore by their compatriot 'coolie brokers' into the western Malay states and Sumatra, where they worked the rubber plantations and tin mines. This was a dreadfully exploitative indentured labour system whereby the recruits were tied to three-year contracts. The coolies suffered appalling living conditions, high death rates and were permanently hounded by, and indebted to, secret society and clan headmen. Indentured labour has been described as a new system of slavery. Some Chinese in Malaya became fabulously wealthy, such as Yap Ah Loy, the Kapitan China of Kuala Lumpur, between 1868 and 1885 who owned one in three of the town's buildings, many of which were used as brothels, plus substantial tin-mining and plantation

Yap Ah Loy, leader of the Chinese in Kuala Lumpur, Malaysia, as portrayed in 1878

interests. But most Chinese immigrants remained impoverished tin miners, rubber tappers and smallholders. By the 1930s, about 40 percent of British Malaya's population was Chinese, provoking fears amongst indigenous Malays that they were about to suffer the same fate as the native peoples of North America.

The other great area of Chinese settlement in South East Asia was independent Siam. A large Chinese population had existed in Siam since the seventeenth century, but in the nineteenth century this increased even further; by 1910 Chinese were nearly ten percent of Thailand's population. Bangkok – like Singapore, Saigon and Batavia – grew as a Chinese centre. Chinese merchants continued to dominate Siam's internal and external trades but lower-class immigrants arrived from the late nineteenth century to work on the plantations and mines or engage in market gardening.

Indian merchants and moneylenders were to be seen on the streets of the Straits Settlements from the early 1800s and had been major players in the Melaka emporium since the 1400s. But from the 1880s a new, much larger proletarian wave of Indian workers arrived to tap rubber on the European estates. Indians were increasingly favoured by British managers over the Chinese because they were allegedly more docile. Indian labourers in Malaya were mainly Tamils, recruited by foremen or *kangany* on the indentured system in southern India and Sri Lanka. By the 1910s, then, about ten percent of Malaya's population was classified as 'Indian'. But there was little interaction between the different ethnic groups in colonial South East Asia. Tamil labourers, for example, lived in their isolated, self-contained estate villages and rarely came into contact with the Malays. Distances between the communities were exacerbated by distinct, racially segregated education systems – in Malaya there were separate Malay elite, Chinese language, and Indian estate schools. And Asians rarely mixed with Europeans.

Indeed, the European was isolated at the top of the colonial social ladder. In terms of numbers, the European communities of South East Asia were minute – for example, as late as the 1940s in Malaya only 0.2 percent of the population was European. But the power the white man and woman wielded was immense. Asians were no longer regarded as the equals of Europeans. Absurd pseudo-scientific racial doctrines justified segregation by drawing up a hierarchy of 'civilizations' in which the European brand was definitely at the pinnacle. By the twentieth century, there were great barriers erected between European and 'native' society as the colonials became more settled, especially when larger numbers of women ventured 'out East' due to improvements in tropical medicine and transport. Sexual liaisons between European men and what one British ex-administrator described as the 'good-tempered and good-mannered daughters of the East' were now highly frowned upon. Indeed, as the colonial era neared its close, there was an ever-growing anxiety to 'maintain standards' and 'keep one's distance' to preserve the dignity of the white race. The racial exclusivity of the various European colonial systems was epitomized by the white men's clubs, such as the Royal Selangor Club in Kuala Lumpur, which did not admit Asians, and the hill stations, such as the Cameron Highlands in Malaya and Berastagi in Sumatra, which allowed Europeans to escape for a weekend from the heat and the bustle of the lowland towns. The short stories of Somerset Maugham set in 1920s South East Asia depict a European social world in which Asians do not matter and (almost) seem not to exist. European societies themselves were also stratified into orders – better educated administrators and soldiers were generally considered culturally superior to 'grubby' traders and 'greedy' concession-hunters. In Malaya, for example, the hairy-kneed planters – many of them Scottish – were expected to drink at their own bars rather than rub shoulders with the linen-clad, better educated – and mainly English – officials.

NATIONALIST AWAKENINGS

As time wore on, more and more South East Asians became frustrated by the racial injustices of the colonial order. Colonial schools, designed to churn out office 'boys' and lower-level administrators to assist the 'thin white line' of European civil servants and merchants, increasingly produced Frankenstein's monsters. Modern European history, which was a central part of the colonial syllabus, was littered with revolutions and nationalist struggles for emancipation. Indeed in 1913 the Dutch colonial government insensitively ordered Indonesians to celebrate the centenary of Holland's 'national liberation' from Napoleon's France.

The paradox was not lost on Indonesia's early nationalists! Moreover, Western liberal education preached advancement by merit but in reality it was the colour of one's skin that determined promotion to the top. In both administration and commerce, executive and management positions were the exclusive preserve of Westerners. Racist arrangements and attitudes bred a class of impatient 'angry young men' in the colonial cities. Indonesia's nationalist leader, Sukarno, for example, was born into the Javanese aristocratic administrative class, the *priyayi* and discovered politics between 1916 and 1924 as a student in Surabaya and Bandung. He became a prolific reader and was particularly fascinated by the history of working-class movements in Europe.

The colonialists also shot themselves in the foot by unwittingly creating institutions that knit disparate societies together and made it possible for the inhabitants of particular colonial territories to think of themselves as a 'nation'. In Indonesia, the Dutch forged a unity out of the thousands of islands and hundreds of ethnic groups by insisting on the use of Malay with a new romanized alphabet as the lingua franca. New transport and communications networks, as well as bureaucratic rationalization, further developed what the historian Benedict Anderson has called 'imagined communities'. The huge growth of the colonial cities, particularly Singapore, Saigon, Kuala Lumpur and Batavia, brought people together from all over the colonial territory. These were urban melting pots that represented the emerging 'nation' in microcosm, and it was in the towns and cities that newspapers and pamphlets were circulated and read aloud in coffee shops and self-help groups. It was in the colonial city too that trade unions sprang up after the First World War, organizations that would eventually lend their help to nationalist causes.

South East Asia's educated elites were also gaining inspiration from other parts of Asia by the twentieth century. Japan and China had gone through their own nationalistic self-strengthening movements, and Japan had even defeated a European power, Russia, between 1904 and 1905. After the First World War, Mahatma Gandhi's non-cooperation campaigns in British India provided another powerful example of what could be achieved by Asians. At the same time, Muslim contacts with the Middle East continued to provide a counter-culture to colonialism in the mosques and Islamic schools. The spread of Marxist ideas after the Russian Revolution of 1917 supplied a simple and attractive explanation for, and solution to, the colonial plight. The downfall of colonialism through violent proletarian revolution would lead to the end of exploitation by Western capital and the birth of a new egalitarian society. The proletariat, the industrial working class, was tiny in most colonial settings, but intellectuals such as Ho Chi Minh in Vietnam came to realize that in South East Asia the peasants could be substituted for the workers as the mass base of revolutionary anti-colonial movements. Ho left Vietnam for Europe in 1911 in his early thirties. In France he was drawn to Marxism, even helping to found the communist party there in 1918. As an international communist he travelled to the Soviet Union in the 1920s, and in southern China, Ho saw the possibilities of rural communism first hand as the guest of Mao Zedong. Ho developed a searing critique of French colonial rule in Vietnam, exposing the contradictions between the rhetoric of the 'civilizing mission' and, as he saw it, the realities of capitalist exploitation. As he wrote in 1926, 'To hide the ugliness of its criminally exploitative regime, colonial capitalism always decorates its rotten shield with the idealistic device: Fraternity, Equality etc.'

All sorts of reformist anti-colonial organizations were founded by disaffected South East Asians. In Vietnam, the Indochinese Communist Party was formed in 1930 after Ho succeeded in bringing together various leftist groups. In Indonesia, Sarekat Islam focused from 1912 on a reformist Islam as the basis of a democratic and spiritual renaissance. The PKI (The Indonesian Communist Party) sprang up in 1920 while the PNI (Indonesian Nationalist Party) was formed by Sukarno in 1927, in an attempt to develop a synthesis of nationalism, communism and Islam. In Malaya, meanwhile, disaffected Malay intellectuals – many of them products of the Sultan Idris Training College for teachers – were developing a critique of British rule in Malaya, enhanced by contacts with their radical cousins in Indonesia. In 1937 the Kesatuan Melayu Muda (Malay Youth Union) was established, which according to its leader, Ibrahim Yaacob, 'neither professed loyalty to the Sultans and the British nor spoke of non-cooperation, but worked to promote nationalist feeling and teachings among its members, whose strength lay in the lower classes'. Chinese intellectuals, with the assistance of Vietnam's Ho Chi Minh, formed the Malayan Communist Party in 1930.

The educated urban elites could achieve very little in their anti-colonial struggles, however, without harnessing the anger of the lower orders. The colonial system bred huge disparities of wealth between rich and poor. In Vietnam, for example, only 2.5 percent of land-holders owned 45 percent of the cultivated land. The mass of landless peasants lived in a permanent state of impoverishment. There were increasing numbers of mouths to feed as the South East Asian coun-tryside experienced tremendous demographic growth in the nine-teenth and twentieth centuries; for example, on Java a population of about 5 million in the 1800s had increased some eight-fold by the 1930s. On top of this, were the ever expanding tax demands of colonial bureaucracies. Where peasants secured work on plantations or in mines there was brutal mistreatment and low wages worthy of Scrooge on a bad day. The most notorious and hideous working conditions were on the east coast of Sumatra, where plantation labourers were regarded as 'coolie beasts' who needed to be 'tamed' through frequent beatings, whippings and exorbitant cash fines. It was as a teacher on Dutch estates in Deli between 1919 and 1921 that Tan Malaka became a convinced Marxist, witnessing in his words, 'A land of gold, a haven for the capitalist class but also a land of sweat, tears, and death, a hell for the proletariat'. According to Tan Malaka between 100 and 200 Dutch people were killed or wounded in attacks by coolies every year in eastern Sumatra. Sexual harassment was also common on rubber estates – in Malaya, for example, the strike of Tamil tappers in 1914 demanded an end to the molestation of female labourers by European planters. The consciousness of women was raised, and the possibilities for female emancipation was grasped in the new workplace. As two male Viet-namese Marxists appreciated, 'Knowing that they must work to eat, women no longer simply *follow* their fathers and mothers, *follow* their husbands and sons, as though they were in a state of perpetual bondage'.

The hardships of the lower orders were further aggravated by the Great Depression of the 1930s. The massive downturn in world economic activity after 1929 brought price collapses for all South East Asia's major commodities. The price of rubber, for example, declined by nearly five-fold between 1923 and 1932. Government attempts to restrict output and raise the prices of commodities had little effect. As a corollary to declining profits, wages were cut and labourers were laid off. Probably 40 percent of the wage labour force was sacked in Cochin-China alone after 1931. Those parts of South East Asia, such as Sarawak, that had not been sucked into the world economy emerged relatively unscathed. But, as Elson writes, the 1930s was generally 'a time of considerable distress for rural Southeast Asians, with widespread unemployment or underemployment, a substantial decline in the amount and quality of food available for consumption, and a general fall in living standards'. Hardship and despair spilled over into violent confrontation with colonial states, influenced and co-ordinated by the disaffected intellectuals. Peasants set up 'Red Soviets' in central Vietnam during 1930–31. The Malay peninsula was awash with communist-led strikes between 1934 and 1941 at the docks, in the mines and on the plantations. The coup of 1932 in Thailand also reflected the economic distress of the lower orders.

Yet despite everything, colonial administrations were barely stretched by these isolated incidents. Efficient secret police forces easily dealt with nationalist leaders by imprisoning them – for example, when the PNI took on a more confrontational stance, Sukarno was detained first in 1929 and again in 1933. Superior force was always at the disposal of the colonial state. The Muslim communist outbursts on Java and Sumatra during 1926 and 1927 were simply shot down by the Dutch colonial army. In the aftermath, the PKI was suppressed so effectively that it did not re-emerge until after 1945. The Vietnamese Nationalist Party was liquidated with the assistance of *Madame Guillotine* after its abortive uprising in 1930. The Vietnamese peasant communists of 1930–31 were dealt with in a similar manner. French expatriates in Indochina liked to send postcards home of severed Vietnamese heads, proudly illustrated the ruthless way in which dissent was dealt with.

Moreover before the Second World War there were very few nationalists in colonial South East Asia. The mass of the Indonesian population knew nothing of Sukarno or Tan Malaka. The nationalist movement in Indonesia was highly divided anyway, given divisions between competing secular nationalist, communist and Islamic strands. Sukarno did attempt to produce a federation of anti-colonial parties but it was rent by conflicts over tactics and religion. The Vietnamese communist movement was hampered by internal divisions between Stalinists and Trotskyites and, in the south, it faced competition from the Cao Dai and Hoa Hao eclectic sects, which appealed to the peasantry on a more traditionalist anti-colonial ticket. In Malaya, the Chinese and Indians still tended to look to their homelands for political inspiration rather than think about a Malayan nationalism, and the struggle in the peninsula remained as much a conflict between the various races as a united struggle against colonial rule. The Malays saw the British as their protectors against Chinese and Indian domination. Furthermore, many South East Asians remained deeply loyal to their colonial masters – Christian Ambonese made up the Dutch colonial army; the Straits Chinese, or self-styled 'King's Chinese', of Singapore, Penang and Melaka felt threatened by nationalism, as did the Vietnamese Catholics. Kings and aristocrats still had much to gain from collaboration with the colonial state. Nationalism was hardly developed in Cambodia and Laos before the Second World War largely because the elites in both territories continued to see the French as their guarantee of protection from either Siamese or Vietnamese domination. The huge variety of peoples artificially cobbled together into colonial territories meant that there was an equally huge variety of 'imagined communities'. In such an environment, colonial regimes proved adept at outmanoeuvring, anticipating and containing nascent nationalists while solidifying their alliances with traditional authorities. It was the Japanese Occupation, and its chaotic aftermath, which fundamentally upset the colonial apple cart and brought a new world into being.

CHAPTER SIX

Decolonizing South East Asia, 1941–1965

A dramatic era of far-reaching political change in South East Asia was compressed into a 25 year period in the middle of the twentieth century. The decolonization epoch witnessed the making of today's nation-states. The myth of European invincibility was exploded overnight when the Japanese imperial forces swept their way through South East Asia in the winter of 1941–42. Japan ultimately lost the Pacific War and the European colonials returned to their South East Asian preserves in 1945. But imperial authority was never fully resurrected. In Indochina and Indonesia, the French and the Dutch respectively faced colonial wars that ended in defeat for the imperialists. Britain – although facing its own colonial war in Malaya – lingered longer and was better able to control events in today's states of Malaysia and Singapore. Nevertheless, between 1957 and 1963 Britain withdrew from Malaya, Singapore, Sarawak and North Borneo (Sabah). British influence ebbed away in post-war Thailand too.

Decolonization in some ways represented a victory for South East Asian nationalism. Yet, the heavy-handed policies of the imperial powers in the last few years of colonial rule also brought the colonial edifice crashing down. The retraction of Europe was also a reflection of the growing role of superpower rivalry between the United States, the Soviet Union, and Communist China. South East Asia was sucked into the Cold War.

The Japanese Occupation

JAPAN'S SWEEP INTO SOUTH EAST ASIA

Japan was a major economic player in South East Asia during the early seventeenth century, becoming especially prominent in Thailand's overseas trade. From 1640, however, the Tokugawa shoguns almost completely closed off Japan from foreign contacts. Only at the end of the nineteenth century, were Japanese economic links revived with the Nanyo, as they called the 'South Seas', following Japan's industrialization in the wake of the Meiji Restoration of 1868 and the end of shogun rule. Singapore became the centre of Japanese prostitution. The *karayuki-san* – some as young as ten – were major earners of foreign exchange in the early years of Japan's economic opening. By the 1930s Japan's economic modernization produced a more respectable presence as dynamic Japanese trading firms emerged as major competitors with the Western agency houses, selling cheap, high-quality goods such as textiles and bicycles on a massive scale. The low value of the yen after 1931 made Japanese goods especially cheap. Japan's share of textiles imported into British Malaya increased from 24 per cent in 1929 to 48 per cent in 1933.

In the conditions of global depression, European powers felt increasingly threatened by Japanese industrial power. Colonial markets were protected: quotas established in 1934 on the import of textiles into Malaya resulted in a dramatic reduction of Japan's share. The Japanese also began to feel excluded from raw material supplies, particularly Indonesia's oil. By the late 1930s, the idea of a Great East Asia Co-prosperity Sphere became fashionable in political, business and military circles in Tokyo. A huge yen bloc would allow Japan to dominate the markets and raw material supplies of North Asia and South East Asia.

The Co-prosperity Sphere could be created by force. By the 1930s, Japan had become a formidable military power, possessing a technically superb navy and air force. As the military came to dominate Japanese governments after 1932, Japan began to feel increasingly isolated and surrounded by hostile powers in the Pacific, headed by the United

States and Britain. In 1936, Tokyo moved closer to the other mal-
content powers in signing an anti-communist pact with Nazi Germany
and Fascist Italy. Bogged down in its war with China after 1937, the
Japanese came to an agreement in the summer of 1940 with the French
in Indochina to station troops there. American oil embargoes followed,
alienating Japan further from the Western democracies. The final straw
was Hitler's attack on Soviet Russia in June 1941. Stalin was now added
to Japan's list of enemies.

The military junta took the Pearl Harbor gamble. The bombing of
the Hawaiian naval base on 7 December 1941 put most of America's
Pacific fleet out of action. In the end the bet proved a bad one: the
United States was brought into the Second World War, leading ultimately to the end of Japan's imperial pretensions. Yet, following the
sinking of the British warships, *Prince of Wales* and *Repulse*, off the
Malayan coast, Japan had naval supremacy in the Pacific. The Japanese
army took advantage and moved down the Malayan peninsula toward
Singapore while landings were also made in Bali and Sumatra in pre-
paration for an attack on Java. Preoccupied with war in Europe,
Britain's great naval base and commercial centre in South East Asia was
inadequately defended. But the fall of Singapore on 15 February 1942
was also the product of bad British planning. The guns at the naval base
were pointing the wrong way since the British never envisaged a
Japanese invasion arriving by bicycle down the peninsula. Meanwhile,
the British troops defending the island were hopelessly confused and
disorganized: in one incredible episode, a group of troops opened up
their maps to find that Singapore had changed shape slightly – the maps
were actually of the Isle of Wight! The empire's worst hour was also a
product of colonial racism – Singapore and Malaya were inadequately
defended because Britain's wartime prime minister, Winston Churchill,
simply could not conceive that an Asian power might defeat the British
empire.

Once the Singapore linchpin had fallen, the Japanese swiftly took the
Indonesian archipelago as well as Burma and the Philippines. Only in
Indochina did the colonial regime survive as the Japanese struck a deal
with the pro-German Vichy regime there. The French administration
would stay intact as long as it did not obstruct the Japanese military

occupation of Vietnam, Laos and Cambodia. By the spring of 1942, Japan controlled an empire covering one-fifth of the globe and stretching from northern China to the shores of Australia.

'ASIA FOR THE ASIANS'

The rhetoric behind Japan's advance into the Pacific was based on an ideology of liberation. Japan, as the most economically and militarily advanced independent Asian state, should lead Asia to freedom. In the early weeks of the occupation, all Europeans who had failed to escape were interned and their positions in the various colonial administrations were taken by South East Asians. Singapore, now known as Syonan (Light of the South), became Japan's capital in the region and the most strategically important areas of Malaya and Sumatra were ruled directly by the Japanese military. Outside these areas, the Japanese provided opportunities for budding nationalists – in Indonesia, Ahmed Sukarno and his deputy, Mohammad Hatta, co-operated with the Japanese given the promise of a share in government. In September 1943 a Central Advisory Council materialized on Java and the Japanese even trained and equipped an Indonesian army. In Singapore, meanwhile, a Malayan Consultative Council was formed, representing the various communities. Radical Malay nationalists, such as Ibrahim Yacoob, were given the opportunity to organize paramilitary and political organizations. A Japanese education programme (aimed at promoting Asian, as opposed to Western, values) allowed leading young Malays to study both in Malaya and Tokyo. Singapore also became the centre of Subhas Chandra Bose's Indian National Army, attracting many Indians in South East Asia to the cause of violent struggle against the British Raj. The Japanese actually knew very little about South East Asia; few understood local languages. As a result, the Japanese (like their European colonial forbears) were forced into collaboration with local elites.

The collaborators *par excellence* proved to be the Thai leaders, who successfully preserved Thailand's independence through a pact of friendship with Japan in June 1940. This was followed by Marshall Phibun's declaration of war against Britain and the United States in January 1942. Phibun was rewarded through the creation of 'Greater Thailand' as the 'lost territories' in northern Malaya, Cambodia, Laos and Burma were re-incorporated into Bangkok's imperial administration. The British regarded Thailand's behaviour as traitorous but this was a treachery born of pragmatism. As Phibun allegedly put it when asked which foe Thai military planning should be directed against, 'Which side is going to lose the war? That side is our enemy'.

As Phibun's cynicism reveals, the Japanese failed to generate any deep, heart-felt support from South East Asians for their rule. Advisory and consultative committees were mere talking shops and it soon became clear that 'Asia for the Asians' was code for 'Asia for the Japanese'. Moreover, the Japanese failed to deliver prosperity. Hyper-inflation, food and textile shortages, vast falls in commodity output, extensive ecological damage, and significant increases in the incidence of prostitution, theft and malaria are all indicative of the strain that administering South East Asia placed on over-stretched Japanese resources. Only Indonesia, with its oil reserves, was regarded by the Japanese as economically important. And beyond oil, the Co-prosperity Sphere could not absorb South East Asia's vast rubber, tin and timber outputs, which had previously been sold on global markets. Allied blockades and shortages of shipping also exacerbated shortages. Living conditions declined markedly from 1944 as wartime fortunes took a definite turn for the worse for the Japanese. Successful American and British campaigns in the Pacific and Burma respectively stretched Japanese forces and resources to the limit. But what really exposed Japan's 'Asia for the Asians' myth was the brutal behaviour of some Japanese towards their new colonial subjects.

BRUTALITY AND RESISTANCE

The Japanese in South East Asia were not all cruel. Some civilian administrators were capable of great kindness and earned the respect, and sometimes love, of South East Asians. In southern Malaya, an Indian chief clerk was beaten up, hurled into a drain and ordered off his rubber estate by Japanese officers when a Malaysian woman reported his improper advances. On the other hand, the military police, the Kempeitai, were capable of hideous cruelty to both Europeans and South East Asians. In the internment camps, such as Singapore's infamous Changi prison, conditions for Europeans were atrocious, and, on liberation, POWs were to be found with protruding ribs, given their undernourishment. A favourite humiliation in Changi was to force women prisoners to wash and go to the lavatory in front of their male counterparts. Young Dutch female internees in Indonesia were forced to become so-called 'comfort women' to Japanese officers. To the Japanese warrior code, Europeans had no rights because they had lost on the battlefield.

Yet South East Asians suffered as much if not more. In the building of the 'Death Railway' between Burma and Thailand, it is often assumed (most notably in the film, *Bridge on the River Kwai*) that the Allied prisoners of war were the principal victims. But more than 75,000 Malayans, mostly Indian Tamils, were recruited to work on the railway. Malnourishment, appalling working conditions and the brutality of the Japanese overseers resulted in death rates approaching 40 percent. Thousands of Chinese 'disappeared', following denouncements by hooded informers, in Singapore and Kuala Lumpur in the early days of the occupation; their bodies would be unearthed in mass graves in the 1960s. The Chinese business community of Malaya was ordered to 'donate' $50 million (about £6 million) to the Japanese. The

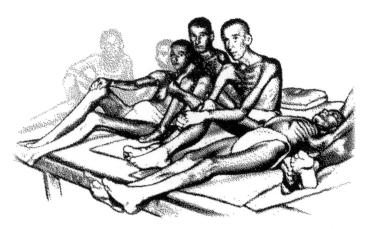

Australian soldiers interned by the Japanese in Changi jail, Singapore during World War II

Chinese communities of South East Asia were particularly targetted by the Japanese as revenge for support given to resistance to the Japanese in China itself. The Indonesians who were forced to build the underground military installations at Bukittinggi on Sumatra were murdered once their work was completed. A devastating famine raged in northern Vietnam during 1944–45 in which between 1 million and 2 million people perished as the Japanese shipped surplus rice from the south for use in Japan as fuel. Indeed, throughout the region it was official army policy to 'maintain the natives' standard of living at the lowest possible level'. In the reoccupation of Malaya, a British official recalled later that the children of Indian rubber tappers were 'in a desperate plight, comparable to photographs I have seen of Biafra or Belsen'.

A worse fate still awaited those interned by the Kempeitai. To make suspected subversives talk, the military police employed a variety of inconscionably inhumane methods. These included beatings with sticks and canes, insertions of needles and heated objects under fingernails, as well as the hideous water torture, which involved pumping vast quantities of water into the victim's body followed by jumping on a board laid across the individual's stomach. Sybil Kathigasu's experience in Malaya was not atypical:

> Policemen, some of whom seemed to hate their task almost as much as I did, would run needles into my finger-tips below the nail, while my hand was held firmly, flat on the table; they heated iron bars in a charcoal brazier and applied them to my legs and back; they ran a stick between the second and third fingers of both my hands, squeezing the fingers together and holding them firmly in the air while two men hung from the ends of the cane, making a see-saw of my hands and tearing the flesh between my fingers; they thrust the rough ragged ends of canes into the hollows of my knees and twisted them until I screamed with pain.

Sybil's resulting injuries caused her premature death in 1949.

Such horrors provoked many South East Asians to resist. In Malaya, anti-Japanese activity was co-ordinated by the communist- and Chinese-dominated Malayan Peoples' Anti-Japanese Army, encouraged by British saboteurs in the underground Force 136. Opposition to both the Japanese and the French in Vietnam was also spearheaded by a communist-led organization, as Ho Chi Minh returned from China and in May 1941 the Vietnamese Independence Brotherhood League, or Vietminh, was formed as a front for the Indochinese Communist Party. Despite their outward appearance of collaboration with the Japanese, Sukarno and Hatta never lost contact with the Indonesian nationalists who chose to go underground, led by the socialist Sutan Sjahrir. In Thailand, meanwhile, the pro-British regent, Pridi, clandestinely organized the Free Thai Movement, secretly in contact with the Allies. Yet, it was not South East Asian resistance that ended the Japanese occupation but the dropping of atomic bombs on Hiroshima and Nagasaki in August 1945. Fearing that the Japanese would never surrender in a conventional war and that the Soviet Union might take the Japanese islands before the United States and Britain, United States President Harry S. Truman brought about a swift termination of the Pacific War. Japan unconditionally surrendered on 14 August 1945. South East Asian nationalists were now presented with what the Vietnamese communists called their 'moment of opportunity'. They could suddenly seize control of state apparatuses in the interregnum between Japanese collapse and European return.

Indonesia: From Dutch Federation to Independent Republic

A DIVIDED HOUSE: THE REPUBLIC OF INDONESIA

Independence for the revolutionary Republic of Indonesia was proclaimed by Sukarno in Jakarta, three days after Japan's surrender, on 17 August 1945. Sukarno himself became president of the new state. It was not until late 1949 that the Dutch finally conceded independence for the islands, but in Indonesia today August 1945 is taken as the date of independence. In the next couple of months of 1945 – before the arrival of British and Australian forces in the name of the Dutch – the republic took power in the major towns of the archipelago. In Brian Aldiss's semi-autobiographical novel, *A Rude Awakening* (1978), set in

Sumatra in October 1945, a young British soldier is told by an Indonesian nationalist in Medan that, 'We now remain in a militant new republic with its own flag, under which certainly no colonialists will be allowed. They will kill off all white foreigners; ten to one'.

Such revolutionary bravado disguised a fundamental lack of unity in the Indonesian nationalist movement as well as a fundamental lack of direction from the centre at Jakarta. The inhabitants of Indonesia were by no means united in a single nationalist movement. For one, the idea of an Indonesian nation was problematic, given that there was never any pre-colonial entity called Indonesia. The medieval empire of Majapahit was often described as the pre-colonial heir to the nation state but, at its greatest extent, Majapahit's authority only covered Java. Paradoxically, the unifying factor in Indonesia was the shared experience of Dutch rule and the widespread encouragement given by the Dutch to use of the Malay language as a kind of lingua franca, linking together the hundreds of ethnic groups and thousands of islands that made up the archipelago. Yet, conversely, since the days of Majapahit an ingrained suspicion of the Javanese existed amongst the 'outer' islanders; a fear reinforced by the Dutch focus on Java and the colonial practice of using Javanese aristocrats in the provincial administration.

As such, the Indonesian revolution represented a number of local struggles rather than a unified struggle against European imperialism. The Japanese occupation turned the world upside down, but it also opened up deep wounds and unleashed a struggle for power amongst competing groups within Indonesian society. In north-central Sumatra, the Christian Bataks fought against the Muslim lowlanders, while in Aceh the Islamic leaders or *ulama* led a social revolution against the traditional aristocracy and the sultan. In Sumatra generally the revolution was out of control: as a republican journalist sent from Jakarta reported in the summer of 1947, the frequent inspections by the army and police in the nationalist zones were 'not to inspect, but to remove cigarettes and money from the pockets of those who passed by . . . It is rough men with no education who now come to the fore, and those who have no shame who do not hesitate to do as they wish towards educated people. . .' In west Java, meanwhile, Muslim fundamentalists (whose movement was called Darul Islam, or 'House of Islam') ousted the Westernized administrators or *priyayi*. Ironically the supposed leader of the revolution, Sukarno, was of the *priyayi* class. The gangsters of Jakarta formed people's militias, which would later be crushed not by the Dutch but by the regular army of the republic who feared the radicalism of this grass-roots movement.

Moreover the leadership was divided at the centre in Jakarta. Several nationalist, communist and Islamic elites vied for leadership of the new republic. Sukarno became president as leader of the reconstructed Indonesian Nationalist Party or PNI. But the PNI's failure to absorb the other nationalist groups was such that Sukarno was forced to form the Central Indonesian National Committee (KNIP) as the basis of the government. Within the KNIP there was general agreement between Sukarno's PNI and the Indonesian Socialist Party under the wartime resistance hero, Sjahrir. But the other major component of the committee was Masjumi (Federation of Muslim Organizations). The Islamic politicians were increasingly alienated from Sukarno's secular Javanese ways, especially as he tried to give a historical basis to Indonesian nationalism by evoking the legendary grandeur of pre-Islamic Majapahit.

Inter-party squabbles notwithstanding, there was also a general division between the government, which favoured negotiations with the Dutch, called the policy of *diplomasi* (diplomacy), and the

President Sukarno, the first leader of independent Indonesia

opposition groups, which abhorred compromise and looked forward instead to a strategy of armed struggle, or *perjuangan*. This was also a generational divide, for the policy of 'struggle' was supported by the restless youth movements, the *pemuda*. Confrontation with the imperialists was also favoured by the Trotskyite wing of the communist movement. In July 1946 the veteran revolutionary, Tan Malaka, led a coup against the republican government. It failed largely because the Stalinist leadership of the communist party (the PKI) assisted in Sukarno's forceful intervention. However, on the return of the PKI leader, Musso, from exile in the Soviet Union, the Stalinist communists abandoned their pacific stance and launched an unsuccessful coup against the government in September 1948 at Madiun in east Java. As a result of these internal disagreements and challenges the republic became steadily more authoritarian as power was concentrated more and more in the hands of Sukarno and his vice-president, Hatta. Both became highly reliant on the republican army to sustain them in power.

Support for the revolution was almost completely confined to Java and Sumatra, and many Indonesian groups, such as the south Moluccans who made up the colonial army, remained intensely loyal to the Dutch. The regional and ideological diversity to the revolution prevented a united front against the returning Europeans. It was not only the war-torn Dutch who were in a weak position in 1945, but also the divided republicans in Jakarta. This weakness, of which Sukarno was only too well aware, delayed the republic's confrontation with Holland.

THE RETURN OF THE DUTCH

Devastated and occupied by Germany during the Second World War, metropolitan Holland lacked resources and manpower to re-occupy the 'girdle of emeralds' as peace was declared in the Pacific. It was left to British and Australian troops during October and November 1945 to restore law and order and disarm and repatriate the 200,000 Japanese soldiers dotted around the archipelago. When the Dutch were ready to re-occupy, the British and Australians would hand over to them. Occupying the eastern islands, the Australians faced few local difficulties in their peace-keeping role. But the British were confronted in Java and Sumatra with an unexpected political problem, namely what to do about the republic and its army equipped with Japanese weaponry. At Surabaya, on Java, in November 1945 a ferocious battle ensued, in which the British commander, General Mallaby, was killed. Britain, overstretched in Asia generally, demanded political consultation between the Netherlands and the republic.

The Dutch were determined to return to Indonesia and, at this stage, Britain and the United States could not envisage any future for Indonesia without some form of Dutch presence. The Dutch badly needed to regain some prestige and influence in the world through reoccupying Indonesia. It was also believed (quite wrongly, as it turned out) that the economy of the Netherlands could never revive or flourish without the markets and raw-material sources of the archipelago. Yet, Holland's postwar vision for the Indies was not completely reactionary and backward looking for it was appreciated that to revitalize and rejuvenate their eastern empire, a place had to be found for Indonesian nationalism. During the war, the Dutch government in exile in London had re-invigorated the pre-war 'Ethical Policy' and devised a gradual, limited decolonization as a means of preserving Holland's interests in a semi-independent Indonesia. Indonesia would be ruled as a federation, in which local government and some central government would be in the hands of Indonesians. The new Indonesian Commonwealth would be united with the Netherlands, and the other Dutch territories in the Caribbean, under the Dutch crown. Once Dutch troops had arrived in Borneo and the eastern islands in the summer of 1946 a conference of co-operative nationalists and Dutch colonials met at Malino on Sulawesi, drawing up a federation consisting of four regions: Java, Sumatra, Borneo and eastern Indonesia. The Dutch believed that the Javanese and Sumatran rebels would be lured into collaboration with this new colonial order.

Indeed, co-operation between the republic and the returning Dutch seemed possible in November 1946 when, encouraged by the British, the Linggajati Agreement was drawn up. Finally signed in March 1947, this treaty delineated republican territory on Java, Sumatra and Madura within a Dutch-supervised United States of Indonesia. In truth, however, there was little meeting of minds between the republicans and the imperialists. Sukarno and Hatta were never fully committed to a loose federation, seeking instead control from Jakarta of a united republic throughout all of the former Dutch realm. The conservative Dutch politicians, military leaders and colonial officials, on the other hand, despised Sukarno and Hatta as traitors for collaborating with the Japanese. They portrayed the republicans as unrepresentative of the mass of Indonesians, who were either bamboozled by their propaganda or cajoled by their terror tactics. On the pretext that the republicans had not lived up to their side of the Linggajati Agreement by failing to maintain law and order in their zones, the Dutch launched their first 'police action' in July 1947. For, while negotiations were going ahead with the republic, the Dutch were engaged in a huge military build-up, which brought imperial forces to 140,000 men by the end of 1948. The first military offensive lasted a fortnight and produced significant territorial gains for the Netherlands. Two-thirds of Java and one-third of Sumatra were now re-occupied. The governor-general, H.J. van Mook, now set about absorbing the newly occupied territories into the Dutch-supervised federation as an alternative to the Republic which still held central Java.

However, the Dutch pacification of Java and Sumatra was increasingly threatened by the actions of the republican guerrillas. The result was a second 'police action' during December 1948 led by the new governor-general, van Beel. The idea was now to liquidate the republic and so complete Dutch-supervised decolonization with the co-operative, Malino politicians. On the surface, the second three-week offensive was a fantastic success for the colonial forces. Sukarno, Hatta and Sjahrir were taken prisoner in Yogyakarta, as the capital of the republic had been re-occupied. The republic now seemed to be collapsing under the weight not only of Dutch military action but also internal schisms with communist and Darul Islam rebellions on Java. But Holland's hard-line tactics brought a new set of political and military problems.

UNITED STATES INTERVENTION

From the end of 1947, Holland found itself bogged down in a costly guerrilla war as some 30,000 republicans went underground in the remoter parts of Sumatra and Java, from where they harassed Dutch troops and installations. The Dutch would not be the only imperial forces in South East Asia to discover that guerrilla armies were far harder to defeat than conventional combatants. The Dutch military completely underestimated the ability of the republicans to sustain an insurgency war, supported by the Indonesian populace. Through attempting to annihilate, rather than negotiate with, the republic, the Dutch got themselves into an unyielding, military trap.

To get them out of that trap required the United States. The newly formed United Nations had intervened in the crisis from the end of 1947. But it was United States pressure that fundamentally decided the issue in favour of the republic. When in September 1948, the Sukarno regime crushed a communist rebellion against it, the Americans believed that they had found in the republic precisely the kind of anti-communist movement they liked. The view in Washington was now that it was better to run with the republic than bolster the Dutch and risk another radical, pro-Moscow coup, which might succeed in toppling Sukarno. At the same time, President Truman was alarmed by the vast Dutch military commitment in Indonesia, which could be better deployed in reconstructing Western Europe and blocking Soviet expansion there. As a result, the United States threatened the Dutch with exclusion from its financial and military aid to Western Europe.

INDEPENDENCE

At the end of 1948, then, the Dutch were blackmailed into co-operating with the United Nations representatives, a process that culminated in the Round Table Conference at The Hague in August 1949. The Dutch came out of these negotiations believing that they had salvaged a Netherlands-Indonesian union and that the new United States of Indonesia, which came into being at the end of 1949, would allow for some regional autonomy from Jakarta. Yet, the state which Sukarno and Hatta constructed after independence was essentially the unitary and untrammelled republic they had fought and negotiated for. Moreover, Dutch economic interests were nationalized in the course of the 1950s.

Nevertheless, the Dutch did hang on in West New Guinea (now

Irian Jaya). The status of the territory was not dealt with by The Hague settlement and the Netherlands government steadfastly refused to give up the underdeveloped region. It would serve as an important resettlement area for Europeans and Eurasians who felt ill at ease in the new republic. When another war threatened in the late 1950s between Holland and Indonesia over Irian Jaya, the Americans again intervened on Sukarno's side and forced the Dutch to back down. Preoccupied anyway with the prosperity of European integration, the Netherlands agreed to allow the United Nations into Irian Jaya, smoothing the path for the territory's absorption into Indonesia in 1962; something the non-Malay peoples of the area have never been very comfortable with.

In the meantime, the early years of Indonesian independence had been fraught with difficulties. Sukarno never solved the cleavages between the secular-nationalist, communist and Islamic strands of the independence movement, and as a result his rule became steadily less democratic as the smooth functioning of parliamentary government was rendered virtually impossible. Political tensions were further aggravated by growing fissures between the political leaders and the armed forces. Furthermore, the centralization of government in Jakarta as the Dutch federal structure was jettisoned, heightened regional disaffection in the outer islands as Dutch rule was seen to be being replaced by Javanese imperialism. The South Moluccans resisted independent rule because of their traditional ties with the colonial army and in 1950 declared their own independent republic. Some 12,000 Moluccans also left for Holland. Dissident political leaders in the regions, often Masjumi Muslim supporters, also joined up with disaffected local military commanders to produce secessionist revolts. One such occurred in Aceh in 1953 and there was a more widespread Sumatra rebellion in 1958, which also linked up with malcontents in south Sulawesi. With the help of the dominant army faction, the regional revolts were crushed by 1962. But Sukarno, showing growing signs of megalomania, now introduced his 'Guided Democracy', in which political parties such as Masjumi and the Socialist Party were banned. The Indonesian revolution, Sukarno declared in 1959, 'had now been infected by dangerous diseases and dualisms'. In confrontations with the Netherlands and Malaysia, and in alignment with the Soviet Union and China, the isolated president grew increasingly reliant on communist support to keep him in power, a factor that came to irritate increasingly both the Indonesian military and the United States who had ironically supported Sukarno as an anti-communist back in 1949.

Vietnam: from French Union to Geneva Division

THE DEMOCRATIC REPUBLIC OF VIETNAM

Only in March 1945 was the French colonial administration in Vietnam displaced by the Japanese. This followed the Allied liberation of metropolitan France. The Japanese now installed the Nguyen emperor, Bao Dai, as puppet ruler of an independent Vietnam within their Co-prosperity Sphere. De facto Japanese rule encouraged the communist-led Vietminh to step up its political and military activities in the countryside beyond the reach of the Japanese-controlled towns and cities. Consequently, when Japan surrendered, the Vietminh led their celebrated 'August Revolution', entering the cities of Hanoi, Hue and Saigon to preside over massive rallies. With no external power to back him, Bao Dai panicked and abdicated, leaving the Vietminh to form a provisional government with Ho Chi Minh as president. On 2 September, 1945, Ho declared the independence of a new Democratic Republic of Vietnam. Adapting both American and French concepts of self-determination and liberty, Ho declared that 'Vietnam has the right to be a free and independent country'. He also ominously predicted that, 'The entire Vietnamese people are determined to mobilize all their physical and mental strength, to sacrifice their lives and property in order to safeguard their independence and liberty'. It would take 30 years of warfare, first with the French and then the United States, to safeguard that independence and liberty.

The genius of Ho's movement was its stress on mass participation. Like Mao in China, Ho seized upon the revolutionary potential of the peasantry, turning orthodox Marxism on its head. As both Mao and Ho appreciated, the industrial proletariat in Asia was minute; instead rural, village communism would herald a new egalitarian society, freed of all

The Vietnamese revolutionary nationalist leader, Ho Chi Minh

imperialist pretensions. Ho fused communism with patriotism to create a truly populist anti-colonial struggle in northern Vietnam. The poverty and economic distress of the 1930s amongst the landless labourers of the Red River delta and Annam, exacerbated by the terrible famine of 1944–45, provided the Vietminh with a fertile ground for mobilization. While other middle-class nationalists in Vietnam ignored or distrusted the masses, Ho openly drew on the strength and anger of the peasants. He drew on traditional Vietnamese patriotism too. In particular, Ho made much of Vietnam's heroic defence against external invaders in the past. Resistance to the French was fired by memories of the pre-modern struggles against the Chinese. Emperors who had resisted Chinese invasions, such as Le Loi in the fifteenth century and Quang-trung (Nguyen Hue) in the eighteenth century, were eulogized as national heroes. That many villages in northern Vietnam worshipped local deities who were symbols of patriotic defence of the fatherland greatly aided Ho's message. In this way, anti-French activities could be seen as part of a long Vietnamese tradition. Ho himself, a wizened figure, riddled with disease, also appealed to the peasantry as a quasi-religious, holy man; an almost Buddha-like figure promising a nirvana on earth.

But the Vietminh, given their international communist connections, also placed the Vietnamese struggle within a modern context, looking forward to a modernized society based on the redistribution of wealth. Through these simple messages, the mere 5,000 members of the Indochinese Communist Party were able to generate a mass following for the revolution of August 1945 and the subsequent struggles against the French and the Americans. But Ho was devious too. In trying to harness as much Vietnamese national support as possible, he deliberately downplayed the communist nature of his movement, stressing instead a nationalist movement for all classes in Vietnamese society. Ho cynically defined his socialism vaguely as merely a system in which the Vietnamese would 'have enough food to eat and enough clothes to wear in cold weather'.

The Vietminh's mass mobilization was greatly assisted by an urban intellectual and cultural renaissance, which had bubbled beneath the surface of French colonial rule since the 1900s. The growing use of a romanized Vietnamese script – far easier to learn than the old Chinese- and Japanese-style characters – created a highly literate society in the towns and cities. Protest poems, historical works, radical political pamphlets and mass underground newspapers flourished and created a literary culture that discussed new ideas and concepts, particularly the issue of national independence. This intellectual ferment drew teachers, lawyers, doctors, lower-level civil servants, and even indigenous businessmen frustrated by French monopolies, to the liberation cause. These groups needed little encouragement from the Vietminh when the Japanese collapsed and much of the August Revolution was spontaneous in the urban context.

Amongst the illiterate peasantry, however, Ho and his followers had to work harder and their technique for mobilization was known as 'armed propaganda'. In 1944–45, the Vietminh gained much kudos for their attempts to alleviate the disastrous famine of that winter by forcibly distributing hoarded rice. Ho and his comrades capitalized upon this goodwill by spreading political ideas and stepping up guerrilla activity against the Japanese and then the returning French. Armed guerrilla units clandestinely carried the political message to the villages; a technique which would be used again and again by the Vietnamese communists in their struggles with the French and later the Americans. 'Armed propaganda' hinged partly on terror. But it also required persuasion and appeals to traditional moral precepts, which legitimized violence against the colonial regimes. The pioneer of 'armed propaganda' was Ho's right-hand man, the school teacher and future military supremo, Vo Nguyen Giap. A French official later described Giap's activities in the Vietnamese countryside:

> In certain remote valleys Van [Giap] opened the path. . . He would arrive alone in a hamlet, destitute like an outlaw offering to work in the fields. In return he received his food. The days passed. First tolerated, then accepted and listened to he assured himself of some solid support. At this moment he had won the game. The village provided intelligence and supplies for the commandos, and then furnished guerrillas. The opposition remained silent or was eliminated.

As a Vietminh training manual of 1945 further explained:

> Clearly outline the long term gains if all the people are liberated and the short term gains if the revolutionary army becomes stronger every day and wins wherever it fights. . . use pamphlets, cartoons, and slogans to carry out propaganda. But the most important means is verbal communication so that the propaganda teams organize meetings and lectures and use theatrical performances and songs (with accompaniment if possible).

Yet the Vietminh was not the only organization with a mass appeal to an alienated and miserable peasantry. In southern Vietnam, two millenarian sects, the Cao Dai and the Hoa Hao, offered an alternative religious vision of the future in a Mekong delta devoid of the corrupting influence of the French. Both looked forward to the coming of 'saviours' who would lead their followers to a promised land. Moreover, more than 1 million Vietnamese Catholics would eventually flee north Vietnam to form the backbone of the southern republic after 1954. A substantial number of Indo-Chinese continued to support the French; more than 150,000 fought in the French-trained Vietnam Army against the Vietminh after 1946. The minority hill peoples of the central highlands, the Montagnards, formed anti-guerrilla units on the French side (and later on the American). The Vietminh was only part, albeit the most important part, of the post-war Vietnamese 'explosion'. Other nationalist, separatist and religious groups presented an alternative to Ho's primacy. The 'democratic' revolution begun in

August 1945 involved a wave of torture and execution of nationalists, Trotskyites, reactionaries and 'collaborators' deemed enemies of the people. On top of internal dissension, the Vietminh faced the problem of what to do about the returning French.

THE RETURN OF THE FRENCH

Immediately after the war, northern Vietnam was occupied by Nationalist Chinese troops and the south by British forces. By early 1946 available French forces in Indochina had risen to 30,000, and in March British responsibilities were surrendered to the ex-Catholic monk, Admiral Thierry d'Argenlieu as French high commissioner for Indochina based in Saigon. The French showed the same determination as the Dutch to return to their treasured South East Asian possessions. Defeated and occupied by Germany during the war, and deeply divided by the issues of collaboration and resistance to the Nazis, France was offered through resurrection of empire a chance to regain some pride and influence in a postwar world likely to be dominated by *les Anglo-Saxons*. France's 'second colonial occupation' after World War Two, just like its original scramble for colonies in the 1880s and 1890s, sprang from an uncompromising French nationalism. Across the political spectrum from communists to conservatives, the French people were agreed on the need to retain the empire.

This was not to be a return to pre-war arrangements: like the Dutch, and as we shall see the British too, the French envisaged a streamlined, rationalized empire, in which colonial peoples would be given a greater say. As part of the new French Union, the various Indo-Chinese states would be given 'associated state' status. Vietnamese would have a large hand in running their own affairs and Vietnamese politicians would be offered the opportunity of taking office in Paris in the central Assembly of the French Union. France would maintain its empire, and bolster its power in the postwar era, by developing a partnership with colonial peoples. The French believed that a deal could be struck with the Vietminh that would satisfy Ho Chi Minh with local self-government. But Ho's authority would be restricted to the northern area around Hanoi.

Remarkably, in March 1946 an agreement was struck between Ho and the French. The French retained close control of Cochin-China, but in the north the Democratic Republic of Vietnam was recognized as the legitimate ruler of an independent 'Free state having its own government, parliament, army and finances'. Crucially, however, the new state would remain *within* the French Union, meaning that France would retain control of foreign affairs, defence and economic policy. As compensation, the French consented to allow a referendum in the south to decide whether the Democratic Republic of Vietnam should comprise the whole country.

How could Ho accept this clearly limited independence and even contemplate a compromise with the colonialists? The answer lies in the military weakness of the Vietminh plus fears of perpetual Chinese domination. As Ho reasoned, it was better to do a deal with an ailing imperialist like France than become completely subservient to or absorbed into a resurgent Nationalist China. As Ho explained to his startled comrades, the deal with France was merely a tactical retreat, because 'the white man is finished in Asia. But if the Chinese stay now, they will never leave. As for me, I prefer to smell French shit for five years, rather than Chinese shit for the rest of my life'. As part of the March accords, the French were permitted to station 15,000 troops in the north for five years. These would replace the existing Chinese contingent, and to Ho's thinking, act as a guarantee of future Vietnamese independence.

French colonial figures like d'Argenlieu were never fully committed to accommodating the Vietminh in the postwar set up. Ultimately, the French wished to devolve power to a number of small Indochinese states within the overarching French-managed Union. This aim was always going to be irreconcilable with Ho's own vision of full independence for Indochina, preferably under the direction of the Indochinese Communist Party. Once the wartime Free French leader, colonial guru and architect of the French Union, General de Gaulle, had left French politics in January 1946, the conservative French officials 'on the spot' in Saigon began to lose faith with liberal and socialist governments in Paris. Horror stories concerning Ho's subservience to Moscow and international communism generally filtered back to metropolitan France. D'Argenlieu increasingly took matters into his own hands. The inevitable showdown came in November 1946 at the northern port of Haiphong when, after a dispute over arms shipments to the Vietminh, French naval bombardments killed 6,000 Vietnamese. Then on 19 December, 1946, after Vietminh forces refused to lay down their arms in Hanoi, full-scale war began as the Vietminh were driven from their capital. The country would not know peace for close to 30 years.

THE FIRST INDOCHINA WAR

From the end of 1946, the main body of Vietminh forces withdrew north to prepare base areas near the Chinese border and so fight a resistance war. Under the military command of General Giap, guerrilla units harried French forces by suddenly concentrating firepower for swift ambushes only suddenly to melt away into the jungle, aided by sympathizers amongst the peasantry. Ho Chi Minh likened this war to a struggle between a tiger and an elephant. The tiger 'will leap upon the back of the elephant, tearing huge chunks from his hide, and then he will leap back into the dark jungle. And slowly the elephant will bleed to death'. Despite holding down French forces in Tonkin, however, the first three years of the war represented a stalemate. The tide was only turned in favour of the Vietminh by the victory of Mao Zedong's communists in China by the end of 1949. Having fought their way to the Vietnamese border, Chinese communist forces now began supplying the Vietminh with weaponry. Between 1950 and 1954 the Vietminh would receive some 80,000 tons of war materiel from China (including 116,000 guns and 4,630 cannons).

As French military fortunes declined, the colonialists attempted political concessions. The colony of Cochin-China was re-united with the protectorates of Annam and Tonkin to form the unitary state, named the Republic of Vietnam. The former Japanese lackey, Bao Dai, was reluctantly recalled from the racetracks and casinos of the French Rivierra to head this new semi-independent state, covering the whole of Vietnam but *within* the French Union. Important economic and strategic privileges remained with France. Concurrently, the French touched the raw nerve of Western Cold War paranoia as they convinced the United States that the war was a crusade against international communism rather than a war of colonial restoration. From May 1950, military assistance from Washington was stepped up to France and the Indo-Chinese states. By the end of the conflict, the United States was shouldering over three-quarters of the costs of the French and their Vietnamese allies.

This assistance all proved too little, too late for the French. Bao Dai never served as a non-communist alternative to the Vietminh because, usually sporting expensive golf shoes and sunglasses, he failed to appeal to the mass of the peasantry. Most Vietnamese recognized the sham independence over which the puppet emperor presided. Meanwhile, buoyed by Chinese weapons, Giap had refined his military techniques. French garrisons near the Chinese border were overrun in the autumn of 1950 and the guerrilla units were increasingly effective. 'Parallel administrations' were set up in supposedly French-controlled villages – in reality, power was wielded secretly by the Vietminh. Most of northern Vietnam was under Vietminh control by the end of 1952. In 1954 the French commander-in-chief, General Navarre, sought to try and stop the Vietminh infiltrating Laos by building up a huge French force at the highland garrison of Dien Bien Phu. The French fortress was finally overrun on 7 May after a 55 day battle. Some 8,000 Vietnamese and 1,500 French died in this battle, which ended both the French phase of the war and the century of French rule in Indochina.

VIETNAM RE-DIVIDED

The news of the Vietminh triumph at Dien Bien Phu reached an international conference on the future of Indochina sitting at Geneva in Switzerland. The Vietminh contingent was ecstatic. But they proved to be the losers at Geneva as the big powers ignored their claims to be the rightful rulers of the whole of Vietnam. Having backed the French in their anti-communist crusade, the United States sulked and took no part in the proceedings. Instead, it was Britain, the Soviet Union and China who came to a remarkable consensus to divide the country along the seventeenth parallel into a communist-controlled North Vietnam and (what would become an American-dominated) non-communist South Vietnam. The somewhat naive strategy of Britain's foreign secretary, Anthony Eden, was that the Geneva division would bring a lasting peace to the region via a compromise between communists and non-communists. The equally naive belief of the Russians and the Chinese was that the agreement would prevent American military intervention in the region and that future elections would reunite the country under the Vietminh. China also had historical reasons to fear a powerful Vietnam on its southern frontier; the communist regime in Beijing was no different from its imperial predecessors in this respect.

Neither British nor Soviet-Chinese assumptions would prove correct. In the north, the French withdrew within a year of Dien Bien Phu. The Democratic Republic of Vietnam was now anything but democratic. The facade of a broad national front with the non-communists was ditched and after 1960 communism became the official ideology of the totalitarian state in the north. Communist control was assured through the official Vietnam Workers' Party as well as the largest army in South East Asia. In the countryside, a forced programme of land collectivization, which was frequently unpopular with smallholders, consolidated communist authority over the peasantry. The regime was further buttressed by aid from China and the Soviet Union. French economic interests were nationalized and North Vietnam's economy was firmly integrated into the communist bloc. Invested with absolute powers, Ho remained as president until his death in 1969. Even so, a personalized dictatorship was avoided as Ho kept a remarkably low profile and ruled collectively with the principal party leaders. Giap, for example, maintained control over the defence forces.

In the south, power passed into the hands of Ngo Dinh Diem and his Catholic, drug-addicted family. In deposing Bao Dai, Diem became president of the southern republic in 1955. Although violently anti-communist, Diem's regime was equally authoritarian as its northern enemy. The backbone of domestic support for the regime were the Catholics who fled the north in 1954, and the government itself was run by a clique of former 'collaborators' with the French. Yet as the French scaled down their activities, the Diem regime became reliant on United States support. The Americans took over from the French in the provision of military aid, despatching first training teams and then Special Forces units. In many ways, the French had transferred power in the south to the United States rather than to a Vietnamese successor state.

In 1956 Diem refused to hold the elections agreed to at Geneva, which would undoubtedly have led to a communist-dominated reunification. Infuriated and also alarmed by the growth of American influence, the northern leaders sanctioned a new phase of military activity in the south. In 1959 the National Front for the Liberation of South Vietnam, or Vietcong was formed. The undercover Vietcong guerrillas launched campaigns of sabotage, assassination and terror. At the same time, they established schools in the villages, redistributed land from rich to poor peasants and encouraged the non-payment of taxes to the regime in Saigon. By the end of 1962 the Vietcong claimed to control two-thirds of the southern countryside. In response to Vietcong incursions, Diem had declared a state of emergency and arrested thousands of political opponents in October 1961. He also agreed to the dispatch of American servicemen to Vietnam so that by the end of 1962 there were some 11,000 in the country.

But Diem did not quite prove the puppet of Washington that his Vietnamese opponents liked to claim. Disenchanted by the excesses and independence of Diem and his family, President John F. Kennedy connived at a plot by Vietnamese army officers to oust and kill their president in November 1963. The United States military build-up continued under the more malleable anti-communist, military-dominated regimes that succeeded Diem. The scene was being set for another Vietnam War.

Independence for Cambodia and Laos

The other constituent parts of French Indochina, Cambodia and Laos, contrasted sharply with the experience of Vietnam. The populations of the feudal monarchies were much smaller – in the 1950s about 4.5 million in Cambodia and 2 million in Laos, compared to about 20 million in North Vietnam and South Vietnam combined. Anti-colonial nationalism was hardly developed before the war and the French reoccupied the kingdoms easily after the Japanese surrender. Shoring up what Osborne describes as the 'comic opera world of royal courts, sacred elephants, ancient temples, and orange-robed monks' in both protectorates became a central element in French strategy for recovering and rejuvenating Indochina as part of the new French Union. Laos and Cambodia became constitutional kingdoms in 1947 as 'independent' members of the union. Yet, as in Vietnam, the pattern of postwar developments in both countries did not follow French plans.

LAOS: ROYALISTS AND COMMUNISTS

The Laotian elite (the royal family and semi-hereditary royal officials) were generally happy to co-operate with the returning French officials in the most populous areas around Vientiane and Luang Prabang. Pre-war networks of collaboration were restored, which made sense for the Laotians given their tiny population, their mainly village subsistence existence, plus Laos's underdeveloped transport networks and absence of international trade links. The Laotian kingdoms were officially melded together under French supervision in 1947, as the country became known as Laos for the first time, with a royal capital at Luang Prabang and an administrative capital at Vientiane. As in Cambodia, the deteriorating situation in Vietnam pushed the French into transferring power to the conservative, traditional elite in 1953. This, the French believed, would be an independent kingdom but one still heavily-reliant on French aid and influence.

The royal family and its supporters were not the only political force of consequence in the country. Under Japanese rule, an anti-French, communist-influenced group emerged under the leadership of a royal prince, Souphanouvong. When the French returned in the autumn of 1945, the radical prince and his comrades went into the jungle to link the Laotian struggle with that of Vietnam. The Pathet Lao, as Laotian communists were known, came to work closely with the Vietminh in their north eastern stronghold. Here, the Pathet Lao gained support from disaffected non-Lao hill peoples (who made up about half Laos's population) as well as Lao intellectuals, youths and workers. Consequently, Laos became crucial to the conflict in Vietnam. The Dien Bien Phu strategy was aimed at preventing Vietminh incursions into Laos. After the Geneva settlement, then, the French lost their interest in controlling Laotian events. A compromise was reached between the communists and the royalists, which anticipated integrating Pathet Lao forces into the country's army and Souphanouvong taking a role in government. Such a deal proved unworkable, however, as the royal elite had no interest in working with the communists while the Pathet Lao had no interest in accepting a subordinate role to the right-wing royals. By 1960, the country was in a state of civil war, exacerbated by the intervention of the United States who now backed a right-wing royalist faction. At the same time, Soviet military aid was directed to the Pathet Lao and its allies. After another international conference on Indochina at Geneva, an attempt was made in June 1962 to bring together the warring pro-American, communist and neutral factions into a coalition government. This deal also broke down and Souphanouvong went into exile. Elections were nevertheless held in 1965. But the next ten years would continue to be dominated by a military struggle in which Laos was divided into two halves – one controlled by the Pathet Lao and the other by the Royal Lao Government.

CAMBODIA: SIHANOUK'S TRIUMPH?

Cambodia too achieved its independence in 1953 but here communism remained an irrelevance until the 1970s. Instead, nationalism became the monopoly of the remarkable King Sihanouk. Crowned in 1941, Sihanouk was initially a reluctant politician. Yet between 1949 and 1953 he led Cambodia's 'crusade for independence' in which the Cambodian people rallied around the King. The French were forced to accept Sihanouk's leadership of Cambodian nationalism and until the 1970s the Cambodian royal remained his country's dominant political figure. But as a constitutional monarch, Sihanouk (who was a democrat and a socialist) felt he could not give the country full leadership. He resigned, therefore, in 1955 in favour of his father, Suramarit. At the subsequent general election, the ex-king's Popular Socialist Community Party swept the board and consigned the Khmer communists to the political wilderness. Sihanouk's party relied on support from the Buddhist monkhood, promoting 'Buddhist Socialism'. Similar electoral successes ensued in 1958 and 1962, and in 1960 when his father died Sihanouk took the title chief of state but did not revert to being king.

Sihanouk would prove himself a skillful diplomat, whose neutral approach in the Cold War allowed Cambodia to receive aid from both the United States and the communist bloc. Sihanouk's strategy was designed to resist Thai and Vietnamese domination of his country as in the past. Unfortunately, this policy would be undermined by the spread of a second war in Vietnam to Cambodian soil in the 1970s. At the same time, Sihanouk's triumphant monopolization of nationalism was ultimately the country's tragedy as Cambodia's communists were encouraged to take an increasingly militant, uncompromising stance.

Malaysia: From Malayan Union to Singapore Separation

THE MALAYAN UNION

The British returned to Malaya after the Japanese occupation in September 1945. In contrast to the French in Vietnam and the Dutch in Indonesia, they were not confronted by a nationalist regime. The chief resistance to the Japanese, the Chinese-dominated Malayan Communist Party (MCP), even disarmed and disbanded its guerrilla units. The main problem facing the British Military Administration (BMA) in the first few weeks of the occupation was actually fighting between Malayan communities as Chinese took revenge on Malays for wartime wrongdoings and vice versa.

It was subsequent British policies that provoked Malayan problems. During the war, officials in London and in India had drawn up a new political scheme for the peninsula called the Malayan Union. The aim was to unite the pre-war mishmash of states and settlements in Malaya under a single administration for the first time. This would revitalize the Malayan raj in a period when the dollar income from rubber and tin was absolutely vital for Britain's reconstruction. The union would also lay the basis for the development of a multi-racial Malayan citizenship as a prelude to eventual self-government within the British Commonwealth of Nations. Malaya would be led through a gradual, controlled decolonization in which Britain's sizeable economic and strategic interests would be preserved.

This was a progressive colonialism for the post-war world, which the British hoped would meet the criticisms of both American and nationalist critics of colonialism. In April 1946 when the BMA disbanded, the Malayan Union was inaugurated. The indirect rule of the pre-war era was abandoned as the sultans, fearing punishment for 'collaboration' with the Japanese, signed away their sovereignty. For the first time, the Malayan peninsula was a single colony. For the first time too, immigrant Chinese and Indians were recognized as having long-term rights of abode in Malaya.

The scheme enraged the Malay *bumiputera* ('sons of the soil'). Citizenship rights for the Chinese and the Indians and the stripping of the powers of the sultans seemed to threaten Malay political dominance. The result was the formation of the Malay political party that still dominates politics in contemporary Malaysia, the United Malays National Organization (UMNO). Its aim was to overturn the Malayan Union, restore the powers of the sultans in their states, and re-assert Malay special privileges. The UMNO's leader was the Johor aristocrat, Dato Onn, who toured the country making a number of impassioned speeches, which united the Malays of the different states for the very first time. The British, completely unintentionally, had provided the Malay intelligentsia with a cause to create a mass Malay nationalism.

Fearing a loss of control and the possibility of a link with radical republican Malays in Indonesia, the British panicked and compromised with UMNO and the sultans. A series of conferences eventually produced a new political arrangement called the Federation of Malaya in February 1948. Far less centralized than the Malayan Union, the federation returned the states to protected status under the sovereignty of the sultans. This federal structure would serve as the basis of the nation-state of 1957 and would be expanded to include Sarawak and Sabah in the Malaysia that emerged between 1963 and 1965.

THE EMERGENCY

The Federation solved the problem of Malay disaffection. Yet, the new constitution only served to create another alienated sector of the population in the form of those Chinese affiliated to the MCP. This tension resulted in the twelve-year shooting war between the government and the communist guerrillas that began in June 1948. Ironically British saboteurs had worked with the MCP-dominated Malayan Peoples' Anti-Japanese Army (MPAJA) during the war, supplying them with weapons and engaging in joint operations with the mainly Chinese guerrillas. Known as the *bintang tiga* (after the three stars on their berets), the MPAJA had gained great kudos amongst the Malayan populace as the principal resistors to the Japanese. The guerrilla leaders were subsequently decorated in the victory parades and expected some form of political role in the new Malaya.

But the British never saw the MCP as possible political partners, fearing their radicalism and Chinese dominance in an MCP Malaya. Yet, the MCP could not be ignored because (amongst the Chinese lower classes, at least) they were a popular force. Through a combination of terror and genuine support, the guerrillas had created a mass support network amongst the Chinese 'squatters' who had escaped from the Japanese in the towns to settle on the jungle fringes during the occupation. These communities would provide the Min Yuen, or 'Masses Organization', which, in replication of the Vietminh's 'armed propaganda' strategy, supplied guerrilla units with food, funds, information and recruits. As well as a large sympathetic population beyond British control in the jungle, the MCP enjoyed control over the Chinese and Indian labourers on the plantations and mines of western Malaya. Continuing where it had left off before the war, the MCP organized labourers into trade unions. In a period of labour shortages after the war, the communists had the potential to disrupt the reconstruction of the Malayan economy. A wave of strikes, often violent and demanding higher wages, threatened the whole position of British capital in the peninsula.

The MCP did rely on terror to mobilize labour. A favourite tactic was to nail strike breakers to trees. But the cadres were able to draw on a number of genuine Malayan grievances in the difficult reconstruction period. In the first place, the turmoil following the defeat of Japan created space for the growth of communist-dominated unions. In the wake of Sino-Malay violence, the communist unions offered a measure of security in an uncertain world. Moreover, once the British had restored order, they exacerbated economic difficulties as the BMA became known as the 'Black Market Association'. Clothing was in such short supply that rubber tyres were worn. There was not enough food either as pre-war rice supplies from Burma, Vietnam and Thailand proved difficult to restore. Smuggling and the black market thrived, with rice prices reaching 20 times their normal level. In a situation of chronic inflation, real wages declined rapidly. The British official response was to resist wage increases in an effort to curb inflation. Moreover, while the Treasury in London desperately wanted Malaya's dollar earnings, it would not allocate more consumer goods. And, as the British managers started returning to their plantations and mines, the Chinese squatters were ejected, often violently. Vast numbers of the immigrant population felt alienated and marginalized, providing a receptive environment for radical doctrines. Radical groups were springing up amongst the normally quiescent rural Malays too. The Malay Nationalist Party of 1945 was more left-wing than the UMNO, leaning as it did towards communism and Indonesian republicanism.

The Federation – representing a return to the alliance of the British colonialists and the Malay traditional aristocracy – was the final kick in the teeth for the MCP and its radical affiliates. By 1948, the MCP leadership had also become less compromising. Back in August and September 1945, the guerrillas were in a potentially strong position, being still armed and in control of many Malayan towns. They failed, however, to take advantage of British weakness because the MCP's leader at the time, Lai Tek, was a triple agent. During the war, Lai Tek had worked for the Japanese and led a number of MCP leaders to their deaths at the hands of Japanese soldiers at the Batu Caves outside Kuala Lumpur. At the same time, of course, he was co-operating with the British officers of Force 136. After the war, Lai Tek resumed working for the British as 'Mr. Wright' and so encouraged his comrades to lay down their arms and co-operate with the returning colonials. In early 1947, the rest of the MCP politburo finally woke up to Lai Tek's treachery and he absconded with a large slice of the party's funds. The new secretary-general, Chin Peng, was totally independent of the British. The policy of co-operating, or at least not openly opposing the British, was discarded. Preparations for the 'armed struggle' were made, based upon the secret stashes of wartime weapons that had not been surrendered at the end of the occupation.

The first shots in the uprising were not co-ordinated by the central party. Rather, on 16 June 1948, three British planters were murdered in Perak by an MCP unit acting without orders. The British reaction, however, was swift: on 18 June a state of Emergency was declared for the whole of Malaya, beginning Britain's most protracted and intensive war of decolonization. Although its origins were chaotic and unplanned, the MCP had a clear plan of campaign during the Emergency: to bring the Malayan economy to its knees, forcing the British to quit. The guerrillas sought to halt rubber and tin production by hit-and-run raids on plantations and mines; killing key personnel, slashing rubber trees, and damaging valuable capital equipment. Ultimately, 'liberated areas' were to be created by winning and retaining control of tracts of country freed of all 'capitalist imperialist' influence. The main areas of primary production in Malaya were surrounded by primary jungle and were particularly vulnerable to attack. As a result, the European planters and miners were forced to carry arms and travel around in armoured vehicles. About one in ten of the European planting community would lose their lives during the Emergency years. The harrowing experiences of one ex-planter during the Emergency (such as narrowly avoiding an MCP ambush) still cause him to sleep unsoundly to this day.

The early years of the Emergency did not go very well for the British. Casualties reached their peak in 1950 as the MCP guerrillas proved tough nuts to crack. The assassination of the British high commissioner, Sir Henry Gurney, as his car made its way to the weekend retreat of Fraser's Hill in October 1951, was a real low point for both European and Asian morale. According to one planter, the colonial government was 'like a sailing ship in a calm sea'.

The turning point in the campaign came in February 1952 when the new Conservative government in London appointed General Templer as the new civil and military supremo. Templer's 'no-nonsense' military approach was illustrated in the town of Tanjong Malim two months after his arrival in Malaya. After the murder of 12 men by communists, the general imposed a 24 hour curfew and reduced the rice ration until information was volunteered concerning the perpetrators. In Britain, there were howls of protests in the media and in parliament concerning such illiberal methods, but, as Templer later confessed, 'this didn't worry me very much'. Alongside the stick, however, Templer also relied on the carrot to defeat insurgency. In this, he was fortunate for the Korean War after the summer of 1950 produced a massive demand for Malaya's rubber and tin. The boosted revenues from the four-fold increase in commodity prices swelled government coffers and permitted an expansion of the police and military. More public money also allowed for a great expansion in the programme of forced re-settlement, which re-located Chinese 'squatters' from the terrorist-infested jungle fringes to supervised 'new villages', cutting off the guerrillas from the Min Yuen and the food, intelligence and money they supplied. As life became more and more miserable in the jungle, increasing numbers of guerrillas were encouraged to surrender and inform on their former comrades. Greater funds were available too for social and economic development, for investment in hospitals, piped water, sewerage, schools, and roads. In contrast to the Dutch in Indonesia and the French in Vietnam, this 'hearts and minds' approach – the idea that counterinsurgency relies on winning the population over to the government side – is often seen as the reason why the British succeeded in Malaya, and British counter-insurgency experts would go on to advise the Americans in Vietnam after 1964.

The colonial regime's victory also relied upon the failings of the MCP. The party never parted from its orientation towards China and its reputation as a party of the Malayan Chinese. Malays did occupy senior positions in the MCP, but this was mere window-dressing, as generally the communists failed to cross communal boundaries. The Malays mostly remained loyal to their sultans and the Islamic faith. As a result, the Malayan guerrillas were never able to mobilize the masses to rival the success of their counterparts in Vietnam, and it was the traditionalist, anti-communist UMNO politicians who became the nationalist heroes and heroines of the Malay villages. Moreover, despite British propaganda campaigns, which portrayed the MCP as the agents of Moscow and Beijing, the Malayan guerrillas received virtually no financial or military support from either China or the Soviet Union. In contrast, war material from China was vital in the Vietminh's victory over the French.

A combination of British counter-insurgency success and MCP failing, then, ensured that the tide of the Emergency was turned in favour of the colonial regime by 1954. From then on it was really just a question of 'mopping up' the few remaining bandits. Nevertheless, the Emergency regulations were only finally lifted in 1960 (three years after independence for Malaya), and only in December 1989 was a truce reached between the Malaysian government and the remaining guerrilla bands exiled in southern Thailand.

INDEPENDENCE FOR MALAYA

As part of the 'hearts and minds' strategy of winning the Emergency, the British also chose to accelerate political change, the aim being to show average Malayans that independence could be achieved without the communists and without violence. The problem for the British, however, was how to forge a united nation from the communally divided Malaya they had helped create from the late nineteenth century. Traditional jealousies between the Chinese and the Malays were a great advantage in preventing the spread of communism. In the approach to independence, however, communism became a thorn in Britain's side as the federal secretariat attempted to 'unite and quit'. The solution, the British believed, was to nurture a truly multi-racial, anti-communist nationalist movement. Before the arrival of Templer, Dato Onn had been encouraged in 1951 to resign the presidency of his exclusively Malay party, UMNO, and form the Independence of Malaya Party, which aimed to represent all of Malaya's communities.

Like Bao Dai in French Indochina though, Onn never really commanded much popular support. He had the reputation of being a British stooge but, more importantly, multi-culturalism was simply not popular with Malayans. An alternative, anti-communist nationalist movement sprang up as an alliance of communal parties. Onn's political destruction was sealed by the actions of UMNO and the pro-business Malayan Chinese Association, who co-operated during the Kuala Lumpur municipal elections of February 1952. UMNO and the MCA essentially came to a bargain whereby Malay political dominance was recognized in return for the retention of Chinese economic power. The 'special position of the Malays' would later be enshrined in the Malayan constitution. The Alliance, led by UMNO's new president and scion of the Kedah royal house, Tunku Abdul Rahman. It later came to include the Malayan Indian Congress (MIC). It is the UMNO-MCA-MIC alliance, with UMNO very much the dominant partner, which presides over government in Kuala Lumpur today.

In the summer of 1955, the Alliance completely trounced Onn, winning 51 of the 52 seats in the elections for internal self-government. British officials now shared power with Alliance ministers in the Malayan cabinet. The British had failed to foster a united multi-racial nationalist party as their successor, but the Alliance proved itself an excellent partner to transfer power to. Although the Tunku had the reputation of being a 'playboy prince', more interested in the racetrack than government, he proved himself a shrewd and highly capable politician. At the Baling talks of December 1955, the Tunku, now chief minister, insisted on the MCP's unconditional surrender as a prelude to ending the Emergency. The guerrilla leader, Chin Peng, could not possibly agree. But this apparent failure gave the Tunku even greater anti-communist savvy in British eyes. In return for assurances that British financial and commercial interests would be upheld in the new successor state, a date of 31 August, 1957, was set for independence.

Tunku Abdul Rahman, the aristocratic Prime Minister of Malaya/Malaysia between 1957 and 1970

The independent federation joined the Commonwealth and the Anglo-Malayan Defence Agreement locked Malaya into the Western camp in the Cold War.

MALAYSIA AND SINGAPORE

For Britain, however, the colonial epoch was not yet over. There remained the problem of what to do with its remaining South East Asian possessions, Singapore, Sabah (North Borneo) and Sarawak, which had been ruled as separate crown colonies since 1946. Going back to the Second World War, the British held a long-term aim of federating Malaya with the rest of British South East Asia to form a self-governing dominion along the lines of Canada or Australia. By 1959, Singapore had achieved internal self-government under the leadership of the People's Action Party of Cambridge-educated lawyer and Chinese leader, Lee Kuan Yew. By the early 1960s, Lee had purged his party of suspected communists and Singapore was settling down to political stability after years of labour unrest. But the big fear for the British, who still retained a huge naval base and vast commercial assets on the island, was that divorced from Malaya, Singapore would not be viable and would simply become a satellite of communist China. The latter nightmare scenario seemed probable given Singapore's majority Chinese population and political unrest during 1961, when Lee's government looked like falling to left-wing extremists. Sabah and Sarawak, meanwhile, might fall foul of Indonesian aggrandizement. The British were greatly relieved in 1961 when the Tunku announced his support for Malaysia – the merger of Singapore, Sabah and Sarawak with Malaya. In 1963, Singapore, Sabah and Sarawak all achieved independence from Britain, but only as new states within the Federation of Malaysia (this despite strong evidence that the peoples of Borneo were far from enthusiastic about the prospects of Malay rule from Kuala Lumpur).

The early years of Malaysia were hardly plain sailing. Brunei thwarted Britain's and Malaya's plans by not joining the federation. Sultan Omar was not prepared to share the oil riches or sovereignty of his small state with his Malay cousins. Instead, Brunei remained a British protected state until 1984. Brunei's last-minute snub was

Lee Kuan Yew, leader of Singapore between 1959 and 1991

followed by Singapore's expulsion from Malaysia by the central government in Kuala Lumpur in 1965 to become a separate independent republic (as it remains to this day). Lee Kuan Yew and the Tunku were genuinely committed to Singapore staying in the federation. Lee famously shed tears on television when he announced the island's expulsion. But UMNO politicians around the Tunku (described by Lee as 'mad Malay mullahs') feared Singapore's Chinese population. Lee's powerbase amongst the Chinese of Singapore might be extended to the urban Chinese of Malaysia as a whole who now outnumbered the Malays. Moreover, Lee's movement, although moderate and constitutional, professed socialism and non-communalism. Both doctrines were feared by the conservative Malays because they might upset the established political dominance of the traditional Malay elite. Meanwhile, Lee was not prepared to see the Malay political and social privileges of the federation extended to his political domain. Nor was the Singapore political and commercial elite best pleased about the taxes and revenues demanded by Kuala Lumpur to fund development in the poorer areas of Malaysia. When bloody Sino–Malay clashes broke out in Singapore in July 1964, the only sensible way to avoid prolonged racial conflict seemed a separation of island and mainland.

Ethnically diverse Sabah and Sarawak did remain part of Malaysia.

Their position was contested by President Sukarno of Indonesia as a 'neo-colonial plot'. British troops fought alongside their Malaysian counterparts in the limited and undeclared war known as Confrontation that began in 1963. By 1964, the Americans too had come to see Malaysia as a handy block to the spread of communism in the region and suspended aid to Jakarta. The United States subsequently connived with the military coup that overthrew Sukarno and brought an end to Confrontation. When the government of Harold Wilson in London announced in January 1968 the withdrawal of British forces by 1971 from Malaysia and Singapore, Washington was distraught. Britain's residual 'East of Suez' presence was much prized by the Americans, because by the mid-1960s Washington had inherited from the French the war against the North Vietnamese communists.

Thailand Remains Independent

THE POST-WAR SETTLEMENT

Thailand managed to avoid colonization in the nineteenth century. Nevertheless, it had fallen under the influence of Britain and the years after 1945 continued the process of decolonization from Albion's circle and the emergence of a new Thai-US partnership in the Cold War. As punishment for Thailand's 'treachery' during the Second World War (i.e., its alliance with Japan and occupation of the northern Malay states) Winston Churchill suggested that southern Thailand might be formally appended to the British empire. This idea came to nothing, but in the post-war settlement the British wished the Thais to 'work their passage home'. Demands were made for rice requisitions without payment and disbanding of the Thai armed forces. Jealous of Britain's economic dominance in Thailand and its political influence with the liberal government of wartime resistance leader, Pridi Phanomyong, the United States intervened and British demands were tempered. Nevertheless, there was mounting concern amongst Thais, particularly in the military, that Thailand was being pushed around by the Allies and that this meant that the monarchy was being insulted. Combined with fears about the 'communist' sympathies of Pridi's government (as well as the large Chinese community), nationalist sentiments would pave the way for the return of wartime dictator, Marshal Phibun.

THE RETURN OF PHIBUN

Various political machinations, including the death of King Ananda in mysterious circumstances in June 1946, culminated in a right-wing coup of 8 November, 1947. Pridi was ousted and Phibun returned to power, first as supreme commander of the armed forces and three months later as prime minister. The former Japanese collaborator was back. Both the British and the Americans were now prepared to accept their former enemy because of his excellent anti-communist credentials. With the outbreak of communist insurrections in Vietnam and Malaya, Phibun's Thailand was described by one British Foreign Office official as 'an anti-Communist oasis in the middle of S. E. Asia'. Yet, given Britain's financial and military impotence, it was the United States that succeeded to the status of Thailand's principal ally. From 1950 American economic, military and technical aid was directed to Phibun, and Thai students and military officers started to receive education and training in the United States. In return, Thailand participated on the Western Side in the Korean War. In 1954 Thailand was brought into anti-communist defence and security planning as a member of the South East Asia Treaty Organization (SEATO), which the United States supported. Provision for American military bases would soon follow. As the United States ambassador in Bangkok reported back to Washington in January 1953, 'Thailand has in effect assumed some of the characteristics of a protégé... That relationship is a definite asset to the United States for it is really remarkable that this small country surrounded by turmoil and exposed to communist aggression should so openly side with us'. The United States did pressurize Phibun to liberalize his regime, however. In 1957 press bans were lifted and political parties were legalized in the prelude to a general election. Phibun just scraped a victory, but this had been achieved through massive corruption that alienated Phibun's former supporters in the military.

THE SARIT YEARS

A bloodless coup of 1957 brought to power Field Marshal Sarit Thanarat, previously a military commander in Bangkok. Sarit announced fresh elections, but parliamentary government was swiftly abandoned and military rule was re-imposed in October 1958. Nevertheless the United States quickly came to admire the new military dictator as he banned strikes, dissolved trade unions and clamped down on the Communist Party of Thailand, while offering favourable tax and land concessions to multinational firms. Bangkok became the centre of many American organizations in South East Asia.

Sarit differed from Phibun, however, in that he was concerned to revive or preserve Thai culture in the face of growing United States influence. He advocated a return to the values of the Thai kings of the nineteenth and early twentieth centuries. The need, according to Sarit, was for the Thai political system to have 'deep roots in Thai soil', growing traditional Thai fruits: 'bananas, mangoes, rambutans, mangosteens, and durians; and not apples, grapes, dates, plums or horse chestnuts'. Sarit was keen to preserve the hierarchical links between government and the people in a system of despotic paternalism; government should be for the people but not by the people. As a traditionalist, Sarit was also concerned to protect the throne and religions. Phibun had previously sidelined the king and concentrated power in his own hands. Sarit, in contrast, brought King Bhumipol into the limelight again as an important source of legitimacy to the military-dominated regime. At the same time, traditional Buddhist ceremonies, particularly processions associated with the monarchy, were once again encouraged. Sarit died in 1963, by which time economic and social tensions within Thai society were showing; stresses that would come to challenge the military conceptions of Thai traditionalism in the 1970s.

CHAPTER SEVEN

Independent South East Asia, 1965 to the Present Day

By the mid-1960s South East Asia's states were once again being run by South East Asians. But the independence epoch has not proved a bed of roses. Given South East Asia's key strategic location astride the Pacific and Indian oceans, the end of the European empires gave way to the region's full entanglement in the Cold War. The most tragic consequences were felt during the wars in Indochina, and by 1975 the region was divided along the so-called 'Bamboo Curtain'. Vietnam, Laos and Cambodia were on the communist side of the curtain while Thailand, Malaysia, Singapore, Brunei and Indonesia were in the capitalist camp. Yet, Cold War divisions aside, almost all the states of the region were united by their authoritarian political systems. One of the ironies of decolonization was to create the strongest states that have ever existed in South East Asia, and regimes where rulers exercise greater power over the ruled than ever before.

The postcolonial period has also seen more rapid and drastic economic and social change than any other era. While many of the communist economies stagnated, the capitalist states went through a tremendous commercial boom from the late 1960s. That economic miracle was brought to an equally miraculous halt, however, during the Asian financial crisis of 1997. Another paradox of political independence has been South East Asia's *increased* dependence on the global economy.

Another Vietnam War

AMERICA'S WAR

The second phase of the Vietnam War in the decade after 1965 was in many senses a Vietnamese civil war between the military-dominated governments of the south and the communist regime in the north. Yet, the involvement of the United States in the struggle came to obscure the Vietnamese nature of the war, transforming it into a very Hot War within the much larger Cold War. Uncle Sam and Uncle Ho had once been friends, as US secret servicemen had supported the Vietminh in its guerrilla war against the Japanese, and in September 1945 Ho Chi Minh based parts of Vietnam's declaration of independence on the famous American version. But the international political environment had changed drastically by the 1960s. Ho's communism now made the Vietnamese leader 'enemy number one'. In an attempt to prevent the South East Asian dominoes falling to international communism, the American military build-up continued after the assassination of President Kennedy in November 1963. Kennedy's successor, Lyndon Johnson, agreed to begin a devastating series of carpet-bombing campaigns in the north from 1965. In the following eight years, United States aeroplanes dropped five times the tonnage of bombs on Vietnam, Laos and Cambodia that fell in all of the Second World War. American combat troops made their presence felt too in South Vietnam through the 'search-and-destroy' and 'selective terrorism' missions designed to flush out communist guerrillas and sympathizers in the countryside. The forced-resettlement programme – as in 1950s Malaya, intended to cut off the terrorists from food and information sources amongst the civilian population – was administered by the American military also. There were the infamous defoliation, or napalm-bombing, programmes as well, which attempted to deprive the Vietcong and the North Vietnamese Army (NVA) of jungle cover. By 1967, over half a million United States troops were deployed in Vietnam, and between 1964 and 1968 alone over 200,000 Americans were killed or wounded. In addition, numerous US servicemen went missing and in 2001 Washington was still spending $20 million a year on recovery operations.

Communist guerillas in Vietnam

The GI experience of the war has become part and parcel of postwar American national mythology through countless films and books. Vietnam was a particularly gruesome war because of the nature of both terrain and enemy. As in the French phase of the war, the communists generally chose to avoid conventional, set-piece confrontations. Instead, the Vietcong and NVA continued the tactics of the Vietminh, suddenly emerging from the jungle and hills to engage in hit-and-run ambushes that relied on surprise and fear. Understandably, such warfare was terrifying for the American conscripts. Worse still, the underground guerrilla networks amongst the civilian population made it virtually impossible to tell friend from foe. As a result, in the 'search-and-destroy' swoops on Vietnamese villages, six civilians were killed for every known communist.

Back home, the sight of waves of GIs returning in wheelchairs or body bags, produced a disenchanted American public. It was difficult for many Americans, university and high-school students especially, to reconcile their country's historic commitment to liberty and freedom with the daily news footage of a peasant society being blown to smithereens by the full military might of an industrial superpower. Antiwar rallies in New York in 1967 attracted up to half a million demonstrators. Disillusion spread further after North Vietnam's surprise

Tet ('New Year') offensive in 1968. Tet was a huge all-out military push engineered by North Vietnam's military supremo, General Giap. For the first time, Vietcong and NVA forces targetted South Vietnam's urban centres, millions of television viewers in the United States watched in disbelief as communist guerrillas went so far as to penetrate the American Embassy in Saigon. For North Vietnam, Tet failed in its immediate objective of dislodging the Americans and overthrowing the military regime in Saigon, and it cost some 40,000 Vietcong lives. Giap was discredited; the north would not risk a total offensive again and returned to its older strategy of 'people's war'. Yet, the intensification of antiwar protests in America, intense media criticism, plus the draining of conscript morale, all culminated in the first peace talks between Hanoi and Washington, held at the end of 1968. News of the My Lai village killing spree (a shocking incident in the aftermath of Tet, in which a platoon from Charlie Company massacred some 500 allegedly pro-Vietcong peasants, including old men, women, children and babies) leaked out in November 1969 and further added to the war's popular image as a brutal, amoral affair. The mother of one GI commented that, 'I gave them a good boy, and they made him a murderer'.

The disillusion after Tet persuaded Johnson not to stand for re-election and in 1969 he was replaced as president by Richard Nixon. Despite his conservative, Cold Warrior credentials and the unleashing of another all-out bombing campaign in the north as well as in Laos and Cambodia, Nixon was committed to ending American participation in an increasingly unpopular and costly war. American Cold War strategy now shifted towards prizing open the split between Russia and China. As such, a remarkable rapprochement between Beijing and Washington was reached in 1971, and the following year Nixon visited China. Beijing now put pressure on the North Vietnamese to withdraw from the south. Characteristically defiant, the latter refused and continued the struggle for reunification. The Americans wished to get out of Vietnam at almost any price. In Paris, therefore, in January 1973 agreement was reached to withdraw all United States personnel, bar a few key advisers, even though North Vietnam was allowed to keep troops south of the seventeenth parallel.

THE WEAK SOUTH

It was not only an American military failure that accounted for the eventual victory of the North Vietnamese communists. Certainly, the United States is to blame for alienating so many Vietnamese through the killing of innocent civilians during bombings and 'search-and-destroy' missions. There were also the forced peasant exoduses to the towns, which followed napalm attacks and the destruction of food crops. But the real failure was in the unpopularity of the military regimes in Saigon. The Vietnamese generals who ran the government in the south had first cut their teeth on the French side during the war of 1946–54. Divorced and distanced from average Vietnamese in the villages, the generals could not win Vietnamese 'hearts and minds'. Moreover, the government of General Nguyen Van Thieu, in power for most of the 1965–75 period, was monumentally corrupt. Supporters amongst the Catholic Church became alienated and Thieu failed also to woo Buddhist leaders or the Cao Dai and Hoa Hao sects as counters to communism. Buddhists were generally disgusted by the lack of popular democracy in the south as well as the excessive pandering to the United States, and it was quite common for monks symbolically to burn themselves to death in protest at the regime. The most famous self-immolation was that of a 55-year-old nun, Thanh Quang, in May 1966 in Hue.

In contrast, the Vietcong had a firmer base of support amongst the South Vietnamese peasantry. Like the 'parallel administrations' of the French era, the National Liberation Front was able to infiltrate the villages and clandestinely portray itself as the protector of the peasants against the tax and labour demands of the regime in Saigon. The generals were frequently compared with the 'robber barons' of medieval and early modern Vietnam. As in the North before 1954, the Vietcong also promised the redistribution of land from rich to poor. Here was something the right-wing generals, drawn from the South Vietnamese land-holding class, just could not contemplate.

THE RESILIENT NORTH

The American withdrawal after 1973 also reflected the tenacity of both government and populace in the north. Like the French before them, the United States and their allies in Saigon consistently underestimated the capacity of the Vietnamese people to 'sacrifice their lives and property in order to safeguard their independence and liberty' (as Ho Chi Minh had predicted back in 1945). There was a tremendous wartime patriotism not only in the armed forces but also in the villages and numerous state-sponsored organizations. The more the Americans threw at the north, the more that patriotism grew. Vietnamese numbers grew as well: through conscription, Hanoi could rely on some 200,000 teenagers to fill the ranks each year. These boy- (and girl-) soldiers were despatched south along the 'Ho Chi Minh Trail', the network of secret mountain paths that ran through eastern Laos and Cambodia, which acted as a supply chain between north and south. The combined strength of Vietcong and NVA forces in the south was probably in excess of half a million by 1968. Indigenous patriotism and numbers were backed up by support from the communist bloc. China, before the Sino-American rapprochement of the early 1970s, supplied guns and ammunition filtered south along the Ho Chi Minh Trail. The Russians provided their high-tech MIG jet fighters to make United States penetration of North Vietnamese airspace increasingly difficult.

REUNIFICATION

The peace agreement of 1973 did nothing to curtail North Vietnam. Rather, military activities were stepped up and more and more territory fell under communist control. Although still supplying military and economic aid to the south, Washington only threatened retaliation. Saigon finally fell in April 1975 after the Thieu government resigned. In the final melee, some 2,000 Americans and Vietnamese caught the legendary 'last chopper out of Saigon' from the roof of the United States Embassy.

The swiftness of this collapse took the north by surprise. It was only in November 1975 that a Political Consultative Conference in Ho Chi Minh City (as Saigon was renamed) discussed plans for reunification. Elections were duly held and a new National Assembly met in June 1976. The reunified Socialist Republic of Vietnam was declared on 12 July. Ho Chi Minh had died in 1969 and thus had not seen the end of the war. But what occurred after 1976 was essentially the imposition of

Ho's northern communist system on the whole of the country. The new setup was far from democratic but did continue to abide by the founding father's principles of 'collective leadership' within the politburo. A collective presidency was enshrined in the new constitution of December 1980, and the State Council replaced the presidency as the supreme decision-making body. In July 1981, the veteran Truong Chinh became chairman of the State Council, confirming the dominance of the political system by the northern old guard. Vietnam was also confirmed as a one-party state; a Russian-style dictatorship of the proletariat under the communist party.

The promotion of socialist ideology and culture, and the transformation of the economy from private to state ownership was now spearheaded as part of the five-year plan of 1976-80. The result was to create as many losers as winners in a southern society that had been dominated by capitalist economic development since the 1860s. It was the urban merchant class, mainly ethnic Chinese, who felt the pinch as their properties and businesses were confiscated. These skilled entrepreneurs escaped the country in droves as 'boat people'. Those who made it to Malaysia or Hong Kong would eventually carve out successful lives in Europe and North America. But thousands more drowned, starved to death, or were murdered by pirates on the jampacked junks that ventured into the savage South China Sea. Within Vietnam, however, the intolerance of capitalism and capitalists continued and was reinforced by the country's heavy reliance on Russia and Eastern Europe for economic and military aid. Incorporation into the Soviet bloc was complete after the 'thousand-year conflict' with China again flared up into full-scale warfare for nine days in March 1979. This followed Vietnam's occupation of Cambodia.

By the mid-1980s, economic decay, consequent upon the huge costs of reconstruction from the war with the United States and the invasion of Cambodia, loss of the dynamic boat people, international isolation, and criticisms from more democratically inclined southern communists forced a re-think. At the end of 1986, the Vietnamese Communist Party endorsed a new strategy called *doi moi* (renovation). This entailed a degree of political openness *within* the communist party, a new economic strategy, which tolerated the free market, and a foreign policy that looked to greater links with the capitalist world. The pragmatism in overseas affairs culminated in the visit of Bill Clinton at the end of 2000. Clinton was the first United States president to step on to the soil of a reunited Vietnam, and everywhere he went, he was mobbed by enthusiastic crowds. However, this has not meant the birth of Western-style, multi-party democracy. Public disenchantment with communism – born of land disputes, widespread corruption amongst party officials and unresponsive government, and manifested in protests by the hill peoples of the central highlands – led to calls for 'grass-roots democracy' at the Ninth Congress of the communist party in April 2001. This was probably little more than tinkering, however, to contain dissent. For, in line with China, Vietnamese leaders continue to stress that economic liberalism, some political reform and the end of international isolation will not mean the surrender of communist control of the state.

Cambodia: Genocide and After

COMMUNISM CAMBODIAN-STYLE

The Vietnam War – in many senses the Indochina War – also left a deep scar on the contemporary history of Laos and Cambodia. Although unable to compete on the formal political stage with Prince Sihanouk after Cambodia's independence in 1953, the Cambodian communists were given increasing support by the Vietminh. Against Sihanouk's monopolization of nationalism, the communists chose an increasingly radical propeasant line. They found significant support amongst those in the villages who were alienated by Sihanouk's intolerance of opposition, heavy tax demands, and support for the Buddhist hierarchy. The Cambodian Communist Party, or Khmer Rouge, was further strengthened by the appointment of Pol Pot (then known as Saloth Sar), a French-educated school teacher, as party secretary in 1962. Pol Pot was deeply influenced by a combination of French marxism and the Chinese peasant communism of Mao Zedong. It was his aim to create a totally new society, emancipated from both the feudalism of the Cambodian monarchs and the capitalism offered by the United States. But, as well as being violently anticapitalist and antitraditional, the Khmer Rouge came also to develop an excessive xenophobic nationalism to counter Sihanouk's claim to be the embodiment of the nation. An armed struggle was launched in 1967 and Pol Pot's forces encouraged peasant revolts in their strongholds in the north west. These were put down brutally by Sihanouk's regime. The Khmer Rouge leaders were forced into hiding. At this stage, Cambodian communism remained a weak and divided entity.

LON NOL AND AMERICAN INTERVENTION

The coup that toppled Sihanouk in March 1970, while the prince was away on one of his many overseas junkets, was actually right-wing, capitalist and backed by the United States. Although Sihanouk had tried to balance American and Soviet influence in his country, the prince fell out with Washington from the early 1960s. He also turned a blind eye to the Vietnamese communists' use of Cambodian territory as part of the Ho Chi Minh Trail. Sihanouk finally eschewed American aid in 1963 on the grounds that, 'We prefer to live in poverty, because at least we will be free'. In the 'reds-under-the-bed' paranoid atmosphere of 1960s Washington, such declarations of independence appeared evidence that Sihanouk had indeed gone 'commie'.

From March 1969 the Americans converted the Vietnam War into an Indochina War when they began a covert bombing campaign in Cambodia to destroy the supply routes between North Vietnam and the Vietcong. The pro-United States prime minister, General Lon Nol then toppled Sihanouk. As the North Vietnamese stepped up their support for the Khmer Rouge in its war against the Phnom Penh regime, Lon Nol appealed to the Americans and the South Vietnamese for military assistance. This finally arrived in the form of an invasion of 30,000 troops. The Cambodian phase of the Vietnam War brought the Nixon government only increased criticism at home. Moreover, it completely failed to knock out Vietnamese sanctuaries inside Cambodia. American intervention also proved Lon Nol's Achilles Heel because it encouraged Sihanouk and the Khmer Rouge to join forces against him. For several months in 1973 the Americans carried out heavy bombing of the guerrilla positions to help their ally in Phnom

Penh. Yet this only served further to increase the popularity of Pol Pot's movement. In the tragedy that followed, the Americans have to accept a large share of the blame.

THE KILLING FIELDS

By early 1975, despite the bombings and the massive aid programme from the United States to Lon Nol, the Khmer Rouge controlled most of the countryside. In April the boy-soldiers of the Khmer Rouge, with their characteristic black suits and red headbands, pounced on the cities and proclaimed a revolutionary government in Phnom Penh. Prince Sihanouk was forced into exile. Pol Pot now sought to eradicate all vestiges of the old Cambodia. Private property was nationalized, Buddhist institutions were banned, the use of money was abolished, and the Cambodian people were required to live in communes. Education was downgraded and Western medicine rejected. In an Orwellian nightmare, 1975 became 'Year Zero' and Pol Pot was now referred to as 'Brother Number One'. Phnom Penh was described as a 'wasteful and consuming city' and its 2 million inhabitants were force-marched into the countryside.

There was a degree of method to Pol Pot's madness: five years of war had left Phnom Penh unable to feed itself. But the brutal intolerance of certain sections of Cambodian society led to a completely illogical reign of terror and murder. The constitution of the new Democratic Republic of Kampuchea was one only for 'workers, peasants and labourers'. In attempting to forge a rural peasant utopia, the ruling and professional classes of the cities were castigated as collaborators with Western imperialism. Members of Sihanouk's family, doctors, teachers and engineers were executed, tortured or exiled. Bourgeois undesirables were infamously identified through the 'hand-test' portrayed in David Puttnam's film, *The Killing Fields* (1984) – smooth hands being an indication of a pampered, non-manual and 'decadent' urban life. Peasants who resisted collectivization were also killed as were many deemed ideologically suspect within the communist party itself. All told, the Khmer Rouge was responsible for about one million Cambodian deaths between 1975 and 1979. Half were executed, the rest died of starvation and illness. Another half a million fled. Additionally,

Exhumed skulls, Cambodia – a vile legacy of the Pol Pot period

the Khmer Rouge's xenophobia culminated in the expulsion of 200,000 Vietnamese from the country as well as a genocide against the Muslim Chams and other ethnic minorities. Isolationism was another expression of this intolerant creed – only with Communist China was the regime on good terms.

THE DOWNFALL OF THE KHMER ROUGE

As news of Pol Pot's excesses reached the outside world, it was easy for 'moderate' Cambodian communists to persuade their Vietnamese comrades to lend assistance in ousting the Khmer Rouge. The Vietnamese gave support to the Kampuchean United Front for National Salvation, led by Heng Samrin and Hun Sen, who had defected from the Khmer Rouge in 1977. During January 1979 Vietnamese-led forces captured Phnom Penh and established a People's Republic of Kampuchea with Heng Samrin as president and Hun Sen (aged just 27) as prime minister. This pro-Hanoi government would rule Cambodia for the next ten years, and Hun Sen (a lover of cigarettes and dark glasses) remains today as the country's most important political figure. Heng Samrin's and Hun Sen's regime was considerably less harsh than its predecessor: it tolerated Buddhism and modified the extreme peasant communism of Pol Pot. But, in emulating the political set-up in Vietnam, and heavily reliant anyway on the continued presence of Vietnamese troops and advisers, there was no room for noncommunist Cambodians in the new government. Instantly this exclusion alienated the anti-Sihanouk and anticommunist Khmer People's National Liberation Front led by a former prime minister, Son Sann. A guerrilla coalition formed against the new government in Phnom Penh, composed of unlikely bedfellows: Son Sann's movement, the remnants of the Khmer Rouge, and Sihanouk's monarchists.

THE UNITED NATIONS SETTLEMENT

Heng Samrin's regime was tolerated by the international community as the lesser of two evils. But, from 1979, the UN refused to recognize the pro-Vietnamese government and tried to promote the coalition of opposition groups as the legitimate government-in-exile. In June 1982, a political coalition finally emerged in Thailand with Prince Sihanouk as president, the Khmer Rouge leader, Khieu Samphan, as deputy president, and Son Sann as prime minister. Given its superior military capacity, the Khmer Rouge remained the main player.

Increasing economic difficulties within Vietnam forced a withdrawal of Hanoi's forces during 1989, and, deprived of military backing, Hun Sen was pushed into negotiation with the opposition. Even so, attempts to reach a peace agreement floundered on the issue of power-sharing between Hun Sen and Sihanouk. But with the ending of the Cold War, an agreement was finally reached in 1991, which looked forward to eventual elections. A United Nations force was despatched to Cambodia, which included the first contingent of Japanese troops in South East Asia since the Pacific War, to oversee the elections in 1993. 'Founding father' Sihanouk was re-installed as king (a position he had last held in 1955). The king's son, Prince Ranariddh led the Funcinpec Party to victory in the polls. But this was far from the end of Hun Sen: Ranariddh was forced to accept a coalition government with Hun Sen's Cambodian People's Party, who controlled the army and the police. Increasingly frustrated with having to share power with the monarchists, Hun Sen forced his senior princely partner into exile after a coup in July 1997. The international community negotiated Ranariddh's return and a new set of elections twelve months later. But the grip of the Cambodian People's Party over the police and army assured Hun Sen's continued dominance as his party won just over half of the seats in the National Assembly. Ranariddh was forced into an agreement in December 1998, which left Hun Sen firmly in control of a coalition government through the allocation of key ministries to his party. Hun Sen, who dropped out of school in 1970 to become a teenage guerrilla fighter, has now settled down to a life of playing golf and opening schools, medical centres and orphanages. At the time of writing, the prime minister maintains an iron grip over the machinery of state and increasingly projects himself as the new father of the nation to replace the ailing King Sihanouk.

THE RETURN OF STABILITY

Throughout all the political chicanery in Phnom Penh, the Khmer Rouge continued their struggle from Cambodia's northern-most reaches. Yet, today, the Cambodian people face the possibility of long-deserved, long-term stability. For, at the end of 1998, the last remnants of the Khmer Rouge laid down their guns, literally limped out of the jungle and accepted the authority of the government in Phnom Penh. Khmer Rouge leaders had long been unhappy about Pol Pot's continued advocacy of open warfare. As more and more of the grass-roots membership defected, the one-legged military commander, Ta Mok, overthrew and arrested Pol Pot in July 1997. Fearing that Ta Mok would hand him over to an international tribunal on crimes against humanity, Pol Pot committed suicide in April 1998. As his wife put it,

Cambodian refugees

'Brother Number One' had died of a broken heart. The Khmer Rouge's 30-year struggle was over. Notwithstanding massive corruption within the army, police and administration, the economy is beginning to recover and tourists are flooding back. But Cambodia faces huge costs of reconstruction. There are the psychological scars of the Khmer Rouge terror, and Ta Mok and his cronies are yet to be tried for war crimes. But the most obvious hangover is the landmines, which still pepper the countryside. Some 9 million were laid by all combatants in the 30 years of warfare. The result was that more than 35,000 Cambodians lost limbs, giving the country the highest per capita rate of amputees in the world – about one in 250 of the population.

Communist Laos

THE END OF THE CIVIL WAR

Like Cambodia, Laos could not avoid being sucked into the struggle for Vietnam. The country was also subject to a tremendous American airborne bombardment after 1965 because the northern stretches of the Ho Chi Minh Trail passed through Laos. After 1973 though, the scaling down of United States involvement in South East Asia provided an opportunity for the communist Pathet Lao forces to gain the upper hand in its war with the Royal Lao Government. After the fall of Saigon in 1975, the Pathet Lao seized power in Vientiane. The US-supported, ex-prime minister, Prince Souvanna Phouma was retained as an adviser to the government. But King Sisavang Vatthana abdicated at the end of 1975 when the Lao People's Democratic Republic was proclaimed, and the new regime became dominated by leaders of the Pathet Lao.

ISOLATION AND IMPOVERISHMENT

Hopes of peace and moderate reform in Laos were swiftly shown to be illusory as the authorities began a programme of collectivization and 're-education'. Royal language was abolished, royal statues demolished and King Sisavang Vatthana was banished to a labour camp and did not return. Although there was talk of 'Buddhist socialism', the government restricted the operations of the monkhood given its former links to the monarchy. In the 1980s, the pace of collectivization was slowed and foreign aid was sought from outside the communist bloc, notably from Scandinavia, for the building of hydroelectric dams. Trade and investment links were also fostered with neighbouring Thailand. Yet the communists remained firmly in control through the monopolization of political power by the Lao People's Revolutionary Party (the political incarnation of the Pathet Lao). In elections in December 1997, only one of four approved noncommunist party members won a seat in the National Assembly, the 98 other seats were won by the Lao People's Revolutionary Party. Communism is buoyed up by Laos's particularly close relationship with Vietnam, and, as such, Laos remains isolated and one of the poorest countries in the world.

Economic liberalization has brought some benefits to the Lao Loum, the Tai-speaking Buddhists of the lowlands who make up about 50 to 60 percent of the population. But the animist non-Lao hill peoples, such as the northern Hmongs, continue to be impoverished and politically marginalized. The insurgency raging in the northern hills, at the time of writing, is a clear manifestation of this. There have also been signs of dissension within the ruling party. And, from Thailand, Prince Soulivong Savang – whom, at the age seventeen, fled across the Mekong River on a bamboo raft in 1982 – leads an international campaign to restore democracy to Laos under a constitutional monarchy. Desperate to earn foreign exchange from tourism, the communist government in Vientiane has recently permitted the revival of the old Buddhist festivals. Inadvertently, this has led to a new wave of Laotian enthusiasm for the mystical cults surrounding the royals. Teenagers in the old royal capital, Luang Prabang, wear amulets devoted to Prince Phetsarath to ward off malevolent spirits. Half-deity, half-royal, Phetsarath is celebrated for his ability to fly away and transform himself into an animal during Laos's struggle for independence with the French. Even so, as the *Far Eastern Economic Review* concluded in August 2000, 'after twenty-five years of heavy-handed rule, including restrictions on freedom of association, prospects for the emergence of a homegrown alternative to the ruling party still seem distant'.

Military Rule and Quasi-Democracy in Thailand

THE TEMPORARY END OF MILITARY RULE

Throughout the Indochina War, Thailand managed to stay on the capitalist side of the Bamboo Curtain. One reason for this was the continued political authority of the Thai military: strong-man Sarit was succeeded as prime minister by Field Marshal Thanom Kittikachorn in 1963. Even so, opposition to military rule was mounting. High rents, landlessness and indebtedness in the Thai countryside, particularly in the neglected north east, increased the appeal of the Communist Party of Thailand. There was disaffection amongst university students too, whose numbers had rocketed in the towns and cities with the expansion of higher education provision in the 1960s. Full-blown antimilitary demonstrations overtook Bangkok during October 1973, protesting about rice shortages, mounting corruption, inflation, and the lack of democracy. After over a quarter of a century on the throne, King Bhumipol abandoned his previously neutral stance, intervening in Thai politics for the first time by ordering Thanom and his leading supporters into exile.

THREE YEARS OF OPEN POLITICS

For three years after October 1973, Thailand embarked upon a bold experiment in democracy – something the country had never fully experienced before. The draft constitution of 1974 aimed to restrict the political power of the military and the civil service. A realignment in Thai foreign policy also seemed likely as the new governments distanced themselves from the United States and ordered an American military pull-out. But, against the backdrop of increasingly aggressive communist mobilization in the countryside and strikes in Bangkok, Thai politics soon descended into traditional patterns of conservatism. The coalition governments of the 1973–76 period were mainly led by Prince Seni Pramoj. Although antimilitary and a prominent Free Thai leader during the war with Japan, Seni was a conservative, elite figure, whose governments were too weak to deal with Thailand's domestic problems. The king now became disillusioned with the bickerings of the politicians that he saw as dividing the nation. The feeling of insecurity was intensified by the communist victories in Vietnam, Laos and Cambodia. By 1976, Bhumipol had come to favour the military again. Rightist groups – supported by the army and big business – clashed with students in October of that year. In the name of restoring law and order, and so protecting the king, military units overthrew Seni's last government.

SEMI-DEMOCRACY IN THE 1980s

The Thai military was back in power but it could not simply turn the clock back to the 1950s. The chattering and business classes of Bangkok no longer regarded the military as the legitimate rulers of the country, and with rising political tensions, the army itself deposed the ultra-conservative general, Thanin Kravichien in 1977. What happened after 1978 was a kind of compact between the political parties and the military-bureaucratic complex. A new constitution represented a fusion of old and new trends in Thai politics. Prominent generals would still be directly appointed prime and cabinet ministers by the king and without links to any political party. But the generals were expected to rule in concert with the House of Representatives, the Lower House of which was now popularly elected. An element of democracy, as well as economic growth, was seen by the military as an antidote to communism. The figure who came to embody this more populist approach was General Prem Tinsulanonda, who was prime minister during the 1980–88 period. Although dissolving parliament on two occasions, Prem generally ruled constitutionally by deftly balancing the interests of the armed forces, the political parties and the monarchy.

DEMOCRACY AFTER 1988

Even so, pressure mounted from the educated urban middle classes, students and intellectuals to introduce a truly democratic regime. Prem bowed to the inevitable in 1988 when he refused another term as unelected prime minister. Chatichai Choonhavan became Thailand's first elected prime minister. Within two years though the military were back, fermenting a coup in the name of the people to cleanse Thai democracy, which had once again become infected with ineptitude and peculation. But when the generals showed no sign of restoring popular sovereignty, massive demonstrations engulfed Thailand's cities. The students and middle classes were concerned that the demise of democratic government would lead to economic stagnation: not least because Washington suspended millions of dollars of economic and military aid. 'Down with the nonelected prime minister! Down with the illegitimate regime!' were the slogans of the huge crowds that bravely and defiantly marched in Bangkok.

Again, the role of King Bhumipol was crucial in avoiding large-scale bloodshed; he appointed an interim prime minister with responsibility to organize new elections. The crisis was resolved and democratic government returned in May 1992. A new constitution, which operated from the beginning of the new millenium, was designed to cement democracy further by reducing military dominance of the Senate. However, in the wake of the financial disaster of 1997, Thai constitutional politics took a farcical turn. In January 2001, the flamboyant policeman-turned-telecoms billionaire, Thaksin Shinawatra, famous for swanning around Bangkok in a bronze Porsche, was elected prime minister. His newly-formed Thai Rak Thai (Thais Love Thais) party won a landslide victory on the back of the leader's personality cult, bolstered by promises of remarkably generous grants to the villages and tax cuts. Shinawatra's proposed solution for Thailand's national debt problem was particularly bizarre: acting on a tale from an elderly monk, parties of officials, soldiers and labourers were despatched in a frenzied search for a stash of gold bars and bonds, allegedly dating from the Japanese alliance with Thailand during World War Two. The legendary treasure trove is yet to be found. Worse still, at the time of writing, Shinawatra faces losing office if a corruption indictment against him is upheld by the constitutional court. It still remains to be seen, therefore, if future Thai politicians can rule efficiently and with integrity so as not to alienate King Bhumipol and provide him with reasons to invite the military to reimpose authoritarian rule.

Malaysia's Quasi-Democracy

THE FALL OF THE TUNKU

By the late-1960s, cracks were appearing in Malaysia's multiracial society. The intercommunal tolerance of the Malay prime minister, Tunku Abdul Rahman – evidenced by his circle of non-Malay friends and his adoption of two Chinese children – was called into question by more militant members of the ruling Malay party, the UMNO. The wealth of the Chinese community was increasingly resented by Malays and, outside of the ruling coalition, the Pan-Islamic Party, PAS, was gaining more support as an alternative protector of Malay rights. PAS sought an Islamic state where nationality would be open to Malays only. On the other side of the racial divide, opposition to the 'special position of the Malays' was led by the urban- and Chinese-dominated Democratic Action Party (DAP). For the younger Chinese, the Malaysian Chinese Association, part of the ruling alliance since the 1950s, was seen as a poor defender of Chinese interests. Elections in 1969 produced another alliance government but big gains were made by both PAS and the DAP. A DAP 'victory' parade through the streets of Kuala Lumpur culminated in a spate of horrific killings and lootings as Chinese and Malay groups clashed on 13 May 1969. The Tunku was discredited and stood down in favour of his deputy, Abdul Razak, in 1970. Malaysia now entered into a period of far less liberal and less tolerant politics.

THE CONSOLIDATION OF MALAY POWER IN THE 1970s

The shattering events of 1969 produced a drastic change of course in Malaysian political and economic life. Parliamentary democracy was temporarily suspended, and discussion of emotive subjects like the special position of the Malays and the role of the sultans was banned. Various national thinktanks were established to assess what had gone wrong. The riots were supposed to have originated from an imbalance in the racial distribution of wealth. Chinese and Indians essentially had too much; the Malays too little. The country's heavy reliance on foreign enterprise, largely ex-colonial British, was also questioned. The result was the formulation of a New Economic Policy (NEP) to try and raise the position of disadvantaged groups in the economy; the official aim being to restructure 'Malaysian society to correct economic imbalance, so as to reduce and eventually eliminate the identification of race with economic function'. This meant a set of 'affirmative action' policies: the Malays and other indigenous groups (such as the Dayaks of Sarawak) were now collectively known as the *bumiputera* ('princes of the soil') and were to be favoured in economic activities promoted by the state.

The era of statist capitalism began. Vast, lumbering public enterprises (such as PERNAS, the National Corporation) were formed to engage in business ventures with the intention of eventually relinquishing control to Malay private investors. Not only were local Chinese businesses being pushed aside, but the NEP also entailed the takeover of a number of the British trading and investment giants during the late 1970s and early 1980s. Foreign enterprises were encouraged (particularly Japanese manufacturers) but joint ventures were now required to reserve at least 30 percent of their shareholdings to Malaysian state enterprises to be held in trust for the *bumiputera*. NEP, then, was a levelling process; a massive project in social engineering, which aimed specifically at creating a Malay commercial middle class.

And, as the governments of Abdul Razak (1970–76) and Hussein Onn (1976–81) became more aggressively pro-Malay, Islamization was necessarily sponsored. This also aimed at undercutting the appeal of the Islamic fundamentalists in PAS. Muslim holidays, Islamic values in education, and missionary movements amongst the animist peoples of the peninsula and Borneo, were all promoted by the UMNO-dominated government. There was also official coordination of the hajj, the annual pilgrimage to Mecca. At the same time, it became increasingly difficult for non-Malays to gain jobs in the civil service, army and police or places at Malaysian universities. Fearing a 'Malay Malaysia', many frustrated Chinese left the country during the 1970s.

MAHATHIRISM

The new Malay assertiveness was embodied in Dr Mahathir Mohamad, Malaysia's outspoken prime minister since 1981. At the time of writing, he is Asia's longest serving elected premier. Under Mahathir, the power of UMNO within the ruling National Front (Barisan) has continued to grow at the expense of the other coalition partners, the Chinese and Indian parties and the major regional parties in Sarawak and Sabah. Malaysia has held elections at regular intervals but has become steadily less-democratic with a dubious human-rights record. This was not always the case under Mahathir: in his first six years in power, Mahathir presided over a relatively liberal era in which criticism of government policies was tolerated in the national media and detainees from the previous regimes were released. But during 1987, the Internal Security Act (ISA; originally intended to suppress communism) was deployed to arrest and detain over 100 politicians and dissidents. The government also closed down three newspapers on the grounds that they were provoking interracial tension. Since 1987, the ISA has been used several times to silence Mahathir's rivals and opponents.

Yet, although hardly democratic in the Western sense, 'Mahathirism' has a populist touch. The son of a commoner, Mahathir is the first nonaristocratic, and nongolfing, Malaysian prime minister. Indeed, as a populist upstart, Mahathir was sacked from UMNO by Tunku Abdul Rahman following the 1969 riots, and his book, *The Malay Dilemma*, was banned for its criticisms of the Tunku's administration. Mahathir attacked the feudal nature of Malay society and once in power eroded the political powers of the Malay sultans, from whose ranks the king and head of state, the Yang di-pertuan Agong, is chosen. The independence of the 'feudal' states has also been dented: a state such as Kelantan, which has been run by PAS-led governments, has been denied federal assistance. The political impartiality of the judiciary and the police can no longer be guaranteed.

Opposition parties do still function in Mahathir's Malaysia. PAS and DAP were joined by a break-away UMNO group, Semangat '46, led by Tunku Razaleigh, a former finance minister, in an alliance to fight the 1990 elections. There are also regional groups, which seek greater autonomy from Kuala Lumpur, such as the Christian Kadazan Party in Sabah. Before his death in 1990, the wheelchair-bound Tunku Abdul Rahman delivered some thundering criticisms of Mahathir in the pages of the Penang-based daily, *The Star*. There has also been growing interest amongst professionals and intelligentsia in environmental groups. But opposition often comes to very little. The PAS-DAP-Razaleigh alliance of 1990 had a very divided programme and was easily defeated by the ruling Barisan. After the elections, the opposition parties once again went their own separate ways, and Razaleigh rejoined UMNO. Despite new working and middle classes, consequent upon economic development, and the fact that the country has no tradition of oppressive military rule (as in Thailand or Indonesia), Malaysia still remains far from Western-style liberal democracy. To Mahathir's thinking, the excesses of Western liberalism have produced drug addiction, single mothers, AIDS and incest throughout Europe and North America. Instead, Mahathir argues that Malaysians should be guided by 'Asian values', which protect the rights of communities rather than the rights of individuals. For Mahathir, economic growth and prosperity can be delivered without democracy. Certainly, Mahathir's economic successes before 1997 underpinned Barisan authority. The prime minister has been careful not to appear too extreme. His 'all-things-to-all-people' approach has involved a more aggressive 'Malayness' and support for Islam but not to the degree that the Barisan has completely alienated Chinese and Indian support.

The tremendous personal authority wielded by Mahathir, particularly over the police and the judiciary, has been confirmed by recent events. The financial crisis of 1997 appeared to deliver a crushing blow to the prime minister's much-publicized 'Vision 2020' – his policy to transform Malaysia into a fully industrialized country by the second decade of the twenty-first century. Now into his seventies, there was talk that Mahathir should step down in favour of his protégé and deputy, Anwar Ibrahim. So fearful was Mahathir of an Anwar challenge, that he fired the deputy prime minister and then arrested him on charges of sodomy and corruption. After drawn out trials in 1999 and 2000 Anwar was jailed for a total of 15 years. Public demonstrations in favour of Anwar – most embarrassingly as Britain's Queen Elizabeth II was attending the Commonwealth Games in Kuala Lumpur during September 1998 – led on to the founding of a broad reform movement and a new political party, Keadilan (Justice), led by Anwar's wife, Dr. Wan Azizah.

But what the reform movement entailed was unclear. Anwar did write a book in 1997 entitled, *The Asian Renaissance*, which called for some political and economic change. But Anwar really only stepped up the volume and intensity of his criticism once he was fired and arrested. What precipitated the clash between Mahathir and Anwar was Mahathir's attempt to bypass Anwar's position as finance minister by appointing the Malay business leader and political fixer, Daim Zainuddin, to head a new national economic committee. The Mahathir-Anwar contest was a power struggle rather than an ideological contest for greater civil rights and economic reform.

Mahathir still commands the loyalty of all the component parties in the ruling coalition and remains wildly popular with average Malaysians. Moreover, many ethnic Chinese and Indians in Malaysia do not trust Anwar, who is seen as an Islamic extremist, given his past as a leader of Muslim youth groups. This was brought home in the elections of November 1999 when the Barisan and Mahathir were returned with a two-thirds majority in parliament. PAS made gains in the northern Malay heartlands, adding oil-rich Terengganu to Kelantan as states under its control, and Wan Azizah won her husband's old seat. Some 70 percent of university students were said to be antigovernment. But, generally, the opposition could not match the funding, media and business support or the electoral knowhow of Mahathir's Barisan. Moreover, the urban Chinese rallied around Mahathir, fearing a repeat of the May 1969 bloodshed if the PAS-DAP-Keadilan opposition triumphed. In the wake of the election, Mahathir once more ruthlessly deployed the Internal Security Act to silence his critics. No doubt, this action would have earned Mahathir sneaking admiration across the Johor Straits in Singapore.

Singapore: the Authoritarian City-State

KARATE-CHOP GOVERNANCE

Like Malaysia, Singapore has held regular elections but can hardly be described as democratic. Since independence in 1963 and separation from Malaysia in 1965, Singapore has been dominated by one man and one party, Lee Kuan Yew and his People's Action Party (PAP). In this, radical socialist and communist Singaporeans have been confined to the margins by the English-educated 'moderates'. Swiftly, cleanly and effectively (like a karate chop) 'subversives' and 'dissidents' have been arrested under the provisions of the Internal Security Act (as in Malaysia, a hangover from British colonial rule). As late as 1987, there were 22 people still detained on the grounds that they were involved in a Marxist conspiracy within the Catholic church to overthrow the ruling regime and institute a communist state.

The result has been the virtual monopolization of politics by the PAP. From the 1970s, PAP governments extended their control over other bodies, which otherwise might have formed a basis of opposition. The trade unions – a source of left-wing support in the turbulent 1950s and early 1960s – were de-politicized through the PAP-controlled National Trade Union Congress, which stressed collaboration rather than confrontation with government and the major employers. In a similar way, the civil service has become part of the ruling structure. Many public servants go on to become PAP politicians. This is true of the armed forces also, where a successful career can lead to political or bureaucratic office. Lee Kuan Yew's son, Lee Hsien Loong, is a case in point. He is currently deputy prime minister, having previously risen to the rank of brigadier-general in the army. In this way, the military has been allowed a major role in the political structure but, in contrast to Thailand or Indonesia, not a dominant one. Even the huge public housing programme is used as a means of political control. By the early 1980s, more than three-quarters of Singapore's population had been provided with new suburban flats as the slums of the old colonial city were cleared. But both building and refurbishment programmes have often been linked to the political loyalties of particular constituencies. In other words, housing provision and other social benefits might be downgraded in wards not supporting the PAP.

By the 1970s Singapore's leaders, like Malaysia's, were justifying their authoritarian rule in terms of 'Asian values'. They spoke of how modernization and national survival in the tiny island republic, perched precariously between unpredictable Malaysia and Indonesia, would be sacrificed under Western-style democracy. Opposition and too much free speech were unsuitable, indeed potentially damaging, to Asian societies. Aged 68, Lee stepped down as prime minister in 1991 in favour of his protégé, Goh Chok Tong (the career of Lee's son having been temporarily curtailed by cancer). Goh emphasized that the 'second-generation' leadership of Singapore should have a more 'human face' and work towards a 'kinder, gentler society', and there were greater attempts in the 1990s at consultation with average Singaporeans through Citizens' and Residents' Committees. But Goh and his colleagues continue to emphasize the vulnerability of Singapore and the need to manage society and political participation. Singapore's leaders still regard people-power as something to be avoided. As one politician has declared, 'People, even with education, tend to be irrational'. Anyway, as a senior minister, the founding father's imprint is still firmly felt on Singapore. As Lee declared in 1988, 'even from my sick bed, even if you are going to lower me into the grave and I feel that something is going wrong, I'll get up'. And it is likely that the Lee dynasty will continue, as Hsien Loong is tipped to succeed Goh as prime minister.

Despite an ever-expanding middle class there has been limited political participation in Singapore. One reason for this is that the PAP government has legitimized its rule through the economic prosperity it has delivered. The Lee government proved adept at delivering economic growth and prosperity. From 1966 it adopted a strategy of export-orientated industrialization to compensate for the scaling down of British military facilities. This was followed in the 1970s by the promotion of Singapore as South East Asia's financial centre, with the development of a modern international banking sector and a world-renowned stock exchange. Today, average income in Singapore is on a par with most Western societies, and in South East Asia is only second to Brunei.

'A FINE CITY'

PAP political dominance also owes much to the high degree of social control, which has accompanied Lee Kuan Yew's rule. Compulsory military service, firmly-controlled media and education systems are all designed to create a strong sense of citizenship, discipline and conformity. Heavy-handed state intervention is epitomized by the draconian penalties imposed for littering, spitting, chewing gum, dirtying public toilets, wasting water, and (for men) long hair-cuts. It is a common local joke, to quip that Singapore is indeed 'a fine city'. The overall result is an incredibly clean and safe city-state, but one which many visitors claim lacks 'soul' and Singaporeans seem to find it difficult to relax and have fun.

Moreover, not all is rosy in the Singaporean garden. The PAP claims to be noncommunal but given that 85 percent of the population are ethnically Chinese, and that most political leaders are drawn from the majority community, other races feel discriminated against. In the reverse of Malaysia, the Malays believe they are second-class citizens vis-à-vis the Chinese. This is exhibited by national housing policies, which have favoured Chinese over Malays in the allocation of scarce apartments.

The Survival of the Brunei Sultanate

In common with Singapore, Brunei's tiny population of a quarter of a million have been soothed by affluence. Brunei lost its British resident in 1959 and became a British-protected state. Having chosen not to join Malaysia, this arrangement lasted until 1984. The Islamic sultanate was not completely autocratic: a new constitution in 1959 provided for a Legislative Council, and this assembly came to be controlled by the radical Party Ra'ayat (literally, 'People's Party'). The experiment in democracy was abandoned after 1962, however, when AM Azahari of the Party Ra'ayat led a revolt against the sultan's autocracy and in favour of full parliamentary democracy within a Brunei-dominated, independent federation of Borneo. The aim here was to re-create Brunei's sixteenth-century glory and its dominance of Borneo island. With the help of British Gurkha troops from Singapore, this popular but hopelessly organized uprising was easily suppressed, the council was abolished, and the control of state finances passed back to the sultan.

Sultan Omar abdicated in favour of his 21-year-old son, Bolkiah, in 1967 but continued to pull the strings from behind the throne. Authoritarian rule was confirmed in Brunei's 1971 treaty with Britain, leaving the sultan in control of all internal matters, while allowing Britain responsibility for foreign affairs and defence. Embarrassed by their last outpost of colonialism in South East Asia, the British government wished to see Brunei federated with Malaysia. But the sultans stuck staunchly to their alliance with Britain – despite criticism from other South East Asian countries – because it provided protection against an unpredictable Indonesia as well as domestic political opponents. But mounting pressure from the UN forced independence upon Brunei in 1984. A defence agreement with Britain, however, permitted the continued stationing of a Gurkha battalion paid for by the sultan, and oil extraction remained in the hands of the giant Anglo-Dutch multinational, Shell. After 1984 political power continued to be the exclusive preserve of the ruler and his family. Sultan Bolkiah took the posts of prime minister, minister for home affairs and minister of finance, while his father was minister of defence, and other royal brothers also held ministerial posts. When his father died in 1986, Bolkiah inherited his post as minister of defence. Indeed, the Brunei armed forces are in essence the sultan's private army. In May 1985 the Brunei National Democratic Party was allowed to register but oil-induced wealth has proved a formidable anesthetic to democracy. This is in stark contrast to Brunei's giant neighbour, Indonesia.

The Rise and Fall of Military Rule in Indonesia

THE FALL OF SUKARNO

The year 1965 is a convenient marker in Indonesia's history: it began a period of military rule which lasted over thirty years. President Sukarno was becoming steadily less democratic anyway following the adoption of 'Guided Democracy' after 1959. In the last years of his increasingly deranged rule, Sukarno balanced on a tightrope between the two props to his power – the military and the communists. Yet Sukarno leaned to the left a little too much. Concessions to communism – such as the redistribution of land in rural Java and the organization of huge demonstrations against 'Western imperialism' – began increasingly to alienate the conservative military. There were fears amongst Muslims too of a communist takeover. When six generals were assassinated in an abortive coup in October 1965, the top brass concluded that Sukarno's hobnobbing with the PKI must end. Indonesia's economy was now going down the proverbial pan. The economy had never recovered from the wars against the Dutch, but the difficulties were compounded by Sukarno's mismanagement and extravagance. Discrimination against the Chinese and expropriation of Dutch investments removed badly needed entrepreneurial expertise. Increases in military spending further exaggerated the collapse of trade and production and resulted in hyperinflation. As a consequence, the average Indonesian became poorer between 1957 and 1965 and food consumption declined, culminating in a dreadful famine on the island of Lombok. Cessation of American aid, as a consequence of Sukarno's campaign against Malaysia, created further difficulties and tied Indonesia even more tightly to Moscow's and Beijing's apron strings.

General Suharto, head of the military's strategic reserve, emerged as the main opposition leader to Sukarno. Although the hero of the independence struggle continued as president until 1967, he was powerless from March 1966. The PKI was banned as the military took control of the state apparatus and allowed the massacre of suspected communists as part of a Muslim *jihad* in Java and Bali; this also involved a pogrom against the Chinese community. All told, probably 1 million died, and in some parts of Java the country lanes literally ran red with blood.

THE NEW ORDER

Suharto was officially made president in 1968 as head of the New Order. This was Sukarno's 'Guided Democracy', but *without* the communists. Military authority was consolidated as army officers were encouraged to take an overtly political role. Suharto himself combined the top military and political positions; until 1973 he remained minister of defence and security as well as commander of the armed forces. Military officers, meanwhile, were given appointments in the judiciary, the civil service, and even in state businesses such as the oil conglomerate, Pertamina.

Party politics was largely circumvented and controlled under the one-group/two-party system devised by Suharto in the early 1970s. The group was the government-run Golkar, established as a means of directing political energies into military-approved channels to unite the nation. It was essentially the army's political party. Golkar sections were formed amongst civil servants, the armed forces, intellectuals, women, youths, workers, peasants, veterans and even the drivers of pedicabs (three-wheeled bicycle taxis). Although not technically a political party, Golkar was extremely successful at mobilizing votes in general elections. In 1971, when the first general election since 1955 was held, Golkar won about two-thirds of the available seats. The only two parties allowed to operate officially were the Muslim United Development Party and the PDI (the Indonesian Democratic Party). But, lacking the resources or official support of Golkar, the parties were always at a disadvantage in elections. Parliament was downgraded anyway as the People's Consultative Congress (MPR) took on the role of an official talking shop. The political parties were also depoliticized by the requirement after 1987 that all political, social and religious organizations should conform to the state ideology of Pancasila (Five Principles), the five principles being: Faith in God, Humanity, Nationalism, Representative Government and Social Justice. Into the 1980s, Suharto's regime proved very successful at co-opting and absorbing potential opposition, for example, through moves to conciliate Islamic interests by the formation of the Muslim Intellectuals' Association as another prop to the regime.

Despite the obvious lack of democracy, Indonesia's jettisoning of Chinese and Russian influences under Suharto restored it to the Western fold. Once again American aid poured in, followed by massive investments from Japanese multinationals. Inflation was brought under control and food production increased. Economic growth, as well as state repression, would underpin the political stability of the 1970s and 1980s.

THE FALL OF SUHARTO

Nevertheless by the 1990s, the PDI emerged as a focus of discontent with the New Order. From 1993 the party was headed by Sukarno's daughter, Megawati Sukarnoputri, despite the government's clear disapproval. Economic growth under Suharto produced a new middle class, which became increasingly disenchanted with the corruption and monopolies of the Suharto clan as well as the lack of political democracy. Despite government intimidation, thousands of politically aware Indonesians descended on the PDI's 1993 congress to elect Megawati as their saviour. The student movement was also increasingly vocal as were the labour organizations, representing the growing industrial working class, frustrated at low wages, poor housing conditions and lack of trade union rights. In addition, mounting regional nationalisms in Aceh, Irian Jaya and East Timor challenged the Suharto regime in Jakarta. But against the repressive power of the Suharto family, backed up by the military, these opposition groups could achieve little.

But then came the student demonstrations of 1997 and 1998 that accompanied the inflation, food shortages and unemployment, which were themselves a consequence of the collapse of Indonesia's currency. Suharto was now persuaded to step down by the military in favour of BJ Habibie. An eccentric former cabinet minister and head of the Muslim Intellectuals' Association, Habibie took a more liberal stance on human rights and introduced more freedom of expression. More importantly, he promised elections for the MPR, which would then choose a president. The taint of the Suharto connection and continued corruption scandals made Habibie unpopular, students could not abide him. It was almost inevitable, therefore, that Megawati's PDI would win the most votes in the general elections of June 1999. But, although wildly popular with the middle classes of Java and Bali, Megawati's secularism came to alienate even moderate Muslims. Controlling little over 30 percent of seats in the MPR, Megawati could not command a majority to become president. Instead, with the army remaining remarkably neutral, a Muslim-Golkar coalition emerged in the MPR during October 1999 to elect Abdurrahman Wahid as Indonesia's new president. Wahid was representative of a dynamic new generation of Islamic revivalists, which sprang up in the 1970s. Although Megawati was later compensated with the position of vice-president, some of her supporters were distraught and there were student demonstrations in Jakarta against the new presidential arrangements. But the result was broadly welcomed by the army, the technocrats and rural Indonesians. Even non-Muslims were satisfied because Wahid had a reputation for moderation and promoting cooperation between all of Indonesia's religious groups.

The tasks facing the new president in post-Suharto Indonesia were always going to be immense. The restoration of law and order in outlying trouble spots proved intractable. Ethnic antagonisms have reached boiling point as a consequence of the 'transmigration' schemes, which settled millions of people from overpopulated Java and Madura in South Sumatra, Kalimantan, Sulawesi and Irian Jaya. The sense of crisis after 1997 led to many outbursts of interethnic brutality, which Wahid's government was unable to curb. Dayaks in West Kalimantan reinvented their 'headhunting' past, beheading and cannibalizing thousands of Muslims from Madura who had been settled on Dayak ancestral lands. On Ambon, meanwhile, sectarian violence festered between Christian and Muslim communities. Other problems stemmed from curbing corruption, which had become endemic. By the spring of 2001, however, Wahid's parliamentary support had collapsed, and student demonstrators were calling for his resignation, particularly because of two corruption cases in which the increasingly ineffectual and nearly blind president was implicated. Meanwhile, in Wahid's political heartland of East Java, the president's Islamic supporters attacked opposition-party offices and threatened to march on Jakarta to save their leader. As political chaos threatened economic recovery, Wahid exposed the shallow roots of Indonesian democracy by seeking refuge in the authoritarian impulses of his predecessors. He asked the military to impose a civil emergency, ironically, along the lines of Sukarno's suspension of the constitution and disbandment of parliament in 1959.

MEGAWATI'S MOMENT

The generals refused and threw their support behind Megawati. In August, Wahid was sacked for constitutional violations and Sukarno's daughter became president. To counter Megawati's secular nationalism, Hamzah Haz, leader of Indonesia's third largest party, the Islamic-based PPP (United Development Party) was elected deputy-president.

Even before Wahid's disastrous political reign, average Indonesians were cynical about the prospects for democracy. As one Javanese village official told a *Guardian* reporter in October 1999: 'We are all little people... We are the flour; they [the politicians] decide what shape to make the cake'. Megawati's moment has finally come but introducing genuine political and economic reform will be no easy task. Indonesia also faces the prospect of national dissolution. In her first speech as president, Megawati apologized to the peoples of Aceh and Irian Jaya for years of human rights abuses. But, at the same time, she made it clear that the provinces would never be allowed to break away from the united republic which her father founded, and the army continues to see as inviolate. Jakarta has offered greater regional autonomy but secessionists in Aceh and Irian Jaya (as well as in Maluku and Riau) are unlikely to be satisfied with anything less than full independence given recent developments in East Timor.

The East Timor Tragedy

THE END OF PORTUGUESE IMPERIALISM

The eastern half of the island of Timor remained a neglected, colonial slum within the Portuguese empire until 1975. It was a hangover from the Portuguese trading realm in South East Asia of the fifteenth and sixteenth centuries. When the Dutch took West Timor, a formal division of the island into Dutch and Portuguese spheres was announced in 1913. But, as the weakest of the European colonial powers, Portugal did little to develop its territory. Most of East Timor's Malay-Melanesian peoples were still engaged in subsistence agriculture in the 1970s and more than 90 percent of its 650,000 people remained illiterate. West Timor became part of the Indonesian republic when control was transferred from the Dutch at the end of 1949. But the prospect of independence for East Timor became realizable only after the coup of left-wing army officers during April 1974, which toppled the right-wing dictatorship in Lisbon. The sudden lifting of restrictions on free speech, and comments by radical members of the Portuguese junta in favour of decolonization, led to a sudden upsurge in political activity in East Timor.

Three political parties sprang up, led by the educated elite who had been given a place in the Portuguese administration from the 1960s. The most important of these was the left-wing Revolutionary Front for Independent East Timor, or Fretilin, whose base was the capital, Dili. A more conservative, pro-Portuguese party was the UDT (the Timorese Democratic Union) while Apodeti, the Timorese Popular Democratic Association, represented the small Muslim community and favoured union with Indonesia. In January 1975, the UDT and Fretilin joined together in a coalition government. However, in August 1975 civil war broke out, as the UDT launched a countercoup against the alleged communist-connections of the Fretilin leadership. Fretilin, however, had both greater support and military superiority. The UDT was forced back to the border with West Timor. Fretilin formed a government as the last Portuguese governor fled the island. The new government in Lisbon, more concerned with negotiating peace settlements in its African colonies, now washed its hands of East Timor. On 28 November 1975, Fretilin declared independence for a Democratic Republic of East Timor.

INDONESIAN ANNEXATION AND TERROR

The situation in East Timor proved unacceptable to Suharto's regime in Jakarta. Having suppressed communism within Indonesia, the president and his generals were far from delighted by the prospect of a small, left-wing nation on Indonesia's southeastern flank. East Timor might become subject to Beijing's influence. Jakarta's initial aim was to absorb the ex-Portuguese territory into its realm by peaceful, political means. But the main support for union with Indonesia amongst the Muslim community of the border areas was too small, so the Indonesian army came to support the UDT in its civil war against Fretilin. The success of Fretilin forces against the UDT culminated in a full-scale Indonesian invasion, beginning on 7 December 1975. This, and the subsequent occupation of East Timor, saw the full deployment of the Indonesian arsenal on a largely defenceless people. Aerial bombardments, the destruction of crops, widescale torture, and the use of concentration camps underscored a ruthless campaign against East Timorese independence. There were the most dreadful abuses of human rights in East Timor and at least 60,000 people were massacred in the first three months alone of the Indonesian occupation.

The Fretilin leaders were forced to flee, and in July 1976 East Timor was integrated into Indonesia as its twenty-seventh province. A bitter guerrilla resistance continued, however, in which Fretilin forces retreated to their bases in the interior led by the charismatic, Portuguese-educated, Xanana Gusmão. The hilly terrain tended to favour the insurgents and an underground network continued to link the guerrillas to sympathizers in the urban areas, especially amongst the student movement.

With the Fretilin leadership in the hills or exiled, Jakarta attempted to assimilate East Timor into Indonesia. But the East Timorese, the majority of whom continued to support Fretilin, proved stubbornly independent. The years of Portuguese imperialism had produced a sense of difference from the rest of the archipelago. The Malay language was not widespread; instead, most East Timorese spoke Tetum. As the Indonesian occupiers banned Portuguese, Tetum emerged as the language of East Timorese nationalism and resistance. The sense of difference was accentuated by the role of the Catholic church. East Timorese Catholics saw themselves as quite different from the Javanese Muslims who made up the bulk of the occupying army. Particularly after the appointment of Carlos Belo as Bishop of East Timor in 1983, the Catholic church emerged as a defender of East Timorese national identity and culture. As Belo himself has put it, 'the Catholic faith for the people is a kind of symbol to unite them, it is a way to express the fact that they are Timorese, they don't like any other religion [and] they [certainly] don't like Indonesia.' Acting as leaders of the passive resistance to Jakarta, Belo and his priests frequently condemned Indonesian atrocities and the general policy of Indonesianization and Islamization.

But the East Timorese independence movement, whether led by the Fretilin guerrillas or the Catholic church, failed to gain powerful backers in the international political community. East Timorese self-determination was sacrificed on the altar of Cold War realities.

Washington did not wish to upset the cozy relationship established with the anti-communist Suharto. As the Indonesian economy opened up to American multinationals, President Nixon labelled the archipe- lago 'by far the greatest prize in the Southeast Asian region'. Given the fact that Indochina had fallen to communist regimes in 1975, the Indonesian government found it easy to convince Washington of the dangers of a left-wing government on East Timor. There was some condemnation of Indonesian actions in the UN, but without US support, words counted for nothing. Moreover, Indonesia's southern neighbour, Australia, with potential oil and gas development in the Timor Sea, did not oppose the invasion. As the Australian ambassador in Jakarta telegraphed Canberra in August 1975: 'We should show as much understanding as we can of Indonesia's position and. . . there is no inherent reason why integration with Indonesia would in the long run be any less in the interests of the Timorese inhabitants than a highly unstable independence.'

INDEPENDENCE FOR EAST TIMOR

During 1993 and 1994, Bishop Belo was instrumental in bringing about a number of 'reconciliation talks' between the Indonesian gov- ernment and both anti- and pro-Indonesian Timorese groups. But a settlement only became possible following the changing of the guard in Jakarta during the summer of 1998. Facing dire financial difficulties, the new president, Habibie, offered East Timor a referendum on inde- pendence. There still remained an obstacle to East Timor's autonomy: the generals were not happy, fearing that East Timorese independence was the tip of the iceberg and would encourage separatist movements all over Jakarta's sprawling and unstable empire. Despite massive intimidation from the pro-integration militias, organized and armed by the Indonesian military, an overwhelming majority of East Timorese defiantly voted in favour of independence in the UN-supervised elections of August 1999. Tragically this only encouraged the militias to step up their attacks on pro-independence East Timorese, to which the Indonesian army turned a blind eye. The unarmed UN overseers were powerless to help the East Timorese and withdrew. Only in October 1999 did UN troops arrive to arrest the pro-Jakarta militias, set up a new civil administration for the territory, and aid the return of the 200,000 refugees forced into Indonesian Timor by the militias and the regular military. The UN's transitional government aims to hand over to a fully independent administration at the end of 2001, thus completing the decolonisation of South East Asia. But many problems will face the new nation. For one, there are the pro-Jakarta militiamen who lurk across the border in Indonesian West Timor. Moreover, there remain bitter political differences between Fretilin and the UDT, and some fear a return to the fighting of 1975, which left the door open for an Indonesian invasion. Let us hope that Xanana Gusmão, East Timor's likely first president, and Bishop Belo, can play roles akin to Nelson Mandela and Archbishop Tutu in South Africa and bring about peace and reconciliation in a troubled land. Boasting oil and gas and world-famous arabica coffee, potentially self-sufficient in rice and maize, and highly attractive to tourists, East Timor is potentially very rich. With political stability, the East Timorese should be able to share in the economic growth that has raised living standards in other parts of the region.

Economic Development: A Tale of Two South East Asias

South East Asia's independence offered economic opportunities to break away from colonial domination. This was particularly the case in the development of manufacturing industry, which had been held back by colonial regimes who feared Asian competition with European goods. But postindependent economic development in South East Asia has not been an even process: while the capitalist states achieved conspicuous economic success from the 1960s onwards, the communist states of Indochina stagnated or grew at much slower rates. Yet, the capitalist states have faced problems too; not least in the late 1990s when boom turned to bust.

THE ASEAN STATES

Malaysia, Thailand, Singapore, Brunei and Indonesia can all be grouped together economically because they have been committed, since the 1960s at least, to capitalist-style development, in which private property has largely been preserved. All were linked together as members of the Association of South East Asian Nations (ASEAN), which began as an alliance of authoritarian but anticommunist states in 1967. Yet even Singapore as an ardent defender of free trade, relied on a high degree of state planning and direction in the growth of its economy. The ASEAN states were hardly free-market exemplars. State intervention was evident in the sprawling state enterprises, such as the Jurong Town Corporation in Singapore or PERNAS in Malaysia, which were intended to act as springboards of economic growth.

The role of the state proved particularly important in diversifying the ASEAN economies away from the export of a few agricultural and mineral products, as in the days of colonial rule, towards the export of light-industrial goods. The growth of industries such as textiles, toys, electrical goods and components and canning led to more rapid growth and reduced South East Asia's dependence on the vagaries of world commodity prices.

Industrialization would have been impossible, however, without improvements in South East Asian agriculture. Benefitting from the higher-yielding crops, fertilizers and machinery of the postwar 'Green Revolution', the productive capacity of South East Asian farms was greatly expanded. A country such as Indonesia, which had to import rice and other foodstuffs in the 1950s, could feed itself by the 1970s because rice production now kept up with population growth. But cheaper and more abundant food also ensured that more people could migrate to the towns from the countryside and find employment in the expanding factories.

Aside from strong, determined states and the Green Revolution, South East Asia's economic growth relied on the efforts of individual entrepreneurs, particularly from the large Chinese communities of the region. The overseas Chinese presence has often been resented by 'indigenous' South East Asians, but Chinese commercial and financial skills remain central to economic growth in most of the capitalist states. Despite various indigenization schemes in Malaysia and Indonesia, ethnic Chinese continue to own about three-quarters of domestic private capital in both countries. So-called 'Ali Baba' networks in both

Malaysia and Indonesia – whereby an indigenous official ('Ali') gains a government concession on behalf of a Chinese capitalist ('Baba') – proved convenient ways of circumventing anti-Chinese policies. Although encouraged to take Thai names, Chinese capitalists remained central to the take off of manufacturing industry in Thailand too.

Capitalist South East Asia also boomed under favourable international economic conditions. The oil bonanza after 1973 boosted the economies of Malaysia, Indonesia and Brunei as crude oil prices quadrupled. At the same time, United States economic aid flooded in to anticommunist regimes – between 1950 and 1975, Thailand alone received a staggering $650 million from Washington. With America's withdrawal from Indochina, Japan emerged as the new lender *extraordinaire*. As Japanese official aid expanded, so too did Japanese trade and investment. Japanese multinationals no longer saw South East Asia as just a source of raw materials but as an area for the location of industrial plant, especially as labour costs were increasing in Japan itself. Japanese companies provided the technology in joint ventures with South East Asians (often ethnic Chinese) to set up manufacturing operations. For example, Japanese computer firms subcontracted the production of silicon chips from Malaysia to make electronics one of the latter country's main export industries in the 1980s. Malaysia's national car, the Proton, was likewise developed out of partnerships between Japanese and Malaysian firms. Memories of the Pacific War died hard, especially amongst the ethnic Chinese of the region, but leaders of South East Asian states generally welcomed economic links with Japan as a means of asserting an Asian identity. The classic example here was Prime Minister Mahathir of Malaysia, who wished to divorce himself from the Anglophile leaders of the past by announcing during the 1980s a strategy of 'Look East' and a campaign of 'Buy British Last'.

Not only in Tokyo and Osaka but also in United States and West European boardrooms, capitalist South East Asia came to be seen as a 'land of milk and honey'. South East Asia's growing absorption into the international capitalist system was assisted by loans from the World Bank and the International Monetary Fund. The strings attached to these loans tied the ASEAN states even more firmly to the global capitalist economy, for example, through the devaluation of currencies, restrictions on the operations of trade unions, reduced government spending on social services, and greater openings to imports and foreign investment. The policy prescriptions of the IMF advisors have often been seen as a new form of imperialism, a 'neocolonialism'. But abiding by the rules of the capitalist system did suck in more development capital from multinational enterprises. And as infrastructures became more developed, states such as Thailand could further expand their tourist industries and further reduce dependence upon commodity exports.

Economic growth produced remarkable changes to South East Asian societies. Urbanization absorbed the massive growth in population from about 150 million people in the region at the end of the Second World War to 400 million by 1990. The skylines of the big cities were transformed. The centres of Singapore, Bangkok, Jakarta and Kuala Lumpur became dominated by high-rise international-style office buildings, hotels and shopping complexes. The overhead rail networks put up in Kuala Lumpur during the 1990s made the city unrecognizable on our second visit in 1997, the year also in which the world's tallest building, the Petronas Towers, was completed.

The old and the new. The former Selangor Secretariat building – British headquarters during the colonial period – is dwarfed by the Telecom tower and modern bank buildings in modern-day Kuala Lumpur

Such change has produced definite benefits to the lives of most South East Asians. Increases in life expectancy, for example, are a result of increases in per capita incomes. The greatest success stories were Singapore and Brunei. Generally, capitalist South East Asian states did far better than other Third World countries. But there were a number of negatives to the dash for growth. Corruption or 'cronyism' seemed to expand in direct proportion to growth in national incomes. Only Singapore, amongst the ASEAN states, avoided the taint of widespread peculation. Import-substitution in particular lent itself to cosy relationships springing up between governments and most-favoured entrepreneurs, for example, in the alliances forged between Thai bureaucrats and Chinese capitalists. The NEP in Malaysia produced a class of Malay 'kleptocrats'. Indonesia was worse, where oil and logging concessions and cigarette monopolies were awarded to President Suharto's relatives and associates.

Avaricious urban elites, then, did very well out of economic development. But much growth merely bypassed the lower orders. Before 1997 Malaysia achieved an average national income probably higher than in the UK but this wealth was very unevenly spread, leaving certain groups in society, for example, the jungle-dwelling Orang Asli and lower-class urban Indians, conspicuously impoverished. The street hawkers, pedicab drivers, piece workers, prostitutes and beggars that live in the slums of Jakarta and Bangkok clearly have received few benefits. For a Jakarta slum dweller in 1999, hiring a pedicab would cost about 20p a day but the driver would earn just 50p.

It was not necessarily the case that the 'rich got richer and the poor got poorer'. Migrants to the big cities made rational choices. While slum houses built of plywood with plastic corrugated roofing, and with no running water, look far less salubrious than the romantic wood-and-thatch homes of the lush countryside, the economic opportunities and standards of living measured in terms of wages are far better in an urban than a rural setting. Even so, income distribution was and remains badly skewed in favour of a small, well-connected elite. Moreover with the breakdown of traditional hierarchies and communities, the new technocrats and entrepreneurs represent a harsher ruling class, largely unconstrained by the paternalism of both the precolonial and colonial orders.

Income disparities manifest themselves on a regional basis too. Jakarta's drain on the wealth of the Indonesian outer islands has long been a source of resentment, and has spurred on regional separatist movements, for example, in Aceh. But in Thailand also, the Bangkok conurbation, where the money and political influence is concentrated, is inevitably favoured in contrast to the outlying provinces. The average income in Bangkok by 1970 was three times the average rural income, and four times average incomes in the impoverished north east, where many minority non-Thai hill peoples live. Gender gaps opened up too, male members of the community being the first to receive the benefits of new employment opportunities in the towns, while women remained locked in the agricultural economy.

Unbridled development also had negative consequences for South East Asia's natural environment. Overfishing and pollution of seas and rivers became widespread, as industry expanded unregulated. Deforestation was an even worse result of the economic 'miracle'. In 1960 more than half of Thailand was still covered in lush forest, but 30 years later probably just ten percent cover survived. The result is loss of habitat for animals but also for forest-dwelling minority peoples. The loss of forest cover intensified soil erosion and facilitated the spread of fire. The most extreme example was Indonesia, where fire was regularly used as a means of large-scale forest clearance. In 1997 the fires ran completely out of control and a pall of smog and soot spread for thousands of miles over Sumatra and Kalimantan, seeping also into both East Malaysia and West Malaysia. The result was long-term respiratory problems for countless numbers of South East Asians, and the loss of wildlife, most tragically many of the endangered orang utan of Borneo and Sumatra. All told an estimated 4.2 million acres, or 1.7 million hectares, burned (an area equivalent to over 4 million football pitches). Most fires seemed to start not from local farmers burning off small plots (as the Indonesian government always claimed) but from clearances to make way for large-scale palm oil or timber plantations. Many of these enterprises were run by individuals with close connections to the ruling Suharto family.

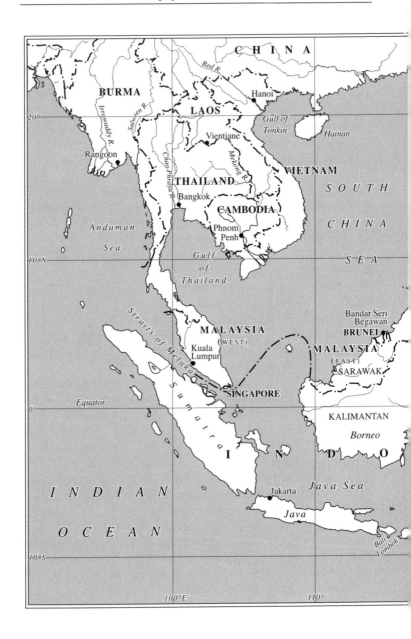

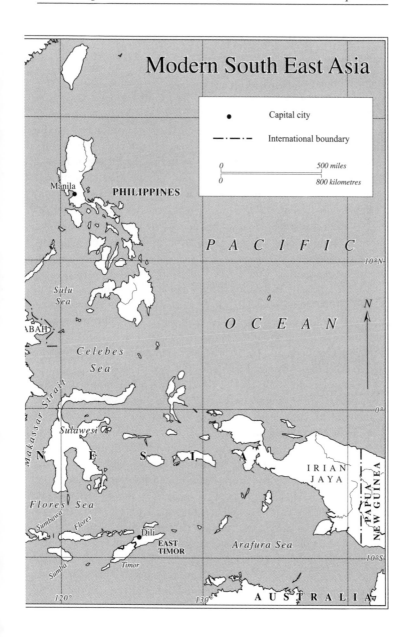

Modern South East Asia

Legend:
- ● Capital city
- —·—·— International boundary

0 — 500 miles
0 — 800 kilometres

PHILIPPINES

Manila

P A C I F I C

10º N

Sulu Sea

O C E A N

N ↑

ABAH

Celebes Sea

Makassar Strait

Sulawesi

N   E   S   I   A

IRIAN JAYA

PAPUA NEW GUINEA

Flores Sea

Sumbawa   *Flores*

Dili

EAST TIMOR

Arafura Sea

0º

Sumba   *Timor*

10º S

AUSTRALIA

120º   *130º*

THE COMMUNIST STATES

The development path in the Indochinese states was very different from the rest of South East Asia. Here socialist regimes monopolized virtually all formal economic activity. The most extreme case was in Pol Pot's Cambodia between 1975 and 1979, in which private property was abolished. The execution, torture and exile of Cambodia's middle class ruined modern industry, education and health care. The country still produced a rice surplus in the 1960s, but the effects of Khmer Rouge economics were to bring famine. Although less extreme and more humane, the governments of Laos and Vietnam also instituted hopelessly inefficient collectivization schemes. After reunification in 1975, socialist economic policies proved extremely unpopular with the more cosmopolitan southern Vietnamese, epitomized by the mass exodus of skilled entrepreneurs as boat people. Collectivization and resettlement schemes in the countryside were resisted or evaded.

The socialist states did benefit from massive aid progammes from the Soviet Union and China to rival American and Japanese support to ASEAN. Unfortunately for the Indochinese nations, the communist bloc only controlled about ten percent of world trade. This meant that Vietnam, Cambodia and Laos had access to comparably less aid and also had to accept less-advanced technology.

Moreover communist South East Asia suffered far more than the capitalist states from international warfare. An emphasis on the development of heavy industry in North Vietnam after independence in 1954 actually produced impressive growth comparable to the capitalist states of the region. But then came the war with the United States; the impact of saturation bombing in the three years after 1965 was to produce a marked decline in production and the forced dispersal of population from industrial centres. Even before the Khmer Rouge, civil war and American bombing in Cambodia between 1970 and 1975 resulted in a decline in output of over ten percent per annum and the deaths of more than half a million people. Laos's economy, meanwhile, was almost brought to a standstill by American bombing, making refugees of one-quarter of the population. Reunified Vietnam faced, and continues to face, breath-taking problems of reconstruction arising from its terrible, ten-year conflict with the United States. Some 58,000 American lives were lost but the Vietnamese death toll was a staggering 3 million, with 300,000 Vietnamese still missing. Agricultural land was polluted with millions of gallons of Agent Orange, and the deadly chemical, dioxin, in the defoliant caused tens of thousands of birth defects. Railways and bridges were destroyed, food was in desperately short supply, and millions of people had been displaced from their homes or found themselves unemployed. Prostitutes, drug addicts and orphans were everywhere in the cities of the south. Unexploded bombs and mines continue to claim three to five victims every day. It is no surprise that the Vietnamese government has, thus far unsuccessfully, sought compensation from Washington.

The cumulative effect of naive planning and warfare was far slower growth than in capitalist South East Asia. In Vietnam economic growth was unable to keep up with the expansion of numbers of people. After 1975 the government attempted to alleviate population pressures in the towns by resettlement in new economic zones in upland areas. More than 2.5 million people were moved, but the population grew by 14 million in the decade following reunification. Massive inflation and agricultural stagnation followed.

From the 1980s, therefore, reform programmes were initiated. In Vietnam, there were attempts to unleash the small-business sector, refugees were encouraged to return and foreign investors were wooed. Japanese government aid and private capital poured in to the country to revitalize the economy, and in 1999 a trade pact was finally reached with the old enemy in Washington. The 1980s witnessed economic recovery in Laos as trade increased with Thailand, especially through the export of electricity from the Nam Ngum project. Despite continued political instability, Cambodia recovered after 1993, as ethnic Chinese business conglomerates resumed operations and reintegrated Cambodia into the 'bamboo network' of overseas Chinese business operations throughout the South East Asia region. The breakdown of economic barriers between 'capitalist' and 'communist' South East Asia was confirmed in the 1990s, when Vietnam, Laos and Cambodia all joined ASEAN. Even so, the three Indochinese states remain the poorest countries in the region.

On the positive side, however, socialist economies have provided less opportunity for corruption. While communism produced a privileged 'official class', few individuals were in a position to accumulate wealth on the scale of a Suharto. A greater stress on social justice has also meant that women have done better economically in Vietnam than in any other country in the region. Adult literacy rates in the 1990s were also very high in Vietnam (about 94 per cent); higher than in Singapore, Malaysia, Indonesia and Brunei and about equal to Thailand. But the reintegration of Indochina into capitalist South East Asia meant that it also faced the blast following the financial disaster of 1997.

THE GREAT CRASH

The economic events of 1997 illustrated that the South East Asian economies were houses built on sand. Following the collapse of the Thai baht, the Indonesian rupiah fell by some 25 percent against the United States dollar and the Jakarta Stock Exchange lost one-third of its value. Malaysia's economy suffered the worst: the ringgit lost one-half of its value against the dollar and the Kuala Lumpur stock market lost some 65 percent of its capitalization, transforming the country's billionaires into mere millionaires. Once Thailand had sneezed, Laos could not avoid catching the flu: its currency nose-dived by a staggering 80 percent. According to the *Guardian*'s economist, Will Hutton, the root of the problem was the system of effectively pegging local currencies to the US dollar. This was greatly beneficial in the short-term, for it encouraged borrowers to borrow and foreign lenders to lend because there was virtually no exchange-rate risk. This risk-free source of capital induced the 'miraculous' growth of the 1970s and the 1980s. But as the dollar rose in value during the first six months of 1997, the South East Asian economies struggled to protect their currencies. International speculators now sold their stocks of Thai, Indonesian and Malaysian currencies, forecasting that they could buy them back cheaper at a later date. Western investors panicked, withdrawing much badly needed capital from the region. The South East Asian governments were forced to devalue, ruining many of the region's overextended businesses, which had taken out huge loans denominated in dollars. Lacking sound management structures, these firms were also entrepreneurially weak because of the ingrained corruption, nepotism and 'cronyism' that characterized South East Asian capitalism. Indeed, it was the collapse of a number of Thai property companies that led to the devaluation of the baht in July 1997 and which set off the regional crisis. The dramatic downturn was subsequently exacerbated by the swift flight of foreign capital from South East Asia's stock markets. Of the capitalist economies, only Singapore came out relatively unscathed; an indicator of its more scrupulous and accountable business system.

In the aftermath, Thailand and Indonesia introduced austerity measures to curb imports, slash government spending, and postpone or reschedule big infrastructure projects, such as highways and dams. These were often the requirements of the huge IMF loans negotiated to prop up currencies. Malaysia followed their strategies too – the unfinished hotels and overhead rail systems in Kuala Lumpur were the very visible relics of 1997. But Mahathir's government also favoured a more independent line of insulation from the world economy, via strict exchange and capital controls. In Vietnam and Laos, meanwhile, governments questioned the wisdom of capitalist-style reforms. Unemployment, food and goods shortages, and political unrest were consequences of the crash. Governments fell in Indonesia and Thailand. Yet, South East Asians, as we have shown throughout the book, have exhibited tenacity and flexibility in facing worse storms in the past. By the new millennium, national economies were showing sure signs of recovery, and in the year 2000 Indonesia, Malaysia and Thailand sported growth rates of 7 per cent. (South East Asian economies remained highly vulnerable, however, in the face of any slowdown in the United States economy of further estrangement between Washington and Beijing.) Within South East Asia, the challenge for the future was to develop more accountable business and political systems in which the benefits of economic growth could be more evenly spread.

Epilogue: Southeast Asia in the Early 21st Century

VIETNAM: CAPITALISM AND COMMUNISM?

Since the beginning of the twenty-first century, relations between communist Vietnam and the capitalist United States have been further consolidated through top-level official visits to Washington. The US has become Vietnam's main trading partner and the two former enemies are now allied in a clean-up operation designed to rid Vietnam of one of the lasting legacies of the 'America War' – the ongoing effects of Agent Orange. The defoliant still causes birth defects, is linked to cancer, and is still making the leaves fall. Compensation remains limited.

Ironically, historical enmity has far greater staying power in relations between Vietnam and communist China. In 2008, the two parties reached an agreement over a border dispute dating back to the 1979 war. This willingness to come to terms on land did not extend to disputes over the South China Sea. Though bilateral agreements were reached over the gas-rich waters in 2010, the issues surrounding ownership and access remain unresolved. Vietnam has accused Chinese vessels of attacking Vietnamese fishing boats or vessels exploring for oil, leading to populist anti-Beijing protests in Hanoi and Ho Chi Minh City.

Vietnam has dealt with the inherent contradiction between capitalism and communism through the adoption of the 'dual model'. Economic reforms were promised and pushed through, and in 2007 Vietnam joined the World Trade Organisation. This has successfully driven growth, making Vietnam the Asia Pacific region's second fastest growing economy after China. This has also led to the creation of more and more Vietnamese millionaires (many of them women), and the growth of an affluent middle-class with its conspicuous consumption of designer goods and luxury cars. Poverty has been reduced from around 60 per cent in the 1990s to around 12.5 per cent in the 2010s. But there are increasing gaps in the distribution of wealth, a divide felt most obviously by Vietnam's rural communities.

These inequalities grew worse as Vietnam suffered the effects of the global downturn. Despite national growth rates averaging 5 per cent, the government was heavily criticised for its economic mismanagement. Inflation, for example, had risen to almost 20 per cent by the end of 2011. Meanwhile, the government's forced eviction programme (with measly compensation payments) adversely affects rural communities. While the Vietnamese state has always been able to take land away from communities if it was deemed to be in the public interest, it now seems that what the public needs is a new golf course, resort or eco-urban dwelling rather than a collective farm. The Communist Party's promises of sweeping land reforms – which won support from the peasantry to fight the Japanese, the French and the Americans – are but a distant memory. Three-quarters of the population still live in crowded countryside areas as land is sold off to multinational investors and well-placed local businesses. Ironically, this had been a principal Vietnamese grievance against French colonialism. *Plus ça change.*

While *doi moi* has led to considerable economic reform, this has not been matched by increased democracy or political freedom. The political scene has been blighted by corruption scandals and embezzlement by civil servants. In 2007, a younger generation of party members replaced the old guard as Party Chairman, Prime Minister and President. This did not mark a new 'opening up': the pro-reform journalists who exposed corruption in the transport ministry during 2006 were subsequently arrested for bringing the state and the party leadership into disrepute, reflecting a growing crackdown on 'subversive' and 'pro-western' activities. Since 2008, the government has banned online bloggers from raising 'inappropriate' subjects, and arrested and imprisoned a number of human rights and democracy campaigners. Moreover, it continues to persecute, arrest, and torture ethnic and religious minorities, most notably Montagnard Protestants and followers of the Hoa Hao Buddhist sect. With 34 per cent of the population now using the Internet, there may be even wider repression in the future.

CAMBODIA: MOUNTING AUTHORITARIANISM

Like Vietnam, Cambodia remains scarred by its recent turbulent history, notably the devastation inflicted by the Khmer Rouge's five-year reign of terror. The on-going process that gives voice to the victims and seeks justice for their cause proves painfully slow. In 2001, the government finally set up a tribunal to investigate the crimes of Khmer Rouge leaders and bring them to justice. It took four years for the Extraordinary Chambers in the Courts of Cambodia to gain full UN backing. It was a further two years before the first five arrests were made, another two years before the proceedings in the first case, and the Tribunal didn't commence its hearing of the second case until 2011. Since 2011, only one of those indicted – Kuang Guek Eav, known as Comrade Duch, the former head of the notorious Tuol Sleng prison camp – has actually been sentenced.

In 2010, Prime Minister Hun Sen, no doubt aware of ties within his ruling Cambodian People's Party (CPP) to the Khmer Rouge, suggested that the prosecution should rest with the conviction of Comrade Duch. Despite a 2013 ruling that made it illegal to deny the atrocities committed by the Khmer Rouge, the good work of the Tribunal remains tainted by allegations of corruption and government interference. This is indicative of increasing authoritarianism and the existence of a de facto one-party state. Following the elections in 2003 the main opposition parties, Funcipec and the Sam Rainsy Party (SRP), formed the Alliance of Democrats in order to gain more leverage in coalition with Hun Sen's party. But Prince Ranariddh sold out his Alliance partners and entered a short-lived coalition with the CPP. Subsequently ousted from his leadership of Funcipec, Ranariddh lost his seat in 2007. The Prince was then found guilty of a breach of trust in what was regarded as a politically motivated verdict. The SRP has fared little better, and is unlikely to see any improvement in its fortunes while its leader is in France avoiding imprisonment in Cambodia for encouraging peasants to defy recent Vietnam-Cambodia border changes. The royal family does remain as an important counter to Hun Sen's power, as evidenced by the thousands of anguished mourners who took to the streets during Sihanouk's funeral in 2012. But the veteran king and political survivor had shocked Cambodians back in 2004 when he abdicated in favour of his son Sihamoni, a former dancer. Sihamoni was regarded as an ideal candidate for the job of monarch because of his neutral political position.

A significant barrier to greater democracy also exists in the close monitoring of the nation's media. A free press exists, but most of the media is pro-CPP. Currently there are no controls over access to the Internet, but this will be rectified by imminent legislation. Moreover, the CPP continues to exert its influence over the police and the judiciary. Cambodia has recently strengthened its ties with China through its support for the superpower's claim to the South China Sea rites, much to the consternation of its ASEAN neighbours. This has only added further speculation that Cambodia's fragile democracy is fast fading.

LAOS: PERSECUTION AND PRESERVATION

Democracy is performing poorly in Laos as well. The People's Revolutionary Party has relaxed its commitment to maintaining an atheist state, but relative freedoms granted to Buddhists have not been extended to the country's Christian communities. Laos has intensified its persecution of Christian and animist groups in an attempt to rid the nation of 'alien faiths'. Meanwhile, the Hmong communities, who supported the United States in the Vietnam War, have maintained low-level resistance to the communist regime. It is estimated that many thousands of Hmong people have been tortured or executed and up to 300,000 have fled the country as refugees, many to neighbouring Thailand before further repatriation. Human rights organisations continue to lobby western governments and ASEAN to do more to question the 'forced disappearance' of activists and to protect the minority, ethnic and religious groups from persecution.

The Lao government has been concerned to present a more positive image to the outside world. Not least, because tourism is of growing importance to the Lao economy – and particularly the UNESCO World Heritage Site of Luang Prabang. Alongside the instinct for preservation of heritage, Laos has begun to reform its economy – along Vietnamese lines – in an attempt to encourage private enterprise but also preserve communist rule. Laos has suffered little from the effects of the global financial crisis due to its limited international trade. Even so, Laos remains Southeast Asia's poorest country, with an estimated 30 per cent of the population still living in poverty. Recent campaigns to remove beggars from the streets of Luang Prabang and Vientiane, in the interests of preserving the tourism industry, are ironic testament to this.

Even so, Laos's economic policies have been welcomed by outside analysts who predict positive growth for the country for the next few years. To raise living standards, the government has invested heavily in the country's infrastructure, including a controversial hydroelectric dam on the Mekong River. Vietnam and Cambodia have strongly criticised the project as the river is a critical watershed, providing vital fishing and irrigation for millions of people downstream. Nevertheless, Laos has pressed ahead with the dam, which it regards as crucial to its economic development.

THAILAND: 'THE GREAT DIVIDE'

Thailand's government has embraced the Laotian HEP project, as a major investor who will profit also from cheaper electricity (a key element, it is hoped, in diffusing recent political discontent). Relations have not been as good with another neighbour, Cambodia. There has been a long running dispute over the ownership of temples on the Cambodia-Thailand frontier, which has even involved exchanges of fire and the evacuation of 500 Thai citizens from Cambodia in 2003. But the temple dispute has proved a mere side show to the main event in twenty-first century Thai politics: the split between those in favour and those against ex-Prime Minister Thaksin Shinawatra. 'The great Thai political divide' has pitted the pro-Thaksin Red Shirts (the United Front for Democracy against Dictatorship) against their royalist, yellow-shirted rivals (People's Action for Democracy). The Red Shirts are made up of rural farmers, the urban working-class and some left-wing activists. The Yellow Shirts, on the other hand, constitute a marriage of convenience between pro-democracy reformers, concerned with the growing 'Thaksinocracy', and conservative, nationalist forces that maintain close links to the military and look forward to a return to the semi-democracy of the 1970s and 1980s.

Thaksin's government of 2001-5 appealed to the masses with land, health and education reforms. But the chattering classes were aggrieved by high-level government corruption, the heavy-handed military response to the Muslim Malay community in the south, and illiberal policies towards Thailand's many drug addicts. Thaksin gambled on reaffirming the support he had gained in the landslide victory of 2005 by calling snap elections in 2006. The Yellow Shirts responded with widespread urban protests, particularly in the capital Bangkok. Thaksin was forced from office, charged with corruption and driven into exile in Cambodia. While in Cambodia, remarkably, Thaksin was appointed economic advisor to the Cambodian regime by his golfing buddy, Hun Sen. This did nothing to calm tensions between the two nations, nor did Thaksin's exit soothe Red and

Yellow Shirt antagonisms within Thailand. Following a period of military-backed rule, the People Power Party (a reincarnation of Thaksin's banned Thai Rak Thai party) swept to victory at the polls in the December 2007 general election. Again, the Yellow Shirts responded in numbers of tens of thousands. Through the blockade of Thailand's airports, their attempt to topple the 'proxy' Thaksin government now struck at one of the country's most important industries, tourism.

Having succeeded in bringing down the government of Thaksin's brother-in-law, Somchai Wongsawat, a new coalition regime of opposition parties was formed. But this had to immediately deal with Red Shirt protests, resulting in the deaths of 91 protesters following a three-month armed struggle in Bangkok during 2010. The July 2011 election was unusually peaceful, and less widely affected by corruption and vote buying. With 48 per cent of the popular vote, Thaksin's sister, Yingluck Shinawatra, became Thailand's first female Prime Minister. But the New Pitak Siam movement led by General Boonlet Kaewprasit united the Yellow Shirts against what was regarded as yet another Thaksin puppet regime. Violent protests in Bangkok starting in November 2013 demanded Yingluck's resignation and the imposition of an unelected 'people's council', culminating in a state of emergency in early 2014. This was ahead of a snap general election in February, which the opposition boycotted. Protestors prevented voting in some constituencies, and so a new government could not be formed. Yingluck has also been accused of corruption because of the lucrative rice subsidies that benefit the farmers who form the core of her support. Political tensions are likely to continue therefore.

The situation in Bangkok is not helped by on-going disturbances in the Muslim Malay-dominated southern provinces of Pattani, Yala and Narathiwat. Since 2004, violence in the region has escalated. In an attempt to bring an end to insurgent activities, in February 2013 the Bangkok government finally acknowledged the leading Malay party, Barisan Revolusi Nasional, and the two sides agreed to talks. But the insurgent movement is deeply fractured and divided between various splinter groups and between the older and younger generations, making a lasting settlement very difficult to achieve.

Political instability has taken its toll on Thailand's economy (as did the devastation caused by the 2004 tsunami and the 2011 floods). To be fair to Yingluck, Thailand's economic outlook in 2013, at least, was improved. The government raised the minimum wage and provided incentives to first-time car buyers. These initiatives were part of a wider economic stimulation package that, as well as cross-border investment in Laos's Mekong Dam project, included improved water-management systems and a multi-billion dollar high-speed railway.

MALAYSIA: POST-MAHATHIRISM

Love him or loathe him, since Mahathir Mohamad's departure from the main stage it is clear that Malaysian politics have become more divisive and less stable. 'Dr. M.' finally bowed out of office in October 2002 to be succeeded by Abdullah Badawi. Since independence in 1957, each Malayan/Malaysian prime minister has groomed his successor. The trouble for Mahathir was that he had virtually strangled any potential talent within the ruling party. In 2004, Badawi's Barisan coalition secured a landslide victory, but it subsequently failed to make good on its promises, notably in curbing corruption and introducing greater transparency. Badawi only just managed to cling on to power after the 2008 election in which, for the first time, the Barisan lost its treasured two-thirds majority. Yet, what really brought Badawi down was Mahathir's continued interference. Dr. M. accused Badawi of corruption and publicly denounced his leadership. The ex-prime minister quit UMNO and urged others to do likewise until Badawi stepped down. In 2009, Badawi was succeeded by Deputy Prime Minister Najib Abdul Razak.

Najib Razak is the son of Malaysia's second Prime Minister, Abdul Razak, the so-called 'father of development' who sought to eradicate the economic disparities that fuelled ethnic antagonism in the late-1960s. Despite entering the job nearly 40 years after his father's premature death, Najib still has to contend with those very same problems. Affirmative action has resulted in spectacular affluence for some well-connected Malays, but the Chinese remain the wealthiest ethnic group in Malaysia. Poverty has increased across the racial divide in the last decade, but particularly amongst the politically marginalised Indian community. Hence, the popular Malaysian quip that 'the Indian problem is no problem'. Not that the government has been complacent about the effects of the global economic crisis, which have hit

Malaysia's exports hard. In 2009, the government pledged $16 billion in spending and tax incentives and, in 2011, an equally huge investment was announced to improve Kuala Lumpur's mass rapid transit system to try and curb the city's nightmarish congestion. KL is also developing its financial sector as the Muslim world's answer to Wall Street.

Despite the government's New Economic Model (need-based, rather than ethnically-based affirmative action) and its 1Malaysia concept, emphasising ethnic harmony and national unity, the results of the 2013 general election revealed on-going ethnic divides. The Barisan achieved an even worse performance than in 2008, gaining a tiny majority of just 11 seats. Supporters of the Pakatan Rakyat ('People's Coalition') – an alliance of Parti Keadilan Rakyat (the People's Justice Party), the Democratic Action Party and the Pan-Islamic Party – turned out in force. This was despite attacks on the country's independent on-line media (which the opposition relies upon to disseminate its message). The Pakatan was charismatically led by former Deputy Prime Minister, Anwar Ibrahim. He has galvanized the opposition into a credible force, having survived attempts to smear his moral character: his conviction for sodomy was overturned in 2004 and in 2012 he was acquitted of the same charge. It remains to be seen whether leading Pakatan figures will be bought off with lucrative enticements into government, or whether they will be subject (as in the past) to Malaysia's new anti-subversion legislation, the Security Offences (Special Measures) Act (Somsa), introduced in 2012.

On the surface, Somsa gave credence to the claim Najib was a reforming prime minister. It was hailed as another milestone in Malaysia's journey to liberal democracy. But there has been considerable cynicism as well. The vaguely worded law still allows for arrest without evidence and imprisonment without trial for 28 days. Intellectuals do talk of a new 'openness' post-Mahathir, but 'reforms' such as Somsa continue to make Malaysians cynical about politics.

SINGAPORE: BUSINESS AS USUAL?

On the surface, little has changed in twenty-first century Singapore. The People's Action Party (PAP) remains in power and the son of founding father Lee Kuan Yew, Lee Hsien Loong, became Singapore's third prime minister in 2004. The enforcement of strict social controls continues and the City-State has maintained its enviable status as the world's number one country in which to operate a business. Singapore's economy is the largest and the fastest growing in the region. It emerged relatively unscathed from the economic downturn of 2009, with record growth figures of around 14 per cent in the years since 2010. Scratch beneath the shiny veneer of affluence, though, and a different picture emerges: one of disaffection, political opposition and growing inequalities. This has led observers to suggest that Singapore has reached a turning point in its history.

Lee Kuan Yew (who continued to wield tremendous influence as Minister Mentor in the cabinet) continued to warn voters that if they voted for the opposition they would suffer the consequences: the PAP would continue to look after PAP constituencies. But the ruling party can no longer count on the allegiance of an electorate simply grateful for Singapore's progress since independence. Younger voters have become increasingly disillusioned, especially as home and car ownership is out of reach for many young Singaporeans. Rising inflation has also forced food prices to increase, and the poorest 20 per cent of the population suffered a 2.7 per cent fall in income in the first decade of the 21st century. Poorer Singaporeans are also feeling squeezed by an influx of foreign workers prepared to work for lower wages than locals, and in 2013 there were mass demonstrations against immigration.

Growing disaffection with the PAP has been reflected at the polls. The PAP's popular share of the vote fell to 60 per cent in 2011 (from 67 per cent in 2006 and 75 per cent in 2001). This is reflective also of an on-line media explosion, facilitating more effective campaigning by opposition groups. The winner-takes-all electoral system still makes it difficult for the opposition to convert votes into seats. But the relative success of the opposition in 2011 led Lee Kuan Yew and his protégé and former Prime Minister Goh Chok Tong to resign from cabinet. They argued that the 'time has come for a younger generation to carry Singapore forward in a more difficult and complex situation.' Lee Hsien Loong admitted that the party would have to undergo some 'soul searching'. It will prove very hard, however, for Singapore's political elite to temper its pro-multinational capitalism stance in favour of poorer and marginalised Singaporeans.

BRUNEI: THE BEGINNINGS OF DEMOCRACY AND DIVERSIFICATION?

The most interesting development in Brunei during the last decade has been the tentative move taken by the Sultan towards democratic politics. Twenty years after he closed parliament in 1984 (following independence from Britain) the Sultan announced the reopening of the state legislature. Later in 2004, the Sultan amended the constitution to include a provision for the addition of a small group of elected representatives. In 2011, a limited ballot was extended to leaders of the sub-districts and heads of villages and longhouses. This select electorate then nominated a total of 53 candidates, and subsequently elected a mere 4 members to represent the Sultanate's four districts in the otherwise wholly appointed legislature. It is unlikely, however, that the franchise will be extended since Bruneians appear to be satisfied with the status quo. It is difficult to tell whether the lack of appetite for democracy is driven by genuine satisfaction with the political regime, the high-standard of living enjoyed by the Sultan's subjects (thanks to its oil-generated wealth and enforced price capping) or the regime's intolerance of any form of dissent and its self-censoring media.

Limited political development has been matched by poor economic growth rates. Brunei remains dependent on its oil and gas reserves. These generate 90 per cent of the sultanate's income but only employ 3 per cent of the population. The major employer is actually the state, accounting for around 90 per cent of all jobs. This current state of affairs is not sustainable. The steady depletion of Brunei's gas and oil reserves and the inability of the public sector to absorb an expanding workforce have raised concerns about the country's future economic viability. *Wawasan 2035* (Vision 2035) is the government's response to these concerns. The aim is to attract foreign investment, stimulate local business creation (which remains very weak) and develop up-market eco-tourism. Given that since the 1950s Bruneians have been grappling with concerns over their dwindling oil reserves and consequent need to diversify the economy, it seems that nothing changes so much in Brunei as it stays the same. That cannot be said of Indonesia, Brunei's massive neighbour.

INDONESIA: DEMOCRACY SUSTAINED

Indonesia has thrown off its 'sick man of Southeast Asia' image. With its vast consumer base and abundant natural resources, foreign investors currently regard it as one of the world's emerging economies. This has been helped by a remarkable degree of political stability, defying previous assertions that the island chain could not cope with democracy. In 2004, the military took a further step back from politics as for the first time Indonesians were permitted to vote directly for their President. Megawati, despite her legitimacy as Sukarno's daughter and as champion of the poor, lost out to retired general Susilo Bambang Yudhoyono. Improving security and delivering economic growth, he was re-elected in 2009. Despite Yudhoyono's ties to the military and the re-emergence of Golkar as Indonesia's largest political party, a peace accord was signed with the Acehnese rebels in 2005. This allowed for the disarming of the guerrillas in northern Sumatra and the withdrawal of government troops. A year later, Aceh held its first direct elections and the former separatist leader, Irwandi Yusuf, became governor of the autonomous province. Following a South African-style 'truth and reconciliation' commission, the President also expressed 'deep regret' in 2008 at human rights violations in East Timor. Indonesia in the 21st century has one of the freest presses in Southeast Asia. It benefits also from a vibrant civil society, underpinned by numerous NGOs (focussing especially on environmental and women's issues) and limited restrictions on access to social media, such as Facebook and Twitter.

Indonesia still has its problems. A downside of the return to political pluralism has been the frightening upsurge of religious extremism. Some militant Islamic groups are allegedly linked to al-Qaeda, most notoriously those responsible for the bombings at two nightclubs on Bali in 2002 that killed 202 people (most of whom were Australian tourists). Not only foreigners have been targeted but also Christian and moderate Muslim Indonesians, as well as local journalists who have criticised Islam or lauded religious diversity.

Corruption and red tape continue to hold back desperately needed infrastructure projects. Highly dangerous 'roof-surfing' on jam-packed Jakarta commuter trains is not only a symptom of poverty but also reflects a general shortage of trains to meet demand. Indonesian trains continue to run on the tracks left behind by the Dutch in the 1940s. In the lucrative forestry industry tax evasion is reckoned to cost the government US$2 billion per annum – equivalent to the archipelago's entire spending on health care. Notwithstanding Yudhoyono's high moral integrity and prosecutions of MPs, cabinet ministers, diplomats and judges, Indonesia still has one of the world's worst corruption ratings. Corruption in Indonesia has been likened to Coca-Cola: 'Everyone, every time, everywhere'.

Millions of Indonesians still live below the poverty line, and the ranks of rural poor migrating to the cities continue to rummage on rubbish tips to eke out a living. Liberal economic reforms have only enriched the already wealthy. Moreover, regional tensions persist in the vast, ethnically and religiously diverse archipelago. Irian Jaya was granted greater autonomy by Jakarta in 2002 and adopted its locally preferred name of Papua. But, there have been protests in the eastern province over the exploitation of gold and copper resources by a Jakarta-backed US company, and in 2013 eight soldiers were shot dead by separatists. The highly unstable physical environment was under-lined at the end of 2004 when a monstrous tsunami crashed into the coast of Sumatra, leaving over 220,000 Indonesians dead or missing. Then, in May 2006 an earthquake on Java killed thousands. Despite these natural disasters, democracy has not been derailed, and the economy in 2010 and 2011 boasted growth rates of over 6 per cent (at a time when Europe and the US were in the midst of recession).

EAST TIMOR: THE CHALLENGES OF INDEPENDENCE

Independent since 2002, East Timor's economic performance has been less impressive than its neighbours. It remains one of Asia's poorest countries and has the unenviable position as world leader in tobacco consumption (a staggering 61 per cent of its population smoke every day). The reconstruction of infrastructure and facilities left in ruins by 25 years of Indonesian occupation, let alone generating new jobs for young people in an agriculture-dominated economy prone to drought, has not been helped by an elusive search for polit-ical stability. UN forces left East Timor in 2005, apparently having achieved one of the organisation's few successes. They would return

just one year later. This followed a repetition of the violent faction-
alism that had plagued nationalist politics in the interregnum between
Portuguese withdrawal and Indonesian occupation back in 1975. The
sacking of soldiers set off a wider struggle for power, as well as looting
and arson by disaffected unemployed youths. The hero of independence and first president, Xanana Gusmão, became increasingly disaffected with his own party, Fretilin, and formed a new political
organisation, the National Congress for Timorese Reconstruction. But
Gusmão's appointment as Prime Minister in the summer of 2007 trig-
gered another round of violent protests. In February 2008 the
President who appointed Gusmão, José Ramos-Horta, was the
subject of an assassination attempt. Investigations into corruption
amongst civil servants further fractured East Timorese unity. But
Gusmão's victory in the elections of 2012 did lead to a more robust
coalition government. The political stabilization was considered sufficient for hundreds of Australian soldiers to withdraw from East Timor.

There is hope now that the East Timorese can settle down to the
task of improving living standards and reducing their dependence on
outside aid. By 2013, the massive oil and gas fields in the Timor Sea
allowed the accumulation of £7.6 billion in government revenues.
Although marred by allegations of Australian spying in the run-up to
the Timorese-Australian agreement of 2006 on the division of the
spoils, Gusmão is now in a position to deploy these funds on
economic development. Reflecting this, the GDP growth rate in 2013
was a highly respectable 10 per cent.

Notes

Notes

Chronology of Major Events

BC

c. 500,000	*Homo Erectus* living in Java
600–300	Rise of the Dong-son culture in northern Vietnam
207	Co Loa founded in northern Vietnam
111	Co Loa falls under Chinese rule

AD

c. 1–99	Kingdom of Fu-nan in Cambodia founded
192	Kingdom of Champa in central Vietnam founded
c. 300–399	Mahayana Buddhism arrives in Vietnam from China
c. 540	Chen-la defeats Fu-nan in Cambodia
c. 600–700	Srivijaya founded on Sumatra
706	Chen-la divided
790	Sailendra dynasty invades and defeats Chen-la
c. 800	Construction begins on Borobudur on Java
802	Reign of Jayavarman II begins, unifying the Khmers in Cambodia
889	Yasovarman I founds Angkor in Cambodia
939	Chinese rule in northern Vietnam ends
1002	Khmers move into central Thailand under the reign of Suryavarman I
1006	Srivijaya defeats the central Javanese kingdom of Mataram
1009	Later Ly dynasty begins in Vietnam and promotes Theravada Buddhism
1039	Airlangga re-establishes order in Mataram
1025	Cola invades and occupies Srivijaya
1049	Airlangga's death prompts the division of Mataram into Jangala and Kediri
c. 1113	Construction begins of Angkor Wat
c. 1186	Jayavarman VII begins building spree at Angkor

1222	Ken Angrok (Rajasa) defeats Kediri and Singhasari is founded on Java
1225	Beginning of the Tran Dynasty in Vietnam
1238	Sukhothai becomes centre of Tai authority
1257	Mongol invasion of Vietnam
c. 1275–99	Islam makes first appearance in South East Asia
1283	Theravada Buddhism introduced in Thailand
1290	Kertanagara of Java defeats Srivijaya
1293	Majapahit founded in east Java
1296	Mangrai founds Chiang Mai in northern Thailand
1351	Kingdom of Ayutthaya founded in central Thailand
1353	Fa Ngum founds Lan Sang in Laos
1364	Death of Gaja Muda begins the decline of Majapahit
1403	Kingdom of Melaka founded on Malay peninsula
1407	Chinese occupy northern Vietnam
1431	Fall of Angkor, following attack by Tais from Ayutthaya
1434	Cambodian capital moves to Phnom Penh
1471	Champa defeated by Dai Viet
1511	Afonso de Alberquerque conquers Melaka
1527–8	Majapahit collapses; beginning of the Mac dynasty of Vietnam
1531	Beginning of the Thai-Burmese wars
1539	Trinh dynasty founded, Vietnam
1540	First formal partition of Vietnam
1602	VOC (Dutch East India Company) founded
1605	Formation of sultanate of Makassar
1607	Beginning of Aceh's age of greatness under Sultan Iskandar Muda
1619	VOC seizes first slice of Java and founds Batavia (Jakarta)
1621	Massacre of Bandanese by Dutch in Maluku Islands
1641	Dutch conquer Melaka with aid of Johor
1666–69	VOC allies with Bugis of Bone to defeat Makassar
1667	Dutch victory over Aceh; treaty between Holland and Minangkabau confirms the latter's domination of west Sumatra
1692	Champa kingdom finally destroyed by Vietnam forces
1707	Lan Sang splits into Vientiane, Champasak and Luang Prabang
1755	Mataram divided into sultanates of Surakarta and Yogyakarta
1767	Ayutthaya sacked by Burmese
1773	Tayson rebellion begins in Vietnam
1782	Chakri dynasty founded, Thailand
1784	Dutch victory over Johor-Riau
1786	British settlement on Penang founded

1802	Nguyen Anh becomes Emperor Gia-long as Vietnam is re-unified under the Nguyen dynasty
1811	British occupy Java
1819	Singapore founded by Sir Thomas Stamford Raffles
1824	Anglo-Dutch Treaty (Benkulen traded for Melaka)
1825	Rebellion on Java begins against Dutch rule led by Prince Dipanagara
1826	Anglo-Siam Treaty begins process of opening up Thailand to Western trade
1827–28	Lao-Thai wars
1841	Vietnam exiles Cambodia's queen, James Brooke becomes rajah of Sarawak
1848	Monarchy restored in Cambodia but under joint Thai and Vietnamese protection
1859	French attack Saigon and found colony of Cochin-China
1867	Straits Settlements of Singapore, Melaka and Penang come under control of British Colonial Office; French protectorate over Cambodia
1873	Aceh wars against the Dutch begin
1874	Resident system begins in Malaya
1875	British military expedition to Perak, Malaya restores resident system
1877	*Hevea brasiliensis* (the rubber tree) introduced to Singapore Botannical Gardens
1881	North Borneo Company chartered by British government to administer Sabah
1884	France imposes protectorates on Annam and Tonkin in Vietnam
1893	French protectorate over Laos
1896	Federated Malay States formed with a capital at Kuala Lumpur
1901	Dutch introduce Ethical Policy in Indonesia
1904	French acquire Battambang and Siem Reap from Thailand
1906	Brunei becomes a British protectorate
1909	Thailand cedes four northern Malay states to Britain
1912	Sarekat Islam founded in Indonesia
1913	Timor divided into Dutch (west) and Portugese (east)
1920	PKI (Communist Party of Indonesia) founded
1926	PKI launch an uprising against the Dutch
1927	PNI (Indonesian Nationalist Party) founded; VNQDD (Vietnamese Nationalist Party) founded
1929	Oil is discovered at Seria, Brunei
1930	ICP (Indochinese Communist Party) founded
1932	Bloodless revolution in Thailand ends absolute monarchy

1938	Marshall Phibun takes power in Thailand and establishes military dictatorship
1941	Vietminh founded
1942	Japanese occupation of South East Asia begins following fall of Singapore; Thailand recovers 'lost territories' in Malaya, Burma, and Indochina
1944	Free Thai movement removes Phibun from power in Thailand
1945	Atomic bombings of Japan bring end to Pacific War; Republic of Indonesia proclaimed with Sukarno as president; Ho Chi Minh proclaims Democratic Republic of Vietnam in Hanoi
1946	Franco-Vietminh agreement; French naval bombardment kills 6,000 and sparks the First Indochina War; UMNO (United Malays National Organization) formed to challenge British inauguration of the Malayan Union; parliamentary democracy restored to Thailand and King Ananda dies under mysterious circumstances; Republic of Indonesia-Dutch conflict begins in Java and Sumatra; end of the Brooke dynasty and the North Borneo Company as Sarawak and Sabah come under direct British Colonial Office control
1947	Dutch launch first 'police action' in Indonesia; Cambodia and Laos become independent states within the French Union; bloodless right-wing coup launched in Thailand
1948	Federation of Malaya founded and Malayan Emergency begins; Marshal Phibun returns as Prime Minister of Thailand; Dutch launch second 'police action'
1949	Malayan Chinese Association founded (MCA); Republic of Vietnam founded; Dutch transfer power to Republic of Indonesia
1950	South Malukans declare an independent republic in Indonesia
1951	Sir Henry Gurney, the British high commissioner is assassinated in Malaya by communist guerrillas
1953	Cambodia and Laos gain independence; secessionist rebellion begins in Aceh
1954	9,500 are killed at the battle of Dien Bien Phu, ending the French phase of the war in Vietnam and French rule in Indochina; the partition of Vietnam into north and south is agreed at Geneva and a Republic of Vietnam is declared in the south
1957	Government of National Union proclaimed in Laos; Malaya gains independence; bloodless coup in Thailand ends the rule of Phibun
1958	Secessionist rebellion takes place in Sumatra and spreads to

	Kalimantan and Sulawesi; military rule is re-imposed in Thailand
1959	Singapore achieves internal self-government and Lee Kuan Yew becomes prime minister of Singapore; Vietcong founded in South Vietnam and begins campaign against government in Saigon; Brunei loses its British resident and becomes a British-protected state
1960	Malayan Emergency ends
1961	Diem declares a state of emergency in South Vietnam
1962	Regional secessionist revolts crushed in Indonesia; Brunei rebellion
1963	Malaysia founded in 1963 (Singapore, Sabah and Sarawak join with the Federation of Malaya); three-year Confrontation begins between Indonesia and Malaysia
1965	Singapore separates from Malaysia; military rule follows the fall of Sukarno in Indonesia while the PKI is brutally suppressed and pogroms are unleashed against the Chinese community; United States President Lyndon Johnson orders the 'carpet bombing' of North Vietnam
1966	Buddhist monks protest against General Thieu's regime in South Vietnam; end of Malaysia – Indonesia confrontation
1967	Formation of ASEAN (Association of South East Asian Nations)
1968	General Giap engineers North Vietnam's Tet offensive; first peace talks between Washington and Hanoi take place
1969	Ho Chi Minh dies; parliamentary democracy is suspended in Malaysia following inter-communal rioting in Kuala Lumpur
1970	Tunku Abdul Rahman resigns as Malaysia's prime minister; Prince Sihanouk is overthrown in Cambodia; ex-president of Indonesia, Sukarno, dies as General Suharto consolidates military power
1971	British troops withdraw from Malayasia and Singapore; British relinquish control of internal affairs in Brunei in favour of the sultan
1973	Student uprising topples military rule in Thailand and the country begins a three-year experiment with democracy; the United States directs bombing campaign against guerrilla positions in Cambodia in support of Lon Nol; US troops leave Indochina
1975	Victory in Cambodia for Khmer Rouge and the fanatical Pol Pot era begins; Saigon falls to the North Vietnamese Army; communist takeover in Laos; Civil war breaks out in East

	Timor as an independent Democratic Republic of East Timor is declared
1976	Indonesian occupation of East Timor begins; Vietnam is reunified and the Socialist Republic of Vietnam is declared; Thailand reverts to military rule
1978	Vietnam invades Cambodia
1979	Vietnamese occupy and set up satellite government in Phnom Penh as Khmer Rouge regime falls
1981	Dr Mahathir becomes first non-aristocratic prime minister of Malaysia
1984	Brunei becomes independent
1991	Massacre at Dili, East Timor
1992	Democracy returns to Thailand
1993	UN sponsored elections in Cambodia; Reconciliation talks begin between the East Timorese and the Indonesian government
1995	Normalization of US-Vietnam relations
1997	Students begin demonstrations against the Suharto regime in Indonesia; in Cambodia, Hun Sen forces Prince Ranariddh into exile; currency crisis overwhelms South East Asian economies; forest fires in Indonesia run out of control
1998	Suharto's presidency ends; students protest against the arrest and trial of Anwar Ibrahim, the former deputy prime minister of Malaysia; the Khmer Rouge lay down their weapons and Pol Pot commits suicide while Prince Ranariddh is forced to accept Hun Sen's dominance of a new governing coalition in Cambodia
1999	Anwar Ibrahim is sentenced to six years imprisonment for abuse of power in Malaysia; East Timorese vote in favour of independence from Indonesia; UN troops are called in to assist in the creation of a new civil administration; BJ Habibie is replaced as president of Indonesia by Abdurrahman Wahid
2000	South East Asian economies show signs of recovery; normalization of US-Vietnam relations with visit of Bill Clinton to Vietnam; Anwar receives a further nine-year sentence for sexual misconduct
2001	Megawati replaces Wahid as president of Indonesia; UN hands over power to an independent government of East Timor; Thaksin Shinawatra becomes prime minister of Thailand

2002	Mahathir succeeded at Malaysian prime minister by Badawi; Bali bombings kill 202 people; Irian Jaya granted greater autonomy as Papua; East Timor achieves independence
2003	Alliance of Democrats formed after elections in Cambodia; evacuation of Thai citizens from Cambodia
2004	Sihanouk abdicates as King of Cambodia; escalating violence in southern Thailand; tsunami hits Indonesia, Malaysia and Thailand, killing 220,000 in Indonesia alone; landslide victory for Barisan in Malaysia; Anwar Ibrahim's conviction for sodomy overturned; Lee Hsien Loong becomes Singapore's third prime minister; Sultan of Brunei reopens legislature and amends constitution to allow for greater elected representation; Yudhoyono becomes Indonesia's first directly elected president
2005	Landslide victory for Thaksin in Thailand; peace accord signed with Acehnese rebels in Indonesia; UN forces leave East Timor
2006	Snap elections in Thailand lead to street demonstrations and force Thaksin from office and into exile; UN forces return to East Timor following political violence; agreement reached between Australia and East Timor on division of oil and gas revenues in the Timor Sea; thousands killed by earthquake in Java; exposure of corruption in Vietnam's transport ministry
2007	Vietnam joins World Trade Organization and younger generation replace old guard at top of Vietnamese politics; Prince Ranariddh loses his seat in Cambodian elections; election victory in Thailand for People Power Party provokes Yellow Shirt protests; Xanana Gusmão becomes prime minister of East Timor, sparking violent protests
2008	Vietnam and China reach agreement on disputed land border; Vietnam increases restrictions on online bloggers; Barisan loses its 2/3rds majority in Malaysian elections; Indonesia's president expresses 'deep regret' for human rights abuses in East Timor; assassination attempt on President Ramos-Horta in East Timor
2009	Najib replaces Badawi as Malaysian prime minister and \$16 billion economic stimulation package announced; Yudhoyono re-elected as Indonesian president
2010	Limited agreement reached between China and Vietnam over South China Seas; Red Shirt protests in Bangkok
2011	Vietnam's inflation rate approaches 20 per cent; Khmer Rouge's Comrade Duch sentenced in Cambodia; Yingluck Shinawatra becomes Thailand's first female prime minister following peaceful elections; upgrade of Kuala Lumpur's rapid transit system announced; floods inflict further damage on poorly performing Thai economy; PAP's share of the vote falls to 60 per cent in

Singapore elections; Lee Kuan Yew and Goh Chok Tong resign from Singapore cabinet; first elected members in Brunei legislature

2012   Death of Sihanouk, former King of Cambodia; Anwar Ibrahim acquitted of sodomy charges and Security Offences (Special Measures) Act introduced in Malaysia; political stabilization in East Timor leads to withdrawal of Australian troops

2013   Denial of Khmer Rouge atrocities becomes a crime in Cambodia; street protests in Bangkok demand Yingluck's resignation; talks between Thai government and Barisan Revolusi Nasional over future of Muslim Malay provinces in southern Thailand; worst performance on record by the Barisan in a Malaysian election; mass demonstrations in Singapore against immigration; 8 Indonesian soldiers shot dead by Papuan separatists

Selected Rulers & Heads of State

BRUNEI

Sultans
Muhammad, r. *1363*
Abdul Majid, r. *1402*
Ahmad, r. *1408*
Sharif Ali, r. *1426*
Salaiman, r. *1432*
Bolkiah, r. *1485*
Abdul Kahar, r. *1524*
Saiful Rijal, r. *1535*
Shah Brunei, r. *1581*
Muhammad Hasan, r. *1582*
Abdul Jalilul Akbar, r. *1597*
Abdul Jalilul Jabbar, r. *1659*
Haji Muhammad Ali, r. *1660*
Abdul Hakkul Mubin, r. *1661*
Muhyiddin, r. *1673*
Nasruddin, r. *1690*
Husin Kamaluddin, r. *1710*
Muhammad Aliuddin, r. *1730*
Husin Kamaluddin (second reign), r. *1737*
Omar Ali Saifuddin I, r. *1740*
Muhammad Tajuddin, r. *1795*
Muhammad Jamalul Alam I, r. *1804*
Muhammad Tajuddin (second reign), r. *1804*
Muhammad Kanzu Alam, r. *1807*
Muhammad Alam, r. *1826*
Omar Ali Saiffudin II, r. *1828*

Abdul Mumin, r. *1852*
Hashim Jalilul Alam Aqamaddin, r. *1885*
Muhammad Jamalul Alam II, r. *1906*
Ahmad Tajuddin, r. *1924*
Omar Ali Saifuddin III, r. *1950*
Hassanal Bolkiah, r. *1967*

CAMBODIA

Fun-nan
Kaundinya, r. towards the end of the first century AD
Hun P'an-h'uang, r. second half of second century
P'an-p'an, r. earlt third century
Fan Shiman, r. first quarter of third century
Fan Chinsheng, r. second quarter of third century
Fan Chan, r. second quarter of third century
Fan Chang, r. second quarter of third century
Fan Hsun, r. third quarter of third century
Chu Chantan, r. middle of fourth century
Kaundinya II, r. first quarter of fifth century
Che Li pa-mo, r. middle of fifth century
Jayavarman, r. late fifth century to early sixteenth century
Rudravarman, r. *539*

Chen-la
Bhavavarman I, r. *c. 550*
Mahendravarman, r. *c. 600*
Isanavarman I, r. *c. 611*
Bhavavarman II, r. *c. 635*
Jayavarman I, r. *c. 650*
Jayadevi, r. early part of eighth century
Sambhuvarman, r. first half of eighth century
Rajendravarman, r. third quarter of eighth century
Mahipativarman, r. end of eighth century

Angkorian Period
Jayavarman II, r. *802*
Jayavarman III, r. *850*
Indravarman I, r. *877*

Yasovarman I, r. *889*
Harshavarman I, r. *900*
Isanavarman II, r. c. *922*
Jayavarman IV, r. *928*
Harshavarman II, r. *942*
Rajendravarman II, r. *944*
Jayavarman V, r. *968*
Udayadityavarman I, r. *1001*
Suryavarman I, r. *1002*
Udayadityavarman II, r. *1050*
Harshavarman III, r. *1066*
Jayavarman VI, r. *1080*
Dharanindravarman I, r. *1107*
Suryavarman II, r. *1113*
Dharanindravarman II, r. *1150*
Yasovarman II, r. *1160*
Jayavarman VII, r. *1181*
Indravarman II, r. *1221*
Jayavarman VIII, r. *1243*
Indravarman III, r. *1295*
Indrajayavarman, r. *1308*
Jayavarman Paramesvara, r. *1327*
Nippean-bat, r. *1362*
Kalamegha, r. *1371*
Kambujadhiraja, r. c. *1362*
Dharmasokaraja, r. c. *1385*
Po Pi-ya, r. *1389*
Naranya Ramadhipati, r. *1404*
Sodaiya, r. *1429*
Ponhea Yat, r. *1432*
Dharmarajadhiraja, r. *1444*
Srey Sukonthor, r. *1486*
Kan, r. *1512*
Ang Chan, r. *1516*

Kingdom of Cambodia
Barom Reachea I, r. *1566*
Chey Chetta I, r. *1576*
Raemea Chung-prei I, r. *1594*
Barom Reachea II, r. *1596*

Barom Reachea III, r. *1599*
Chau Ponhea Nhom, r. *1600*
Barom Reachea IV, r. *1603*
Chey Chetta II, r. *1576*
Ponhea To, r. *1628*
Ponhea Nu, r. *1630*
Ang Non I, r. *1640*
Chan, r. *1642*
Batom Reachea IV, r. *1659*
Chey Chetta III, r. *1672*
Ang Chei, r. *1673*
Ang Non (usurper), r. *1674*
Chey Chetta IV, r. *1675*
Outey, r. 1*695*
Chey Chetta IV (second reign), r. *1695*
Ang Em, r. *1699*
Chey Chetta IV (third reign), r. *1701*
Thommo Raechea, r. *1702*
Chey Chetta IV (fourth reign), r. *1703*
Thommo Raechea (second reign), r. *1706*
Ang Em (second reign), r. *1710*
Satha, r. *1722*
Thommo Raechea (third reign), r. *1738*
Ang Ton, r. *1747*
Chey Chetta V, r. *1749*
Ang Ton (second reign), r. *1755*
Preah Outey II, r. *1758*
Ang Non II, r. *1775*
Ang Eng, r. *1779*
Ang Chan II, r. *1806*
Ang Met, r. *1834*
Ang Duong, r. *1841*
Norodom, r. *1851*
Sisovath, r. *1901*
Monivong, r. *1927*
Norodom Sihanouk, r. *1941*
Norodom Suramarit, r. *1955*
Norodom Sihanouk – Chief of State, *1960*
Lon Nol – Chief of State, *1970*

Democratic Republic of Kampuchea
Pol Pot – Prime Minister, *1975*

People's Republic of Kampuchea
Heng Samrin – President, *1979*
1991 UN agreement – new elections in 1993

Kingdom of Cambodia
Norodom Sihanouk, r. *1993*
Norodom Sihamoni, r. *2004*

De facto authority remains with the former communist leader, Hun Sen, who has monopolized sate power.

EAST TIMOR

PRESIDENTS
Xanana Gusmão, *2002*
José Ramos Horta, *2007*
Taur Matan Ruak, *2012*

INDONESIA
Only the rulers of Java and Aceh have been listed from the many dynasties of the too-numerous islands to mention.

West Java
Purnavarman, r. *c. 400*
Po-to-kia, r. *424*
Dvaravarman, r. *c. 435*
N.B. No names known between *435–1030*
Jayabhupati, r. *1030*
Niskalavastu (dates unknown)
Deva Niskala (dates unknown)
Ratu Devata, r. *1333–57*
Sanghyang, r. *1552*

Central Java
Sanjaya, r. *737*

Pacapana, r. *778*
Panunggalan (dates unknown)
Varak (dates unknown)
Garung, r. *829/39*
Pikatan, r. *864*
Kayuvangi, r. *879*
Vatu Humalang, r. *886*
Balitung, r. *898*
Daksa, r. *915*
Tulodong, r. *919*
Vava, r. *924–28*

East Java
Airlangga, r. *1019–49*
Janggala, r. *1060*
Jayavarsa, r. *1104*
Kamesvara I, r. *1115–30*
Jayabhaya, r. *1135–57*
Sarvvesvara, r. *1160*
Aryyesvara, r. *1171*
Gandra, r. *1181*
Kamesvara II, r. *1185*
Sarvvesvara II, r. *1190–1200*
Kertajaya, r. *1216–22*

Singhasari and Majapahit
Rajasa, r. *1222*
Anusapati, r. *1227*
Tohjaya, r. *1248*
Vishnuvardhana, r. *1248*
Kertanagara, r. *1268*
Jayakatwang, r. *1292*
Kertajasara, r. *1293*
Jayanagara, r. *1309*
Tribhuvana, r. *1329*
Rajasanagara, r. *1350*
Vikramavardhana, r. *1389*
Suhita, r. *1429*
Kertavijaya, r. *1447–51*

Mataram
Senapati, r. *1582*
Djolang, r. *1601*
Agung, r. *1613*
Amangkurat I, r. *1646*
Amangkurat II, r. *1677*
Amangkurat III, r. *1703*
Pakubuwana I, r. *1705*
Amangkurat IV, r. *1719*
Pakubuwana II, r. *1725*
Pakubuwana III, r. *1749*

Yogyakarta
Hamengkubuwana I, r. *1749*
Hamengkubuwana II, r. *1792*
Hamengkubuwana III, r. *1810*
Hamengkubuwana IV, r. *1814*
Hamengkubuwana V, r. *1822*
Hamengkubuwana VI, r. *1855*
Hamengkubuwana VII, r. *1877*
Hamengkubuwana VIII, r. *1921*
Hamengkubuwana IX, r. *1939–99* (Vice President of the Republic of Indonesia, *1973–8*)
Hawengkubuwana X, r. *1989*

Aceh
Ali Mughayat Shah, r. *1496*
Salah ud-din Ali, r. *1528*
Husain, r. *1537*
Muda, r. *1575*
Sri Alam, r. *1575*
Zainal Abidin, r. *1576*
Mansur Shah, r. *1577*
Boyong, r. *1589*(?)
Ala'ud-din Riayat Shah, r. *1596*
Ali Riayat Shah, r. *1604*
Iskandar Muda, r. *1607*
Iskandar Thani, r. *1636*
Safiyat ud-din Taj al-Alam bint Iskandar Muda, r. *1641*
Naqiyat ud-din Nur al-Alam, r. *1675*

Zaqiyat ud-din Inayat Shah, r. *1678*
Kamalat Shah Zinat ud-din, r. *1688*
Badr al-Alam Sharif Hashim Jamal ud-udin, r. *1699*
Perkara Alam Sharif Lamtui, r. *1702*
Jamal al-Alam Badr al-Munir, r. *1703*
Jauhar al-Alam Amin ud-din, r. *1726*
Shams al-Alam, r. *1726*
Ala'ud-din Ahmad Shah, r. *1727*
Ala'ud-din Shah Jahan, r. *1735*
Mahmud Shah, r. *1760*
Badr ud-din, r. *1764*
Sulaiman Shah, r. *1775*
Ala'ud-din Muhammad, r. *1781*
Ala'ud-din Jauhar al-Alam I, r. *1802*
Sharif Saif al-Alam, r. *1815*
Ala'ud-din Jauhar al-Alam II, r. *1818*
Muhammad Shah ibn Jauhar al-Alam I, r. *1824*
Mansur Shah, r. *1838–74* (Dutch Occupation)

Republic of Indonesia
PRESIDENTS
Ahmed Sukarno, *1945–67*
General Suharto, *1968*
BJ Habibie, *1998*
Abdurrahman Wahid, *1999*
Megawati Sukarnoputri, *2001*
Susilo Bambang Yudhoyono, *2004*

LAOS

Lan Sang
Fa Ngum, r. *1353*
Sam Sen Thai, r. *1373*
Lan Kham Deng, r. *1416*
Phommathat, r. *1428*
Kham Ten, r. *1429*
Sai, r. *1430*
Fa Khai, r. *1430*
Kon Kham, r. 1433

Yukhon, r. *1434*
Khamkeut, r. *1435*
Sainyachakkaphat, r. *1438*
Suvanna Bulang, r. *1479*
La Sen Thai, r. *1486*
Som Phou, r. *1496*
Visoun, r. *1501*
Photisarat I, r. *1520*
Setthathirat, r. *1548*
Soulinthara, r. *1571*
Nakhone Noi, r. *1582*
(interregnum *1583–91*)
Nokeo Kumane, r. *1591*
Thammikarat, r. *1596*
Oupagnouvarat I, r. *1622*
Photisarat II, r. *1623*
Mone Keo, r. *1627*
Oupagnouvarat II (dates unknown)
Tone Kham (dates unknown)
Visai (dates unknown)
Soulingavongsa, r. *1637*
Tian Thala, r. *1694*
Nantharat, r. *1700*
Sai Ong Hue, r. *1700*

Vientiane
Sai Ong Hue, r. *1707*
Ong Long, r. *1735*
Ong Boun, r. *1760*
(interregnum *1778–82*)
Chao Nan, r. *1782*
Chao In, r. *1792*
Chao Anu, r. *1805*

Champasak
Soi Sisamout, r. *1713*
Saya Koumane, r. *1737*
Fay Na, r. *1791*
Chao Nou, r. *1811*
(interregnum *1811–13*)

Phromma Noi, r. *1813*
Chao Nho, r. *1813*
Chao Houy, r. *1826*
Chao Nak, r. *1841*
Chao Boua, r. *1852*
Chao Kham Nhai, r. *1856*
Kham Souk, r. *1863–1900*

Luang Prabang
Kitsarat, r. *1707*
Khamone Noi, r. *1726*
Inta Som, r. *1727*
Sotika Koumane, r. *1776*
Tia Vong, r. *1781*
(interregnum *1787–91*)
Anourath, r. *1791*
Manta Thourath, r. *1817*
Souka Seum, r. *1836*
Tiantha, r. *1851*
Oun Kham, r. *1872*

Modern Period
Zakarine, r. *1894*
Sisavangvong, r. *1904*
Sisavang Vatthana, r. *1959–75*

Lao People's Democratic Republic
PRESIDENTS
Prince Souphanouvong, *1975*
Kaysone Phomvihane, *1991*
Nouhak Phoumsavanh, *1992*
Khamtai Siphandon, *1998*
Choummaly Sayasone, *2006*

MALAYSIA

Melaka
Paramesvara, r. *1403*
Sri Maharaja, r. 1425

raja Ibrahim, r. *1445*
Raja Kasim, r. *1447*
Mansur Shah, r. *1459*
Ala'ud-din Riayat Shah, r. *1477*
Mahmud, r. *1488–1511* (arrival of Portuguese)

Malaya/Malaysia
Since Independence in 1957, the constitutional head of state has been the Yang di-Pertuan Agong (paramount ruler or king). This position rotates every five years amongst the hereditary rulers of the nine Malay States. In reality, however, the most powerful figure has been the prime minister.

Federation of Malaya
PRIME MINISTER
Tunku Abdul Rahman, *1957*

Federation of Malaysia
PRIME MINISTERS
Tunku Abdul Rahman, *1963*
Tun Abdul Razak, *1970*
Tun Hussein Onn, *1957*
Dr Mahathir Mohamad, *1981*
Abdullah Badawi, *2002*
Najib Adbul Razak, *2009*

SINGAPORE

PRIME MINISTERS
Lee Kuan Yew, *1959*
Goh Chok Tong, *1991*
Lee Hsien Loong, *2004*

THAILAND

Sukhothai
Sri Intaratitya, r. *1238*
Ban Muang, (dates unknown)

Ramakamhaeng, r. *1279*
Lo Tai, r. *1317*
Thammaraja Lutai, r. *1347*
Thammaraja II, r. *1370*
Thammaraja III, r. *1406*

Ayutthaya
Ramathibodi, r. *1351*
Ramesuen, r. *1369*
Borommaracha I, r. *1370*
Thong Lan, r. *1388*
Ramesuen (second reign), r. *1388*
Ramracha, r. *1395*
Intharacha I, r. *1408*
Borommaracha II, r. *1424*
Trailok, r. *1448*
Borommaracha III, r. *1488*
Ramathibodi II, r. *1491*
Borommaracha IV, r. *1529*
Ratsada, r. *1534*
Prajai, r. *1534*
Kero Fa, r. *1546*
Khun Worawongsa, r. *1548*
Mahachakrapat, r. *1549*
Mahin, r. *1569*
Thammaracha, r. *1569*
Naresuan, r. *1590*
Ekathosrot, r. *1605*
Intharacha II, r. *1610*
Jattha, r. *1628*
Athityawong, r. *1630*
Prasat Thong, r. *1630*
Chao Fa Jai, r. *1656*
Sri Suthammaracha, r. *1656*
Narai, r. *1657*
P'ra P'etraja, r. *1688*
P'rachao Sua, r. *1703*
Thai Sra, r. *1709*
Borommakot, r. *1733*
Uthumphon, r. *1758*

Borommaracha V, r. *1758*

Bangkok

Phraya Taksin, r. *1767*
Rama I (Chakri), r. *1782*
Rama II, r. *1809*
Rama III (Nang Klao), r. *1824*
Rama IV (Mongkut), r. *1851*
Rama V (Chulalongkorn), r. *1868*
Rama VI (Vajiravudh), r. *1910*
Rama VII (Prajadiphok), r. *1925*
Rama VIII (Ananda), r. *1935*
Rama IX (Bhumipol), r. *1946*

PRIME MINISTERS
Pridi Phanomyong, *1932*
Field Marshal Phibun, *1938*
Khuang Aphaiwong, *1944*
Seni Pramoj, *1945*
Khuang Aphaiwong, *1946*
Pridi Phanomyong, *1946*
Thamrong Nawasawat, *1947*
Khuang Aphaiwong, *1947*
Field Marshal Phibun, *1948*
Sarit Thanarat, *1957*
Thanom Kittikachorn, *1963*
Sanya Thammasak, *1973*
Kukrit Pramoj, *1975*
Seni Pramoj, *1976*
Thanin Kravichien, *1976*
Kriangsak Chomanan, *1977*
Prem Tinsulanonda, *1980*
Chatichai Choonhavan, *1988*
Anand Punyarachan, *1991*
Suchinda Kraprayoon, *1992*
Chuan Leepkai, *1992*
Banharn Silpa-Archa, *1995*
Chavalit Yonkchaiyudh, *1996*
Chuan Leepkai, *1997*
Thaksin Shinawatra, *2001*

Surayud Chulanont, *2006*
Samak Sundaravej, *2008*
Abhisit Vejjajiva, *2008*
Yingluck Shinawatra, *2011*

VIETNAM

Thuc Dynasty (Kingdom called Au Lac; capital at Co Loa)
Thuc An Duong Vuong, r. *257–208* BC

Trieu Dynasty (Kingdom called Nam Viet)
Trieu Vo Voung, r. *208* BC
Trieu Van Voung, r. *136* BC
Trieu Minh Voung, r. *124* BC
Trieu Ai Voung, r. *112* BC
Trieu Voung Kien Duc, r. *111* BC, falls under China

Early Ly Dynasty
Ly Nam Viet De Bon, r. *544* AD
Trieu Viet Voung Quang Phuc, r. *549*
Ly Hau De Phat Tu, r. *571–602*, falls under China

Ngo Dynasty
Ngo Vuong Quyen, r. *939*
Duong-Binh Vuong, r. *945*
Ngo Nam Tam, r. *951*
Ngo Thien Sach, r. *951–4*
(interregnum *965–68*)

Dinh Dynasty
Dinh Bo Linh, r. *968*
Dinh De Toan, r. *979*

Early Le Dynasty
Le Dai-Hanh, r. *980*
Le Trung-Ton, r. *1005*

Later Ly Dynasty (Kingdom now known as Dai Viet)
Ly Tai To, r. *1009*

Ly Tai Tong, r. *1028*
Ly Thanh Tong, r. *1054*
Ly Can Duc, r. *1072*
Ly Than Tong, r. *1127*
Ly Anh Tong, r. *1138*
Ly Cao Tong, r. *1175*
Ly Hue Tong, r. *1210*
Ly Chieu-Hoang, r. *1224*

Tran Dynasty
Tran Thai Ton, r. *1225*
Tran Thanh Tong, r. *1258*
Tran Nhon Tong, r. *1278*
Tran Anh Tong, r. *1293*
Tran Minh Tong, r. *1314*
Tran Hien Tong, r. *1329*
Tran Du Tong, r. *1341*
Duong Nhut Le, r. *1369*
Tran Nghe Tong, r. *1370*
Tran Thuan Tong, r. *1388*
Tran Thieu De, r. *1398*

Ho Dynasty
Ho Qui Li, r. *1400*
Ho Han Thuong, r. *1400*

Restored Tran Dynasty
Tran De Qui, r. *1407*
Tran De Qui Khoang, r. *1409*

Later Le Dynasty
Le Loi, r. *1428*
Le Thai To, r. *1433*
Le Nhon Ton, r. *1442*
Le Thanh Ton, r. *1460*
Le Hien Ton, r. *1497*
Le Tuc Ton, r. *1504*
Le Ui-Muc De, r. *1504*
Le Tuong-Duc De, r. *1509*
Tran Cao, r. *1516*

Le Du, r. *1518*
Le Hoang De-Xuan, r. *1522*
(Mac interregnum *1527–33*, see below)
Le Trang Ton, r. *1533*
Le Trung Ton, r. *1548*
Le Anh Ton, r. *1556*
Le The Ton, r. *1573*
Nguyen Duong Minh, r. *1597*
Le Khin Ton, r. *1599*
Le Thanh Ton, r. *1619*
Le Chan Ton, r. *1643*
Le Than Ton, r. *1649*
Le Huyen Ton, r. *1662*
Le Gia Ton, r. *1671*
Le Hi Ton, r. *1671*
Le Du Ton, r. *1705*
Le De Duy-Phuong, r. *1729*
Le Thuan Ton, r. *1732*
Le I Ton, r. *1735*
Le Hien Ton, r. *1740*
Le Man Hoang-De, r. *1786–1804*

Mac Dynasty
Mac Dang Dung, r. *1527*
Mac Dang Doanh, r. *1530*
Mac Phuc Hai, r. *1540*
Mac Phu Nguyen, r. *1546*
Mac Mau Hop, r. *1562*
Mac Toan, r. *1592*
Mac Kinh Chi, r. *1592*
Mac Kinhn Cung, r. *1593*
Mac Kinh Khoan, r. *1623*
Mac Kinh Hoan, r. *1638–77*

Trinh Dynasty
Trinh Kiem, r. *1539*
Trinh Coi, r. *1569*
Trinh Tong, r. *1570*
Trinh Tang, r. *1627*
Trinh Tac, r. *1657*

Trinh Con, r. *1682*
Trinh Cuong, r. *1709*
Trinh Giang, r. *1729*
Trinh Dinh, r. *1740*
Trinh Sam, r. *1767*
Trinh Can, r. *1782*
Trinh Khai, r. *1782*
Trinh Phung, r. *1786–7*

Tayson Rulers
Nguyen Nhac, r. *1778–93*
Nguyen Hue (Quang-trung), r. *1788–92*
Nguyen Quang-toan, r. *1792–1802*

Nguyen Dynasty
Nguyen Hoang, r. *1558*
Nguyen Nguyen, r. *1613*
Nguyen Lan, r. *1635*
Nguyen Tan, r. *1648*
Nguyen Tran, r. *1687*
Nguyen Chu, r. *1691*
Nguyen Chu, r. *1725*
Nguyen Khoat (Chua Vo Vuong), r. *1738*
Nguyen Thuan, r. *1765*
Nguyen Anh (Gia-long), r. *1778*
Gia-long, r. *1802*
Minh-mang, r. *1820*
Thieu Tri, r. *1841*
Tu-duc, r. *1848*
Duc Duc, r. *1883*
Hiep-hoa, r. *1883*
Kien Phuc, r. *1884*
Ham Nghi, r. *1885*
Dong Khanh, r. *1886*
Thanh Thai, r. *1889*
Duy Tan, r. *1907*
Khai Dinh, r. *1916*
Bao Dai, r. *1925–45*

Champa

Sri Mara, r. *192*
?
?
Fan Hiong, r. *270*
Fan Yi, reign ended in *336*
Fan Wen, r. *336*
Fan Fo, r. *349*
Bhadravarman I, reigning in *377*
Gangaraja, (dates unknown)
Manorathavarman, (dates unknown)
Wen Ti, (dates unknown)
Seven rules with title Fan, r. *c. 420–c. 510*
Devararman, r. *c. 510*
Vijayavarman, r. *c. 526*
Rudravarman I, r. *c. 529*
Sambuvarman, r. *c. 605*
Kandhardpadharma, r. *c. 629*
Bhasadharma, r. *c. 645*
Bhadresvaravarman, r. *645*
?
Vikrantavarman I, r. *653*
Vikrantavarman II, r. c. *686*
Rudravarman II, r. c. *731*
Prithindravarman, r. c. *758*
Satyavarman, r. c. *774*
Indravarman I, r. c. *787*
Harivarman I, r. c. *803*
Vikrantavarman III, r. c. *854*
Indravarman II, r. c. *875*
Jayasinhavarman I, r. *c. 898*
Jayasaktivarman, (dates unknown)
Bhadravarman II, r. *c. 910*
Indravarman III, reign ended in *959*
Jayaindravarman I, r. *c. 960*
Paramesvaravarman I, reign ended in *982*
Indravarman IV, r. *c. 982*
Lieou Ki-Tsong, r. *c. 986*
Harivarman II, r. *c. 991*
Yan Pu Ku Vijay, r. *c. 999*

Harivarman II, r. *c. 1010*
Paramesvaravarman II, r. *c. 1018*
Vikrantavarman IV, reign ended in *1030*
Jayaindravarman II, r. *1044*
Jayaparamesvaravarman I, r. *1044*
Bhadravarman III, r. *c. 1061*
Rudravarman III, r. *1061*
Harivarman IV, r. c. *1074*
Jayaindravarman II (first reign), r. *1080*
Paramabhodisatva, r. *1081*
Jayaindravarman II (second reign), r. *1086*
Harivarman V, r. *c. 1114*
Jayaindravarman III, r. *c. 1139*
Rudravarman IV, r. *c. 1145*
Jayaharivarman I, r. *1147*
Jayaharivarman II, (dates unknown)
Jayaindravarman IV, r. *c. 1167*

(Division into two kingdoms)

A. KINGDOM OF VIJAYA
Suryajayavarman, r. *1190*
Jayaindravarman V, r. *1191*

B. KINGDOM OF PHAN RANG
Suryavarman, r. *1190*

(Kingdom reunified)

Suryavarman (of Phan Rang), r. *1192–1203* (incorporated into Cambodia)
Jayaparamesvaravarman II, r. *1220*
Jayaindravarman VI, r. *c. 1254*
Indravarman V, r. *c. 1265*
Jayasinhavarman II, reign ended in *1307*
Jayasinhavarman III, r. *1307*
Che Nang, r. *1312*
Che Anan, r. *1318*

Tra Hoa, r. *1342*
Che Bong Nga, reign ended in *1390*
Ko Cheng, r. *1390*
Jayasinhavarman IV, r. *1400*
Maha Vijay, r. *1441*
Moho Kouei-lai, r. *1446*
Moho Kouei-yeou, r. *1449*
Moho P'an-lo-yue, r. *1458*
P'an-lo T'ou-ts'iuan, r. *1460–71*

(In 1471 Champa was defeated by the Le dynasty of northern Vietnam and the Cham kings became vassals of Dai Viet. In 1832 the Cham kingdom was formally aboloshied by which time Cham lands has been fully incorporated into Nguyen Vietnam).

Democratic Republic of Vietnam (North Vietnam)
Ho Chi Minh – President, *1945–69*

After Ho's death there was a collective leadership, the 'inner-circle of five'.

Associated State of Vietnam
Bao Dai, r. *1949*

Republic of Vietnam (South Vietnam)
Bao Dai – President, *1954*
Ngo Dinh Diem – Prime Minister, *1954*
Ngo Dinh Diem – President, *1955*
Nguyen Ngoc – Head of State, *1963*
General Nguyen Khan – Head of State, *1964*
Tran Van Huong – Head of State, *1964*
Nguyen Xuan Oanh – Head of State, *1965*
Phan Huy Quat – Head of State, *1965*
Nguyen Cao Ky-Nguyen Van Thieu – coalition, *1965*
Nguyen Van Thieu – de facto Head of State, *1967*

Socialist Republic of Vietnam (reunited Vietnam)
The de jure heads of state have been as follows:

PRESIDENTS
Nguyen Huu Tho, *1980*

CHAIRMEN OF THE COUNCIL OF STATE
Truong Chinh, *1981*
Vo Chi Cong, *1987*

PRESIDENTS
Le Duc Anh, *1992*
Tran Duc Luong, *1997*
Nguyen Minh Triet, *2006*
Truong Tan Sang, *2011*

Further Reading

General Surveys

ALAC-APPA, MUTHIAH (ed.) *Political Legitimacy in Southeast Asia: The Quest for Moral Authority* (Stanford, California: Stanford University Press, 1995).

BROWN, IAN, *Economic Change in South-East Asia, c. 1850–1980* (Kuala Lumpur, Oxford University Press, 1997).

COEDÈS, G., *The Indianized States of South East Asia*, English edn. (Honolulu, East-West Center, 1968).

HALL, D.G.E., *A History of South-East Asia*, 4th edn.(London, Macmillan, 1981).

OSBORNE, MILTON, *South East Asia: An Introductory History*, 6th edn. (St. Leonards, NSW, Allen and Unwin, 1995).

RAWSON, PHILIP, *The Art of Southeast Asia* (London, Thames and Hudson, 1967).

REID, ANTHONY, *South East Asia in the Age of Commerce, 1450–1680* (2 vols) (New Haven, Yale University Press, 1988).

SARDESAI, D.R., *South East Asia, Past and Present* (London, Macmillan, 1997).

STEINBERG, DAVID (ed.) *In search of South East Asia, A Modern History* (London, Pall Mall Press, 1971).

TARLING, NICHOLAS (ed.) *Cambridge History of South East Asia, Vols. I & II* (Cambridge, Cambridge University Press, 1992).

Individual Country studies

ANDAYA, B.W. and ANDAYA, L., *A History of Malaysia*, 2nd edn. (London, Palgrave, 2001).

CHANDLER, DAVID, *A History of Cambodia*, 2nd edn. (Boulder, Colorado, 1993).

CRIBB, ROBERT and BROWN, COLIN, *Modern Indonesia since 1945* (London, Longman, 1995).

HODGKIN, THOMAS, *Vietnam: The Revolutionary Path* (London, Macmillan, 1981).

JOLLIFFE, JILL, *East Timor: Nationalism and Colonialism* (St. Lucia, Queensland, University of Queensland Press, 1978).

KAMM, HENRY. *Cambodia: Report from a Stricken Land* (New York: Arcade Publishing, 1998).

KARNOW, STANLEY, *Vietnam: A History* (London, Century Hutchinson, 1983).

KRATOSKA, PAUL, *The Japanese Occupation of Malaya, 1941–45* (Honolulu: University of Hawaii Press, 1997).

LEE, E. and CHEW, C.T., *A History of Singapore* (Singapore, Oxford University Press, 1991).

LOCKHART, GREG, *Nation in Arms: the origins of the People's Army of Vietnam* (Sydney, Allen & Unwin, 1989).

RICKLEFS, M.C., *A Modern History of Indonesia since c. 1300*, 2nd edn. (London, Macmillan, 1993).

RUANE, KEVIN, *War and Revolution in Vietnam, 1930–75* (London, UCL Press, 1998).

SAUNDERS, GRAHAM, *A History of Brunei* (Kuala Lumpur, Oxford University Press, 1994).

STUART-FOX, MARTIN, *Laos: Politics, Economics and Society* (London, Pinter, 1986).

TAYLOR, JOHN G., *Indonesia's Forgotten War: The Hidden History of East Timor* (London, Zed Books, 1991).

TURNBULL, C. MARY, *A History of Singapore, 1819–1998*, 2nd edn. (Singapore, Oxford University Press, 1989).

___, *A Short History of Malaysia, Singapore and Brunei* (Sydney, Graham Brash, 1980).

WYATT, D.K., *Thailand: A Short History* (New Haven, Yale University Press, 1984).

Travellers' Accounts

BASTIN, JOHN, *Travellers' Singapore: An Anthology* (Kuala Lumpur, Oxford University Press, 1994).

COOPE, A.E., *The Voyage of Abdullah: A Translation from the Malay* (Singapore, Malaya Publishing House, 1949).

GULLICK, J.M., *They Came to Malaya: A Travellers' Anthology* (Singapore, Oxford University Press, 1993).

KING, VICTOR T., *The Best of Borneo Travel* (Singapore, Oxford University Press, 1993).

MAUGHAM, W. SOMERSET, *The Gentleman in the Parlour: A Record of a Journey from Rangoon to Haiphong* (New York: Marlowe & Co., 1994).

MILLER, GEORGE, *To the Spice Islands and Beyond: Travels in Eastern Indonesia* (Kuala Lumpur, Oxford University Press, 1996).

MURPHY, DERVLA, *One Foot in Laos* (London, John Murray, 1999).

REID, ANTHONY, *Witness to Sumatra: A Travellers' Anthology*, (Singapore, Oxford University Press, 1995).

REITH, G.M., *1907 Handbook to Singapore* (Singapore, Oxford University Press, 1985; first edn., Singapore, Fraser and Neave Ltd., 1892; second edn., 1907).

RUSH, JAMES R., *Java: A Travellers' Anthology* (Kuala Lumpur, Oxford University Press 1996).

SMITHIES, MICHAEL, *Descriptions of Old Siam* (Kuala Lumpur, Oxford University Press, Smithies 1995).

VICKERS, ADRIAN, *Travelling to Bali: Four Hundred Years of Journeys* (Kuala Lumpur, Oxford University Press, 1994).

Works of Fiction

ALDISS, BRIAN, W., *A Rude Awakening* (New York, Random House, 1978).

BALABAN, JOHN, and NGUYEN QUI DUC. *Vietnam: A Traveler's Literary Companion* (San Francisco: Whereabouts Press, 1996).

BOULE, PIERRE, *Sacrilege in Malaya* (London, Fontana, 1961).

BURGESS, ANTHONY, *The Malayan Trilogy* (Harmondsworth, Penguin, 1978).

CLAVELL, JAMES, *King Rat* (London, Coronet, 1975).

CONRAD, JOSEPH, *Victory* (first published 1920/London, Pan Books 1975).
___, *Lord Jim* (Doubleday, 1920/Oxford, Oxford University Press, 1983).

FARRELL, J.G., *The Singapore Grip* (Weidenfeld & Nicolson 1978/London, Fontana 1984).

FAUCONNIER, HENRI, *The Soul of Malaya* (Kuala Lumpur, Oxford University Press, 1965).

GREENE, GRAHAM, *The Quiet American* (London, Heinemann, 1956).

HAN SUYIN, *. . . And The Rain My Drink* (London, Cape, 1956).

KOCH, CHRISTOPHER, *The Year of Living Dangerously* (London, Grafton, 1978).

LUBIS, MOCHTAR, *Twilight in Djakarta* (Kuala Lumpur, Oxford University Press, 1983).

LULOFS, MADELON, *Rubber* (Cassell, 1933/Singapore, Oxford University Press, 1987).

MAUGHAM, W.S., *Collected Short* Stories, Vols. Two and Four (London, Mandarin, 1991).

MEEKER, CLARE HODGSON. *A Tale of Two Rice Birds* (Seattle: Sasquatch Books, 1994).

NGUYEN DU. *The Tale of the Kieu* (New Haven: Yale University Press, 1987).

Historical Gazetteer

Numbers in bold relate to the main text

BRUNEI

In the sixteenth and seventeenth centuries, Brunei was one of South East Asia's most powerful states, with influence extending throughout the island of Borneo and as far as the Philippines in the east. This power was superseded, however, by the Sulu sultanate of the southern Philippines. The arrival of the British on Borneo in the nineteenth century confirmed Brunei's eclipse and restricted the area over which the sultans ruled to the tiny north west region that the state occupies today. In contemporary times, however, Brunei has re-emerged as a considerable force within South East Asia, due mainly to its vast oil reserves, which have made the Sultan of Brunei one of the world's richest men. To some extent this wealth has 'trickled down' to the average Bruneian through a system of welfare and educational provision and an enviable freedom from taxation.

Bandar Seri Begawan is the country's capital city, with attractions ranging from the traditional to the strikingly modern. Of the traditional variety, **Kampung Ayer** is a sight to behold. A network of wooden bridges connects the sprawling villages, or *kampung* of wooden houses, built high on stilts above insanitary water below. People have lived in such dwellings for centuries, but today's inhabitants have electricity and piped water to make life considerably more comfortable.

Bandar's museums are also worth visiting, the most impressive being the **Brunei Museum** with its fabulous collection of Islamic art and an informative gallery on Muslim cultural traditions. If royalty is of interest to you, then the **Royal Regalia Building** is the place to head for. The museum has an opulent feel to it, which is derived not only from its extravagant exhibits but also from the sumptuous surroundings in which photographs, anecdotes and memorabilia are displayed to chart the current sultan's life from childhood.

Brunei is a strictly Islamic state, which, combined with the sultanate's wealth, ensures that there are numerous impressive mosques. The most formidable is the **Sultan Omar Ali Saifuddin Mosque**. The mosque, which was completed in 1958 at a cost of US$5 million is built in a classical style and makes the finest use of Italian marble, Venetian stained glass, chandeliers and gold leaf. It is both awesome and beautiful and the building's full architectural glory is reflected in a circular lagoon on which a *mahligai*, a royal barge, sits dormant awaiting its next ceremonial function. The wealth of Brunei is also reflected by the sultan's magnificent **Nural Iman Palace**. The Istana (palace), which cost an estimated US$350 million is rarely open to the public. However, good views can be obtained from a nearby park, or from a trip in a water taxi.

CAMBODIA

Cambodia has a history that is both rich and turbulent. From the latter, this troubled country is only now starting to emerge. The kingdoms of Fu-nan and Chen-la ruled over much of the country between the first and the seventh centuries, when it was superseded by the grandeur of the Angkorian period and the mighty Khmer empire. Cambodia's rich architectural heritage owes much to this classical period up to the sixteenth century (although the actions of the Khmer Rouge have taken their toll on many of the country's and some of the world's most important monuments). The country was also subjected to an 85-year colonial interregnum under the French from the 1860s when it was known, along with Laos and Vietnam, as French Indochina. As with neighbouring Laos to the north, Cambodia became a target of American bombing raids during the Vietnam War, and it also

suffered incursions by South Vietnamese troops seeking out communists. Bitter fighting in the country resulted, culminating in the brutal regime of Pol Pot and the Khmer Rouge, who sought the radical transformation of society along extreme Maoist principles. Overthrown in 1979, the Khmer Rouge have since remained outside mainstream Cambodian politics. Guerrilla warfare tactics have only recently been given up by the Khmer Rouge, granting the population welcome relief, and the world's travellers greater access to some of the greatest architectural treasures. **218–24**

Angkor is located in north western Cambodia outside Siem Reap. It was the capital of the Khmer empire and was founded under Jayavarman II in the ninth century. A visit to Cambodia would not be complete without a tour of the magnificent temples found at Angkor, which range in date from the ninth to the thirteenth centuries. Unfortunately, however, there has been terrible vandalism inflicted on the wonderful statuary around Angkor. Many statues are without their heads, dynamited by thieves who then sell them on the black market – indicative of both Cambodian poverty and the lack of control excercised by the government in Phnom Penh over the Angkor area until very recently. Angkor Wat is the name commonly given to the series of temples found at Angkor, but it is in actual fact only one of Angkor's many architectural masterpieces. The successive cities, centred around the temples, were constructed under the influence of Hindu cosmology. The temple-table, upon which the religious shrine was erected at the top, represents Mount Meru, the home of the gods, and the Khmer kings were identified with the gods represented in the temples' architecture and art, thus helping to reinforce the regal cults. The temples are some distance apart, and most travellers find that taxis or motor cycles are the best ways to get around, but it is not advisable to veer from the marked pathways.

The most famous of all the temples is **Angkor Wat** itself – its temple towers are shown on the modern-day Cambodian flag. Angkor Wat is the largest of the temples at Angkor, and is undoubtedly one of the world's greatest architectural achievements. It took 30 years to build, and the amount of stone used was equivalent to that of the great pyramids of Egypt. Suryavarman II (r. 1113–52), ordered the construction of the temple to honour the god Vishnu with whom he was associated. The temple was also to serve as Suryavarman II's funeral temple, in which he would achieve immortality. Angkor Wat was surrounded by a moat that may have served as the water supply for its inhabitants and was 200 yards wide and four miles long. The entrance to the complex is along a causeway lined with huge stone *nagas* (mythical snakes). This roadway represents the bridge between the world of man and the world of the gods. The symmetry of the temple is testament to the outstanding skills of the architects and craftsmen responsible for the construction of the temple, which extends over some 81 hectares. Indeed, nothing you read will ever prepare you for the sheer size and magnificence of Angkor Wat. The temple complex as a whole faces westwards and represents a universe in concentric circles, six of land and seven of oceans. The complex is crowned by five perfectly symmetrical towers, which represent the five peaks of Mount Meru, the highest of which towers 168 feet (50 metres) above ground. The city of Brahma,

Angkor Wat

the home of the gods, is located at the summit and is protected at cardinal points by eight guardian divinities. Surrounding the central temple complex is the world's longest continuous bas-relief. Intricately carved, the reliefs depict scenes from Hindu mythology. Of the many scenes, one on the southern side of the temple depicts the Churning of the Ocean of Milk by 88 devils and 92 gods, both seeking to extract the elixir of immortality, and watched over by Vishnu, Siva and Brahma.

North of Angkor Wat stands the walled city of **Angkor Thom**, which covers almost four square miles. Built under the reign of Jayavarman VII (r. 1181–1221) it housed more than 1 million inhabitants. At the centre of Angkor Thom is the Bayon, a table-temple of towering and mysterious smiling faces which, combined with its smoky colour, gives the temple its eerie atmosphere. The faces are said to represent Jayavarman II, as the omnipresence of the Bodhisattva Avalokitesvara. Scenes from twelfth-century life in Angkor are depicted in the temple's 1,312 yards (1,200 metres), of masterfully carved bas-reliefs.

Further to the north west is **The Baphuon**, another representation of Mount Meru. Pyramidal in style it was built by Udayadityavarman II (r.1050–66); the door frames and lintels are particularly fine examples of Khmer art. In the fifteenth century, a reclining Buddha, 44 yards (40 metres), in length was fashioned from the second-level western wall of the temple.

Ta Prohm, overgrown by jungle, offers a unique opportunity to experience the vision that confronted French archaeologists when they discovered the site in the nineteenth century. Much more intimate than the other larger and restored temples of Angkor, Tha Phrom is delightful for the contrast it offers. The towering trees give the seventeenth-century temple a mystical quality and although its friezes are partially obscured by the overgrowth, Tha Phrom is not to be missed. Most visitors to Angkor include a trip to the great lake, **Tonle Sap**, from whence Angkor received its water supply.

While at Angkor you may wish to travel further north to visit the temple of **Banteay Srei**. Although the temple is only small, it is well worth a visit. Banteay Srei is about 1,000 years old, but it is very well preserved and very ornate. It is advisable, however, only to take this trip with a driver. **51–8, 76**

Phnom Penh is situated on the confluence of the Mekong, Bassac and Tonle Sap rivers. It dates back to 1327 when Wat Phnom Don Penh was built by a rich widow on the Hill of Lady Penh. The city was completed in 1434 under the reign of King Ponhea Yat, and has served as a capital for most of the time since Angkor was abandoned in the fifteenth century.

There are many sites of historical interest in Phnom Penh, not least is the **Royal Palace**. Built in 1866 by King Norodom, it was opened in 1870 and, although the main palace compound is closed to the public, there is still a great deal to see. In the compound that is open to the public fresco paintings depicting episodes from the Khmer version of the *Ramayana*, the *Reamker*, decorate the walls. **Wat Preah Keo** (Temple of the Emerald Buddha) more commonly known as the Silver Pagoda is also worth seeking out. It is so called because of the 5,000 silver tiles, each weighing nearly 2.5 pounds, which cover the floor and make it a priceless piece of religious art. In the centre, sits an Emerald Buddha made of baccarat crystal and, before it, a 14 stone solid-gold Buddha encrusted with 9,584 diamonds. The Gold Buddha, which was made in 1906, is said to have been constructed to the exact proportions of King Norodom and was fashioned from his melted down jewellery. It is flanked on either side by more Buddhas, one of which is encrusted with 1,000 diamonds. Gifts to the Khmer kings from foreign nations are displayed in cabinets that line the perimeter.

North of the Royal Palace is **The National Museum**, which is an impressive structure built between 1917 and 1920, and a fine example of Khmer architecture. The museum houses some 5,000 works of art, which date from Fu-nan and Chen-la through to the nineteenth century. Among its collection are ceramics and sculptures as well as royal barges and costumes.

The city's other museum **Tuol Sleng** is an old schoolhouse, which was taken over in 1975 by Pol Pot's security forces and turned into a prison known as S-21. Thousands of victims passed through security prison 21, where they were tortured by the black-suited, red-head-banded boy soldiers of the Khmer Rouge before being sent to the extermination camp known as the Killing Fields at Choeung Ek. Those who did not make it to Choeung Ek were buried in mass graves on site. The blood-splattered museum walls are lined with carefully catalogued photographs and other documentation on those who passed through S-21. The documentation, preserved by the Khmer Rouge torturers, was uncovered by the Vietnamese in 1979 when they took over the city. **107, 108, 145, 219–21**

From Phnom Penh you can travel south west to the Killing Fields of **Choeung Ek**. The remains of 8,985 people, who were bludgeoned to death between 1975 and 1978, were exhumed in 1980 from 86 communal graves. Those disinterred graves still have pieces of cloth and fragments of bone scattered within them. Another 43 graves remain untouched. In 1988, a memorial stupa was erected; behind its glass panels are the carefully arranged skulls from the mass graves. *Tonle Bati* is the site of **Ta Prohm Temple** and the smaller **Yeah Pean Temple**. Ta Prohm Temple was built in the twelfth century by Jaya-varman VII on the site of a sixth-century Khmer shrine. Ta Prohm Temple has five chambers and in each stands a statue or *linga*. Unfortunately these statues were damaged by the Khmer Rouge. There is an interesting story, which accompanies the temples, however. The king of

Angkor fell in love with the beautiful Yeah Pean and left her a ring, which she was to give to their unborn child Phrom, to identify him when he later called at Angkor. Upon his return, Phrom built the temple of Ta Phrom and later that of Yeah Pean to honour his mother. The site is a popular spot for family picnics at weekends.

INDONESIA

The phrase 'Unity in Diversity' is indeed appropriate to a nation that is home to more than 200 different ethnic groups, inhabiting more than 10,000 different islands. The Republic of Indonesia was proclaimed in August 1945, but the emergence from being a colony was by no means easy, and wars against the Dutch continued until 1949 when they finally withdrew. But long before the arrival of the Dutch, and the Portuguese before them, the various islands of Indonesia had been part of powerful empires that thrived on commercial trade and swapped tributes with China, while Europe remained buried in the Dark Ages. It was in the classical era, between about 500 and 1500 AD, that Indonesia's greatest architectural and religious monuments were constructed, and to which tourists and pilgrims flock today.

Bali still has many examples of Hindu art and architecture, dating from the eleventh century, and many Balinese continue to practice a form of Hinduism combined with some indigenous elements. Perhaps the most important and the largest of Bali's historical monuments is the temple at **Besakih**, or the **Mother of Bali Temple**, as it is known. Nearly 3,000 feet up the side of Gunung Agung, this temple is more than 1,000 years old. The temple is dedicated to the Hindu trinity of Siva, Brahma and Vishnu; their statues are covered in cloth and decorated with gifts of flowers. There are 18 smaller sanctuaries dedicated to different regents and favoured by different groups of Balinese who celebrate at their particular sanctuary during each group's unique annual festival.

Travelling south west from Besakih brings you to the site of a sacred spring and another of Bali's temples at **Tampak Siring**. The sacred spring waters are said to have curing powers and people have traditionally bathed at the temple of **Pura Tirta Empul** in hope of health and prosperity. Regular ceremonies are held at the 1,000 year old temple to give praise for the sacred spring and to preserve its purity. **Gunung Kawi** is not far from Tampak Siring and is arguably one of the island's most impressive sites. The attraction is a series of memorials cut into the cliffs of the river valley. They are linked to the cave complex and it is thought that the memorials are dedicated to an eleventh-century east Javanese king and his four most favoured wives – the five *chandi* (temples) are known as the Royal Tombs. Nearby are some more interesting rock-face carvings at **Yeh Pulu**. Unlike the *chandi* at Gunung Kawi, the significance of these rock-face reliefs is unknown as the scenes depicted are unidentified (although there is a carving of the Hindu elephant-god, Ganesa). The carvings are thought to date from the late eleventh or early twelfth centuries and are located at one of Bali's many sacred fountain sites.

Goa Gajah gives its name to a cave sometimes referred to as the Elephant Cave, which is believed to have been a monastery in the eleventh century. The cave contains a statue of Ganesa, hence the temple's popular name. In 1920, the cave was rediscovered and excavations have since uncovered a sacred bathing area surrounded by six statues of nymphs holding water carriers. The statues are pierced, and it was through these holes and through the spouts of the water-carriers that water would have flowed from an under-ground tank, which was fed by a local spring. Two statues stand either side of a carving of a hideous and demonic monster. The carving guards the entrance to the cave, and it is thought that the demon face may depict the spirit of the cave. The cave has a rustic feel to it, which may be synonymous with the sacred Hindu symbol of the mountain. Despite the cave's Hindu images, it has also been suggested that the cave was used by Buddhist monks.

South west Bali is where you will find the most-photographed temple in Bali, which means that it is extremely popular with tourists, especially in the late afternoon. The temple sanctuary at **Tanah Lot** is built on top of a huge rock, which is surrounded by the sea. Local sources believe that poisonous seasnakes found at the base of the rock guard the temple from evil spirits and intruders, and ritual ceremonies are performed to pay tribute to these 'guardians of the sea'. The temple is believed to have been built during the sixteenth century, under the instruction of one of the last priests to escape from Islam on Java by fleeing to Bali.

Java is home to the nation's capital, **Jakarta**. The Indonesian tourist board would no doubt direct you to **The National Monument** as the first stop in Jakarta. Known as Monas, the monument is a symbol of the nation's determination to rid Indonesia of its colonial yoke and drive the Dutch out. It was built during the Sukarno post-independence era, which was characterized by its fierce nationalism, and is constructed from marble – apparently Italian. At the base of the monument is a hall for meditation, and a museum that charts the struggle for *merdeka* (independence). At the summit is a gold-plated flame, which required 77 lbs of gold. A trip to the top of the monument (450 feet high) affords a superb view across the city. The monument is nicknamed 'Sukarno's last erection' and is only one of the many Stalinesque monuments, which attest to the struggle for independence as well as Sukarno's megalomania. **178–86**

Jakarta was known as Batavia under the Dutch, and a wander through the **Old Town** still conveys a Dutch feel to it thanks to some impressive colonial buildings. Many of the buildings were constructed by the Dutch East India Company, and some of them now function as museums. One such building is the **Jakarta Museum**.

Finished in 1627, the building originally acted as the town hall but was extended and renovated between 1705 and 1715. It gives a good overview of Jakarta's history and contains fine paintings, furniture, porcelain and maps from the Dutch era. The building was also used as a prison and it is said that the Indonesian hero, Dipanagara, who led a revolt against the Dutch between 1825 and 1830 was held in its basement cells before being exiled to Sulawesi.

There is also a relic from the city's Portuguese colonial past in the form of a large cannon. The cannon, **Si Jagur** is nicknamed 'Mr Fertility', as women used to sit astride it in the hope that it would cure barrenness. They were encouraged in this belief by its strange clenched fist, believed to be a symbol of fertility, and its inscription, which translates to, 'Out of myself I was reborn'. We do not know whether this practice was in any way successful. The so-called Portuguese Church, **Gereja Sion**, was built outside the city walls in 1695 for the Portuguese residents of Batavia or the 'black Portuguese'. From the outside it is not a very appealing building, but inside it houses an impressive baroque pulpit and organ. The 'black Portuguese' were the slaves, who were brought to Indonesia by the Portuguese in the sixteenth century and were granted their freedom if they joined the Dutch Reformed Church.

The National or **Central Museum** is a real treasure trove of ceramics, bronzes, coins and religious artefacts. It contains relics dating as far back as the Stone Age and has fine examples of Hindu and Buddhist sculpture. An impressive collection of cultural artefacts provide insight into the lifestyles of the various ethnic groups of Indonesia. The museum, which was founded in 1778 by the Dutch, is commonly known as the 'elephant building', so called because of the stone elephant found on the front lawn of the museum, which was a gift from King Chulalongkorn of Thailand in 1871.

Indonesia's most famous and popular historical site can be found not far from the modern-day city of **Yogyakarta**. At the centre of Yogya, as it is known, is the **Ngayogakarta Hadiningrat Palace**, or **Kraton**. The palace was built in 1755, when Prince Mangkubumi (Sultan Hamengkubuwana I founded Yogyakarta, which today is a city within a city. Visitors can gain a glimpse of the past through the live gamelan performances, the collections of artefacts and the displays of traditional palace ceremonies. Yogya makes the ideal stopping-off point or base from which to visit nearby Prambanan and Borobudur. **123, 146, 183**

The Saivite temple at **Prambanan** is the largest, and some would say the most beautiful, Hindu temple in Indonesia. The complex was built by Central Java's Hindu Kings between the late-ninth and early-tenth centuries and, like the temples found in Cambodia, it was influenced by Hindu cosmology. It was designed to incorporate 232 temples, with the eight most important and largest temples in a central square surrounded by an outer wall and 224 smaller temples, miniature versions of the central temple. Many of the temples are still in ruins after the devastation of a sixteenth-century earthquake, but the central temples and some of the smaller temples were restored by the Dutch. The largest of the temples stands at about 120 feet high and is dedicated to Siva. It is flanked to the north and south by temples dedicated to Brahma and Vishnu, and together the three temples represent the Hindu divine trinity. Known locally as the **Loro Jonggrang Temple**, or Temple of the Slender Virgin, the central temple contains a magnificent statue of the goddess Durga, Siva's consort. The temples are beautifully decorated with scenes from the *Ramayana* and contain niches with the usual celestial beings, but the actual architectural structure of the central temple, being a series of six storeys crowned by a large stupa, is reminiscent of the earlier Buddhist temples found in central Java, such as those at Borobudur.

Borobudur, one of Indonesia's – and indeed the world's – greatest historical and religious monuments is located 26 miles (42 kilometres), north west of Yogya. The Buddhist temple was built about 800 AD, was abandoned around 100 years later, and was only rediscovered in 1814 when Sir Thomas Stamford Raffles sent expeditionary forces into the interior of Java when the island was temporarily under British control. It is thought that the design of Borobudur

may have provided a template for some of the temples at Angkor. Six diminishing square terraces surround an inner complex of three diminishing circle terraces crowned by a huge stupa, towering 131 feet (40 metres) above the ground. The circular terraces are covered with many smaller stupas of open lattice work, inside each of which is a barely visible huge stone Buddha. The fact that the images can be seen through the lattice work is an indication that enlightenment has not yet been achieved. The monument as a whole acts as a sort of school of instruction of Buddhist thought, with each stage in the ascent representing a stage of enlightenment. The terraces are lined with relief sculptures that detail the deeds of the good and the bad and reveal stories from the life of the Buddha. Within niches in the terrace walls, images of the Buddha reflect the stage of enlightenment reached at that particular point on the monument. Thus the person arriving at the summit has progressed according to the Buddhist teachings on each level, has travelled through the many stages of consciousness, has reached the ultimate spiritual enlightenment and can now see the hitherto-invisible image of the Buddha in the stupa on the final level.

Before a pilgrim could begin his or her ascent at Borobudur, he or she would first have to pass through the levels of the nearby **Mendut Temple**. The series of smaller temples form an integral part of the Borobudur complex, and it is from Mendut Temple that processions to

Borobudur start during Buddhist festivals. Mendut Temple, which was also built around 800, is said to point towards India where the Lord Buddha taught his first followers. It was constructed to house a collection of sculptures, which, along with the temples' decoration, are meant to illustrate the combined doctrines of Garbhadhatu and Vajradhatu. Both are complex Buddhist theories but Vajradhatu is a horizontal group of five Buddhas each presiding over realms corresponding to the five major psychological categories; Garbhadhatu is the other Javanese grouping of Buddhist divine principles – this time on a vertical basis in which the Buddha has two divine projections – the Bodhisattva Avalokitesvara and the Bodhisattva Vajrapani. Some of the statues are missing and, therefore, the exposition of the doctrine is incomplete, but those which remain, and the exquisite decorations of the temple, betray what a truly awe-inspiring experience Mendut must have been. One of the smaller temples en route from Mendut to Borobudur is **Pawon Temple**. Pawon Temple, despite being relatively plain in decoration, is dedicated to Kuvera, the god of wealth, with many of the relief carvings depicting wish-trees surrounded by pots of gold and jewels. A temple dedicated to the god of wealth may seem strange today, but it is thought to be indicative of the important role played by international merchants in carrying Buddhism to new shores along the trade routes. **9, 65, 78–9, 129**

Just as Borobudur is not to be missed for those interested in religious monuments, then the small town of **Sangiran** ought not to be missed if you are interested in the origins of mankind. Sangiran is the site where, in 1891, Eugene Dubois, a French anthropologist, discovered fossils of Phitecantropus Erectus, the oldest 'Java Man'. Some 40 years later, more fossils were found of man dating from the Pleistocene period, as well as fossils that are said to show human evolution from the ape. There is a small museum at Sangiran, which houses a fine collection of fossils including those of mammoths. Meanwhile, a short walk on from the museum may reward you with sight of the fossils and bones that remain in the exposed earth. **21–2**

Not quite as old as the fossils, are the temples on the **Dieng Plateau**, which stands 60,000 feet above sea level. Dieng was an area of hermitages during Java's medieval period where devout Javanese could escape the grind of everyday life. The temples stand on a crater, which is swampy and emits sulphurous fumes: pongs aside, however, the site is impressive to behold. The exact date of the Saivite temples is unknown; it is thought that most predate Borobudur. The site is thought to be an auspicious one because of its elevation and, therefore, its mountain-like symbolism, which is important in Hindu religion. The temples vary in shape and size and, although they are not as ornate as those of the later period, it is said that their beauty lies in their proportions. Many of the temples' sculptures have been removed, but this does not detract in any way from their majesty, nor from the skill of the Javanese architects, which is readily apparent.

Travelling to east Java brings us to the centre of the Hindu empire of Majapaphit, which dominated Java from the thirteenth to the sixteenth century. Although much of the former glory has faded, some impressive temples and ruins remain, which date from the early thirteenth century. **Trowulan**, the capital of Majapaphit, has several ruins from the period that should be distinguished from the ruins of central Java. It was during the thirteenth century that an art form developed, which was much akin to the modern-day *wayang* or shadow-puppet play, with sculptures and reliefs dominated by less realistic figures with unnatural angular features. A good starting point to explore Majapahit would be the **Trowulan Museum**, which has a map showing the location of the ruins and the shrines. Other sites of interest in eastern Java include those of the kingdom of Singhasari with its ruins, not far from **Malang**. It is common for visitors to do a round-trip of the main sites in a single day. The three main sites are **Singhasari Temple**, **Jago Temple** and **Kidal Temple**. Singhasari Temple dates from the early thirteenth century, and it is thought that it was built to honour a king who died in a tantric orgy. The temple artistry marries both Buddhist and Hindu influences with tantric rituals, but both pure Buddhist and Hindu images have been found there.

Jago Temple was built between 1268 and 1280 and it is thought that it was to be the funerary monument to King Vishnuvardhana. The design of the building is unusual in that the temple's central cell is situated towards the back, rather than the centre of the temple. Originally the temple contained a statue of a Bodhisattva, but now it does not even have a roof. It remains an important Buddhist monument, however, and has interesting relief carvings, which should be viewed in an anticlockwise direction. In addition, to the stories of the *Mahabarata*, the sculptures reportedly tell the story of a traveller to the kingdom of the dead: the temple itself faces north west, the direction of the kingdom of the dead. Older than Jago Temple is Kidal Temple, which was completed in 1260 to honour one of the Singhasari kings. The porticoes of the temple are shrouded by a demon head, otherwise known as the Face of Glory. The temple is dedicated to Siva, although it no longer contains its icon, which is thought to have been taken to Amsterdam. Kidal Temple is regarded as a gem of Singhasari art. **68–70**

Maluku is the name given to the collection of 'spice' islands, which were famed for their valuable mace and nutmeg, and over which the Spanish, Portuguese, English and Dutch vied for influence during the sixteenth and seventeenth centuries. Many Malukans adopted Christianity, became integrated into Dutch colonial society and were favoured by the Dutch as trustworthy administrators and soldiers. Thus when Indonesia achieved independence, many Malukans felt that they had been abandoned by the Dutch and sought support to gain independence from the new nation. Most visitors to these islands are attracted, not only by the scenery, but also by the colonial heritage. Many forts and relics of the colonial past are well preserved and of interest to the traveller with an eye for history. The Portuguese **Fort Victoria** at **Ambon** (the provincial capital) dates from 1575 and its fortifications along the seafront are well preserved. At nearby Hila, **Fort Amsterdam**, originally a Portuguese fort was rebuilt by the Dutch in the eighteenth century. The central fortification remains intact, but it is now home to the contorted roots of a giant banyan tree. Ambon's other main attractions are the **Siwalima Museum**, with its interesting collection of local arts and crafts, and the **ANZAC war cemetery**.

Ternate, an island off the west coast of Halmahera in northern Maluku, is another of the many islands that carry a firm imprint of the region's colonial past, despite being an Islamic stronghold. The ruins of the large **Fort Orange** in the town centre are an indication of the importance attached to the island by the Dutch, who erected the fort in 1637. Also in Ternate town is the old **Sultan's Palace**, which is now a museum and, nearby, yet more ruined forts. Rusting guns and wrecked aircraft, relics from World War Two, can be seen strewn about the island of **Morotai** off the north coast of Halmahera. The island was an

important strategic base for both the Allies and the Japanese who fought over the region during the Pacific War. **34, 41, 67, 87–92**

Sulawesi is a diverse island with many different ethnic groups, of which perhaps the Toraja are the most memorable. **Tana Toraja (Torajaland)** provides a unique experience in Indonesia for the traveller interested in the cultural tenacity of Indonesian peoples to withstand external influences and maintain their own indigenous belief system, known as Aluk Todolo. Although converted to Christianity by Dutch missionaries in the early twentieth century, the Toraja continue to practice ancestor worship, and this may go some way to explaining why all their houses face the same direction – north. It was from that direction that, according to legend, the founding Toraja migrated to the island. The first Toraja are said to have descended from heaven in a boat, which explains why the roofs of their houses are pointed upwards at either end like the bows of a ship, and why the entrance to Torajaland is marked by a boat-like gate structure. Funeral festivals are particularly spectacular in Torajaland and usually take place some time after death, because of the need to raise enough money for the festival and to equip the deceased with necessary goods for the afterlife. Because of the time lapse, funeral festivals are often ceremonies that last for a few days and are occasions during which more than one deceased is buried. If you are lucky enough to be in Torajaland when a festival is taking place, then it is likely that you will be invited to join in the feasting in order to add to the confusion. The Toraja believe that noise (of which the squealing of sacrificial pigs is just one element), bustle and general confusion disorientate the evil spirits, easing the safe passage of the dead to the afterworld. The Toraja are a strictly hierarchical community, and this is reflected in the numbers of animals that must be sacrificed at the funerals: the greater the number of sacrifices, the more important the person. The dead, in their coffins, are then placed deep inside caves in the local hills. The entrances to the caves are guarded by huge statues, or wooden effigies. Two caves that are easy to visit, and to which guided tours are often given, are Lemo and Londa, skeletons and coffins can be seen inside.

Ujung Pandang (formerly known as Makassar) is the provincial capital of South Sulawesi and is the region's chief port, and it is here that the Bugis famous fleet of *perahu* (sailing boats) can be seen at Paotere Harbour. As well as sailing their vessels to Australia many centuries ago, the Bugis also launched attacks on the high seas against the opportunistic Europeans in the sixteenth, seventeenth and eighteenth centuries. Bugis vessels still trade throughout the archipelago. **Bentung Ujung Pandang** is perhaps the city's most important landmark. Construction of the fort began in 1545, during the reign of the tenth ruler of Goa. But when Makassar finally capitulated to the Dutch in 1669, the fort was renamed Fort Rotterdam and was reconstructed in a Dutch style. The outer walls of the fort remain intact and are well preserved, and along with the educational and cultural government offices, there is a museum that houses archaeological finds, manuscripts, costumes and ornaments. As a dedicated centre of culture, lessons are given in traditional dance to local children within the fort walls.On the outskirts of the city, are the **tombs of the Makassar kings**. The most well known was Sultan Hasanuddin, famed for his bravery in resisting the Dutch but eventually forced to accept the terms of the Treaty of Bungaya in 1667. In a small fenced-off plot near to the tombs is the Tomanurung Stone, the seat on which the kings were crowned. The rulers resided at Sungguminasa in a wooden palace built on stilts, which is now home to the **Ballalompoa Museum**. Among the museum's collections are the weapons and the costumes of the Makassar kings. **83, 89, 118–19, 151**

Sumatra lies to the north west of Java, and has a rich culture and a population who seem to be unusually gifted in the arts. At the north west tip of the island is the region of **Aceh**. Known as Po-Li to the Chinese in the sixth century, the region rose to the height of its power in the first half of the seventeenth century, when it was an important centre for Muslim trade and proselytisation. The Acehnese went on to mount a campaign of strong resistance to Dutch colonial rule between 1873 and 1942. More than 10,000 Dutch lost their lives in the wars against the Acehnese. Aceh would also play a significant role in

Indonesia's final struggle for independence after the Second World War. Having rid themselves of one colonial master, the Acehnese are now seeking to gain greater autonomy from Jakarta. Known for their Islamic devotion, the Acehnese have a fine collection of mosques, of which the **Masjid Raya Baiturrahman**, in **Banda Aceh**, is one of the most outstanding. The present mosque was built in 1875 and has been extended and renovated over time. The earlier mosque, which stood on the same site, was constructed of wood and burnt down at the beginning of the Aceh wars in 1873. The state museum, or **Museum Negeri** is regarded as another of the city's jewels. Among the museum's exhibits are a large clock, which was a gift from the emperor of China and was brought to the island by Admiral Cheng Ho in 1414, a large cast-iron bell presented to the Acehnese by the Chinese some time in the first century AD, as well as a fine collection of clothing, jewellery, household tools and weapons. **114–17**

The island's capital city, **Medan**, is a typical Sumatran city. It is unattractive and congested but it does have a few sites of historical interest. Perhaps most spectacular is the Grand Mosque, or **Masjid Raya**. The mosque was built in 1906 by the Sultan of Deli, who also built the impressive **Istana Maimoon**, the sultan's palace in 1888. On a less specific, but still architectural theme, there are a number of Dutch colonial buildings in Medan, remaining from the days when the city was the centre of the east-coast plantation belt, which prospered from the early 1900s. The **Museum of North Sumatra** is in Medan and has a fine collection of cultural artefacts as well as offering a good historical overview of the region. **149**

In west Sumatra, the town of **Bukittinggi** is well worth visiting for it has several interesting sites, and makes an ideal base for exploring the surrounding countryside. The major landmark of Bukittinggi is its clock tower with its pointed horn-shaped roof, reminiscent of Minangkabau architecture. The clock tower is known locally as **Jam Gadang**, and so the town is often known as Kota Jam Gadang, or Big Clock Town. Not far from the clock tower (in fact all the sites in Bukittinggi are within walking distance), is **Fort de Kock**, as the town was known under the Dutch. There is not too much to see at Fort de Kock, which was built by the Dutch during the 1820s, but it affords fine views of the town and is en route to the **Minangkabau Museum**. The museum is a must for anyone interested in the Minangkabau culture. Housed in a traditional Minangkabau building, built in 1934 by the Dutch controller, the museum provides an excellent example of the region's architecture and even has the obligatory rice barns at the front of the house. The rice barns would be used to store grain, one for use by the family, and the other as a provision for unexpected events and guests or travellers. The museum contains many cultural artefacts and tools, which are well displayed with informative commentary in English, and it provides a very useful oversight into the matrilineal culture of the Minangkabau, who combine Islam with the traditions of *adat*, local law. **The Military Museum** at Bukittinggi is also worth visiting with its many interesting photographs and weaponry from the war of independence against the Dutch, fought between 1945 and 1949, and subsequent suppression of the communists in 1965. On the way back from the museum to the town is the **Panorama Park**, which is home to a troop of friendly monkeys, but of greater historical interest are the Japanese caves inside the park. The caves – actually a series of tunnels – were secret underground bunkers used by the Japanese military during the occupation (1942–45). Many Indonesians were imprisoned and lost their lives there. Necessarily the caves have quite an eerie and sinister feel to them. At Bukittinggi it is easy to arrange tours of the surrounding area that take in **Batu Sangkar** – the centre of the Minangkabau kingdom in the fourteenth century. Nearby, you can see some stones with ancient Sanskrit inscriptions, known as the **Written Stone** and the **Stabbed Stone** – indications of early Indian influences on Sumatra. Other attractions include a large-scale model of a **Minangkabau-style palace**, and a visit to the restored 'original', as well as visits to traditional villages where it is likely that the way of life has changed little for centuries. **117–18, 132, 148**

In the south of the island is **Bengkulu**. The town was the site of the British presence on Sumatra from 1685 until 1824 – a period when the British vied for control of the region with the Dutch. Bengkulu was traded for Melaka in Malaysia, and so ended the brief interim of British rule. There are a few vestiges of the British presence, notably **Fort Marlborough**, which was finished in 1719 and has since been restored. Its most famous inhabitant was Sir Stamford Raffles who arrived in 1818. During his short stay on the island Raffles devoted much of his time to studying the region's flora and fauna and discovered the world's largest flower, the *Rafflesia arnoldii*. **129**

LAOS

Laos has long suffered from the incursions of expanding kingdoms and empires. Its diversity reflects these intrusions as well as migrations from Thailand, Burma and China. Perhaps the greatest incursion was made by a power that sought neither to populate, nor to colonize, but to suppress communism in neighbouring Vietnam: Laos was an unfortunate casualty in Vietnam's war against the United States. Few people realize that Laos bore the brunt of American bombing raids in the 1960s. These have left much of the countryside pock-marked: a constant reminder of the devastation wreaked by a war that began some six centuries after the creation of the first Lao kingdoms in the Luang Prabang area.

Luang Prabang, situated on the confluence of the Mekong and Nam Khan rivers in northern Laos, was the centre of the first Lao kingdom, Lan Sang and was constructed by Fa Ngum in the 1350s. Fa Ngum successfully united the group of Tai-speaking *muang* (villages), which had developed alongside the Mekong and its tributaries between the fourth and eighth centuries. Xiendong Xienthong, as Luang Prabang was known, was the kingdom's capital until 1560, when the administrative centre moved to Vientiane, the modern-day capital. But Luang Prabang warlords continued to act as contenders for the throne, and in 1707 Lan Sang split into three smaller kingdoms centred on Vientiane, Champasak and Luang Prabang. These smaller kingdoms existed in competition with one another. They were weakened and vulnerable to external threats and, as a result, the kingdoms were forced to pay tribute to the neighbouring Vietnamese and Thais.

Fa Ngum, who was sponsored by Khmer rulers, introduced Buddhism to Lan Sang in the fourteenth century. Over the centuries, the monarchs at Luang Prabang became the patrons of temple building. Many of these temples survive today and are in part responsible for the UNESCO decision to designate the city of Luang Prabang a World Heritage Site. **Wat Xieng Thong** is a must. The temple was built in 1560 by King Setthathirat, and is a real feast for the eyes. Reflecting a pure Luang-Prabang-style, the temple with its graceful, low-sweeping roofs and wonderful glass mosaics is a real treasure trove. Inside the temple's several chapels, a rare bronze reclining

Buddha, and a 40 feet high royal funeral chariot are among the attractions. The latter is elaborately carved and gilded, and was last used in 1959 for the funeral of King Sisavangvong. The temple walls are decorated with gilt panels, depicting scenes from the *Ramayana*, and there is a beautiful mosaic of a bodhi tree on the rear wall. There are many more memorable and charming temples in Luang Prabang – UNESCO noted 33. Of these, the next most interesting are: **Wat Wisunalat**, Luang Prabang's oldest functioning temple, which dates from 1513 (rebuilt in 1898), and is home to an interesting collection of wooden Buddha images, and a sixteenth-century lotus stupa; **Wat Mai**, built in 1796 with wonderful gilded stucco bas-reliefs revealing images of village life, incarnations of the Buddha and scenes from the *Ramayana*; and **Wat Long Khun**, a temple that dates from the eighteenth century but has been added to and restored over the years. This latter temple is of interest because it was customary for the regent to spend time here in meditation and reflection before accession to the throne. Luang Prabang's other architectural wonders include a curious blend of French and Lao styles; another factor which influenced the UNESCO decision. One of the most notable of these sites is the **Royal Palace Museum**. Built between 1904 and 1909, the building married the two architectural styles in an attempt to establish friendly relations between the colonizer and the colonized. For example, at the entrance to the building the columns bear the *fleur-de-lys*, while a crest above the entrance is of Erawan, a three-headed elephant and symbol of the three Laotian kingdoms; the theme continues inside, with French mirrors reflecting traditional Lao lacquered and gilded furniture. The building was initially home to King Sisavangvong, who was allowed to stay on at Luang Prabang after Laos became a French protectorate in 1893. The seat remained the home of the Laotian royal family until 1975, when the Lao People's Democratic Republic was established and the royal family was exiled to northern Laos. Today, the museum's exhibits include the **Pha Bang**, a gold standing Buddha three feet in height and weighing in at a hefty 8.5 stones; the statue is displayed at Wat Mai during the Lao New Year. Other highlights include some fantastic murals of Lao village life painted by a French artist; silk screens decorated by the former queen and a collection of Luang Prabang-style standing Buddhas. **61, 107, 145, 196, 225**

Moving to the south east from Luang Prabang brings you to the **Plain of Jars** in Xieng Khouang province. The mysterious origins of these jars meant that they remained untouched for millennia. The curious jars, which date from the Neolithic period, were scattered in their hundreds across the plain. The area was heavily bombed by American B52s during the Vietnam War but there are still over 100 jars remaining. Many of the smaller jars have been removed by collectors, while none of the largest jars, which weighed up to 15 tons,

survives and others have been transported to Vientiane. They come in a variety of sizes and shapes and for years archaeologists disputed their function. One theory put forward was that of huge 'storage jars' for rice. It is more likely that they were used for storage of a different kind, however, as sarcophagi: human remains have been found inside the jars, and it is believed that the size of the jar reflected the social status of the interred. The plain makes for an interesting detour on the way to Vientiane.

Vientiane became the capital of Lan Sang in 1560. King Setthathirat built a wooden rampart to protect his new capital and surrounded it by a moat. The name Vientiane derives from the description of the capital's defences: 'the rampart of sandalwood'. During the seventeenth century, under the reign of King Soulignavongsa, the kingdom of Lan Sang entered a golden age and was held in high repute by foreign visitors. But when Soulignavongsa's reign came to an end in 1694, Lan Sang descended into civil war and Vientiane lost its status as Laos's premier city. Only with the arrival of the French in the 1890s was capital-city status restored to Vientiane and a re-united Laos. In the meantime, however, a weakened Vientiane had become the plaything of powerful neighbours. During an invasion of 1828 the Thais destroyed much of Vientiane's rich architectural heritage. One site that has been restored, however, is **That Luang Stupa**. Built by King Setthathirat in 1566, the venerated shrine is now the national symbol of Laos. Legend has it that the shrine was built to house a piece of Lord Buddha's breastbone, but archaeologists have found Khmer statues near to the site and believe it was chosen due to its close proximity to a twelfth-century Khmer monastery. The central stupa is surrounded by mini stupas, and at the lower levels are encoded messages to be read by the devout on their pilgrimage around the stupa, which represents an elongated lotus bloom – the symbol of enlightenment. A statue of King Setthathirat stands at the entrance to the compound, and in the month of November, worshippers pay homage to his spirit. Another casualty of the Lao-Thai wars was **Wat Phra Kaew**. The temple was built by King Setthathirat in 1565 to house the sacred Emerald Buddha. The Buddha, actually made of jasper, originates from Lan Na in northern Thailand, and in 1779 the Thais recovered their venerated statue, which is now housed in Wat Phra Kaew in Bangkok. The temple was reserved for royal worship until in 1828 the Thais took the 'Emerald Buddha's revenge', by razing its former resting place to the ground. The present temple dates from 1936 and is now a museum with a fine collection of Khmer and traditional Lao sculptures, as well as Hindu-inspired carvings. Most unusual of all is a 'European-style' Buddha image; unusual because the seated Buddha's legs are hanging down and not crossed, or in the lotus position.

Wat Sisaket is the oldest surviving

temple in Vientiane, dating from 1818. The temple was built by King Chao Anu (Anuvong), whose exact physical proportions are said to have been given to a standing Buddha image inside the temple. The Anuvong Buddha is only one of 6,840 housed at the temple. The reason that there are so many Buddhas results from the Lao-Thai wars, when many Buddha images were left homeless after the destruction of their sanctuaries. The square cloister – a Thai influence – houses more than 2,000 of the smaller Buddha images in niches in the walls; below them are 200 larger Buddha images resting on shelves – more reside inside the temple. The temple is expecting a 'face lift' sometime in the near future, restoring the faded murals that tell the story of the Buddha's life.

From Vientiane's oldest to its most popular temple: **Wat Simuang**. Another temple founded by King Setthathirat at the very centre of his new capital is said to be the home of the city's guardian spirit, Sao Si. Apparently the *wat* received its name from the woman who died tragically after she jumped into the foundations of the temple's central sanctuary or *sim*. As she did so, the ropes holding the central column were released. The temple thus received the name of Simuang, meaning Si's town. The lives of those who died in the Indochina wars are commemorated in an arch of triumph called **Patousai**. The arch, which was built in 1958, is reminiscent of the *Arc de Triomph* in Paris but is decorated with Lao motifs. The monument should be dis-

tinguished from the **Unknown Soldiers' Memorial** erected after the
communist takeover in 1975, and so
Patousi is sometimes referred to as the
Old Monument. **61, 107, 108, 145,
146, 196, 224**

MALAYSIA

Long before Malaya became the
jewel in the Britain's South East Asian
crown, a kingdom on the Malay
Peninsula had risen to rival the
empires of Thailand and Indonesia.
Melaka emerged in the fifteenth
century, and it was not long before
the European imperialists saw the
strategic and economic importance of
this rich trading post. The Portuguese
were the first to arrive but were
ousted by the Dutch, who then traded their Malayan interests for a clear
run in Indonesia. It was under the
British that Malaya reached its full
potential as a colony in the early
twentieth century. At first the British
saw great value in the peninsula's
strategic position, particularly in
relation to the control of the Straits of
Melaka, but before long the colony
had become an important and valuable economic asset – through its
rubber and tin production. Malaya
would become crucial to Britain's
postwar recovery in the 1940s and
1950s. Since independence in 1957,
and the 1963 union with Sarawak,
Sabah and Singapore (from which the
latter withdrew in 1965), Malaysia has
grown to become the region's second
most vibrant and diverse economy,
and is now on the road to economic
recovery after the currency crisis of
1997.

Kuala Lumpur, which means
'muddy-river junction', was founded
in 1857 by an expedition of 87 Chinese tin miners at the confluence of
the Gombak and Klang rivers. It
became capital of the Federated
Malay States under the British in
1896. The British built a number of
grand buildings worthy of the new
capital. But KL – as the locals call it –
has undergone a vast transformation
in recent years. As one guidebook
remarked, maps are virtually out of
date before the ink has dried. There is
not that much to see in Kuala Lumpur, but one particularly impressive
and grand structure, which was
known as the Selangor Secretariat and
served as the centre of the colony's
administration under the British,
should be on the agenda. The
Moorish-style red and grey brick
building was designed by AC Nor-
man and was completed in 1897. It
has since been renamed the **Sultan
Abdul Samad Building** and is now
home to the Supreme Court and a
textile museum. Its impressive facade
of intricate colonnades is best viewed
by day; by night it looks like something from a fairy grotto.

Of the other grand relics of
Malaya's colonial past, the **Railway
Station**, is also worth a special visit –
if you haven't arrived in the city by
train. The designer, AB Hubbock,
was heavily influenced by north
Indian Islamic architecture, and this is
reflected in the station's spiralling
minarets, cupolas and arches. The
building was completed in 1911 and
has stood the test of time well, having
been designed to weather all storms,

including the unlikely eventuality of six feet of snow! Hubbock also designed **Masjid Jame**, which marks the very spot where the Gombak and Klang rivers meet and the site where the Chinese miners first landed. The mosque, the oldest in the city, was completed in 1909 by Hubbock, who took his inspiration from the mosques of north India, which he had greatly admired during his time there. It was his success at Masjid Jame that influenced Hubbock's design for the railway station; the similarities between the two structures are readily apparent. Masjid Jame was once the centre for Islamic worship in Malaysia, until the **National Mosque**, a modern and unusual but not as impressive a structure, superseded Masjid Jame in 1965.

The **Museum Negara** is not the best museum in Malaysia, and perhaps the building itself (a 1963 version of a traditional Minangkabau-style house) is more interesting than some of the exhibits. However, there is an exciting transport collection at the back of the museum, including locomotives and vintage cars, and an even more fascinating form of transport inside, in the form of a chariot used to carry the son of the sultan of Kelantan to his circumcision ceremony in 1933. The museum also has a cross-section of a Baba-Nonya house replete with fine furniture, a replica of an ancient Malay palace and a gallery of traditional Malay musical instruments.

Kuala Lumpur is home to the world's largest building, the **Petronas Towers**, which are 1,483 feet (452 metres) high and were finally completed in 1997 as testament to Malaysia's rapid economic modernization since the 1970s. The huge silver-tiled towers were inspired by the Five Pillars of Islam, and during low cloud and the rainy season, the top 20 floors or so become a sort of city in the sky obscured from view. Unfortunately, the towers are not open to the public but, although they are a sight to behold at any time of day, at night strategic lighting gives the towers a jewelled appearance and they become truly spectacular. If you are going to see the towers at night, then it might be worthwhile combining your visit with **Le Coq D'or**, which nestles between the skyscrapers just around the corner. The restaurant and bar function in what was once a Chinese tin-mine owner's mansion, and was one of many on the Ampang Road leading out to the tin-mines. The European-style food is fantastic, but the other reason for going is the building itself, which, although run down, still has some fabulous features: among them original art-deco lighting; Rennie Mackintosh inspired tiling in the bathrooms; beautiful mosaic floors and murals of old KL. The owners, who are bound by the legacy of a will stipulating that they could not alter any of the building's features, are most happy for visitors to wander around free to enjoy the mansion's many faded treasures. Further along Jalan Ampang is the tourist information centre, **Matic**, which was also once a *towkay* mansion. Built in 1935 by Eu Tong Seng, a wealthy tin-mine owner, the mansion acted as the War Office for the British and later as the headquarters of the Japanese during the Pacific War. It was also the site of the first sitting of the Malaysian Parliament and has served as the venue for the coronation ceremonies of several of Malaysia's kings. Another experience of colonial KL can be had at the **Coliseum Hotel**. Now famed for its sizzling steaks and the patronage of Lat, Malaysia's foremost satirical cartoonist, the Coliseum Hotel has changed little since it was a popular drinking venue for European rubber planters; it remains a haven for expats and tourists. **132–3, 165–6, 229, 249**

Melaka is Malaysia's most historic town, although its sites can easily be taken in a day or two. In the fifteenth century, Melaka was the centre of a powerful trading empire, which ruled over the west coast of the peninsula from Perak to Singapore, as well as most of the east coast of Sumatra. But in 1511 the Portuguese, under Don Afonso de Albuquerque, led a successful campaign of conquest in a bid to capture the region's ports; naturally Melaka was targeted. In a symbolic act, to ensure that there was no doubt as to who was in charge in Melaka, the Portuguese constructed a fort, **A Famosa**, in 1511 on the site of the sultan's palace. The fort was a grand feat of engineering but was not able to withstand the invading Dutch in

The Portuguese fort, Melaka, Malaysia

1641, who damaged the fortress only to repair it and claim it for their own by adding the Dutch East India Company crest to the Porta de Santiago – the gateway that still stands today. The rest of the fort was destroyed by the British when they relocated their Straits Settlement headquarters to Penang in 1807. Another legacy left by the Portuguese is **Our Lady of the Mount Chapel**, built by Duarte Coelho in 1521, which was the burial place for nobility and important visitors. In 1553 the missionary, St. Francis Xavier, was buried in the church, but all that remains is a plaque that marks the place of his brief interment, before his body was moved to Goa in India. A statue of the saint now stands in front of the chapel, which was renamed **St Paul's Church** by the Dutch in 1641. St. Francis's important role – spreading Catholicism throughout South East Asia – is honoured in the Gothic-style **St Francis Xavier's Church**, which was built in 1849 in remembrance of the 'Apostle of the East'. In 1753, as part of the Dutch centenary celebrations **Christ Church** was built, and St Paul's fell from favour. The brightly painted exterior of Christ Church is a foil for a more sedate interior without chancel or aisles, reflecting a typical Dutch design. The church with its hand-carved heavy beams and fine pews carved from single pieces of wood, together with inscribed tombstones on the floor and commemorative plaques on the walls, is well worth a visit.

The Dutch also left behind the **Stadthuys**, the official residence of the Dutch governors. Constructed in 1650 from a combination of stone and wood, the building continued to perform a central administrative function under the British as the town hall. The Stadthuys has been faithfully preserved and has a real seventeenth-century feel to it. The building is now home to a very fine **Historical and Ethnographic Museum**. On display are diorama of decisive moments in Melaka's history and artefacts and relics, including traditional costumes, and photographs of old Melaka, which, you will notice, has changed little.

A wander round the old town will bring you into contact with a number of treasures, among them the oldest and one of the most unusual mosques in Malaysia. In 1728, Dato Shamsuddin built **Masjid Kumpung Hulu** in a Sumatran style with a pagoda-inspired minaret. It is thought that the architectural influence came to the peninsula with the arrival of the Minangkabau. Another typical mosque of the Melakan style is **Masjid Kampung Kling**, which dates from 1748 and has Chinese and Hindu carved images on the pulpit, over which hangs a chandelier suspended from a beautifully carved wooden ceiling. This mosque also has a pagoda-style minaret and an unusual sloping three-tiered roof.

Melaka also claims to have the country's oldest Chinese temple, which dates from 1646. **Tokong Cheng Hoon** (Merciful Cloud Temple) was built with materials imported from China and is dedicated to the goddess of mercy. A visit to the temple is rewarded by its fine carvings, woodwork and mythological statues. The early successes of Melaka brought waves of Chinese entrepreneurs to the town, who helped to turn the trading post into a thriving economic concern and married Malay wives. Their descendants, the Babas and the Nonyas have a unique culture, which is revealed at the **Baba-Nonya Heritage Museum**. The museum is an amalgamation of three homes all owned by one family. Fronted by Greco-Roman columns, the museum holds cultural artefacts, which are surrounded by intricately carved and gilded fittings, inlaid mother-of-pearl furniture and beautifully lacquered screens; all indicative of the financial success of this unique community. The most famous Baba family was that of Tan Cheng Lock, leader of the Malayan Chinese Association between 1949 and 1958. It was at **Tan Cheng Lock's House** that the alliance between the MCA and UMNO was formalised in 1953, which finally led Malaya to independence. Heeren Street, upon which both the museum and Tan's house are found, is commonly known as 'millionaires' row', and has since been renamed Jalan Tun Tan Cheng Lock in honour of the Chinese statesman's achievements. Also worth visiting in Melaka is the former Melaka Club building. Built during the British colonial period in 1912, it is now the **Proclamation of Independence Memorial**, a repository of relics, manuscripts, video tapes, films and slides relating to the Malayan

independence movement. This is fitting because Malaysia's first prime minister, Tunku Abdul Rahman, announced in February 1956 that the Federation would become independent in August 1957 at a site near the memorial. At the foot of St. Paul's Hill, there is an excellent replica of the **Melaka Sultanate's Palace**. The architectural design of the building, which houses a small cultural museum, is based upon the description in the *Sejarah Melayu* (Malay Annals) of the early-seventeenth century, and it is the only one of its kind in Malaysia. **70–72, 86–93, 109–15**

Penang holds the title of food capital of Malaysia, but it has far more to commend it to the visitor than its culinary delights. Penang, from the early-nineteenth century, was once one of the foremost ports of the British Empire and has a fine collection of colonial buildings and a fort to testify to its grand and historic past. If most of Penang's attractions are found on Pulau Penang, then there is an even greater concentration of attractions in **Georgetown**, the state capital. Despite Georgetown's grandiose past, much of the city has been deprived of cash for renovation, which may be unfortunate for the inhabitants but is advantageous to the traveller, since many parts of the old town retain their traditional character, making it a real gem of old Malaya. Most of its sites can be taken in a day or two but you will probably want to linger longer to soak up the atmosphere.

The oldest building in Georgetown is **Fort Cornwallis**. The fort marks the spot of the British landing at Penang in 1786 by Captain Francis Light, who established a port at Penang that same year and began the construction of the emplacement that was named after the governor-general of India, Lord Charles Cornwallis. The most interesting object at the fort is Sri Rambai cannon, which is said to have mystical powers that can cure infertility. The cannon was originally a Dutch possession, which was captured by the British and discarded to the sea at Penang. Legend has it that when the cannon refused to yield to the efforts to remove it from its watery bed a local prince, Tunku Qudin, tied a rope around the cannon and ordered it to rise from the sea, which it obediently did, hence its magical powers. Not far from the fort, are some impressive administrative and commercial colonial buildings, which are evidence enough of Penang's importance in the British empire; among them, the **old town hall** and **the state legislature building**, as well as the impressive **Chartered Bank**.

Georgetown became a thriving port and its success made it attractive to immigrants, particularly the Chinese who set up *kongsi*, or clan houses, to provide mutual aid and support for new arrivals and existing inhabitants. The best example of such a clan house is the **Khoo Kongsi**, which was built in 1894 on an elaborate and grand scale, only to be destroyed by fire in 1902, perhaps at the hands of jealous members of another clan. The *kongsi* that stands today, although not as elaborate as the original, is still an impressive building, which is used for ancestor worship and communal gatherings. Plaques, recording the help given to clan members and their subsequent successes at universities across the world, line the walls of rooms, which are filled with heavy, but beautifully crafted, furniture inlaid with mother-of-pearl. The *kongsi*'s heavy roof is supported with equally impressive carved beams and pillars, and the building is replete with colourful statues, dragons and murals.

Another focal point for the Chinese community is a temple dedicated to the Buddhist goddess of mercy. The **Kuan Yin Teng Temple** was Penang's oldest temple, dating from 1800, but, after the devastation of World War Two, the temple was rebuilt in its current form. It is the most popular Chinese temple in Penang and is most often clouded by smoke from burning incense and bonfires of imitation money, which is burned to bring luck and wealth in the afterlife.

Pulau Penang is also home to Malaysia's largest Buddhist temple at Ayer Itam. The **Kek Lok Si Temple** was begun in 1890 and took some 20 years to complete and it is not difficult to see why. The temple is an elaborate and highly colourful structure of statues and staircases and has an imposing pagoda, which stands just under 100 feet high: a beautiful view of Georgetown rewards those who climb its 193 steps. Another temple on the tourist trail is known as the **Snake Temple**. If you are afraid of snakes, then this temple is to be

Kek Lok Si Temple, Penang, Malaysia

avoided, for it is home to many venomous snakes, which give the temple its popular name. The temple is dedicated to Chor Soo King, who was famed for his ability to heal the sick, and his statue sits before the entrance. According to legend, when the temple was completed in 1850, snakes suddenly appeared and have remained ever since, living freely inside the temple and in its surrounding gardens. Nowadays the temple is popular with tourists, and informative guides will take you through the temple's various chambers, all of which seem to lead to an in-temple photographic studio, where visitors are snapped with defanged snakes draped about their person, making for a memorable holiday souvenir. **128–32, 136, 149**

Sarawak on the island of Borneo can commend itself to the historical tra-

veller for at least two reasons. The first is a brilliant museum at **Kuching**, the state capital. The **Sarawak Museum** has a fascinating collection of artefacts from the various indigenous peoples who live in the interior of the East Malaysian state. Many of these artefacts were collected by the museum's influential but controversial curator, Tom Harrisson, in the 1950s. Another of the museum's valuable collections are the items discovered by the nineteenth-century naturalist, Alfred Russell Wallace who spent two years on Borneo in the 1850s. Wallace was a contemporary of Charles Darwin, who, having travelled and studied independently of Darwin, reached the same conclusions about man's evolution ten years after Darwin had first formulated his ideas. Wallace's work was important and added scientific weight to Darwin's theories, and together the two pioneers coined the term, *Evolution of the Species*, work which is more often accredited solely to Darwin's efforts. Other exhibits include some excellent examples of early Chinese ceramic jars, which were traded for spices and rhinoceros horns, which were highly valued among the tribes of Borneo. A Dayak longhouse is another of the attractions. Visitors are invited to enter and climb up to the storage loft where Dayak villagers would store their handicrafts and traditional sleeping mats. Visits to longhouses are easily arranged, which is the second obvious attraction in Sarawak.

Many of the Dayaks, the biggest of the indigenous groups who populate Sarawak, still live in traditional **longhouses**, which can house up to 100 families – a whole village under one roof. Each family has its own private living space for eating and sleeping with its own entrance door. The houses are built upon stilts, with livestock residing on the lower level, and entrance to the house is achieved via ladders, which lead to a communal veranda. The veranda is the place where the occupants of the house socialize and perform traditional tasks such as textile- and basket-weaving; skills which they will most usually be happy to demonstrate. The Dayaks have maintained their own cultural identity and continue to practice an animist religion, in which all living things possess a spirit. Many longhouses are still decorated with shrunken heads collected by the

Dayaks when they were infamous headhunters. The ritual was once part of a rites-of-passage ceremony for young men, but today the men gain status by returning after making their way in the world (usually through working in Kuching), bringing home far more innocuous prized items, such as electrical gadgets, as proof of their manhood. **4, 161–3, 206–8, 231**

SINGAPORE

From the 1830s to the 1960s, Singapore was at the heart of the British presence in South East Asia. The British were able to exercise control over the traffic that passed from the Melaka Straits through to the South China Sea; thus Singapore became a vital strategic outpost of the empire as well as an important commercial centre and trading port. The settlement was founded by Sir Thomas Stamford Raffles in 1819 and has thrived ever since, becoming South East Asia's most successful economy after its separation from Malaysia in 1965.

Downtown Singapore is the location of Singapore's most famous monument, or perhaps institution, **Raffles Hotel**, where the famous 'Singapore Sling' cocktail was first mixed back in 1915. Raffles started as a private villa but opened its doors to the public as a hotel in 1887, reaching its heyday in the early part of the twentieth century, when it became the byword for colonial luxury. Faded grandeur best described Raffles appearance until 1987, when the hotel was declared a national monument and a $160 million facelift restored the 'grand old lady of the East'. If a Singapore Sling in the Billiard Room is beyond your budget, then visitors can soak up the colonial atmosphere through a relaxing stroll around the hotel's courtyards and exclusive shopping arcades. There is also a museum at the hotel with a trove of Raffles memorabilia. Singapore's other monument to its founder is the **Raffles Statue**, which at today's Boat Quay is said to mark the spot where Thomas Stamford Raffles first set foot on the island.

Fabulous colonial architecture, reflective of the island colony's great status, can be found at the **Padang**. Raffles set aside the Padang as an area for recreation and cricket is still played there today. At one end is the **Singapore Cricket Club**, founded in the 1850s with strict 'members only' rules, a factor that prompted the Eurasian community to found their own club in 1883, the **Singapore Recreation Club**, which is located at the other end of the Padang. If the cricket fails to absorb your attention, then take time to appreciate Singapore's **Supreme Court** and the **City Hall** next door. The neoclassical Supreme Court was once the site of Singapore's premiere accommodation, the Hotel de l'Europe. Further along from the City Hall is **St. Andrew's Cathedral**, which was built by Indian convict labour and consecrated in 1862. Amazingly the cathedral now has closed-circuit TV: state of the art technology employed to observe ancient rituals, ensuring complete coverage of the proceedings for the congregation.

The island republic's **National Museum** is also located in the colonial district. The building is impressive in itself, and its contents are even more so. The museum contains several very interesting galleries, which offer insights into the various aspects of Chinese culture and life, including Rumah Baba, which takes you through a series of rooms of the Peranakan house, in which you witness the luxury and the lavish lifestyles enjoyed at the beginning of the twentieth century by the successful Straits Chinese families. A gallery of fine nineteenth-century natural history drawings commissioned by William Farquhar, Singapore's first British resident, as well as the fabulous Aw Boon Haw collection of jade statues are also among the museum's attractions. Also worth checking out is the Colony to Nation Gallery; the highlight of which is video footage of an emotional young Lee Kuan Yew, crying on national television on the occasion of Singapore's divorce from Malaysia in 1965. The museum also has an audiovisual theatre with free films on the transformation of Singapore shown four times daily.

Chinatown is one area upon which the museum film shows concentrate. As immigrants flooded into Singapore, Raffles's solution was to create separate living quarters determined by ethnicity. This may have had its advantages for the immigrants, who were able to find lodgings and places of worship in a local community with which they had common ties of culture, language and religion but, of course, this lessened the chance of integration in an island increasingly populated by various ethnic groups. If you manage to take in one of the films at the museum, then you will find the Chinatown of the quay virtually unrecognizable. The bars and restaurants that line the quay are reminders of the value of the area for tourism, rather than a desire to retain some of the character of old Singapore. Behind this facade, however, a wander through the back streets reveals traditional shopfronts that have not altered much over the last 50 years. One of the highlights of Chinatown has to be the **Thian Hock Keng Temple**. Hokkien in style, the temple was completed in 1842, to cater to a Hokkien quarter of Chinatown. The temple of 'heavenly happiness' was built with materials imported from China, including a statue of the queen of heaven, to which offerings are made by worshippers. Unfortunately, it is difficult to immerse yourself in anything like old Chinatown due to the overbearance of the skyscraper and the high-tech shopping mall, a constant reminder of the nation's thriving economy. The same must be said of Little India, which was originally a Eurasian quarter. **Little India** developed when the area became centred on the cattle trade, reflected by street names such as Buffalo and a hospital called Kandang Kerbau, or Buffalo Pen. A walk around these streets, and those of the neighbouring **Arab Quarter** will take you past some wonderfully colourful Hindu temples and some impressive mosques. One in particular, the **Sultan Mosque** is worth seeking out. The present mosque dates from the early twentieth century, and was built to replace an earlier mosque, which had been built with money donated by the East India Company. Next door to the mosque is the **Istana Kampong Glam**, the former residence of Sultan Hussein of Johor, with whom Raffles successfully negotiated in 1819. The sultan's descendants are still in residence in this unusual building.

East Singapore is the location of **Changi Prison**, which is still in use today, but its infamous claim to fame dates from the Japanese occupation of the island (1942–45). The prison was a POW camp, and it was here that Allied prisoners were subjected to harsh treatment by their Japanese jailers. A museum attached to the prison charts the invasion and the occupation of the island by the Japanese and catalogues the treatment of the prisoners through photographs, sketches and literary sources.

Sentosa Island is really an island playground, but there are quite good historical attractions, which offer information on Singapore's maritime history at the **Maritime Museum**, and good displays and diorama at the **Pioneers of Singapore**, **Surrender Chambers and Festivals of Singapore** exhibition, which charts Singapore's development from the fourteenth century through to the Japanese occupation at the Surrender Chambers, and culminates with displays depicting the nation's annual celebrations in the Festival of Singapore. **128–36, 233–6, 246–50**

THAILAND

Of all the nations visited in this travellers' history, Thailand was the only nation to maintain its independence from foreign colonial rule, while its neighbours were all absorbed into the European imperial design during the nineteenth century. Skilled Thai politicians were able to play the colonial powers, the British and the French, off against one another in order to maintain the king's rule over the Thai nation, while allowing the British, in particular, certain privileges with regard to trade. British pre-eminence came to an end in the late 1940s, when the United States emerged as Thailand's new protector. But Thailand has always been subjected to foreign interest, incursions and immigration. The Mons, the Khmers and the Chinese have all made their presence felt in Thailand, but, equally, Thais have spread their influence into neighbouring Burma, Laos and Malaysia. The powerful kingdoms of Thailand have left behind some fabulous ruins and temples, making the country a truly fascinating one to visit.

Ayutthaya was the administrative centre of Thailand from 1351 and the capital only moved to Bangkok in 1767 when Ayutthaya was sacked by the Burmese. The ancient capital is definitely worth a visit, as there are many interesting sites and ruins, which are testament not only to its glorious past but also explain the UNESCO designation of World Heritage Site. There is an **Historical Study Centre** at Ayutthaya, which may be worth perusing before moving on to explore either the ruins or the wats. The centre is dedicated to the study of classical and early-modern Ayutthaya and it contains reconstructions of the past and provides an information service. Among the many ruined palaces and wats, which date from the thirteenth century to the seventeenth century, are some magnificent stupas as well as many damaged Buddhas. According to local sources, the Buddhas, many of which are without arms or heads, were desecrated by the Burmese in 1767. Two temples of note are **Wat Buddhaisawan**, which houses particularly fine examples of seventeenth-century Buddhist painted wall panels, and **Wat Suanluang Sopsawan**, which contains the Queen Sisuriyothai Memorial Chedi. Queen Sisuriyothai became an Ayutthayan heroine in 1548, when she sacrificed her life (to save her husband) while engaged in elephant-mounted combat with the invading Burmese.

Visitors to Ayutthaya often avail themselves of the chance to visit the **Summer Palace**, which is not far from the old capital at **Bang Pa In**. The site was used as a summer residence from 1630 until 1782, when it was abandoned for 80 years. Under King Mongkut (Rama IV), a new summer residence was built, but it was his son, Chulalongkorn (Rama V, 1868–1910), who popularized the site, returning every year on many occasions throughout his reign. The Summer Palace is, in fact, a series of small palaces mostly built in miniature and many on a European theme. Chulalongkorn was attracted to

European architecture, which he saw on his many travels on the continent, and this inspired him to build the replicas at Bang Pa In, as royal palaces for his own family, and those of his brothers. The Thai-style pavilion, Aisawanthipphaya-At, in the centre of an ornamental lake, was built by Chulalongkorn in 1876. Chulalongkorn's son, Rama VI, had a bronze statue of his father placed in the pavilion, which is a well-known Thai landmark. Less well known, and more unusual, is **Wat Niwer Thammaprawat**. The Buddhist temple was built in 1878 in the architectural style of a gothic English church, complete with stained-glass windows. Architecture was not all that held interest for Chulalongkorn in Europe, however. Thai-British links were strengthened during Chulalongkorn's reign by a visit to Queen Victoria in 1897. The secret treaty that emerged from the meeting of the two monarchs extended British influence in Thailand but allowed Thailand to maintain its independence and avail itself of the opportunities for trade within the British Empire. **58–61, 64, 72, 99–106**

Bangkok is the capital of Thailand and has been since the Burmese sacked Ayutthaya in 1767 and has stood on the present site since 1782, having previously been located across the River Chao Phraya at Thonburi. Bangkok can appear to be a city of a thousand temples, although in actual fact there are only around 400. Although each has its own charm, there are certainly a few that should not be missed. The most spectacular temple is **Wat Phra Kaew**, or **Temple Of The Emerald Buddha**. The temple was consecrated in 1782, and is located within the **Grand Palace** complex. It is home to the Emerald Buddha, made of jasper, which was found inside a stucco Buddha at Chiang Rai in 1464. Today it is the subject of a dispute between Thailand and Laos. The Laotians claim the Emerald Buddha for themselves as they took it to Luang Prabang in the sixteenth century, from where it was retrieved by the Thais in 1779. A permanent exhibition of Royal regalia, decorations, medals and Thai coins, dating from the eleventh century, is also housed within the Grand Palace complex. Chulalongkorn built the Chakri group of buildings as a residence and a series of reception rooms, of which the latter are still used today. The main building of the Chakri group is an unusual marriage of European architectural design topped off by a typical Thai-style tiled and gilded roof. The gold tiled and mosaic walls of the palace buildings and temples almost defy description in their intricacy and beauty, and are testament to the skill of the architects and craftsmen as well as the wealth of the Chakri dynasty. **106, 107, 108, 155**

Just across the road from the Grand Palace is **Wat Pho**. Wat Pho is also tiled, although less ornately than the Grand Palace, but it does have a spectacular attraction of its own, the Reclining Buddha. The gold-plated Reclining Buddha gives Wat Pho its popular name and is 50 yards in length and 49 feet high, with huge inlaid mother-of-pearl feet. Wat Pho is both the oldest and the largest temple in Bangkok and, apart from the Buddha, there are bas-reliefs, wall panels, stupas and statues to view. The many bas-reliefs at Wat Pho make them a popular source for temple rubbings, which can often be purchased at Wat Pho (although not always at competitive prices!) The temple, despite its attractions and size, is very calming, especially in late afternoon.

Wat Traimit, or the Temple of the Golden Buddha contains, as the name suggests, a Golden Buddha. There is, however, an interesting story of the discovery of the golden-seated Buddha. After many years in storage a large stucco Buddha was transported by crane to Wat Traimit. The stucco was damaged in the move when it was dropped by the crane. What could have been a disaster revealed a five-and-a-half ton solid-gold Buddha, which had probably been concealed to prevent its plunder by invading Burmese.

Wat Benchamabophit, a relatively new wat, was built in 1899 by Chulalongkorn. Commonly known as the Marble Temple, it contains an excellent collection of bronze Buddha images from many different periods and consequently many different styles. It was once thought that there existed an authorized image of the Buddha and, in order to obtain the spiritual powers of the Buddha, images should be recreated as closely as possible to the original. Although this has inevitably been attempted, the variation on display at Wat Benchamabophit shows that such perfect

imitation has not been achieved; artistic licence or interpretation of the craftsman prevails, along with fashionable trends. The temple itself is unusual in its marble construction, and European influences can be noted in the addition of stained-glass windows.

The **National Museum** provides an excellent place for an overview of Thai culture and has a good collection of Thai art and artefacts, which date from the Bronze Age. There are numerous cabinets filled with models of reconstructed battles and invasions suffered or perpetrated by the Thais. But, there is also a good example of a traditional Thai house as well as the magnificent collection of royal barges, which are truly spectacular. An interesting take on very early history in Thailand can be viewed. The museum shop is also worth perusing.

Another fine collection of Thai art and furniture can be found in **Jim Thompson's House**. The teak house itself is of interest, as it is in fact a number of traditional Thai-style houses joined to form one dwelling. Jim Thompson was an American silk trader, and the existence of the house and the contents are testament to the success that American businesses enjoyed in Thailand from the late 1940s onwards. Thompson's mysterious disappearance in 1967 in Malaysia's Cameron Highlands has made him the subject of much speculation and debate. It has since been suggested that Thompson's public image, that of an entrepreneur, was a foil for his undercover intelligence work for the CIA. **105, 106, 154–5, 249–51**

Chiang Mai in northern Thailand is, the nation's second largest city. The city of Chiang Mai, founded by King Mangrai in 1296, was the capital of Lan Na in the north while Sukhothai was its southern counterpart. In addition to the power struggle between Chiang Mai and Sukhothai, Chiang Mai also came into conflict with the neighbouring Burmese. The city was fortified against attacks, however, by a moat, which was further reinforced by the city walls. Although you can still see the moat that surrounded the old city, what remains of the city walls are, in the main, reconstructions. Unfortunately, the fortifications did not prevent the invading Burmese from capturing the city in 1556; it was regained by the Thais in 1775. Today Chiang Mai is a popular base for travellers embarking upon jungle treks, but there are also a number of sites of historical interest for the less adventurous traveller.

Wat Jet Yot, a shrine for Buddha, was built in 1458 to a design that emulated the most sacred of Buddhist shrines at Bodhgaya in India, the site where it is said that Buddha gained enlightenment more than 2,500 years ago. The seven-towered monument has a central tower of pyramidal design with a small bell stupa at the top. The other four spires are on the same theme only smaller, and there are recessed porticoes at the end of the building guarded on either side by identical Buddhas. The shrine was damaged in the Burmese invasion of 1566.

Dating from 1383, **Wat Suan Dok** is particularly picturesque, with several of the temple's white *chedi* containing the ashes of Chiang Mai's royal family. The temple is also noteworthy for its huge bronze Buddha – 500 years old and one of the largest in Thailand – and its colourful murals depicting images of the Buddha's life. Another temple worth seeking out is **Wat Phra Singh**. Built in 1345, this popular temple contains a much-revered image of the Buddha. But the Phra Singh image is the subject of some controversy; although it is thought to be 1,500 years old, its exact history is unknown. The temple's Lai Kham chapel contains some beautiful wood carvings and northern Thai-style murals, along with an impressive bas-relief. **Wat Chiang Man** is Chiang Mai's oldest temple, and was home to King Mangrai during his reign. The temple contains two famous Buddha images, one of which, like the Emerald Buddha at Bangkok, has been the subject of a dispute between the Laotians and the Thais. One of the resting places of the Emerald Buddha can also be seen at Chiang Mai, at **Wat Chedi Luang**, which has a magnificent *naga* staircase to the front of the chapel.

Of greater significance is **Wat Phra That Doi Suthep**, which overlooks the city from a hilltop and is one of Chiang Mai's most important landmarks. The temple dates from 1383, is 3,520 feet above sea level and is approached via a staircase of 290 steps. Do not be deterred by the climb, as there is a funicular railway, which will take the hard work out of the ascent for those less energetic. The temple not only offers splendid views of Chiang Mai and the surrounding area, but its golden pagoda contains holy Buddhist relics, making the site an important one for pilgrimages each year by the devout. **58, 59, 102, 105, 155**

Kanchanaburi has become a tourist attraction since it was immortalized in the film *Bridge Over the River Kwai* (1957). Many travellers to Bangkok take a day trip to see the **Death Railway Bridge** at Kanchanaburi. The black iron bridge that spanned the Kwai Yai River was brought from Indonesia by the Japanese and was reassembled by Allied prisoners of war under Japanese supervision. The Death Railway Bridge was just one link in the railway between Thailand and Burma, and it cost the lives of thousands of Allied prisoners-of-war and Asian forced labourers. The bridge that stands today was built after the end of the Second World War; the original was destroyed by Allied bombing in 1945. The **JEATH War Museum** has been constructed in the form of an Allied prisoner-of-war camp, and it gives some idea of the cramped conditions endured by the prisoners. The bamboo-hut construction contains photographs and memorabilia donated by the survivors of the camps.

Lamphun and Lampang, two provinces not far from Chiang Mai, are endowed with some of Thailand's most impressive sites. **Wat Lampang Luang** is Lampang's oldest temple but was entirely rebuilt in the sixteenth century. It is believed to have been the only remaining structure from the fortressed city, which, it is

thought, was founded by Queen Chamma Thewi during the eighth century, when the provinces were ruled by Mon kings. Lampang contains many fine examples of Burmese-style temples, which were built during the seventeenth century. Most notable are **Wat Phra Kaew Don Tao** with its multi-roofed chapel and **Wat Chedi Sao**, which has 20 white pagodas within its complex. **Wat Phra That Hariphunchai** can be found at Lamphun. It is thought that the ancient Mon kingdom of Hariphunchai had its capital at Lamphun, and it is from this that the early-twelfth century temple gets its name. The temple complex's most striking feature is a golden pagoda, which towers at 151 feet high and has a base of 20 square yards. It is widely regarded as a fine example of Lanna Thai architecture. **Ku Kut Pagoda**, also at Lamphun, was built during the eighth century and houses the remains of Queen Chamma Thewi. The queen is the subject of many folk tales, which concentrate on her amorous and diplomatic exploits. The temple was constructed by Khmer artisans and its main pagoda is in the Bodhgaya style, most common in northern India. More examples of Burmese style temples can be found in nearby Mae Hong Son, Nan and Phayo. **58**

Lopburi, around 90 miles (150 kilometres) north of Bangkok, was an ancient Khmer capital dating from the tenth century. **Phra Prang Sam Yot**, meaning sacred three spires, is the town's greatest attraction. Built in the twelfth century, the shrine is one of the finest examples of Khmer provincial art found in Thailand. It was constructed from sandstone and stucco and, like most other Khmer monuments, the shrine provided a focal point for the cult of royalty. The sacred three spires signify the Hindu trinity of Brahma the creator, Vishnu the preserver and Siva the destroyer, through which the monarch's position was reinforced as was his rule over the province of the Menam Plain.

Khmer art was married with French influence in the seventeenth century at Lopburi to design **Phra Narai Ratchaniwet**. The building, which took 12 years to complete, was the former palace of King Narai (r. 1657–88) of the Ayutthaya period. Inside are the remains of the stables, which housed the much loved and worshipped royal elephants. Royal elephants received truly regal treatment, sleeping on large silk pillows, and eating out of and defecating in bowls made of solid gold. They were tethered by gold-plated chains and adorned with silks and perfumed oils. So adored were they by their royal masters, that an elephant death demanded an elaborate funeral, in which it was not unusual for the elephant keepers to offer themselves as sacrifices to travel with the elephant to serve it in the afterlife.

Sukhothai, meaning dawn of happiness, became the first capital of a truly independent Thailand in 1238. Historical research has shown that the Thai language and alphabet, supposedly the creation of King Ramkamhaeng (r. 1275 to 1317), originate from Sukhothai. Sukhothai is also noted for its achievements in art, literature and law, all of which are considerable given that its period of strength was short lived before it was superseded by Ayutthaya in the 1350s. As with Ayutthaya, UNESCO has also designated the ancient city a World Heritage Site. The ruins of Sukhothai evoke the splendour of the ancient capital, and the city walls house some of the most important historical and religious sites in Thailand. The moated **Royal Palace** contains **Wat Mahathat** with its massive stone Buddhas, lotus bud towers, beautiful pagodas and ornamental ponds offering wonderful reflections of the splendid ruins. Sukhothai has several other wats of importance, which are variously influenced by Khmer- and Sri Lankanstyle architecture. Artefacts recovered from Sukhothai and the surrounding area can be seen in the **Ramkamhaeng National Museum**.

Nearby, at **Si Satchanalai Historical Park**, more ruins from the Sukhothai period can be seen, including **Ko Noi Thuriang Kilns**, which were at the centre of Sukhothai's famous Sangkhalok pottery in the fourteenth and fifteenth centuries. **Wat Nang Phaya**, the Temple of the Queen, is also worth seeking out for its exceptionally fine stucco decorations, which are in excellent condition. **59, 60, 75, 99**

VIETNAM

Vietnam is probably the best known of all the South East Asian countries, simply because of the proliferation of films and books about the Vietnam

War, but there is much more to commend Vietnam to the traveller than its many museums that focus on the Vietnamese struggle against the Americans.

Hanoi has a history of importance and splendour that long predates its nomination as independent Vietnam's capital city. In the fifteenth century Thang-long was at the centre of Le Thanh Ton's empire, but when the city was abandoned it became known as Ha Noi, or 'city within the river's bend'. It would not flourish again until the arrival of the French in the nineteenth century, when the city bloomed under French architectural influence, style and design. The French influence is still very much in evidence, especially in the aptly named **French Quarter**, where a wander through the residential area reveals the highly sought-after villas, which range in style from neoclassical to the art deco of the 1930s. Splendid as the villas undoubtedly were, it was the **Opera House** that was the *pièce de la résistance* of colonial Hanoi. The opera house took ten years to construct using the finest materials, many imported from France, and from 1911 it was at the cultural heartland of francophone Hanoi until the disruption of the Pacific War, which was followed by the nationalist revolution, proclaimed from the balcony of the opera house by the Vietminh in August 1945.

The neo-Vietnamese building further along the block from the opera house is the **History Museum**. The museum's most interesting exhibits are those from the Dong-son culture, including ceremonial burial-drums and cooking utensils and tools. Other exhibits include statues, poetry, depictions of military conquests and the struggle against the French. The museum's history stops abruptly in August 1945, when the story is taken up by the **Museum of the Vietnamese Revolution**, but there is a distinct lack of English signs in this museum. Travelling in the opposite direction from the opera house brings you to the **Governor of Tonkin's Residence**. This splendid classical-style building has been restored to its former glory and is now used as a VIP residence for foreign dignitaries, which means that the public is not admitted but the facade is impressive enough to demand a walk by.

When the Later Le Dynasty was at the pinnacle of its power and Thang-long was a thriving city, **Quan Su Pagoda** was built on the southern gate of the capital. The temple is sometimes referred to as the Ambassadors' Pagoda, as it was located nearby Quan Su house, which was built to receive foreign envoys and ambassadors. Since 1942 the temple has been restored and expanded many times into the much larger architectural structure which stands today. The temple is now the headquarters of Vietnam Central Buddhist Congregation and, as well as being a popular centre for worship, it also acts as an important centre for Buddhist learning.

Much older still is Hanoi's famous **One Pillar Pagoda**, which was built by the Emperor Ly Tai Tong

(r. 1028–54). The current structure dates from the 1950s, however, as the departing French blew the temple up when they left the city. Yet, there is an interesting story attached to the pagoda, which is dedicated to Quan Am, who appeared to Ly Tai Tong in a dream holding an infant boy while sitting upon a lotus throne. According to the story, the emperor married shortly after this vision and when a son was born to him, he built the temple in thanks. A statue of Quan Am sits in the central sanctuary, which rises as a single pillar from an artificial lake, representing a lotus blossom, the Buddhist symbol of enlightenment. The temple is overshadowed by the nearby **Ho Chi Minh Museum**, which charts Ho's life and the pivotal role he played in the development of the nation. The displays include photographs and some personal articles as well as an unusual collection of metaphoric images, which are sometimes difficult to work out. Not surprisingly all the displays carry underlying messages. Ho's embalmed body can be viewed at his nearby **Mausoleum**. A much better museum is the **Army Museum**, which charts the nation's history since the 1930s, focusing on the wars against the French and the Americans. The museum is full of arms and weaponry, including a Russian-built MIG 21 fighter plane, and has many good displays including one on the Battle of Dien Bien Phu (1954) and the communist takeover of Saigon (1975). Also of great historical interest in Hanoi is the **Temple of Literature**, one of the few surviving remnants of the Ly Kings' original city and the centre of Confucian learning in Vietnam from the eleventh to the nineteenth centuries.

A symbol of Vietnamese independence, which outdoes the manufactured images of the museums has to be that of **Co Loa Citadel**, just nine miles outside Hanoi. The citadel was a stronghold of independence for around 150 years but was abandoned in the late second century BC after repeated Chinese incursions. In its hey day Co Loa ruled over a vast area and commanded allegiances far and wide from more than a million people. The citadel itself was built by King Thuc An Duong Vuong (257–208 BC), who reigned over Au Lac. His citadel was constructed inside fortifications built on three concentric embankments, upon which walls of up to 26 feet wide were built, separated by moats wide enough for ships to navigate. Co Loa Citadel has proved a rich vein for archaeologists; agricultural tools and arrowheads are among their finds, many of which are on display in the nation's museums. The site's best attraction is Den Vua An Duong Vuong temple, in which the king is honoured. **42–9, 98, 140, 186, 192, 214**

Ho Chi Minh City was known to the French as Saigon and was the capital of French Indochina. Not surprisingly, the city has more than its fair share of museums, which illuminate various aspects of the struggle for independence, the best being the **Revolutionary Museum**. The former Gia-long Palace, which was built in 1886 as the residency of the governor of Indochina, is home to the museum. It is somewhat ironic that this former residency now serves as a venue in which French colonial rule, or 'colonial fascism', comes under scrutiny. Photographs and newspaper articles are among the exhibits charting the growth of nationalism and the struggle against the French. For many, this colonial period is overshadowed by the subsequent war against the Americans, which forms the second focus of the museum. Here the nationalist struggle hots up, with exhibits demonstrating the ingenuity of the Vietnamese smuggling techniques, and the adaptation of bicycle parts into mortars. This theme is continued at the **War Crimes Museum**. Hideous and shocking are words that best sum up the exhibits, which include photographs of torture, mutilations, disfiguring napalm burns, and those which reveal the devastating effect that chemical sprays had on the landscape and the people who fell victim to its poisonous effects. On a lighter note, the **History Museum** contains relics and artefacts that predate French colonial rule, including fine examples of Asian art and numerous Buddha images, as well as displays that chart the rise and fall of the Vietnamese dynasties and decisive military battles.

With French colonial rule came Catholicism and in October 1877, the first brick was laid for the foundations for **Notre Dame Cathedral**. The neo-Romanesque building was completed under the direction of French engineers three-and-a-half years later, at a cost of 2.5 million francs. The square twin towers topped by metal spires are 130 feet high, which makes Notre Dame one of the city's most visible landmarks. There is little else outstanding about this cathedral, save a beautiful stations of the cross marble relief. The city's other main attraction, as far as its French colonial heritage goes, is the **Hotel de Ville**. The hotel, today the city's town hall and home to the People's Committee, stands in Nguyen Hue, which in its colonial heyday was a Far Eastern Champs Elysées. Unfortunately much of the splendour and opulence has disappeared from the thoroughfare, but the building still betrays its former grandeur with its classical Corinthian columns and sculptures.

But Saigon, as many still refer to the city, was by no means culturally barren before the arrival of the imperial civilization, and on the outskirts of city is a temple that is evidence enough of this. **Giac Lam Pagoda** dates from 1744 and is believed to be the city's oldest temple. The first room upon entering is the funerary chamber, which is lined with photographs of the deceased, and has a statue of Chuan De in the centre. Chuan De is a manifestation of Quan Am, the goddess of mercy, who in turn is an incarnation of the Bodhisattva Avalokitesvara. To the left of this room is the main sanctuary, which has quite a collection of Buddhist and Taoist statues and a tree of lights. Worshippers pin their hopes, in the form of small paper messages, to the wooden frame of the tree and then make an offering, which involves topping up one of the lights with oil. A similar tree of lights can be found at **Giac Vien Pagoda**, which was built in 1805 in honour of the Emperor Gia-long, who is said to have been a frequent visitor to the temple. The temple was originally a thatched-roofed hut and was named Kuan Yin, but its name was changed to its present form in 1850. The temple houses over 150 statues and engravings from the late nineteenth and early twentieth centuries. **Xa Loi Pagoda**, built in 1953, offers little to compare aesthetically with the older temples. There is, however, a shrine commemorating the sacrifices made by Buddhist monks, who set themselves ablaze in opposition to the Diem regime's suppression of Buddhism. Diem was South Vietnam's Catholic president after 1955 and his suppression of Buddhist protesters led to popular demonstrations and a subsequent military coup in 1963. The **Jade Emperor Pagoda** offers a very pleasing contrast with Xa Loi Pagoda. It was built by the city's Cantonese community in 1909 and is arguably the most spectacular temple in the city with its splendorous gilt work and its wooden carved panels, as well as its many colourful statues including the Jade Emperor.

Not far from the city are the **Cu Chi Tunnels**. Cu Chi was strongly antigovernment and a haven for Vietcong guerrillas who controlled the area. The villagers were targeted for their alliances with the Vietcong and took evasive action by digging themselves underground. By 1965 a 400-mile-long network of tunnels existed, with one section even passing underneath the United States' Cu Chi base. The tunnels were only about 3 feet high by 3 feet wide, and cramped conditions were made worse by the tunnels less-friendly inhabitants: snakes, scorpions and rats. But the ingenuity of the Vietnamese saw advantages in these otherwise unwelcome guests, which were hidden in bamboo pipes and empty boxes to act as booby traps for the unsuspecting GI. Food was scarce, especially after chemical sprays and scorched-earth policies left the land barren. Scorched earth was one of the tactics adopted by the Americans in an attempt to 'smoke' the Vietcong out of their tunnels. When that failed, the US dropped propaganda leaflets from the sky, only to replace the leaflets with bombs when propaganda had failed. The United States 'carpet bombed' the landscape beyond recognition and killed at least 10,000 Vietnamese in so doing. The tunnels have since been widened in places to allow for the greater dimensions of the Western tourist.

Those who were not sympathizers with the Vietcong often owed their allegiance to Cao Daism. Cao Daism was officially recognised as a religion by the French administration in 1926 and **Tay Ninh** became its Holy See in 1927. The cathedral at Tay Ninh is quite startling and appears to be sinking around a staircase, which rises inside the building. It is not surprising that this colourful building should mimic both cathedral and temple as

Cao Daism is an eclectic mixture of religions – its sources being predominantly Buddhist and Catholic. Cao Dai first appeared to Ngo Van Chieu, a civil servant who practised spiritualism. It revealed to him that Cao Dai had appeared to man on several occasions: notably as Jesus, Mohammed, Lao Tzu and Confucius, and on each occasion Cao Dai had tailored a religion to suit local needs. But this had resulted in religious intolerance, and what was needed was a unifying religion, which could be transmitted through saints. Among Cao Dai saints are Napoleon Bonaparte, Joan of Arc, William Shakespeare and Winston Churchill. Cao Dai told Ngo to adopt the Divine Eye as the symbol of the religion and it is a constant theme throughout the cathedral, recreated in colourful stained-glass windows and watchful over the entrance to the cathedral. Flanking the entrance to the cathedral are two statues, one representing the first female cardinal of Cao Daism, Lam Huong Hanh, and the other representing the religion's first pope, Le Van Trung, a former high-living bureaucrat who realized the error of his ways after Cao Dai appeared to him at a seance. **96–8, 139, 214–16**

Hue and the Central Provinces offer rich pickings for history-minded tourists, particularly of interest is the ancient capital of **Hue**, which UNESCO has recognized as a World Heritage Site. Hue was the capital of the country during the Tayson and the Nguyen dynasties, thriving under the reign of the latter in the early nineteenth century, when many of the city's attractions were built. When the emperor Bao Dai abdicated in 1945, Hue lapsed as the nation's capital, but it is still one of the country's favourite spots for tourists, and rightly so. The **Royal Citadel** is situated on the banks of the Perfume River and was built entirely from bricks, with the construction beginning in 1805 during the reign of Gialong. The outer wall is 20 feet high and has a depth of 65 feet, it has ten entrance gates and the wall is surrounded by a moat. Within the citadel walls, the Imperial Enclosure lies at the centre, with its many temples and royal gardens which were built over a period of some 30 years. At the very centre of the Imperial Enclosure is the **Forbidden City**. Under Gialong, the Forbidden City was known as Cung Thanh, or City of Residences, but two years after coming to power Minh-mang (r. 1820–41) renamed it the Forbidden Purple City. Connected to the Imperial Enclosure by seven gates, the Forbidden Purple City was restricted to the emperor and his immediate entourage, including an array of concubines. Among its many buildings were several royal palaces, a royal library and a royal theatre both built by Minh-mang, as well as Ta Huu Vu, the Left House and Right House. These houses, which face each other, acted as waiting rooms for dignitaries who sought an audience with the emperor.

Hue Museum of Antiquity has an unusual history of its own. The impressive building was commissioned by the Emperor Thieu Tri in

1845 and was known as the Long An Palace. Its original home was the Imperial Enclosure, but in 1909 the building was dismantled and moved to its present location to act as the National University Library (Hue has no fewer than five universities). It was not until 1923 that it was converted into a dynastic museum by the emperor Khai Dinh, to house the costumes and belongings of the former Vietnamese emperors. Among the many attractions at the museum are its wooden panels, which are inscribed with poetry and essays written by the Emperor Thieu Tri himself. **50, 95–8, 139–43**

The Central Provinces are also the location of two other important historical sites, one being **Hoa-lu**, the capital of Dai Viet. Hoa-lu was founded by the Emperor Dinh Bo Linh (r. 968–79) who seized power and moved the capital from Co Loa, which had recently been resurrected as an auspicious site of Vietnamese independence. There is little but ruins remaining of the original structures at Hoa-lu, but its temples were faithfully restored in the seventeenth century. One of the temples is dedicated to Dinh Bo Linh and contains a statue of the king with his three sons, two of whom were assassinated along with the king in 979. The commander of the king's forces Le Dai-Hanh then seized power, and it is to him and his short-lived dynasty (lasting only 25 years), that the second temple is dedicated. **43, 44**

Another important site is that of **Mi-son**, capital of the kingdom of Champa. Cham kings authority res-

ted on the cult of their divinity, hence the proliferation of temples that honour the Cham kings at Mi-son. The site dates back to the fourth century, but most of the temples date from the seventh century to the thirteenth century. When French archaeologists investigated the site, they catalogued each of the temples and gave them an identifying number, prefixed by letters A to G. The most spectacular of the temples was A1, but sadly raiding B52 bombers did their best to obliterate the Vietcong, and the magnificent A1 tower, a wonderful example of Cham art, was a casualty of the war. The temples that remain are small and modest, which is an indication of the transient nature of the Cham kings' power, but this does not detract from their beauty. The Chams found inspiration in both Indian and Chinese architectural styles and themes. Chinese influence is said to be responsible for the pedestal altars, which are found within the temples. The altars were often decorated with ornate sculptures and are testament to the skill and artistic talents of the Chams. Statues would have been placed upon the altars, many of which have been removed to be preserved in museums. The Hindu deities such as Siva, Ganesa and Garuda were worshipped in these temples; the gods and other celestial beings and beasts reappear in some fantastic bas-relief work adorning the temples. **50**

To the south of Hue lies the large port of **Da Nang**, the site of a huge US Air Force base during the Indochina conflict. Its real historical attraction, however, is intrinsically Vietnamese – the unique **Cham Museum** contains statues and friezes from the classical Kingdoms of Champa and serves as a prelude to the ruins at Mi-son, which can be reached from Da Nang.

Index